DATE DUE

APR - 4 2002	

Cat. No. 23-221

Sexual Investigations

Books by Alan Soble

Pornography: Marxism, Feminism, and the Future of Sexuality

The Structure of Love

The Philosophy of Sex: Contemporary Readings (editor)

Eros, Agape, and Philia: Readings in the Philosophy of Love (editor)

Sex, Love, and Friendship (editor)

Sexual Investigations

Alan Soble

NEW YORK UNIVERSITY PRESS

New York and London

Library of Congress Cataloging-in-Publication Data
Soble, Alan.
    Sexual investigations / Alan Soble.
      p. cm.
    Includes bibliographical references and index.
    ISBN 0-8147-8004-0 (alk. paper)
    1. Sex. 2. Sexual ethics. I. Title.
HQ12.S64 1996
306.7—dc20   96-9937
              CIP

New York University Press books are printed on acid-free paper, and their binding materials are chosen for strength and durability.

Manufactured in the United States of America

10 9 8 7 6 5 4 3 2 1

For Rachel Emőke

CONTENTS

Preface   ix
Acknowledgments   xiii

ONE

Ethics   1

Grim Scenarios. St. Augustine. Paul and Kant. Thomas Aquinas.
Contraception. Re-eroticization. Love. Need. Exonerations. Nature.
The Necessity of Consent. The Sufficiency of Consent. Paternalism. Beyond Consent. Polysemous Words. Antioch. Orgasmic Justice. No Pair.

TWO

Masturbation   59

The Concept. Fulfilling Desire. Completeness. Communication.
Two Frameworks. Novel Pleasures. Utility. Men's Liberation. Conjugal Union. Transcendental Illusions. Compulsory Pairing. Guilt.

THREE

Analysis   111

Adultery. Counting Sex. Body Parts. Polysemous Behavior. Fellatio
Insemination. Pleasure. Intentions. Reproductive Form. Sexual Reproduction. Polymorphosity.

FOUR

Health   143

Clean Sex. Eryximachus's Dream. Medicine's Dominion. The Examination Room. Constructivist Health. Functioning Sex. Political
Science. Evolutionary Health. Progress. Freedom.

FIVE

Beauty   175

Relevant Traits. Receptionists and Models. Money. Personal Relations. Arousal. The Beauty Hoax. Equality. Future Sex. Pornographic Beauty.

SIX

Pornography   214

Oral Sex. The Beaver. Polysemous Pornography. Other Animals. Fantasy. Academic Lies. Brutality. Reality. Romanticism.

Notes   251
Bibliography   289
Index   311

The driving force which this male portion of the body will develop
later at puberty expresses itself at this period of life mainly as an urge
to investigate, as sexual curiosity. Many of the acts of exhibitionism
and aggression which children commit, and which in later years would
be judged without hesitation to be expressions of lust, prove in analysis to be experiments undertaken in the service of sexual research.
　　　　—Sigmund Freud, "The Infantile Genital Organization"

I appreciate Freud's tying together sexual research and sexual pleasure. In
writing this book, even more than in writing my earlier books, I found the
connections between investigating sex and instigating sex becoming real
for me. Investigating—reading, thinking, writing—is already undeniably
erotic; investigating sex doubly so. In reading the book, the reader should
similarly experience as real the link between investigating sex and being
the object of instigation, between being provoked into thought and being
provided with intellectual and sensual pleasure.

Don Milligan ominously begins the preface of his *Sex-Life: A Critical
Commentary on the History of Sexuality* with an apologetic disclaimer:
"Books on sexuality generally fall into three categories: theory, practice,
and entertainment. This book is about theory. It is an advanced introduction to the discussion of sexuality." Milligan warns, do not expect to be
entertained; this treatise is difficult and stuffy. But Milligan sells theory
short; it can very well be entertaining, otherwise no one would bother to
do it. I have written a book that wanders through the theory of sex
searching for something true, or at least pleasurable; a book that approaches its task with an analytic frame of mind and method; but also, was
the plan, a book that is theoretical, practical, *and* entertaining.

Words can be sexual; they can also be sexy. The shocking and powerful words in some feminist antipornography writings are sexual but not, for me, very sexy; they arouse, but not in a comfortable, welcome way. Because I analyze the sexual theories and claims of others, the nonsexy sexual in their words cannot always be excluded from my own. But I have tried to make some of the words of my own sexual investigations sexy. Using words to instigate pleasure is nothing new. But analytic philosophy? The formidable problem is to make the cold logic of necessary and sufficient conditions pleasurably arousing. Words, however, tend to be sexual even when we do not want them to be. Lecturing about sex, its history, philosophy, and mechanics, is therefore unavoidably sexual. Circumlocutions and euphemisms only make the arousal subliminal, more dependent on a perceptive and imaginative listener; they do not eradicate the sexual undercurrent. Without much trying on my part, then, the words in these essays will be, even if analytic, sexual. But maybe I have been fortunate enough to have made them also pleasurably pornographic.

One concept that runs through the book is pleasure; it is fitting that the words that talk about sexual pleasure should themselves instigate pleasure. In the first chapter, "Ethics," principles of sexual morality are criticized insofar as they do not sufficiently acknowledge the value of sexual pleasure sought for its own sake. Traditional Christianity of the Augustinian-Thomist kind is the main offender, although, as later chapters elaborate, some contemporary feminism is sewn from the same cloth. My guiding principle is that sexual activity is to be morally justified in its own terms and not in virtue of its contingent, instrumental links with other things (reproduction, love, money, revenge) that have their own and supposedly often greater value. In chapter 2, "Masturbation," it emerges that the enemies of sexual pleasure—in particular, the enemies of an act that has nothing to say for itself except its pleasure—are not only Christian and secular conservative philosophers, but also liberals and leftist men's liberationists. Masturbation, like the apocryphal snuff film, is hated by all sides, regardless of political or metaphysical leaning, and so needs to be defended, yet again, but this time against the *whole* field. In the third chapter, "Analysis," the yielding of sexual pleasure is put forward as an ingredient important to the nature of sexual activity; even if the production of sexual pleasure is not necessary, but only sufficient, for an act to be sexual, its role in sexual activity is significant enough to provide a good (albeit not geometrically demonstrative) argument against the social constructivist idea that sexuality has no essence.

In "Health," the fourth chapter, I argue that social constructivism is nearly right about sexual health and related normative judgments about sex, even if wrong about sexuality per se. Healthy sexuality is, essentially, pleasurable sexuality; this is not to say very much about it. But the further substantive judgments often added by various professionals in the field of sexuality have both the mark and the weakness of social norms: the "healthy" is too readily defined in terms of suspicious values and arbitrary conventions. In the fifth chapter, "Beauty," I inquire whether the pleasure humans derive from being in the presence of physically attractive people is a guiltless pleasure, and whether preferring to associate with the attractive in friendship, marriage, and romance is culpable because wrongly discriminatory. I argue that discrimination against unattractive persons in relationships would be much less morally suspicious in a more egalitarian society, one we should attempt to establish in any event. The final chapter, "Pornography," is saturated with the assumption that sexual depictions are good just because they elicit arousal and pleasure. What applies to sex often applies to pornography as well, hence there is no need to defend pornography per se in terms other than its power to produce pleasure, and there is no warrant to condemn it because its aspirations are so narrow. Sometimes, however, sex is rape, and sometimes a person takes unfair advantage of another's situation. Similarly, if men or women are coerced into the sex acts depicted in pornography, or if they are motivated primarily by poverty, that would make the production of some pornography wrong. Can more be said by way of condemning the content of pornography as degrading? I think not, or not as much as claimed by "unmodified" feminists.

Another theme that runs through the book is polysemousness: the fact that multiple meanings attach to our words (and sentences), our actions, and the representations we construct of ourselves and the world. In particular, our sexual words, our sexual acts, and our sexual pictures, paintings, and photographs are polysemous, allowing of multiple interpretations that both present danger to communication and add to our lives something playful and exciting. Although sexual words, sexual acts, and sexual pictures can be discussed separately, and I do so, note that the speaking of sexual words can also be the performing of a sexual act or the representing and describing of a sexual event. Thus the polysemousness of words, acts, and depictions is all of a piece. I hope to have exhibited this continuity among the fluidity of pornographic representations, the ambiguity of sexual speech, and the indeterminateness of sexual acts.

ACKNOWLEDGMENTS

Most of this book is new, but essays already published provided structure as it was being written. These essays have been surgically dissected and cannibalized to yield a few passages I wanted to retain; but colleagues who have read the earlier pieces will not recognize what is contained here. In several places my conclusions are different from the views I once defended; but even where the position or line of argument is the same, it has been clarified and deepened. I acknowledge the assistance of the editors and other staff involved in the publication of these essays, and thank the journals and publishers for permission to reprint those few passages that do appear in this book.

Chapter 1 descended from "Sexuality and Sexual Ethics," in Lawrence and Charlotte Becker, eds., *Encyclopedia of Ethics* (New York: Garland Press, 1992), 1127–33; "Le morale sexualle," in Monique Canto-Sperber, ed., *Dictionnaire de philosophie morale* (Paris: Presses Universitaires de France, 1996); and "A szexualitás filozófiájáról" (The philosophy of sex), *Magyar filozófiai szemle* (Hungarian Philosophical Review) 36, nos. 5–6 (1992): 1046–68 (translated by Módos Magdolna). Parts of the chapter were aired publicly: "The Philosophy of Sex: Budapest Version" at the Philosophy Department of the Budapest Technical University, November 18, 1991; "Consent to Kiss" at the Philosophy Department of Tulane University, February 24, 1995; and "Antioch's 'Sexual Offense Policy' " at the Eastern Division meetings of the American Philosophical Association, December 1995.

The first version of chapter 2 was "Masturbation," *Pacific Philosophical Quarterly* 61, no. 3 (1980): 233–44; the essay was reprinted, much revised, as "Masturbation and Sexual Philosophy," in my *The Philosophy of Sex*, 2nd ed. (Savage, Md.: Rowman and Littlefield, 1991), 133–57. The present version is an even more extensive revision and elaboration. My treatment of the views of Alan Goldman, Thomas Nagel, and Robert Solomon on masturbation have been greatly modified, and sections have been added on

Sara Ruddick, Janice Moulton, John Stoltenberg, John Finnis, and Roger Scruton.

Chapter 3 also descended from the essay in the Becker *Encyclopedia* and "A szexualitás filozófiájáról." Some of it was taken from "Changing Conceptions of Human Sexuality," the preface to Earl Shelp, ed., *Sexuality and Medicine*, vol. 1 (Dordrecht: D. Reidel, 1987), xi-xxiv. Chapter 4 is a thorough revision of "Philosophy, Medicine, and Healthy Sexuality" from Shelp, *Sexuality and Medicine*, vol. 1, 111–38; and chapter 5 is a thorough revision of "Physical Attractiveness and Unfair Discrimination," *International Journal of Applied Philosophy* 1, no. 1 (1982): 37–64.

Small parts of chapter 6 came from "Pornography: Defamation and the Endorsement of Degradation," *Social Theory and Practice* 11, no. 1 (1985): 61–87; "Pornography and the Social Sciences," *Social Epistemology* 2, no. 2 (1988): 135–44; and "Reply to Critics," rebuttals to three critiques of my book *Pornography*, which exchange occurred at a meeting of the Philosophers for Social Responsibility, during the Central Division meetings of the American Philosophical Association, Chicago, April 1987.

Sexual Investigations was begun during my sabbatical semester, spring 1994. Since then, assistance was provided by the University of New Orleans and its College of Liberal Arts, through the release time of a research professor appointment (thanks go to the Research Council, Vice Chancellor Shirley Laska, and Dean Philip Coulter) and by the Research Support Scheme of the Open Society Institute (grant 1520/706/94). Portions of the book benefited from other grants. The National Endowment for the Humanities sent me to Atlanta to study Kierkegaard with Sylvia Walsh in the summer of 1985; this trip was instrumental for my "Pornography and the Social Sciences." A Fulbright teaching grant allowed me to spend the 1991–92 academic year in Budapest and its Gerbeaud coffee shop, where I wrote "A szexualitás filozófiájáról." I returned to Budapest in May 1994, delivering lectures and conducting seminars at the philosophy departments of the Budapest Technical University and the Hungarian Academy of Science, in which I discussed material that became part of chapters 1 and 6; travel to and living in Budapest were funded by the International Research and Exchanges Board and the Hungarian Ministry of Culture and Education.

From 1975 through 1995, while the essays and then the book were conceived and written, many people contributed to their progress in as many different ways. I am grateful for the help, advice, ideas, and support of Sandra Bartky, Fred Berger, Tony Browning, Ronna Burger, Ruth Colker, Judy Crane, Fehér Márta, Forrai Gábor, Ann Garry, Denise Hatton, Richard Hull, Alison Jaggar, I. C. Jarvie, Edward Johnson, Gale Justin, Kathrin Koslicki, Barbara Lammi, Leonore Langsdorf, Peggy McDowell, Margitay Tihamér, David Mertz, Módos Magdolna, Richard Mohr, Yayoi Naragushi, Norton Nelkin, Lynn Hankinson Nelson, Dolores O'Connor, Niko Pfund, Lynn Powell, Nancy Radonovich, Mary Ann Raney, Yolanda Scott, Jeannie Shapley, Rayford Shaw, Irving Singer, Jim Stone, Rosemarie Tong, Russell Vannoy, Sylvia Walsh, Celia Caroline Winkler, Kenneth Winston, and the personnel at Plantation, PJs, and Coffee & Co. And especially Mom and Dad, Sára and Ráhel (who suspects, at the age of two, that her Daddy's "no"—with enough persistence—doesn't always have to *mean* "no").

Ethics

Respect is absolutely essential. In the sex that you have, treat your partner like a real person who, like you, has real feelings.
—John Stoltenberg, *Refusing to Be a Man*

"Why don't you ever use your strength on me?" she asked. "Because love means renouncing strength," said Franz softly. Sabina realized two things; first, that Franz's words were noble and just; second, that they disqualified him from her love life.
—Milan Kundera, *The Unbearable Lightness of Being*

Sex, even when monotonous, is momentous. Its yearnings make us wonder about how our wants and needs are pulled by and become attached to the bodies and personalities of other people, and even of handsome things; the absence of yearning makes us wonder about the ability of bodies and minds, ours and others, to repel. In sex we are doubly vulnerable to another's seductive touch and coercive force. Flesh is weak, so we are exposed to but also awakened by the other's engulfment or invasion of our bodies. If physical liability weren't enough to worry about, there's also psychological susceptibility to betrayal, embarrassment, shame, loss of self-esteem. A partner's laughter at our pleasure might celebrate our shared joy, or victoriously trumpet our surrender, defeat, our humiliating fall from grace. The other's searching, judgmental gaze examines our comportment and station, exiting the screening room delighted or disgusted. In sex we come face to face with our ambiguous relationship to the interplay of Strength and Respect. We want to be equals, but we are moved and stirred

1

by power—of money, position, and beauty. Such facts about sexuality already provide reason for taking sexual ethics seriously, but the consequences of sexual activity also demand attention: the transmission of disease, the causing of death; a child's existence *in utero* and beyond; exquisite pleasure and happiness, on the one hand, jealousy, anguish, envy, and resentment on the other.

Grim Scenarios

I promise never to describe sexuality again in such pious and overblown terms. Nor will I countenance Gilbert Meilaender's confectionery view that sex (heterosexual coitus, specifically) is "the act in which human beings are present most fully and give themselves most completely to another,"[1] or Robert Nozick's absurdity that sex is "metaphysical exploration, knowing the body and person of another as a map or microcosm of the very deepest reality, a clue to its nature and purpose."[2] Even after rejecting such grandiose portraits, one can still insist on the significance of sexuality in human life and urge that morally evaluating sexual behavior is important. After all, as much as children are one of life's supreme delights, they also require labor. It does not follow that sexual ethics must be highly prohibitive. Yet, given the intricate psychology and far-reaching consequences of sex, it can be argued that engaging in sex is justifiable only by weighty nonsexual considerations, that sex must be renounced unless certain severe conditions are met. Countless theologians, plus the grocer on the corner and her husband, agree among themselves that because procreation has unique meaning as a couple's contribution to God's ongoing work of creation, sex is profoundly important and redeemable only when it occurs within a loving, committed marriage. As a contender for the allegiance of the grocer's children, this precept is very much alive; in one way or another, it figures into almost everything written about sexual morality. Even while some deny this principle of sexual ethics and fashion alternatives, their attempt is colored by the Christian outlook, its haunting presence forming the conceptual and normative background.[3] In the sadomasochist subculture, for example, a slap to the face is spoken of and justified as the top's expression of *love*.[4] And the bottom makes "a total gift of self

[that] requires . . . strength and courage"[5]—a phrase that could have been lifted from the philosophy of love of Pope John Paul II.[6]

Grim secular views of sexuality also abound, which describe sexuality in equally macabre terms. Ponder Jean-Paul Sartre's idea that the reciprocal incarnation comprising our mutual sexual desire always threatens to disintegrate, and often does, plunging us into metaphysical brutality:

> sadism and masochism are the two reefs on which desire may founder— whether I surpass my troubled disturbance toward an appropriation of the Other's flesh or, intoxicated with my own trouble, pay attention only to my flesh and ask nothing of the Other except that he should be the look which aids me in realizing my flesh. It is because of this inconstancy on the part of desire and its perpetual oscillation between these two perils that "normal" sexuality is commonly designated as "sadistic-masochistic."[7]

Then there's Montaigne's depressing "To enjoy it is to lose it,"[8] the ancient ruthlessness of Petronius—"Doing, a filthy pleasure is, and short; And done, we straight repent us of the sport"[9]—and the mercilessness of Shakespeare (Sonnet 129):

> Th' expense of spirit in a waste of shame
> is lust in action; and, till action, lust
> Is perjured, murd'rous, bloody, full of blame,
> Savage, extreme, rude, cruel, not to trust;
> Enjoyed no sooner but despisèd straight.

No wonder sexual activity is seen as unbefitting the virtuous character. The message has been conveyed by others in less poetic but still gloomy terms. The quest for sexual pleasure not only threatens the self's wholeness, the other's personhood, and society's viability, but insults the human spirit and God. Sexual desire by its nature objectifies, making us view the people who are our targets as mere things, and compels us to seek pleasure without much sensitivity to our partners. Because in sex much is at stake, the temptation to use others is pervasive; sex breeds deception, exploitation, and manipulation. Ethics must be a meticulously vigilant watchdog.

These sentiments embody a sexually conservative spirit, a sibling of prohibitive Christian sexual ethics, and one that is still popular, despite its bleakness. Consider Roger Scruton's suggestion that the sexuality of the young be reined in, firmly guided away from the licentiousness of liberal society, on the grounds that "there are sexual habits which are vicious, precisely in neutralising the capacity for love."[10] Scruton means that teaching our children well entails preventing them from falling into pornography, Wilt Chamberlainian promiscuity, sadomasochism, perversions, prostitution, even masturbation. A similar ethics is advanced by Karen Green, who wants to sustain the "psychic connections between sexual desire, love and self-esteem."[11] On Green's view, being a dutiful, loving parent means providing for the well-being and self-esteem of one's children. To do that, the parents must have their own self-esteem. Sexual activity engaged in by the parents in the context of their mutual love makes each feel loved and reinforces their self-esteem (529–30). On the basis of this folk psychology, Green condemns prostitution as "immoral," since it "involves the suppression of a structure of moral sentiments"—the prostitute and client separate sex from love—"which has its moral value in promoting the altruistic behaviour that is necessary if a just society is to reproduce itself" (531). That the loveless carnality of the prostitute and john undermines the just society is improbable enough. But Green confidently extends her argument to casual sex: "the tendency to treat sex as an arena of self-gratification, divorced from love or duties of care, is destructive of family life, even in its milder forms."

Note the resemblance of Green's late twentieth-century thought to Aquinas's medieval argument designed to show that extramarital sex is unnatural:

> it is evident that the bringing up of a human child requires the care of a mother who nurses him, and much more the care of a father, under whose guidance and guardianship his earthly needs are supplied and his character developed. Therefore indiscriminate intercourse is against human nature. The union of one man with one woman is postulated, and with her he remains, not for a little while, but for a long period, or even for a whole lifetime.[12]

I find it eerie that this passage, written so long ago, sounds familiar. Let us, then, review Paul, Augustine, and Aquinas. Doing so will illuminate current debates about sexuality among conservatives, liberals, and feminists.

St. Augustine

Sexual desire and activity, because they produce pleasure, are ordinarily viewed as at least prima facie good. Several themes in Augustine's writings on sex imply that for him, by contrast, they are in themselves bad. Augustine always describes sex in unflattering terms: concupiscence is a "disease," "evil," and "shame-producing."[13] Even marital sex involves "boundless sloughs of lust and damnable craving."[14] For Augustine, people seek "darkness and secrecy" when they engage in sex because sex is shameful;[15] "the evil of concupiscence . . . everywhere shuns sight, and in its shame seeks privacy."[16] The ideal state would be to beget without desire or passion; the penis would, by an act of volition, erect and deliver sperm to the vagina.[17] A man would create children in effect by his will alone, as God by His Will alone created heaven and earth. Witness, in this happy state, the adorable efficacy of spirit: humans would not be plagued by the "perturbations" and "discomforts" of bodily desire. Indeed, this was, for Augustine, the situation of prelapsarian Adam. Although Adam never shared intercourse with Eve, had he done so he would have erected voluntarily, not by reflex at the sight of her body or her odor.[18] Even if men after the Fall cannot regulate the penis voluntarily, at least they can try to control sexual desire, exerting effort that the act be done for its proper procreative purpose:

> A man turns to good use the evil of concupiscence . . . when he bridles and restrains its rage . . . and never relaxes his hold upon it except when intent on offspring, and then controls and applies it to the carnal generation of children . . . , not to the subjection of the spirit to the flesh in a sordid servitude.[19]

Hence sex is a sin, a forgivable one, when not engaged in by the spouses for procreation but for pleasure. "This gratification . . . receives forgiveness owing to the married state in which it is indulged. This . . . must be reckoned among the praises of matrimony; that, on its own account, it makes pardonable that which does not essentially appertain to itself."[20]

For dreary sex-negativity, for the denunciation of the passionate, visceral, animal, involuntary portion of human nature, Augustine is unsurpassable.[21] Sex represented for him the revolt of man against God, the evil victory of body over spirit. So "the time after Christ," for Augustine, is "a time for abstention from sex, time for spiritual regeneration"[22] in which the body finally receives its due disregard. Not even Aquinas, who repeats much of this sex-negativity, condemned sex per se: "It is impossible for carnal union to be evil in itself," he concluded, because heterosexual coitus results from a natural inclination implanted by God and in it certain organs fulfill their natural purpose.[23] But these reasons for judging coitus unobjectionable provided Aquinas with just the axioms he needed to condemn everything else in the sexual universe, including masturbation and homosexuality.

Paul and Kant

Augustine's predecessor, Paul, thought that the ideal Christian life would be celibate (1 Corinthians 7:1; see also 1 Cor. 7:8):

> [1]*It is* good for a man not to touch a woman.
> [7]I would that all men were even as I myself.

The other extreme, promiscuous fornication, is also unsuitable for a Christian and human being (1 Cor. 5:1, 9–11; 1 Cor. 6:9, 15, 18). But ordinary human beings find it impossible to be celibate; they are pulled by desire in the direction of sinful fornication. Paul, a shrewd fellow, applied Aristotle's doctrine of the mean, offering people a way to live between the extreme of celibacy and the extreme of promiscuity. He decreed it allowable (1 Cor. 7:6), even if not ideal, to engage in sex in, but only in, the state of matrimony. "To avoid fornication, let every man have his own wife, and let every woman have her own husband" (1 Cor. 7:2). This was no ordinary marriage; it had to abide by these principles:

> [3]Let the husband render unto the wife due benevolence: and likewise also the wife unto the husband.
> [4]The wife hath not power of her own body, but the husband: and likewise also the husband hath not power of his own body, but the wife.
> [5]Defraud ye not one the other, except it be with consent for a time, that ye may give yourselves to fasting and prayer; and come together again, that Satan tempt you not for your incontinency. (1 Cor. 7)[24]

If the spouses are accessible to each other sexually, if they yield body and behavior when summoned by the other's urges, marital sexual pleasure will keep them from fornicating. Except for spiritual or religious reasons, the partners may not refuse each other sexually. Marriage *ad remedium concupiscentiae* would be useless, it would not be a solution to Paul's sexual dilemma, if access to the spouse's body were limited by headaches, disinterest, or a television program.

"Pauline access," as a solution to the dilemma, is untenable. If, as Paul claims, we have sexual urges tempting us toward fornication and, as a result, celibacy is difficult, then within Paul's matrimony solution to this dilemma arises another dilemma: the same urges will make it difficult to be sexually faithful to one's spouse, in which case the choice is smoldering, resentful faithfulness or sinful fornication. Paul's solution to the original dilemma assumes that constant access to the same partner will be sexually satisfying and will thereby thwart fornication. But constant access to a partner in matrimony kills desire, makes the marriage bed boring, and sends us, anyway, toward fornication.[25] The danger of Pauline access, as Lisa Cahill says about sexual relations in general, is that "sex pursued for the *sole* purpose of physical enjoyment . . . is likely to become technical, depersonalized, and ultimately boring."[26] There is some truth here; however, sex gets boring even when it is not done "solely" for pleasure but for any of the myriad reasons people have for engaging in sex.[27] Indeed, Cahill's own Thomistic philosophy of sex, that we must acknowledge its "total essential reality" (41), that is, the fact that

> persons are not just individuals, but members of a species, and procreation . . . is one mode of their connection to the dignity, purposes, and welfare of the species, and to the ecology of the universe (42)

does not obviously put the zip back into marital, or any other, sex. (Nor is it fair to homosexuality.) To the contrary, we often praise contraception, which severs Cahill's connection between sex and the welfare of the species, for its contribution to pleasure (even if sometimes that contribution is only temporary).

In Romans 7:23–25, Paul suggests a solution to the new dilemma:

> I see another law at work in the members of my body, waging war against the law of my mind and making me a prisoner of the law of sin at work

within my members. What a wretched man I am! Who will rescue me? . . .
Jesus Christ our Lord!

But if the answer is to call on the strength of God to help us overcome the
horrible tension between wanting to be faithful to our spouse (in effect,
being celibate, since desire in marriage is dead) and committing adultery
out of sexual frustration, we could have done *that* in the first place, instead
of marrying, to overcome the tension between trying to lead the celibate
life and being tempted into fornication. And if appealing to Jesus had
helped *there*, the new dilemma would never have arisen. So let us imagine
Paul solving the new dilemma, our being torn between frustrating faithfulness and the pleasures of fornication, in a way that remains true to the
pragmatism of his solution to the original dilemma. Imagine that Paul
blesses masturbation as an Aristotelian mean between fidelity and adultery; even though having sex with one's spouse is ideal, masturbating
alone is allowable in order to cheat Satan. So rewrite 1 Cor. 7:9, "It is
better to beat off than to burn with passion." There is something to this
joke. Paul, in comparison with Augustine, is sexually liberal; but once he
takes that first gentle step, permitting sex for pleasure in marriage on the
grounds that a worse state, sinful fornication, is thereby avoided, the
conclusion is irresistible that oral sex, anal intercourse, pornography, rubber toys, and costumes are legitimate *within marriage* if they keep the
Satan of adultery away.[28] Of course, these things lose their erotic power
after a while, too, which means that Paul's dilemma is ultimately unsolvable. We get old and our bodies fall apart. We achieve Paul's ideal, in
behavior at least, by default.

Pauline access has a further, moral problem: sexual access in which
each partner has power over the other's body seems dehumanizing and
objectifying. Prima facie, the relationship between wife and husband is
fine: their marriage is equal, since the wife has the same power over the
husband's body.[29] What could be sweeter than each pledging himself or
herself to the other forever for the purpose of avoiding sin? If the marriage
is freely entered by two competent adults, why lodge a complaint? But
since a major element of Pauline marriage is sexual activity, the partners
are in danger of being reduced from their full humanity to providers of
pleasure. Further, each spouse consents once to a subsequent lifetime of

sexual acts, and thereafter has a duty, the marriage debt, to provide sexual relief. Therefore marital rape is conceptually impossible—unless the compelled spouse would rather pray. The fact that Pauline access to one's spouse causes boredom rather than lust, attenuating the motive to objectify one's spouse, is the only consolation.

In this regard, comparing Paul's account of permissible sex with Immanuel Kant's is instructive:

> The sole condition on which we are free to make use of our sexual desire depends upon the right to dispose over the person as a whole. . . . If I have the right over the whole person, I have also the right over the part and so I have the right to use that person's *organa sexualia* for the satisfaction of sexual desire. But how am I to obtain these rights over the whole person? Only by giving that person the same rights over the whole of myself. This happens only in marriage. Matrimony is an agreement between two persons by which they grant each other equal reciprocal rights, each of them undertaking to surrender the whole of their person to the other with a complete right of disposal over it. [30]

When two people enter a Kantian marriage, granting each other rights over the whole person, they end up having Pauline power over each other's bodies; this is what the right *to dispose over* the other means. The question remains. Do Paul's and Kant's notions of marriage—consider Paul's talk of power over, ownership of, another's sexuality, and Kant's talk of obtaining rights over another person's genitals—reduce the spouses to sex objects, or is the voluntary agreement of the spouses to the arrangement sufficient to justify it?

Further, is the contention that sex is permissible only in marriage supportable? Aquinas has a reply: having sex only in a monogamous marriage is required for the progeny's well-being and is part of the natural design. Paul, too, has a reply: anything less than lifelong, monogamous marriage—say, a series of marriages, peppered with divorce—would *be* the fornication for which marriage was supposed to be the remedy. But for Kant that question is troublesome: it seems to be conceptually possible, and thus morally admissible, for two people—gay or straight—to grant each other reciprocal rights to dispose over their persons for a specific, limited period of time, either for three years in a contracted marriage or the few hours of a casual encounter. Apparently, nothing in the idea of an exchange of rights per se entails it must be forever or exclusive.

Thomas Aquinas

St. Thomas's sexual ethics, it is often said, are "inhumane." In particular, Aquinas is guilty of "firmly laying it down that masturbation is a graver sin than rape."[31] Let's examine his sexual ethics to discover how he reached this conclusion.

A sexual act can be morally wrong in two distinct ways (*Summa theologiae*, 2a2ae, question 154, article 1, 207). First, "when the act of its nature is incompatible with the purpose of the sex-act [procreation]. In so far as generation is blocked, we have unnatural vice, which is any complete sex-act from which of its nature generation cannot follow." Aquinas means anal sex, masturbation, and bestiality, which are not procreative. Second, "the conflict with right reason may arise from the nature of the act with respect to the other party." Aquinas mentions incest, rape, seduction, and adultery. If a man seduces another man's unmarried and virgin daughter into coitus, the seduction is not unnatural vice; but it is morally wrong in violating proper relations among men. This seduction would (also) be unnatural if the act performed were anal coitus. At this place in the *Summa*, Aquinas only describes two types of immorality; he has not yet defended his hierarchy in which acts of the first kind (mortal sins) are morally worse than acts of the second kind (venial sins).[32]

Later in the *Summa*, Aquinas mentions four examples (q. 154, a. 11, 245) of sexual acts that are unnatural vice because they are not procreative: first, "the sin of self-abuse"; next, "intercourse with a thing of another species"; third, acts "with a person of the same sex"; and, finally, acts in which "the natural style of intercourse is not observed, as regards the proper organ or according to other rather beastly and monstrous techniques." (He means heterosexual anal and oral sex.) Eventually, Aquinas arranges these four into a hierarchy, in which the morally worst (since the most unnatural, the least connected with procreation) appears at the top (249):

- bestiality: wrong species,[33]
- sodomy (homosexuality): right species, wrong sex,

- heterosexual perversions: right sex, wrong holes,
- masturbation: improper use of organ (semen misses every hole).

Masturbation is at the bottom; it is an unnatural vice, although a wimpy one.

But since "unnatural vice flouts nature by transgressing its basic principles of sexuality, it is in this matter the gravest of sins" (247). Aquinas is here replying to an interlocutor who argues that unnatural vice is *not* the morally worst sex. "The more a sin is against charity," says the interlocutor, "the worse it is. Now adultery and seduction and rape harms [*sic*] our neighbour, whereas unnatural lust injures nobody else, and accordingly is not the worst form of lust." Aquinas rejects this thinking, concluding that unnatural vice, including masturbation, *is* "the gravest of sins" and worse than rape (but rape is still always a sin). He constructs another hierarchy, this time *between* unnatural vice and the other group of offenses, employing this rationale: "unnatural sins," the worst, are an "affront to God," since they violate the plan of His creation, whereas seduction, rape, and adultery violate only "the developed plan of living according to reason" (for example, property rights), which "comes from man" (249). Then Aquinas constructs a hierarchy of wrongs *within* the natural category: raping a wife is worse than adultery, adultery is worse than seduction, and so forth.

No wonder Aquinas's ethics have a bad reputation. On Aquinas's view, every sexual act—homosexual anal intercourse, heterosexual oral sex, masturbation—that would ordinarily be performed purely for the pleasure of it, because by its very nature it could not fulfill a procreative intent, is the gravest of sins. Aquinas's pro-procreative natural law ethics are anti-pleasure for its own sake. There is not that much difference between him and Augustine.

Contraception

Aquinas's treatment of sex in the *Summa* makes no mention of contraception. Why, in his hierarchy of unnatural vice, does he not explicitly insert "using contraception" *(right sex, right hole, but as if no hole)* between heterosexual fellatio *(right sex, wrong hole)* and masturbation *(no hole)*?

Not condemning contraception by name is curious because contraception is, tautologously, anti-procreative, the sort of thing Aquinas's natural law ethics were designed to prohibit. In a liberal mood, the Paul of 1 Corinthians 7, not much concerned with procreation, might allow contraception in marriage as a way to increase sexual pleasure and rebuff sin (which tactic could backfire, if the spouses were tempted to use contraception outside marriage). But Augustine confidently denounced contraception; if conception is prevented "by wrong desire or evil appliance" (anal coitus or mechanical devices), the spouses "are really not" husband and wife; their "criminal conduct" in blocking conception (or aborting a fetus) means "they have not come together so much by holy wedlock as by abominable debauchery."[34] Aquinas, by contrast, equivocates:

> every emission of semen, in such a way that generation cannot follow, is contrary to the good for man. And if this be done deliberately, it must be a sin. Now, I am speaking of a way from which, *in itself*, generation could not result; such would be any emission of semen apart from the natural union of male and female. For which reason, sins of this type are called *contrary to nature*. But, if by accident generation cannot result from the emission of semen, then this is not a reason for its being against nature, or a sin; as for instance, if the woman happens to be sterile.[35]

Apply the *beginning* two sentences to contraception: heterosexual intercourse with contraceptive devices (olive oil, acacia gum, a sponge soaked in vinegar)[36] involves an emission of semen in such a way that conception cannot occur, or is less likely, so it is contrary to the good of man. And since a device is deliberately used in order to block conception, it must be a sin. Further, a contraceptive intention fulfilled through coitus interruptus would be unnatural and morally wrong; as in masturbation, semen would fly off into dead space. Now apply the *final* sentence: if sterile intercourse is permissible because it only accidentally fails to be procreative, contraception, which fails by design, is sinful. But in the *middle* portion Aquinas apparently says that *all* acts of heterosexual coitus are natural. Coitus, when contraceptive, does not involve the "emission of semen apart from the natural union of male and female," for the penis occupies, and semen is deposited in, the right place, even if that space is occupied also by leaves or latex. The question is whether Aquinas can speak meaningfully of heterosexual coitus per se as an act "in itself." If not, if contraceptive coitus is a distinct act, the naturalness of heterosexual coitus per se would not automatically transfer to contraceptive intercourse.[37]

Two Catholic authorities, Popes Paul VI and John Paul II, are as confident as Augustine that contraception is wrong. The earlier pope asserted that, by natural law, "each and every marriage act . . . must remain open to the transmission of life," and therefore "conjugal acts made intentionally infecund" are immoral.[38] He also argued, in Kantian style, that the use of contraception can make a husband "lose respect" for a wife (175). Since using contraception implies that the act is for pleasure,[39] the husband might see the wife as "a mere instrument of selfish enjoyment." John Paul II expressed a similar thought:

> When the idea that 'I may become a father' / 'I may become a mother' is totally rejected in the mind and will of husband and wife nothing is left of the marital relationship, objectively speaking, except mere sexual enjoyment. One person becomes an object of use for another person.[40]

John Paul hides nothing from us: "pleasure," for him, is only "an incidental accompaniment of the sexual act."[41] So much the worse for Paul's idea that the rationale of marriage is the pleasure afforded by mutual access; later Christians, as we had worried, interpret Pauline marriage as a school in sexual objectification. In this "abominable debauchery" of marital contraceptive sex, writes Augustine, "the woman is, so to say, the husband's harlot; or the man, the wife's adulterer."[42]

Thus Augustine would be shocked to hear that a contraceptive technique used by the Manichees, which he roundly condemned, was eventually blessed by a gaggle of popes.[43] In "Humanae Vitae," Paul VI, picking up on an idea voiced by Pius XI in his 1930 encyclical "Casti connubii,"[44] asserts that regulating birth by restricting the conjugal act to infecund periods is "licit" (174). But if "every action which, either in anticipation of the conjugal act, or in its accomplishment, or in the development of its natural consequences, proposes . . . to render procreation impossible" (173) is wrong, then how can deliberately avoiding sex during fecund periods be licit? Doing so "in anticipation of the conjugal act" is an express "proposal" to prevent conception. What, as my students want dearly to know, is the difference between smart spacing of the conjugal act and smart use of contraception, when the intention is the same, to engage in sex without worrying (as much) about conceiving a child? Paul VI's reply is brief: "in the former, the married couple make legitimate use of a natural disposition; in the latter, they impede the development of natural processes" (175). *Intending* to avoid conception has apparently turned out to be a red herring; it is licit to avoid conception by relying on natural processes, illicit to do so by interfering with natural processes.

But isn't refusing to act on the sexual urge during fecund periods *unnatural*? Even Aquinas said that the urge was natural, since implanted by God. And if nature has any sensible design, the sexual urge would be strongest during fecund periods; that is, the impulse tied to procreation is meant to be acted on, not squelched, when conception is likely.[45] Abstaining from sex at fecund times is therefore an interference with a natural process, although not an interference that uses *artificial* devices. Is this the difference? Judge and legal scholar Richard Posner thinks not, and believes he can improve on Paul VI:

> The Church's approval of the rhythm method may seem to undermine . . . [its] disapproval of artificial contraception. It does not. The rhythm method can be characterized as a form of (periodic) abstinence. So it is not nature versus artifice but abstinence from sex versus indulgence in sex that distinguishes the rhythm method . . . from other methods.[46]

In this description of the "rhythm method," Posner contrasts (1) refraining from sex during fecund periods, to avoid conception, and engaging in sex during infecund periods, and (2) engaging in sex in both periods, and using contraceptive devices to prevent pregnancy. But how accurate is it to say that the distinction between (1) and (2) is one between "abstinence" from and "indulgence" in sex? Compare two people, following (1), who screw their brains out during infecund periods, having built up sexual tension during the fecund period, and two other people, following (2), who do it regularly twice a week. Abstinence versus indulgence? Where is the abstinence in the abstinence? And whether people follow (1) or (2), isn't their intention the same?[47]

Posner is on the right track, but he omitted the central detail, which shows that abstinence per se is not what matters. John Paul II solves the problem thus: "periodic continence as a means of regulating conception" is licit when the spouses "are prepared to renounce sexual intercourse for other reasons (religious reasons for instance) and not only to avoid having children."[48] Hence, abstaining from sex merely to avoid procreation is not permitted; that is abstaining for the wrong reason. Periodic abstinence, like chastity, is a virtue to be pursued for its own sake and not merely for family planning; it is therefore wrongly conceived as a *method of birth control.* The "periodic" does not mean "every other two weeks," on and off; periods of religious abstinence might last a continuous six months or much longer.[49] Students groan when they hear this explanation; it solves the analytic, but not the pastoral, problem. The distinction, then, is between (1) engaging in sex, *during any period,* trying to prevent conception, by whatever method (which is illicit), and (2) abstaining from sex, *during any period,* even infecund, for weighty religious reasons (permissible). Paul in Corinthians tells the spouses to have sex for pleasure, because that is the purpose of sex in marriage, and adds that abstaining is permissible for the sake of prayer; John Paul tells the spouses to have sex for procreation, because *that* is the purpose of sex in marriage, and adds that abstaining is permissible, in effect, for the sake of prayer.

Re-eroticization

What my students need is re-eroticization, not preaching. "Re-eroticization" means making over, by adding, subtracting, or modifying, sexual preferences and desires, refashioning our personal inventory of the things, people, movements, pressures, sensations, and thoughts that arouse and bring us pleasure (or disgust and pain). Expanding the sexual by regaining the ability to get pleasure from taboo acts, partners, and zones of the body is one kind of re-eroticization.[50] But what my students need, to please the Vatican, is either to enjoy sex less or to be more aroused by the idea of procreative copulation. Using contraception is not the Aristotelian mean between spouses' not having any sex and being encumbered with too many children. Periodic abstinence is that mean.

Re-eroticization has its uses; these can be, like any other technique, for Good or Bad. It has been employed by psychiatry to deal with homosexuality. Turn them (back) into heterosexuals, is the philosophy. Rapists and pedophiles have been treated by "masturbatory satiation," a method of inducing sexual boredom: endlessly repeat the stimulus pornographically during bouts of masturbation, and keep presenting the stimulus post-orgasmically while masturbation continues.[51] If unlimited access to one's spouse in Pauline marriage can kill desire, why not a surfeit of orgasms coupled with too many photos of young kids in provocative nude poses?

Re-eroticization is also promoted by safe sex advocates: we are counseled to learn to enjoy safe activities even if they are repugnant to, or fail to excite, our current erotic nature. How marvelous it would be to overcome the cheerlessness of safe sex by being able to enjoy fellatio when the penis is covered by a latex condom, or to cathect the condom itself, changing it from a desiccated shell to a lovely layer of skin, a second prepuce. To be really safe, how felicitous it would be to cathect the cubitus or patella. Annie Sprinkle (a true student of Diotima) thinks everything can be eroticized: "make love to the earth and sky and all things and they will make love to you," she promises. Sexual pleasure will no longer be a scarce resource: "orgasm is possible from breathing alone, without any touching."[52] When the whole of the body and components of the solar system are eroticized, the concept of the sexual must change as well: re-eroticization and re-conceptualization proceed apace. We learn "cat," and we learn what cats are, together.

Safe sex advocates assume that the demand for sex is inflexible; because sex is a joy of the first rank, expecting people to abandon sex altogether in the face of even deadly disease is unrealistic. Re-eroticization is necessary: if people won't give up sex, at least get them to recast their desires and focus on safe acts. This is a Pauline strategy; the Aristotelian mean between deadly fornication and celibacy is safe sex. (Some also argue that to ask teenagers to abstain from sex is silly; instead, teach them about and make condoms available.) But what if it is not the desire for sexual pleasure that is inflexible, but the desire for sexual pleasure produced in certain ways? If the advocates of safe sex are right about the general inflexibility of sex, but wrong about that which in the sex is inflexible, we should expect people to engage in risky sex because they cannot relinquish their distinctive avenues of pleasure. We have to catch everyone much earlier in life to make breathing orgasmic, about the time they are learning "cat." In the meantime, Paul's religious permission to enter marriage in order to avoid sin can be transformed into secular advice: get married or form a couple, and do all you can within that monogamous (straight or gay) state to keep yourself and your partner satisfied. Make your bodies accessible to each other not to escape sin, but to avoid AIDS.

Germaine Greer thinks it irrational that our culture employs drugs and mechanical devices to prevent pregnancy, since we have such natural and effective means as oral sex, anal intercourse, mutual masturbation, coitus interruptus, and homosexual acts.[53] You want pleasure but you don't want progeny? No need to play around with noxious chemicals or metal loops; try anal sex. Indeed, Greer draws a cosmic lesson from the fact that humans, unlike animals, engage in sexual variations: "we might ask what the point of all the versatility is if not to avoid unwanted pregnancy." That's a cute twist; natural law gave us sodomy, not rhythms, to rely on in family planning. Note that the answer Greer spurns, as too narrow, is that the point of versatility is as an end in itself, the pleasure of variety its own justification. Greer boosts the recovery of our lost nongenital sexuality, a re-eroticization of the de-eroticized intended to serve the laudable instrumental purpose of contraception, turning on its head the procreatively motivated de-eroticization of nongenital sexuality. What a shame, though, that we live in a world in which these zones and acts are to be re-eroticized not for their intrinsic joy, but for the bland utilitarian reason that our families might otherwise be too soon or too large and the planet too crowded.

Love

Fortunately for Catholic ethics, John Paul II solved the riddle of how to make periodic abstinence logically compatible with the prohibition of contraception, for the Church, once it accepts the "rhythm method" of birth control *as* birth control, was in danger of sliding down a vicious slippery slope. If rhythm is licit, and no significant distinction exists between rhythm and contraceptive devices, then contraception is licit. If conjugal sex with contraception is licit, as long as the act expresses and reinforces spousal love and the pursuit of mutual sexual pleasure does not lead spouses to treat each other as means, then a whole previously untapped repertoire of nonprocreative sexual practices unfolds for the married couple, who can rejoice in Greerian versatility as a gift from God. And if these acts are deemed licit for *this* reason, that they express and reinforce love, the door is open to homosexuality, not only because when nonprocreative acts are no longer illicit the sexual acts of homosexuals cannot be judged intrinsically objectionable, but also because when love itself plays a central role in redeeming marital sex, homosexual love will equally justify homosexual sex.[54] Indeed, the popular idea that love between X and Y is not merely necessary, but also sufficient, for their sexual relations to be licit has immediate application to homosexuality, if homosexuals can love in that Shakespearean sense—"Let me not to the marriage of true minds / Admit impediments" (Sonnet 116)—our culture admires. Of course they can, and do, which fact is often invoked both to justify gay sex and to promote gay marriage: "As gay men, we do not believe our love is of any less magnitude or importance than that of any other couples in a long-term committed relationship. For that reason we want the legal recognition of our Holy Union."[55]

The crucial claim that waxes the slope is that sex acts, including nonprocreative acts, express and bolster the love that spouses have for each other; pleasurable sexual acts are both a result of and a contributor to love. If one does not want to go whole hog—that is, to justify sex in its own terms, as intrinsically valuable for the pleasure it yields—then once it is admitted that sex acts, to be licit, need not be instrumentally valuable in terms of procreation, the instrumental value of sexuality in terms of expressing and cementing love must instead be asserted. To hear moderate Protestants or radical Catholics making this claim is no longer unusual. But coming across gay and feminist writers who embrace this hoary link between sex and love is startling.

Consider, for example, the views of Richard Mohr, an outspoken gay philosopher. Mohr is not reluctant to acknowledge that sexual "pleasure is its own bottom"—it can justify itself—because "sex as the most intense of pleasures is one of the central free-standing components of the good life."[56] If sex provides the most intense pleasure we can experience, that would appear to be justification enough for sex, and it protects gay sex as convincingly as it protects heterosex. Why would one, in addition, need or want to appeal to sex's power to secure love? Mohr surprisingly proceeds to do so: "Further, if matrimonial love is central to the good life, sex will be central for this reason as well." Mohr offers this justification of sex, at first, to those persons for whom the self-justification of sex is too incredible. But Mohr soon admits that he, too, finds special beauty in the sex-love connection: "the relation of sex to love is like the relation of a figured bass to a piece of music with a figured bass or . . . the repeating bass line of a passacaglia to the passacaglia as a whole" (114). Mohr's concern is not merely aesthetic; it is, more importantly, legal. *Because* sex makes "a necessary and positive contribution" to love, the state, "in blocking gays from having sex," as in *Bowers v. Hardwick*, "would also deny them love." At bottom is a strategic motive for asserting the sex-love connection; Mohr employs as his lever a dominant value of mainstream society, love, to get the criminal law off the backs of gays. This is a worthy goal, but one that logically requires only the claim that sex is its own bottom.

Indeed, Mohr asserts the idea that sex does not need defense by love or matrimony in terms so elaborate and emphatic that one might conclude— this is how far we have come from Augustine—that we have a moral right to engage in sex. Mohr expands the instrumental defense of sex: "for those people with a sex drive, . . . appropriating [sex] to oneself in some way or another is probably necessary to fulfilled life" (109). We all need food; most need sex, not only for love but for life itself. But Mohr goes farther: "it is not merely as a need that sexual pleasure is central to human life" (113). Sex is truly its own bottom:

> in intensity and in kind it is unique among human pleasures; it has no passable substitute from other realms of life. For ordinary persons . . . orgasmic sex is the only access they have to ecstasy.

In praising sexual pleasure, Mohr slights Plato on the pleasure of beautiful ideas and Aristotle and Montaigne on the bliss of friendship; and he clearly does not play chess, or play it very well. It is curious that this philosopher, who must as gay take for granted the plurality of human interests and aims, would so blatantly homogenize and pretend to speak for the multitudes of ordinary people who *enjoy* sex but *would die* for their pots, or dances, or stamps, or drugs, for the ecstatic pleasure these things, not sex, make possible. Still, Mohr is right that the joys of sex can be enormous, especially if the acts are prolonged and varied rather than quick and repetitive. So sex, including gay sex, is justifiable, and worthy of admiration and protection, on the grounds that sexual pleasure can be divine. But to make this argument one need not overstate the joys of sex or denigrate the pleasures of other activities.

Need

Mohr's applause for sexual pleasure as unique "in intensity and in kind" is hardly alone among hyperbolic philosophies of sex, and is amply rivaled by Janice Moulton's sweet words: "sexual behavior differs from other behavior by virtue of its unique feelings and emotions and its unique ability to create shared intimacy."[57] Sex is looking pretty good; it is exceptional in its ability to foster such vital, even if disparate, things as love and pleasure. This dual goodness of sex is the foundation of Ellen Willis's defense of women's access to abortion.

An antiabortion position that refuses to die says this: a woman's choice is surely important, but it is operative exactly when she decides whether to engage in sex. She knows that if she engages in sex, there is some chance she will get pregnant. If she doesn't want that, she should refrain from sex to begin with, instead of relying on the cushion of abortion. Women who become pregnant through the coercion of rape are entitled to abortion. Apart from that, if a woman does not want a child, she should not perform the first step in the procreative causal chain. Let her abstain until she is ready to mother.

We need a broader notion of rape, or of coercion, than the conservative or antiabortionist usually presumes. The cushion of abortion is necessary at least because women are vulnerable to a kind of male force (not merely physical, but also psychological and economic) to engage in coitus that might not legally count as rape or even be acknowledged as rape by either party, a pressure that men exert on women not only during college dating but also in urban ghettos and the suburbs.[58] This is not what disturbs Willis here. Instead, she replies:

> In 1979, it is depressing to have to insist that sex is not an unnecessary, morally dubious self-indulgence but a basic human need, no less for women than for men. Of course, for heterosexual women giving up sex also means doing without the love and companionship of a mate. . . . "Freedom" bought at such a cost is hardly freedom at all, and certainly not equality.[59]

Willis's rebuttal is not about women who are pressured into sex; she has in mind women who freely engage in sex. For Willis, sex is a "basic human need"; in fulfilling that need women should not have to endure obstacles such as inadequately available abortion. Further, in order to begin, develop, and sustain meaningful love relationships, women must be sexually free. They must not be obstructed by worries about unplanned pregnancies.

Willis's rebuttal is a variation of Mohr's one-two punch. The "basic human need" for sex itself justifies sexual freedom for women. But the grounds for causing the death of a fetus cannot be the raw pleasure, no matter how ecstatic, to be obtained from sex. The right of homosexuals and others to engage in homosexual sex can easily be justified, logically if not politically, by appealing to the intrinsic value of sex; but to defend feticide only on the basis of an orgasm would be morally crass, even if sex is a "basic human need." Willis goes beyond this, as Mohr did, by reaching for the sex-love link. Now her argument for feticide turns on more weighty considerations: sex is essential for meaningful love relationships, so denying women the freedom to engage in sex is to deny them love, companionship, and mates.

Mohr argues that when the state prohibits homosexual sex, it thereby prohibits or interferes with homosexual love; Willis argues that when the state interferes with women's sexual freedom, it threatens women's heterosexual relationships. Although Willis uses Mohr's strategy, there is an important difference. Willis wants to establish more than the weak Mohrish conclusion that the state should not prohibit women from engaging in sex; more than this, access to abortion is required if the freedom to engage in sex is to be the real thing. Or, more precisely, if women are to have the same quality of freedom to engage in sex as men have (or as men themselves would like to have), women must be relieved fully of the worry of pregnancy. Access to abortion is therefore justified as a way of achieving equality between the freedoms of men and women.

But Willis's claim that access to abortion is necessary for women's sexual freedom, and so for their maintaining close, or even casual, heterosexual relationships, assumes that the desires of their partners include an inflexible preference for coitus. This assumption can be challenged à la Greer: women practicing during fecund periods (even if it takes re-eroticization) oral sex, anal sex, aural sex, elbow sex, and mutual masturbation, and neglecting coitus, would be able to have their cake and eat it. They would avoid pregnancy *and* fuse the pair-bond with varied sexual pleasure. Further, a woman's doing without sex hardly means giving up companionship or losing the opportunity to acquire a mate; it means only that a certain kind of mate is forfeited. Rushing into sex under the pressure to form a couple might be to make a concession to mainstream sexist values. For the traditional women and men Willis was trying to answer, doing without sex is required for getting a good mate, not opposed to it, and the premarital sexual tension induced by abstinence might itself weld the pair-bond. In their view, women can combine good sex and intimacy within a monogamous marriage marked by responsible and abortionless parenthood.[60] Women can have this cake, and eat it.

Willis wants women to have the cushion of abortion because women, not men, are the ones who become pregnant and hence women need relief from fears about pregnancy. But the equality between the sexual freedoms of men and women that Willis desires could be attained other than by making it possible for women to behave more like Willis believes men behave or are free to. Equalizing sexual freedom could be accomplished, instead, by reducing men's sexual freedom, or inspiring men to conform more to a Christian sexual ethic. Or equality could be achieved by increasing men's worries about pregnancy rather than decreasing the worries women have: men are to be put on notice that they are responsible for a child. These replies to Willis are standard conservative fare, but sometimes also feminist fare. Catharine MacKinnon, for one, derides abortion rights for making women "available to be freely fucked" by relieving them, like men, of "having to be responsible for children."[61] Sidney Callahan, similarly, thinks that

> women will only flourish when there is a feminization of sexuality, very different from the current cultural trend toward masculinizing female sexuality. . . . [Men's] sexual orientation has been harmful to women and children. It has helped bring us epidemics of venereal disease, infertility, pornography, sexual abuse, adolescent pregnancy.[62]

The fact that Willis speaks more in terms of freedom (of women, to be like men) than of responsibility (of both) shows the difficult gap to be bridged between liberal and conservative thought, especially when gender and feminism are thrown into the mix.

In raising an eyebrow at Mohr's and Willis's reliance on a justificatory sex-love connection, I do not mean to question the legal gains made by homosexuals and women or the expansion of their freedoms. But I do think that pursuing these goals by espousing a traditional sex-love link is intellectual treason to both movements. Nor do I deny that sex can create shared intimacy or that close relationships contribute to a full life. Sexuality is a bonding mechanism that often forges a joint interest out of two separate interests, at times miraculously allowing us to resolve moral and psychological tensions between egoism and benevolence. When sex involves pleasing both the self and the other, such exchanges can generate gratitude and affection. But the thought that sexual pleasure is precious in its own right, that seeking it requires no external vindication, is a more spirited alternative to the sex-negativity of Augustinian Christianity than an instrumental justification of sex in terms of love. No contradiction arises in the assumption that persons who exhibit all the virtues—they are compassionate, courageous, courteous, dependable, fair, honest, and tolerant—could and do lead lives in which sexual pleasure is sought for its own sake. Neither love, nor marriage, nor any sort of commitment must be invoked to justify sex.[63]

Sexuality *is* significant, not as a corrupting influence of the flesh on the psyche, but as a cardinal affirmation of the goodness of bodily existence. The opportunities to attain sexual pleasure should be expanded—for the old and young, the mentally or physically challenged and the well-bodied, the straight and the gay, the educated and the untutored, women and men alike—and social and legal arrangements devised to reduce the evil effects of sexual encounters. Sexual ethics is still serious business; what follows, however, is not that prohibitive moral rules are called for, but weak ones. This does not mean we have a moral right to engage in sex. Reasons for asserting such a right do exist: the value of pleasure per se and its role in the good life; the contribution shared pleasure makes to personal intimacy. But the strongest argument for a right would be that the "basic human need" for sex requires, as does eating and breathing, doing what is hardwired into the human design. But this kind of argument is scorned, by many liberals, socialists, and feminists, as granting too much to Natural Law.

Exonerations

We often exculpate wrongful acts motivated by hunger, because we think we have a "basic human need" for food; filching apples when one is starving can be excused, if the deed does not endanger others. Or we might excuse indigent Heinz if he steals the drug his wife needs. Then why should we not excuse those who commit wrongs in attempting to satisfy Willis's "basic human need" for sex, in particular (to draw the closest analogy), the frustrated rapist who believes he has no other option? The answer is that the rapist, in quenching sexual thirst this way, does so at too great a cost to another person. Not satisfying one's need for sex is not life-threatening, so rape is a kind of inexcusable theft or, perhaps better, an imperialist colonization. Sex should not be treated differently: it is bound, like anything else, by a weighing of harms and benefits. Even if there were a right to sex, it would not entail that we must refuse to condemn sexual misconduct (rape or adultery) or nonsexual behavior that is sexually motivated (a promotion based on attractiveness). Constraints would limit this right as they do any other.

Still, we sometimes do excuse sexual behavior, or behavior motivated sexually, apparently relaxing our standards, treating the event as an exceptional case. An old, discredited theory as to why we should be willing to go overboard to forgive in sexual matters claims that of all the human passions, sexual desire has the strongest capacity to defeat logic and pervert the rational calculus that governs our lives. Sexual desire is an Augustinian disease that vanquishes the will and submerges reason, a malady to which men, more than women, are acutely or chronically susceptible and which can be brought out of remission by perfume, tight jeans, or a smile. Under the influence of "urgent" sexual desire, says Bertrand Russell, "all other interests fade for the moment, and actions may be performed which will subsequently appear insane to the man who has been guilty of them."[64] Sexual desire and arousal invade and occupy us, compelling or tricking us to do unwise things. So men and women under the mind-crippling pressure of sexual desire might be pardoned for rudely discounting, during noncontraceptive coitus, the possibility of progeny. Exculpating sexual misconduct on the grounds that uncontrollability is inherent to sex would be an *internal* exoneration of sex: by its very nature, sex would excuse itself. We do not and should not exonerate shady sexual acts by claiming they were irresistible, although other considerations might be found to support the idea of an internal exoneration of sex.

Catharine MacKinnon seems convinced that, in our culture, sex has internal exonerating power. According to MacKinnon, Susan Brownmiller's 1975 book, *Against Our Will*, was a great advance in feminist thought, since (on MacKinnon's reading of the book)[65] it conceived of rape *not* as a sexual act but as a piece of violence.[66] This was a major event, on MacKinnon's view, because "labeling virtually any act sex was considered exonerating—as in fact it still is."[67] The internal power of sex to exonerate itself applied even to rape, but once rape was seen as violence, not sex, the exoneration blessedly evaporated. MacKinnon's tale is remarkable, for her claim, that "labeling virtually any act sex" was then, and is now, to exonerate it, is extravagant and rash. We have always and mostly been *less* lenient in our judgments of sexual misconduct, rather than more. We do treat sex as a special case, but in the opposite sense that sexual acts are more carefully scrutinized for possible flaws and we punish sexual acts more harshly when they overstep boundaries. Not for one moment did we exonerate Clarence Thomas or Robert Packwood because their acts were sexual or sexually motivated. To the contrary, calling attention to any imaginable sexual component of any action, whether in the act itself or as motive, is precisely the way to make the perpetrator appear as bad a person as possible, not as good as possible, in the public forum. "There is no disgrace," whether in 1946, 1976, or 1996, "that is more feared than that which may result from sexual scandal."[68] We are, as was Augustine, distrustful of sexual pleasure sought for its own sake. We do not exonerate sex by sex, just as we do not acknowledge the justification of sex by sex.

The fact that justifying sex by love is more effective than justifying sex by sex suggests that love is what exculpates sex: the exoneration proceeds externally and instrumentally, not intrinsically. The exoneration, if there is any, comes from the acts being labeled acts of *love*, perhaps blissful romantic love. Humans can be forgiven if they are tempted away from duty by the anticipation of tasting this rare Beauty before it vaporizes. It

is not now, and never was in recent history, lusty, sweaty, masculine/
Greek sex that exonerates; the encounter has to have something uplifting
and feminine/Christian about it, or at least the accused must be able to
pass off a tawdry quickie as if it were divinely inspired, in order to achieve
even a smidgen of exculpation. Had Clarence Thomas told the world he
had felt a deep and profound *love* for Anita Hill, and envisioned being
united with her in the eyes of the Lord, eventually sitting together on the
Court, and he hoped, in his own Black Republican way, that his sexual
provocations would initiate the repeating bass line of the passacaglia of
their love, he might have garnered more tears of sympathy than he did
with his indignant tales of being lynched. Thomas should have pictured
himself the lover described by Pausanias in the *Symposium,* so enchanted
by Anita that he was reduced to "praying for the fulfillment of his
requests, making solemn promises, camping on doorsteps, and voluntarily
submitting to a slavery such as no slave ever knew," but for a purpose that
was "supremely noble." [69] Perhaps he had too much character, after all, to
appeal publicly to the sure winner of Mohr and Willis, that all was done
"in the name of love."

The exoneration of sexual misconduct by love can get out of hand.
Bonnie Steinbock opines:

> People do fall in love with others and out of love with their spouses. Ought
> they refrain from making love while still legally tied? I cannot see much, if
> any, moral value in remaining physically faithful, on principle, to a spouse
> one no longer loves. [70]

This judgment presumably applies as well when one *never* loved one's
spouse (Prince Charles). Whether the spurned spouse still loves the adulterous spouse who has found love elsewhere is not recognized by
Steinbock's pronouncement to have any significance. But if it is already
odd to think that just because X no longer loves Y, X has carte blanche to
sleep with a new beloved Z, the judgment that when Y still loves X, X may
still do as X cavalierly pleases is chilling. Further, in addition to X's not
loving Y any longer, has Y been terribly nasty to X, to deserve such
treatment? In "Faded Leaves," [71] Matthew Arnold positively rejects exonerating adultery by love:

> Each on his own strict line we move,
> And some find death ere they find love;
> So far apart their lives are thrown
> From the twin soul which halves their own.
>
> And sometimes, by still harder fate,
> The lovers meet, but meet too late.
> —Thy heart is mine! —*True, true! ah, true!*
> —Then, love, thy hand! —*Ah no! adieu!*

It is, says Arnold, sad to belong to someone else when the right one comes along; but the tragedy is not earth-shaking, not enough reason alone for throwing one's mate overboard. (And even less reason when there are children.) Recall the adultery in Hawthorne's *Scarlet Letter.* Even the author was unsure of the exonerating power of love, as indicated (in chapter 17) by Hester Prynne's nearly pitiful declaration to Arthur Dimmesdale: "What we did had a consecration of its own. We felt it so! We said so to each other!" Listen to a Steinbockian adulterer pleading his case: "It was, unlike my stale marriage, true love! I felt it so!" Adultery, in being justified by love, is in this higher court not adultery at all, but its antithesis. Ponder Victoria Woodhull's pompous and more extreme declaration:

> marriage consists of a union resulting from love. . . . It is certain by this Higher Law, that marriages of convenience, and, still more, marriages characterized by mutual or partial repugnance, are adulterous.[72]

Funny logic: the marriage is the adultery, the affair the loving union. Self-righteous Woodhull won't permit a plurality of possible reasons for marriage. Any motive other than love is sinful.

Nature

Oral and anal sex, gay and lesbian sex, bisexual and group sex, contraceptive coitus, promiscuity, prostitution, adultery, making or viewing pornography, masturbation, bestiality, and the various paraphilias: if these activities can sometimes be done without harm befalling the participants or others, by consenting adults who can be presumed to know what they want and are doing, how could they be wrong? This question is often posed rhetorically, as asserting that "they could not be wrong," but it can be asked seriously. Aquinas begins his treatment of sexual morality in *Summa contra gentiles* by expressing a similar point made by his interlocutor:

> Suppose there is a woman who is not married, or under the control of any man, either her father or another man. Now, if a man performs the sexual act with her, and she is willing, he does not injure her, because she favors the action and she has control over her own body. Nor does he injure any other person, because she is understood to be under no other person's control. So, this does not seem to be a sin.[73]

Aquinas rejects this libertarian view, as he rejected his interlocutor's claim that "the more a [sexual] sin is against charity, the worse it is," on the basis of natural law.

Natural law philosophy sits in opposition to the liberal or humanist outlook that derives from both Kant and the British utilitarians. The sexual liberal justifies permissive sexual ethics by appealing to the values of pleasure and autonomy, while the natural law theorist justifies prohibitive sexual ethics by appealing to the design of nature to which human behavior ought to conform. If sexual acts are *unnatural,* contrary to nature (say, anal coitus, bestiality), they will be morally wrong, in this ethical system, just for *that* reason. To one standard list of reasons sexual acts might be wrong—they are dishonest, cruel, unfair, manipulative, coercive, exploitive, selfish, unfaithful, or negligently dangerous[74]—Aquinas adds "unnatural." So, too, does Kant, who condemns a slew of sexual acts as *crimina carnis contra naturam.*[75] Not so the utilitarian and many contemporary Kantians, for whom fellatio and cunnilingus, anal intercourse, mutual masturbation, and, for more radical Kantians, consensual sadomasochism, can be performed with "charity" and full respect between sexual partners.

A continuing problem with Aquinas's line of thought is the difficulty of formulating a coherent and cogent account of the design of nature, an account that perceptively illuminates *human* nature. I think Aquinas realized the problem. Is incestuous heterosexual coitus natural, an affront only to proper social relations, or is it a perversion of nature and a violation of

God's design, as much as homosexuality? Although Aquinas, in stating that unnatural sexual vice is the worst kind, does not include incest, he places incest at the top of the list of the venial sins: incest "offends the inborn respect we should show for those linked to us by family ties."[76] His wording (*inborn* respect), and the fact that incest is the worst sin in the second category, hints that Aquinas was divided between judging incest an unnatural, grave sin and judging it a natural, lesser insult to proper relations among people. Perhaps Aquinas was following Augustine, who, trying to understand the incest that occurred if God created only Adam and Eve (all other humans deriving from them), admitted that incest had taken place, "dictated by necessity," but argued that the later religious prohibition against incest was perfectly right because it served important social purposes (such as maintaining Aquinas's relations among men).[77] It is the social, not the natural, that becomes confused when X is both Y's father and grandfather or Z is Y's mother and aunt.[78]

A resurgence of the application of the natural sciences to the human understanding of human beings has contributed to both the intractability of and fascination with this problem. If we are to believe recent sociobiology, promiscuity in men and women's inclination toward monogamy are genetically entrenched, the result of evolutionary mechanisms, which fact turns Aquinas's reliance on nature—in his argument that the male, too, is programmed for monogamy—on its head. Aquinas is more radically upended if Mary Jane Sherfey is right, that the human female is "biologically determined" to be sexually insatiable, not "biologically built" for monogamous marriage.[79] Further, the new research supporting the idea that homosexual orientation has a nontrivial biological basis implies that the Church might have to concede that homosexual desire, behavior, and pleasure are part of nature's design, a feature of Lisa Cahill's "ecology of the universe."[80] If having homosexual desire is little different from being green in the eye, the Church would be hard pressed to withhold moral acceptability from homosexual love relationships.

Incompatible with Aquinas's biology of the function and proper use of sex organs is this remark in John Paul II's *Love and Responsibility:*

'nature' . . . does not mean 'biological nature' . . . [but] the nature of man in the deeper sense, which takes account of and indeed gives pride of place to, those elements which are not and cannot be embraced by physical and still less by physicalist conceptions of man. (296, n. 22)

If this is true, we shall never have a firm empirical grasp on the humanly natural, and that concept will forever be the plaything of politics. The problem with the idea of the superbiological "nature of man in the deeper sense" is just the flip side of the problem of arguing (almost equivalently) from the inescapably vague "nature of God" instead. This is why the *form* of Christine Gudorf's Christian defense of sexual pleasure,

> If the placement of the clitoris in the female body reflects the divine will, then God wills that sex is not just oriented to procreation, but is at least as, if not more, oriented to pleasure.[81]

often yields jokes rather than a serious point of the kind she wants to make. If God had wanted us to be thin, he would have made pizza logically impossible.

The Necessity of Consent

Consent is widely recognized to be a moral requirement for sexual activity. With the exception of the Marquis de Sade's sexual philosophy — according to which everyone has a right to sexual satisfaction, and no one has a right to refuse anyone's advances (that's a robust right to sex) — it is agreed that participation in sexual activity should not be coerced by force or intimidation, nor should it depend on deception, ignorance, or fraud. This is easy to say, more difficult to apply in practice.

Raymond Belliotti judges sex between a living person and a corpse to be "immoral," on the grounds that it "involves the involuntary participation of one of the parties."[82] This makes it look like there could be both consenting and nonconsenting corpses. (A Stoltenbergian corpse demands to be treated with respect, while the Kunderan variety snaps, with the voice of a ghoulish Camille Paglia, "take me, damn you!") Although *something* is fishy about necrophiliac sexual acts, the view that they are immoral *because* the corpse participates involuntarily — did not consent — is odd. A corpse, like a rug, has no will, can neither consent nor withhold consent; if to masturbate on a rug is not to sexually use the rug involuntarily, against its will, we cannot say that masturbating on or in a corpse involves its "involuntary participation." Thus, there is a difference between masturbating on or in a corpse and masturbating, during an act of rape, on or in a living person. Despite what he says, Belliotti means that if the person who is the corpse-to-be never consents in advance to sex after death, then carrying out a sex act with that corpse would be a wrongful use of the corpse; if a person consents before death to a later sexual act, the use of the corpse by the sexual beneficiary would not be wrong. This does not mean that the corpse participates involuntarily *or* voluntarily; it means only that well in advance of the act, a decision by the corpse-to-be is made, and to the extent that we are obligated *(ceteris paribus)* to abide by the pre-death wishes of the deceased, we will carefully guard, or not, the remains. Something significant therefore does emerge from our contemplation of this queer behavior. Belliotti's view makes an assumption, one that has lately been questioned, that a person can—logically and morally—consent to a sexual act in advance of the time it occurs, even if one has no firm idea when it might occur. Belliotti's view about the morality of necrophiliac sexual acts resembles a principle of Pauline marriage: one consents on the day of marriage to sex acts that will occur some indefinite time in the future. And if marriage is indissoluble, the spouses, like the corpse, have no power of retracting consent.

If consent is necessary, should we not conclude that adult-child sex is wrong? Children are susceptible to the various physical and psychological harms that sexual activity can cause, and any verbal agreement on the part of the child, if it exists, cannot be taken at face value. Children, gullible or trusting by their nature, cannot make a wise selection of partner or act, and find it difficult to withstand manipulation. They are not mentally and socially equipped to give or withhold consent to significant acts. Schopenhauer is unequivocal in his condemnation:

> Pederasty ... encroaches on justice, and the dictum *Volenti not fit injuria* cannot be brought to bear against it. For the wrong consists in the moral corruption of the younger and less experienced members of the community who are thus physically and morally perverted.[83]

This passage is just one of thousands of examples of one of the most commonly held views in the universe.

But adult-child sex might not be an easy case. Robert Ehman argues that we overestimate the harmfulness of sex for children. Further, the inability of children to consent to sex is not necessarily a strike against it.[84] We do many things to and with children to which they do not or cannot consent; so consent should not always be a requirement of permissible sex, dispensable at least, say, when the child has expressed desire for the activity. Pat Califia argues that we patronize children by discounting their initiating sex. From her libertarian perspective, consent is required, but children can give it: "any child old enough to decide whether or not she or he wants to eat spinach, play with trucks or wear shoes is old enough to decide whether or not she or he wants to run around naked in the sun, masturbate, sit in somebody's lap or engage in sexual activity."[85] No paternalism here. From the other side of the political spectrum, Ann Ferguson argues that in a future nonsexist, socialist, nonracist, nonhomophobic, and democratic society, "we could expect the issue of adult-child sex to be much more open for experimentation than it is today. But only when social conditions are egalitarian enough so that children themselves organize a sex-for-youth movement will the conditions be right for such a change."[86]

These views exhibit an innocent lightness. Ehman finds no harm in adult-child sex, besides the guilt trip laid on kids by zealously sex-negative parents; Califia puts having sex into the same category of California after-school activities as getting a tan, skateboarding, and shopping; Ferguson envisions children marching with placards, maybe on St. Patrick's Day, demanding legal recognition of their right to sex. For some, then, Marilyn Frye's gloomy dissent will be a welcome breath of fresh air:

> Sex, unlike baking cookies, going camping, or playing catch, engages some of our strongest emotions and most desperate needs in an enterprise powerfully associated with dominance and subordination, violence and victimization, a mythology of ladies and whores, queers and Real Men, ideas of "dirt" and "filth," and so on and on.[87]

But if Frye's overly sober perceptions are right, and the whole of the sexual world is corrupt in this Augustinian way, I wonder why we bother to bring children into it, with sex, let alone try to teach them that sex is not "filthy." Still, if we should be concerned that women's agreement to acts of prostitution does not always amount to genuine consent, we should worry about children being exploited by their elders. Even if what some children are manipulated to do sexually—like what some women are paid to do in prostitution—is not physically or psychically harmful to them, the bribery, the conniving, is itself contemptible. Whether this ugliness in adult-child relations would disappear, as Ferguson hints, in a society of thorough equality is an obscure question we are in no position to answer. We would have to try it. [88]

The Sufficiency of Consent

For the Thomist, the fact that adults engage in sex consensually is not enough for the act to be licit, because even when third party harm is absent, if the act is unnatural it would be for that reason immoral. The fact that a sexual act abides by human law and respects proper relations among humans is not sufficient justification, for Aquinas. Similarly, for a pater-nalist, it is morally wrong for X to harm Y or for Y to allow X to harm Y, even if X and Y participate voluntarily in this activity, and so their act might be wrong even if it harms no third party. Anyone who worries that sexual objectification is the fruit of the constant access built into Pauline marriage also questions the sufficiency of consent. A "moral libertarian," by contrast, claims that the fact that X and Y participate consensually in their sexual act means that they are being treated as ends by each other and not merely being used; when participation is voluntary rather than coerced, each person is respecting the other as an autonomous agent capable of making up his or her mind about the value of the activity. Hence mutual consent that is free and informed is, in the absence of third party harm, sufficient for the morality of sexual acts. No law of God or nature supplements this basic principle of proper relations among humans.

One issue is whether consent is, ceteris paribus, morally sufficient. A distinct issue concerns what genuine consent is. Can we state the conditions in which to agree verbally is to consent? Does every kind of pressure invalidate an apparent consent? The interplay of these two issues is nicely illustrated in Igor Primoratz's criticism of Bertrand Russell's view of prosti-tution. [89] Russell offered the principle that

> Morality in sexual relations . . . consists essentially of respect for the other person, and unwillingness to use that person solely as a means of personal gratification without regard to his or her desires.

and decided that "prostitution sins against this principle."[90] Primoratz replies to Russell that prostitution "does not offend against the principle of respect for human beings as such as long as [prostitution] is free from coercion and fraud" (173); that is, "informed and freely given consent absolves the relation of any such charge, and thereby also of the charge of degradation" (174). Primoratz, as a moral libertarian, claims that consent is morally sufficient; but it is not obvious that Russell's worries about the morality of prostitution are based on the insufficiency of consent. Note that Russell reflected, at the same time, on the sexual activity of married couples and concluded that much of this sex *also* sinned against his principle: "the total amount of undesired sex endured by women is probably greater in marriage than in prostitution" (122). This suggests that Russell was not impugning the moral power of consent to justify sexual activity, but was insisting on a more critical account of genuine consent.

Sounding like a contemporary socialist feminist, Russell admonished, "the intrusion of the economic motive into sex is always . . . disastrous. Sexual relations should be a mutual delight, entered into solely from the spontaneous impulse of both parties" (121). Women, Russell observes (as did Woodhull), have economic reasons for acquiescing to the sexual demands of their lawful husbands. Hence *one* way to understand Russell's discussion of women's participation in "undesired sex" is to read him as recognizing that wives verbally or silently agree to sex, but do so with enough (unexpressed) reluctance to make their consent dubious or absent. Russell understands the feminist critique of marital sex more clearly than Judge Posner: "Marital rape may be uncommon, since few wives will refuse their husband's demand for sexual intercourse," Posner says.[91] But, *pace* this reading of Russell, the fact that wives do not refuse the demands is evidence that this marital sex is, rather than is not, rape. Russell was voicing in the 1920s something similar to Robin Morgan's account of rape: "how many millions of times have women had sex 'willingly' with men they didn't want to have sex with? . . . How many times have women wished just to sleep instead or read or watch the Late Show? . . . [M]ost of the decently married bedrooms across America are settings for nightly rape."[92]

Russell's fundamental idea is sound: ideally consensual participation in sex requires substantial economic, social, and psychological equality between the persons involved; further, a society that contains poverty is one in which people are exposed to economic coercion, even as it appears that they freely consent to what they do. But it is implausible to conclude that women who engage in prostitution, either now or in some egalitarian future, do not ever genuinely consent just because they have economic motives. The intrusion of money as a reason to engage in sex, as the intrusion of motives other than the plain desire for sensual delight (for example, wanting to have a child, needing to exercise, getting revenge), does not always destroy consent. We can see this, and learn something about consent in prostitution, by thinking about elective euthanasia.

The question of voluntariness is crucial in euthanasia: do the ill persons who elect early death (by active intervention in the life process, or by the withholding of surgery or medication) genuinely consent to that option? There is the pain, and the thought of even more pain, that cannot always be alleviated by drugs, or not alleviated without the loss of mental capacity; there is the fear and guilt of being a burden to loved ones who have their own enormous problems, and the frightening prospect of vegetating, becoming a sorry sight in one's own (present) eyes. These are good reasons for electing euthanasia; but these factors can also be seen as coercive, as nullifying the ability to give consent. Whether they are the first or the second cannot be decided, in advance of inspecting a particular case, by general considerations according to which the factors are, by their very nature, good reasons or coercive. When we are concerned about the quality of consent in a case of proposed euthanasia, we think about the ill or disabled person as an individual with his or her own set of desires and values, we carefully probe his or her mental state, and we investigate the specific pressures that bear on him in his familial and social context. In this personalized determination of the patient's ability to consent to euthanasia, we do not allow ourselves to get bogged down trying to unearth vast, insidious social influences that undermine the consent of all patients and that make untrustworthy the whole "institution" of euthanasia.

By contrast, in sexual matters there is a tendency to take seriously the idea that women's consent is, in virtue of the social system of male dominance, largely chimerical: "there can never be objectively consensual [sexual] relations between members of oppressor and oppressed groups."[93] If women's consent to heterosexual acts within patriarchy is not genuine, this will be especially true of prostitution, which can be seen as rape perpetrated by men with economic power rather than by physical assault or the threat of a knife.[94] But whether women can consent to the sex acts of prostitution would seem to be as much a matter of their mental state, their particular needs and values, and the details of their lives as of their membership in a victimized class. The need to earn money can be a good reason to do something; it can also be coercive. Which it is in a given case cannot be established by sweeping claims about gender oppression; instead, we must do the hard work of hunting for the flyspecks of personalized evidence. For an uneducated, unskilled, and unemployed woman with low self-esteem, the promise of much-needed money for a quick, impersonal sexual act in a car is coercive exploitation that makes her consent phony. But it is implausible to claim that a woman who has some education and a decent command of the language, is personable and attractive, and selects the better-paying life of a Heidi Fleiss call girl in preference to working in Burger Queen must have been coerced and her consent bogus. Simone de Beauvoir's reply is not altogether convincing:

> the prostitute would often have been able to make a living in other ways. But if the way she has chosen does not seem to her to be the worst, that does not prove vice is in her blood; it rather condemns a society in which this occupation is still one of those which seem the least repellent to many women.[95]

Granted, there might be a viable notion of "degradation" according to which a woman's consent to acts of prostitution itself makes the sex degrading, or adds to it, or, more simply (*contra* Primoratz's libertarianism), according to which consent to degradation does not have the power to erase degradation.[96] And a woman's choice of prostitution over Burger Queen does not prove, or even insinuate, that she is evil.

But, on the other hand, there is little reason to conclude that a woman's choice of prostitution is necessarily a ringing critique of a society that tells her, "Burger Queen or whoredom." Not every woman, not every man, can be a neurosurgeon. And the fact that one job (neurosurgery or modeling) pays more than another (waiting on tables) is a weak reason, by itself, for concluding that one did not employ one's "free choice" in selecting the higher-paying (or lower-paying) job. Many women would reply to Robin Morgan's question, "Why be a secretary when you can make more money taking off your clothes?" with "I prefer not to; I choose to do something else."[97] Condemnation, then, seems best saved for the society that has no Burger Queen at all, and offers a woman *only* whoredom. (Many men are told, "Burger Queen or nothing at all.") Thus, when economic inequality between the sexes is erased and coercive poverty is abolished, some people (we cannot predict, but must wait to find out) might still select prostitution or modeling for pornography as a way of earning money.

Paternalism

The rhetorical question—if persons of sound mind and adequate fore-knowledge consent to engage in sex together, and do only the acts that both agree to, and do not wrongfully affect third parties, how could their acts be morally wrong?—has another serious, non-Thomistic answer. The moral paternalist (who is often accused of treating adults as children) claims that one person's harming another—and perhaps a person's allowing himself to be harmed—is wrong, even when both enter into the act fully voluntarily. Paternalism has been used to criticize consensual sadomasochism, but the argument has lost its appeal; people in the sado-masochist community have stressed that their sexual activities are fully consensual and do not involve uncontrolled brutality. But paternalism can be appealed to in contending that much ordinary sex is morally question-able. For example, instead of saying, with Morgan, that in virtue of eco-nomic or other pressure women are routinely raped by their husbands, we could make the less dramatic point that women do consent to this sex, the pressure they accede to does not amount to coercion, yet because they do not desire this sexual activity they are harmed by it. If we now add the paternalist principle, we get a different critique of heterosexual practice.

This argument has been advanced by Robin West, who thinks women are harmed by consenting to sex that they do not desire.[98] A woman might consent to undesired sex, according to West, because she and her children are financially dependent on a man; or she does not want to experience the "foul humor," anger, or abuse that might result from refusal; or she has sex with him in order to gain protection from the unwanted advances of other, "more dangerous" men; or she has sex with him because she thinks it is her duty or "lot in life" or because of "peer expectations" (53). West does not go Morgan's route of saying that in these cases the pressure felt by women is coercive and so the sexual acts are rapes because the women do not participate "willingly." West claims, to the contrary, that a woman's participation in sex in these situations is rational and consensual.

Nevertheless, women's participation in undesired sex harms them; it damages "their sense of selfhood" (53). The women "sustain injuries to their capacities for self-assertion"; they "injure their sense of self-*possession*"; "they injure their sense of autonomy"; and they injure "their sense of integrity." I do not want to quibble over whether West has described four distinct injuries suffered by women or only one, namely, the blow to autonomy, which encompasses the others. Nor do I want to quibble over the nature and extent of the harm women endure in consensual sex, except to say that to engage in undesired sex to silence a nagging husband is not, *contra* Morgan, to be a victim of rape nor, *contra* West, to suffer any insult to one's autonomy. What is more important is the moral lesson West teases out of the existence of harms women experience in consensual sex:

> the considerable harms women sustain from consensual but undesired sex must be downplayed if the considerable pleasure men reap from heterosexual transactions is morally justified—*whatever* the relevant moral theory. Men do have a psycho-sexual stake in insisting that voluntariness alone ought to be sufficient to ward off serious moral or political inquiry into the value of consensual sexual transactions. (54)

One implication is that libertarian sexual ethics, which insist that voluntariness is sufficient to justify sexual activity, are, in their application to heterosexual relations in our culture, male-biased: in being blind *in principle* to the harms women endure in consensual sex, libertarian sexual ethics bless, as morally licit, activity that provides pleasure to men at the expense of women. Another implication is an answer to the question, What else might be required, if sexual activity is to be morally acceptable, beyond consent? Since the fault shared by West's examples of morally suspicious sexual activity is that the sex is *undesired*, the answer must be that the woman participates in the sex only when her own desire, her heart, is wrapped up in the act.

The libertarian has three replies. First, the accusation of male bias cannot stick if men, too, suffer similar, even if unannounced and less frequent, harms from consensual sex: the devoted husband who tries to please his wife sexually out of a sense of duty or to dissuade her from leaving him. If men endure any harm from consensual sex, libertarian sexual ethics would be *equally blind* to its existence and hence would not be biased in favor of either gender. At the least, a defender of libertarian ethics could claim that within the context of a nonsexist society, libertarian insistence on the sufficiency of consent would have no biased application, so the problem West uncovered does not eliminate libertarianism from the ranks of viable moral theories. Second, a reconstructed libertarian, tipping a hat to Morgan, could say that the extreme cases described by West do involve coercion; no genuine consent exists on the woman's part to begin with. If so, libertarian sexual ethics are not biased against women even in this culture; the libertarian does not bless the acquisition by men of sexual pleasure in acts that harm women.

Finally, a libertarian could remind us that the alternative principle West embraces is moral paternalism: a woman's consent does not have enough power by itself to justify sexual activity, because *she* will experience harm from participating voluntarily in it. The libertarian will point out that the principal rationale behind its traditional rejection of moral paternalism is precisely—to turn West's argument against itself—that moral paternalism is a threat to *autonomy*. To claim that a woman's rational, consensual choice is harmful to her, and so a matter of our externally situated "serious moral inquiry," is to declare that women need to be protected from their own rational choosings and that men who abide by the rational and consensual decisions of adult women engage in morally suspicious treatment of them. To demand, in order that sexual activity be morally licit, that in addition to giving consent a woman must be motivated exactly by her own sexual desire for the act itself is to place a meddling limit on what is a respectable reason to engage in sex, in the same way that Russell's critique of prostitution did not sufficiently acknowledge the multiplicity of reasons to engage in sex, and Woodhull's concept of marriage allowed only one acceptable reason for it.

Beyond Consent

Alan Goldman's view is that sexual partners are able to satisfy Kant's Second Formulation—treat one another as ends and not merely as means—by recognizing each other's "subjectivity." How is this done?

> Even in an act which by its nature "objectifies" the other, one recognizes a partner as a subject with demands and desires by yielding to those desires, by allowing oneself to be a sexual object as well, by giving pleasure or ensuring that the pleasures of the act are mutual. [99]

For Goldman, each person's effort to produce pleasure for the other is what is required, beyond consent, to make sexual encounters morally legitimate. But if providing pleasure for each other is included in the terms of their agreement—if what the persons have consented to is that while engaging in sex they try to please each other as they are pleasing themselves—we have not moved beyond consent as that which morally justifies sexual activity. Goldman's principle can be construed, that is, as a logical extension or embellishment of Primoratz's libertarian ethics: mutual consent to engage in sex, when that involves the intention to provide reciprocal pleasure, constitutes moral respect and negates the possibility of persons' merely using each other.

But Goldman's odd-sounding expression, "allowing oneself to be a sexual object," opens the question of whether the presence of consent to be used sexually as an object by another might fail to guarantee that one is not merely being used as an object. On the one hand, X's allowing Y to use X need not entail that X sees himself or herself as a mere toy or the tool of Y's pleasure. After all, X is insisting on X's own pleasure as well, so X is not necessarily engaged in treating himself or herself without respect. (It's cute that X's being self-interestedly concerned for X's own pleasure prevents the encounter from being a case of self-objectification.) On the other hand, however, if two people allow themselves to be used as sexual objects by the other, the instrumentality of their relationship seems to multiply, not reduce. It has been suggested that "by yielding oneself [to another], body and soul, one shows respect for the other as an end."[100] That might very well be true. In satisfying your desires, I treat you and your goals as intrinsically valuable; in offering myself to you, I recognize your personhood. But the claim has a similar air of paradox. In giving myself to you, in devoting myself to your goals, am I not treating myself as a means or object? Something else seems required, beyond yielding, to avoid multiplying the objectification.

If the mutual consent of the partners to be used sexually by the other does not negate their merely being used, we can assert *either* that the moral value of the voluntary nature of the act overrides the fact that it involves mutual use, so the activity is still morally licit (a view indistinguishable in practice from Primoratz's libertarianism); *or* that two mutual uses cannot ever combine to make a virtuous act, since using another person is a supremely significant moral fault and the voluntariness of the act counts for nothing. Kant and Pope John Paul II take the second route. According to them, it is always wrong for two people to use each other as sexual objects, or for one person to allow himself to be used, even when that use is designed for their equal pleasure. More than Goldmanesque consent is required. About lesbian sadomasochism, Claudia Card says, on the positive side, that its "participants generally wish each other well and respect each other's choices." But she continues by expressing a puzzled, and perhaps paternalistic, worry: "the only things distinguishing the behavior of [a top] from battery and other abuse may be the motivations of the parties and the consent of the [bottom]."[101] But what *more* could Card want in distinguishing respectful sadomasochism from battery, other than the parties' motivation and consent to experience mutual pleasure? To say, along with Kant and the pope, that more is needed is to jeopardize all unconventional sex, not just consensual sadomasochism.

If we rule out the additional ingredients a paternalist or a natural law theorist insists on, what else might be required beyond consent? At this point, once the easy negative work has been done of arguing that consent alone might not always be powerful enough, positive and unfuzzy accounts of the magical ingredient are hard to come by. According to John Paul II, long-suffering, patient, forgiving, altruistic, committed love, which can truly exist only in marriage, justifies sexual relations. "Only love can

preclude the use of one person by another," because love is the unification
of two persons into one achieved through the mutual gift of their selves. [102]
Kant, too, argues that sexual activity avoids being mere mutual use only
when it occurs within marriage, since here the persons have surrendered
their selves to each other and have achieved a "unity of will" through
reciprocal ownership. [103] The contemporary philosopher Onora O'Neill
offers an account of what else is necessary, a view reminiscent of Karen
Green's, and almost as woolly:

> Avoiding deceit and coercion are only the core of treating others as persons
> in sexual relationships. In avoiding these we avoid . . . obvious ways of using
> as (mere) means. But to treat another as a person in an intimate, and
> especially an intimate sexual, relationship requires far more. These further
> requirements reflect the intimacy rather than the specifically sexual charac-
> ter of a relationship. However, if sexual relationships cannot easily be merely
> relationships between consenting adults, further requirements for treating
> another as a person are likely to arise in any sexual relationship. Intimate
> bodies cannot easily have separate lives. [104]

Her argument, which talks of "intimacy" instead of Green's "love," is this.
In intimate relationships we are able to treat another as an individual
person: "intimacy . . . offers the best chances for treating others as the
persons they are" (272), since in a close and constant relationship, we
acquire the knowledge of that which makes the other the person she is.
Further, sexual activity requires this sort of intimacy; it "cannot easily be"
a casual affair. Hence mutual consent, the only significant moral feature of
casual sexual encounters, is not enough to generate treating the other as
an individual. But O'Neill's argument collapses in its reliance on the
claim that sexual relations "cannot easily be" casual affairs; the argument
amounts to the tautology that consent is not enough when (or for those
people for whom) it is not enough, or that treating another as a person in
sexual activity requires an intimate relationship, unless, of course, for you
sex *can* be easily casual. The equivocation on "intimate" in the passage is
symptomatic of this flaw: "intimate bodies" most certainly can have separate lives, if we mean the physical intimacy of casual sexual relations.

Perhaps the mutual consent of the parties is not sufficient for their
sexual activity to be permissible, and their loving each other is also neces-

sary; love insures, in the presence of consent, that they do not merely use each other. But let us pursue, instead, a different question: if the partners' loving each other is *not* sufficient to justify their sexual acts, is this because consent is necessary? Assume that love (with mutual sexual desire) itself morally justifies sexual activity.[105] Then the only way that consent could *also* be important for the moral quality of sex is for love (or mutual desire) to incorporate consent: even if the lovers' loving and desiring each other never yields an explicit verbal request for and consent to sex (my goodness, it doesn't even always yield an explicit declaration of love), when the lovers take each other into their arms and experience the sweetness of loving touches, both know that the other is willing and has done as much consenting as required. The libertarian claim that consent entails something as disparate as respect turns out not to be far-fetched, if love and desire entail something as disparate as consent. This idea is resisted by those who think that consent must be verbally explicit.

Polysemous Words

How *specific* must consent be? The problem of vagueness arises here. When X agrees "to have sex" with Y, is X consenting to any caress that Y desires or any coital position selected by Y? How *explicit* must consent be? Might it be implied by nonverbal cues?

In order to gain some understanding about these matters, we may find it helpful to examine another moral judgment issued by Belliotti:

> "teasing" without the intention to fulfill that which the other can reasonably be expected to think was offered is immoral since it involves the nonfulfillment of that which the other could reasonably be expected as having been agreed upon.[106]

This looks right. Lingering flirtatious glances *sometimes* can reasonably be taken as an invitation to engage in sex. Hence flirting and not fulfilling its meaning, or never intending to fulfill its meaning, is, like failing to honor other promises, *ceteris paribus* a moral fault. (But not a mortal sin; false flirting is not, for Aquinas, unnatural.) How we should grasp "can *reasonably* be taken as" is not, however, immediately clear. A woman's inquisitive glance might be taken as a sexual invitation by an incredibly optimistic guy, and he and his peers might judge his perception "reasonable." This is why Catharine MacKinnon says that to use "reasonable belief as a standard" can be "one-sided: male-sided."[107] (But a man's innocent glance might be taken as a leer by an anxious or sensitive woman, and she and her peers might judge her perception "reasonable.") Belliotti writes as if all were well with "reasonable":

> Although sexual contracts are not as formal or explicit as corporation agreements the rule of thumb should be the concept of reasonable expectation. If a woman smiles at me and agrees to have a drink I cannot reasonably assume . . . that she has agreed to spend the weekend with me. (9)

I suppose not. But why not? We do not have in our culture a convention, like the display of colored hankies, in which a smile before an accepted drink has that meaning. But nothing intrinsic to this action prevents its having, in the proper circumstances, exactly that meaning. And an optimistic fellow might think the *special* sort of smile she, or another he, gave him constituted a sexual invitation. Belliotti resumes his example:

> On the other hand if she did agree to share a room and bed with me for the weekend I could reasonably assume that she had agreed to have sexual intercourse with me.

Oh? Not true at all for many couples as they travel together. Or maybe she only agreed to snuggling. The problem is that cues indicating sexual interest, and the kind of sexual interest, are fluid and vague; at one time, if a woman asked a man to her apartment or room, the invitation carried more sexual meaning than it does now, even if that meaning still lingers on college campuses.[108] To forestall such objections, Belliotti offers these instructions:

> If there is any doubt concerning whether or not someone has agreed to perform a certain sexual act with another, I would suggest that the doubting party simply ask the other and make the contract more explicit. . . . [W]hen in doubt assume nothing until a more explicit overture has been made.

What could be more commonsensical than this? But it is wrong. A man who thinks it reasonable to assume that a woman has agreed to have sex will not have any doubt, and hence will have no reason to ask more explicitly what she wants. His failure to doubt whether she has consented to engage in sex is brought about by the same factors that cause, for him, the reasonableness of his belief in her consent. It is silly to suggest *"when in doubt, ask,"* because the problem is that not enough doubt arises in the first place, that the brief, inquisitive look is taken too readily as conclusive evidence of sexual interest. [109]

Susan Estrich argues that a man who engages in sex with a woman on the basis of an unreasonable belief in her consent ought to be chargeable with negligent rape; only a genuinely reasonable belief in her consent should exonerate an accused rapist. She would like it to be legally impossible for a man accused of rape to plead that he believed that the woman consented, when that belief was unreasonable even though he thought it was reasonable. Could there be such a robust notion of "reasonable"? Estrich realizes that "reasonable belief" is slippery. She heroically proposes that "the reasonable man in the 1980s should be the one who understands that a woman's word is deserving of respect, whether she is a perfect stranger or his own wife." The reasonable man—and, we might extrapolate, the man who treats a woman with Kantian respect—"is the one who . . . understands that 'no means no.' " [110] The man pawing the arm of the woman who pulls abruptly away—the physical equivalent of "no"—had better immediately doubt the quality of his belief in her sexual interest in him. At the cognitive or psychological level this man might not doubt that she is interested; Estrich's normative proposal is that he is to be held liable anyway, since he *should* be doubtful. Beyond this crude case, I think Estrich means that for the reasonable man, a woman's qualified locution ("Please, not tonight, I think I'd rather not," "I don't know, I just don't feel like it") is not an invitation that he continue trying, but "no." Her wish is expressed softly because she is tactful or frightened. For the reasonable man, her polysemous "I'm not sure I want to" is either a delicate "no" or a request to back off, stop pressuring, while she autonomously makes up her mind.

As congenial as Estrich's proposal is, she muddies the water with a provocative piece of logic (102):

Many feminists would argue that so long as women are powerless relative to men, viewing a "yes" as a sign of true consent is misguided. For myself, I am quite certain that many women who say yes to men they know, whether on dates or on the job, would say no if they could. I have no doubt that women's silence sometimes is the product not of passion and desire but of pressure and fear. Yet if yes may often mean no, at least from a woman's perspective, it does not seem so much to ask men, and the law, to respect the courage of the woman who does say no and to take her at her word.

Estrich's reasoning seems to be as follows: if something as antithetical to "no" as "yes" can mean "no," then something as consistent with "no," "no" itself, means "no." This argument has a curious consequence. If "yes" can mean "no," at least from a woman's *own* perspective (the woman who consents for financial or duty reasons, but whose heart and desire are not wrapped up in the act), [111] then it will be difficult to deny that "no" spoken by some women can mean "maybe," "try harder to convince me," or "show me how manly you are." From their own traditional perspective, "no" is wonderfully ambiguous. Indeed, Charlene Muehlenhard and Lisa Hollabaugh reported in 1988 that some women occasionally say no but do not mean it; 39.3 percent of the 610 college women they surveyed indicated that they had offered "token resistance" to sex "even though [they] had every intention to and [were] willing to engage in sexual intercourse." [112] As a partial explanation, Susan Rae Peterson suggests that "typical sexual involvement includes some resistance on the part of women . . . because they have been taught to do so, or they do not want to appear 'easy' or 'cheap.' " [113] Thus, both "yes" and "no" turn out to be polysemous— rather dangerously.

Men cannot always tell when a woman's resistance is real, token, or playful; men are, moreover, often insensitive as to what a woman does intend to communicate; and, after all, the figure is only 39 percent and not 99 percent, and of that 39 percent, many offered fake resistance only a few times. For all these reasons, in addition to her own, Estrich's proposal, that for the reasonable man "no" means "no," should be understood as wisely suggesting that men and the courts should always assume, in order to be cognitively, morally, and legally safe, that a woman's "no" means "no," even in those cases when it might not. A man who takes "no" as "no" even when he suspects that a woman is testing his masculinity with token resistance is advised to risk suffering a loss of sexual pleasure and a blow to his ego, in order to secure the greater good, for both, of avoiding rape. A normative convention must be established to override the inherent polysemousness of even little words; "no" might of course mean "yes," but we are never to take it that way.

But if men are always to assume that "no" means "no," even though there is a nontrivial chance that it means "yes" or "keep trying," then Estrich should permit men to assume that a woman's "yes" always means "yes"[114]—even though, on her view, a woman's "yes" sometimes means "no." If, instead, Estrich wants men to sort out when a woman's "yes" means "yes" and when it does not, to decide whether to proceed or refrain, she should propose some workable procedure. Yet her description of the reasonable man mentions only what his response to "no" should be, not what his response to "yes" should be. Encouraging women to abandon the token resistance maneuver, to give up saying no when they mean "yes,"[115] is proper and helpful, but it will not take theorists of sex, or men in the presence of apparently consenting women, very far in deciphering when the polysemous "yes" means "no."

Antioch

I propose that we understand Antioch University's well-known, even infamous, "Sexual Offense Policy" as an inchoate attempt to address and solve the problems exposed in our discussion of Belliotti and Estrich. The central assertions of the Antioch policy are these:[116]

A1. "Consent must be obtained verbally before there is any sexual contact."

A2. "[O]btaining consent is an on-going process in any sexual interaction."

A3. "If the level of sexual intimacy increases during an interaction . . . the people involved need to express their clear verbal consent before moving to that new level."

A4. "The request for consent must be specific to each act."

A5. "If you have had a particular level of sexual intimacy before with someone, you must still ask each and every time."

A6. "If someone has initially consented but then stops consenting during a sexual interaction, she/he should communicate withdrawal verbally and/ or through physical resistance. The other individual(s) must stop immediately."

A7. "Don't ever make any assumptions about consent."

In an ethnically, religiously, economically, socially, and sexually diverse population, no common and comprehensive understanding might exist of what various bits of behavior mean in terms of expressing interest in sex. In the absence of rigid conventions and a homogeneous community, a glance, either brief or prolonged, is too indefinite to be relied on to transmit information; an invitation to one's room, or sharing a room, or a bed, on a trip might not have some settled meaning; clothing and cosmetics in a pluralistic culture are equivocal. (Young men, more so than young women, take tight jeans and bralessness to signal interest in sex.)[117] Because physical movements and cues of various kinds can be interpreted in different ways, sex entered into on the basis of this sort of (mis)information is liable to violate someone's rights or be indecent or offensive. Antioch insists that consent to sexual activity be verbal (A1) instead of behavioral.[118] Following this procedure will minimize miscommunication and the harms it causes; it will also encourage persons to treat each other with respect as autonomous agents. Further, bodily movements of a sexual sort that occur in the early stages of a possible sexual encounter can also be ambiguous or indefinite, and do not necessarily indicate a willingness to increase the intensity of, or to prolong, the encounter (hence [A2], [A3]). Protracted verbal communication is supposed to prevent misunderstandings rooted in indefinite, polysemous body language: we should not assume consent from expressions of desire (groans, lubrication) or failures to resist an embrace (A1). Neither reacting with sexual arousal to a touch nor not moving away when intimately touched means that the touched person welcomes the touch or wants it to continue. Sometimes one's body responds with pleasure to a touch but one's mind disagrees with the body's judgment; Antioch's insistence on verbal consent after discussion and deliberation is meant to give the mind decisive and autonomous say. Similarly, the verbal request for, and the verbal consent to, sexual contact must be not only explicit, but also specific (A4). Consenting to and then sharing a kiss does not imply consent to any other act. Nor do the body movements that accompany the sexual arousal created by the kiss signal permission to proceed farther to some other sexual act not yet discussed.

One provision (A7) rebuts Belliotti's advice "when in doubt, ask." Antioch demands, more strictly than this, that the sexual partners entertain *universal* doubt and therefore *always* ask. Doubt about the other's consent must be categorical rather than hypothetical: not Belliotti's "when in doubt, assume nothing," but a Cartesian "doubt!" and "assume nothing!" To be on the cognitive, moral, and legal safe side, to avoid mistakes about intention or desire, always assume "no" unless a clear, verbal, explicit "yes" is forthcoming (A1, A3, A4). Men no longer have to worry about distinguishing a woman's mildly seductive behavior from her "incomplete rejection strategy," about which they are often confused;[119] in the absence of an explicit "yes" on her part, he is to assume a respectful "no." There's still the question of how a man knows, when the obvious consent-negating factors are lacking (for example, she's had too much alcohol), whether a woman's "yes" means "yes." Antioch's solution is to rely on the probing verbal communication that must occur not only before but also during a sexual encounter (A3, A5). The constant dialogue, the "on-going process" (A2) of getting consent during what Lois Pineau calls "communicative sexuality,"[120] is meant to provide a man with an opportunity to assess whether a woman's "yes" means "yes," to give her the opportunity to say a definite if tactful "no," and to clear up confusions created by silence or passive acquiescence. Thus, for Antioch, ordinary consent by itself is not, contrary to libertarians, sufficient; only the *probed* consent is sufficient. At the same time, in agreement with Estrich, the badgering of a woman by a man in response to her "no" is ruled out. A man's query of whether a woman's "no" means "no" is disrespectful of her "no" and fails to acknowledge her autonomy. It is also to embark on a course that might constitute verbal coercion.[121]

It is illuminating to look at the Antioch policy from the perspective of the sadomasochistic subculture, in particular its use of safe words.[122] A set of safe words is a language, a common understanding, a convention jointly created in advance of sex by the partners, to be used during an encounter as a way of saying a definite "yes," "more," or "no," a way of conveying details about wants and dislikes, without spoiling the erotic mood. The use of safe words, which is a kind of Cartesian foundation, attempts to achieve some of the goals of Antioch's policy without the cumbersome apparatus of explicit verbal consent at each level of sexual interaction. And a tactful safe word can gently accomplish an Antiochian withdrawal of consent to sex (A6). But note a big difference between sadomasochism and Antiochian sex: the sadomasochistic pair want the activities to proceed smoothly, spontaneously, realistically, so one party grants to the other the right to carry on as he or she wishes, subject to the veto of safe words, which are to be used sparingly, only when necessary, as a last resort; the couple eschew Antiochian constant dialogue. In dispensing with the incessant chatter of ongoing consent to higher levels of sexual interaction, the sadomasochistic pair violate another provision (A7): consent is assumed throughout the encounter in virtue of the early granting of rights. No such prior consent into an indefinite future is admissible by Antioch.

Does Antioch's policy make sex less exciting by insisting on the use of intrusive safe words? Does it force the couple to slow down, to savor each finger and tooth, when they prefer to be passionately overwhelmed? Julia Reidhead replies to the charge that Antioch's policy begets dull sex.[123] She claims that the policy gives the partners a chance to be creative with language, to play linguistically with a request to "kiss the hollow of your neck," to "reinvent [sex] privately." But Antioch thinks that sexual language needs to be less, rather than more, private; more specific, not less.[124] Hence Reidhead's praise for Antioch's policy misses its point: common linguistic understandings cannot be assumed in a heterogeneous population. To encourage the creative, poetic use of language in framing requests to proceed to a new level of interaction is to provoke the misunderstandings, due to polysemous words and acts, that the policy was designed to prevent. Thus, when Reidhead queries, "What woman or man on Antioch's campus, or elsewhere, wouldn't welcome ... 'May I kiss the hollow of your neck,' " her homogenizing, universalizing "or elsewhere" betrays an insensitivity to cultural differences and their linguistic concomitants.

Reidhead also defends Antioch by arguing that vocalizing creatively about sexual activity before engaging in it mixes the pleasures of language with the pleasures of the body. Indeed, the pleasures of talk are themselves sensual. "Antioch's subtle and imaginative mandate is an erotic windfall: an opportunity for undergraduates to discover that wordplay and foreplay can be happily entwined." Reidhead is right that talking about sex can be sexy, but wrong that this fact is consistent with the Antioch policy and one of its advantages. Reidhead's reading of verbal communication as sexy almost throws Antioch's procedure into a vicious regress: if no sexual activity is permissible without temporally prior consent to it, and consent must be spoken, then if a request for sex is constructed to be a sexually arousing locution, it would amount to a sex act and hence would be impermissible unless it, in turn, had already received specific consent. So Y's consent to nonverbal sex must be preceded by X's request for sex *and* X's request to utter that request. Further, to get consent for the sexual act of kissing the neck by talking sensually about kissing the neck is to use the pleasure elicited by one sexual act to bring about the occurrence of another sexual act. But obtaining consent for a sexual act by causing sexual pleasure and desire with a seductive request interferes with calm and rational deliberation—as much as a shot of whiskey would. This is why Antioch insists that between levels a sexual gap must occur that makes space for three things: (1) a thoughtful, verbal act of request, (2) deliberations about whether to proceed, and (3) consent or denial. A well-timed hiatus re-spected by both parties is the *remedium miscommunicati*. As in Augustine, bodily perturbations must be checked while the mind considers.

But the body should not be totally dismissed. Two people tightly em-bracing, eyes glued to the other's eyes, bodies pulsating, often know, without verbalization, from the way they touch each other and respond, that each wants the sex that will soon occur. Other cases of successful communication, in and out of sexual contexts, are explicit and specific without being verbal. So even if the idea that the mouth can say "no" while the body exclaims an overriding "yes" is rejected, the general point, that the body sometimes speaks a clear language, seems fine. This might be why Antioch, even though it requires a verbal "yes" for proceeding with sex, allows a nonverbal "no" for withdrawing consent (A6); nonverbal acts can have clear meaning across ethnic and gender divides. Certain voluntary actions, even some impulsive, reflex bodily movements, do mean "no," and about these things no mistake *should* be made (as in Estrich). But if such movements are assumed or demanded to be understood unambiguously—*pulling away when touched means "no"*—then some voluntary acts and involuntary bodily movements must reliably signal "yes."

There is another reason for renewing our respect for the body. According to Antioch's policy, a verbal "yes" replaces any possible bodily movement as the one and only reliable sign that proceeding with sex is permissible. If I ask, "may I kiss you?" I may not proceed on the basis of your bodily reply—moaning, you push your mouth out at mine and open it invitingly—because even though it seems obvious to me what these acts mean ("yes"), I might be committing a mistake: I perceive your open mouth presented "invitingly" because I have with undue optimism deceived myself into thinking that you meant to appear inviting. So I must wait for the words, "yes, kiss me," [125] about which interpretive unclarity is not supposed to arise, else the problem Antioch set for itself is unsolvable. A verbal "yes," *after* enough probing, is Antioch's Cartesian foundation. But can the ambiguities of the verbal be cleared up with polysemous language itself? How much probing is *enough*? This question generates a hermeneutic circle that traps Antioch's policy. Her "yes" repeated several times under the third degree of communicative probing can always be probed more for genuineness, if I wanted to *really* make sure. But, losing patience, she will *show* her "yes" to be genuine when she finally grabs me. The body reasserts itself as its own bottom.

My continuing to probe her "yes" over and over again, to make sure that her heart and desire are wrapped up in the act to which she is apparently consenting, is the paternalism that the libertarian found obnoxious in West's account of the harms of consensual sex. The robust respect Antioch's policy fosters for a woman's "no" is offset by the weaker respect it fosters for her "yes," so it seems more accurate to conceive of the policy not as attempting to encourage autonomy but as attempting to prevent harmful behaviors (rape). One Antioch student, Suzy Martin, defended the policy by saying, "It made me aware I *have* a voice. I didn't know that before." [126] Coming in the mid-1990s from a college-age woman, the kind of person we now expect to know better, this remark is astonishing. In effect, she admits that what Antioch is doing for her, at an advanced age, is what her parents and earlier schooling should have already done, to teach her she has a voice. In order to carry out this lesson, Antioch employs a principle in its treatment of young adults—*in loco parentis*—that my college generation had fought to eliminate, on grounds of autonomy. The only warrant for Antioch's doing so is that others have reneged on their responsibility. Thus, the relationship between the policy and autonomy is at best one of paradox.

Orgasmic Justice

Shall we insist, as a matter of morality, that when two people have sex, their orgasms be simultaneous? (It does not matter whether the orgasms are caused by coitus, mutual masturbation, or *soixante-neuf*.) It would be fascinating to discover an argument that made orgasmic simultaneity a moral duty. But even if ethics do not demand simultaneous orgasm, perhaps the nature of paired sex, or the fact that two persons have agreed to have sex, entails that each has a right to an orgasm sometime during a single bout of sex. Even if there is no right to sex, there still might be a right to orgasm *if* we have agreed to engage in sex. Janice Moulton seems to hold this view:

> if a woman spends the time and energy to produce someone else's orgasm, ... it is only fair that her partner do the same for her. If she has to be satisfied with sympathy and understanding alone, then so should her partner. [127]

A moral criterion of one-for-one is too crude. Is it unequal if, during one act of coitus, she comes twice to his once? Maybe not, if she has only two medium ones to his one big orgasm, or if, alternatively, equality is measured in terms of each person's fulfilling his or her orgasmic potential. Anyway, Moulton's criterion is as overly stringent as requiring orgasms to be simultaneous. Indeed, any consideration that inclines us to think that the orgasms need not occur at the same time will incline us to think that they need not occur in the same bout of sex. After all, "during the same bout of sex" is one meaning of "at the same time," and if the orgasms may be separated by minutes, it must be licit for them to be separated by hours, and then also by days, that is, if one bout of sex has ended and another has begun. Justice or fairness is not violated if John has an orgasm during today's sex and his partner Jim or Mary has one tomorrow, as long as the number or intensity of their orgasms over the long haul is fairly distributed or otherwise morally tidy. On this view, microinequalities—in a single sexual bout only one person comes—are ironed out, morally discharged, by a macroequality made possible by future bouts.

Because some people do not insist on orgasm, we could have proposed that each person in a couple has a right to sexual satisfaction in a more diffuse physical and psychological sense. Or perhaps satisfaction is, more narrowly, an orgasm produced in one specific way. Still, the same question arises: must each bout of sex result in equality of satisfaction (in any sense), or can inequalities in single bouts be morally erased by a fair distribution of satisfaction over a long haul? We have these options:

(I) In every sexual act between two people, they must have the sincere intention of satisfying each other, and each sexual act must be left open to equal satisfaction,

and

(II) The partners must strive to make their sexual relationship as a whole equally satisfying, even if by their own design single bouts are not equal,

which principles we might designate Vatican Catholic and Moderate Protestant, on analogy with their respective views about conjugal sex and procreation. It follows trivially from both principles that if the sexual encounter in which the parties are engaged is the only one between them, is not the inauguration of a series of bouts but is the whole series, then this encounter must exhibit equality of satisfaction.

According to (II), then, the standard of morality that applies to sexual bouts that are not part of a series, but are isolated events, is more stringent than that which applies to sexual bouts that are members of a series of bouts. We do not, of course, expect every stranger to be a Mother Teresa of the Bedroom; we do not measure our partners in casual affairs against such lofty ideals. They are, after all, just strangers. Still, perhaps because we *are* dealing with a stranger, it might be appropriate (for Christian swingers?) that more stringent rules be followed. This does not mean, which would be a high paradox of exoneration, that we may get away with murder within a relationship, often or whimsically reneging on a duty to provide pleasure in return, while we must be on our best behavior with a stranger in a one-night stand. But the slack or freedom we have within a relationship, at least on principle (II)—the luxury of committing microinequalities that will be erased by later compensation—is missing from casual sex. Since, in a one-night affair, we will never have a chance to erase a microinequality, we must ensure that no such injustice occurs.

Kant requires a reciprocal exchange of rights, if sexual activity is to be permissible, but insists that the exchange of rights must be for life and exist within the union of marriage. Why could there not be an exchange of rights for an evening, justified by consent? Perhaps Kant reasoned that the achievement of microjustice in one casual bout is unreliable, given the selfishness of human nature; in such a brief affair, deception and manipulation are too tempting or easy. Given our natures, no guarantee of full reciprocity in a single night exists, but only in the long stream of committed marriage. We need time to be moral. And only in a committed relationship can anxiety over sexual justice be quieted. For Kant, then, it misses the point to argue that in casual sex we should abide by a stringent rule in aiming for justice in a single bout, because we will have no chance to set things straight. That we will have no chance to remedy a failure that is very likely to occur is, instead, precisely the reason for not having casual sex at all.

Antioch's policy is, in spirit, closer to (I), in not acknowledging a difference between the morality of isolated, single bouts of sex and of bouts that occur in ongoing relationships. The policy asserts that previous bouts of sex between two people do not relax the rules to be followed during later bouts (A5). Thus, the casual sex of one-night stands and the sex of ongoing relationships are governed by the same standards. Nor does a person's sexual biography count for anything. No historical facts allow us to make "assumptions about consent" (A7). Indeed, in requiring consent at each level in a single bout, Antioch applies a principle of justice to each sub-act within the bout. Earlier consent to one sub-act within a single bout creates no presumption that one may proceed, without repeating the procedure of getting consent, to later sub-acts in the same bout, in the same way that a bout of sex yesterday does not mean that consent can be assumed for a bout tonight. The history of the relationship, let alone the history of the evening, counts for nothing: one cannot consent in advance to a whole night of sex, but only to single, atomistic acts, small pieces of an encounter. In denying the relevance of history, Antioch also makes a Pauline marriage impossible. One cannot consent in advance to a whole series of sexual acts that might make up the rest of one's sex life, so any marriage in which consent to sex is presumed after an exchange of vows is ruled out. In rejecting this arrangement, even if contracted voluntarily, Antioch cuts back on a traditional power of consent. For Antioch, consent is short-lived; it dies an easy death and must always be replaced by a new generation of consents.

Antioch similarly cuts back on the power of consent by making it not binding: one can withdraw consent at any time during any act or sub-act (A6). Nothing in the policy indicates that the right to withdraw is limited by the sexual satisfaction or other (even reasonable) expectations of one's partner; any such Moultonish equalizing qualification would run counter to the policy's spirit. This is a difference between Antioch and Belliotti's libertarianism, according to which breaking a sexual promise is prima facie morally wrong. It is also contrary to the indissolubility of Pauline marriage and the reciprocal exchange of rights over the person of Kantian marriage. But that Antioch would be indulgent about withdrawing consent makes sense, given Antioch's distrust of the historical. Consent is an act that occupies a discrete location in place and time; it is a historical event, and that it has occurred is a historical fact; thus consent is precisely the kind of thing whose weight Antioch discounts. Consenting to a sexual act does not entail, for Antioch, that one ought to perform the act, and not even that one has a prima facie duty to do so; the act consented to need not take place, because the only justification for it to occur is an act of consenting that has already receded into the past and has become a mere piece of impotent history. When consent into the future, today for tomorrow, is ruled out, so too is consent into the future, now for two seconds from now. How could consent have the power to legitimize any sexual act? An air of paradox surrounds the policy: it makes consent the centerpiece of valid conduct, yet its concept of consent is emaciated. Of course, "unless refusal of consent or withdrawal of consent are real possibilities, we can no longer speak of 'consent' in any genuine sense."[128] But that withdrawing consent must be possible does not entail we have carte blanche moral permission to do so. My guess is that Belliotti is right, that withdrawing consent to an act to which one has consented is prima facie wrong. The logical possibility that consent is binding in this way is necessary if we are to take consent seriously as a legitimizer of sexual activity.

If X has promised a sexual act to Y, but withdraws consent and so reneges, it does not follow from libertarianism that Y has a right to compel X into compliance.[129] Nor does that right follow from the terms of Pauline or Kantian marriage. Neither the fact that each person has a duty, the marriage debt, to provide sexual satisfaction for the other when the other wants it, nor the fact that in marriage one act of consent makes rape conceptually impossible, implies that a spurned spouse may rightfully force himself on the other. In patriarchal practice, however, a man sometimes expects sexual access to his wife in exchange for the economic support he provides, and even if rape is conceptually impossible he might extract the marriage debt: "if she shows unwillingness or lack of inclination to engage with him in sexual intercourse, he may wish to remind her of the nature of the bargain they struck. The act of rape may serve . . . as a communicative vehicle for reminding her."[130] Violence is not legitimated by the principles of Pauline marriage, but its possibility might explain why Paul admonishes spouses to show "due benevolence" to each other (1 Cor. 7:3).

Antioch's policy also prohibits "metaconsent," or consent about (the necessity of) consent. Consent, in principle, should be able to alter the background presumption, in the relationship between two people, *from* "assume 'no' unless you hear an explicit 'yes' " *to* "assume 'yes' unless you hear an explicit 'no.' " This power of consent is abolished by Antioch's ahistoricity; consent to prior acts creates no presumption in favor of "yes" tonight. Further, to give consent into the future allows one's partner to make an unwarranted assumption (A7). The policy does not empower a couple to jettison the policy by free and mutual consent; here is another way the policy was not designed specifically to foster autonomy. By contrast, both Paul and Kant allow that one act of consent, the marriage vow, has the power to change presumptions, from "no" to the continuous "yes" of constant access. Thus, for Paul and Kant, the morality of a series of sexual acts is not only a function of the morality of the single acts that constitute it; the whole series could be just, if both partners have freely consented to it in advance. Such is the power of consent for Paul and Kant, that it applies to the future and is binding: we make our bed and then lie in it. Antioch's notion of consent frees us from such stodgy concerns.

No Pair

Simone and her lover were locked in a wet embrace on the grass. Someone approached in the dusk. Their breathing stopped. Her lover thinks:

> Simone's ass, raised aloft, did strike me as an all-powerful entreaty, perfect as it was, with its two narrow, delicate buttocks and its deep crevice; and I never doubted for an instant that the unknown man or woman would soon give in and feel compelled to jerk off endlessly while watching that ass. [131]

Endlessly? That provocative idea reminds us that we have neglected masturbation, never pausing to ask whether justice or fairness demanded that the left hand have access equal to the right, or for how long. Masturbation was mentioned only in passing: for Aquinas, masturbation is morally worse than rape; for Greer, it is a method of birth control; masturbating on a rug, I argued, is little different from masturbating on a corpse. Now we confront the idea of masturbation as an endless source of pleasure. Our energy was spent investigating the pleasure of the pair, trying to distinguish the good sexual pairs from the bad, the right paired sex acts from the wrong. It is time to redress the imbalance. After all, you, the reader, read alone, not as a pair. And I, the writer, write alone, not as a pair. If we meet at all, reader and writer, it is in the same queer space and time in which the masturbator meets the pornographer's models, or in which the undiscovered Marcelle examines, *reads*, Simone's polysemous ass.

Masturbation

This vice, which shame and timidity find so convenient, has a particular attraction for lively imaginations. It allows them to dispose, so to speak, of the whole female sex at their will, and to make any beauty who tempts them serve their pleasure without the need of first obtaining her consent. —Rousseau, *Confessions*

If your right hand causes you to sin, cut it off and throw it away. It is better for you to lose one part of your body than for your whole body to go into hell. —Jesus (according to Matthew 5:30)

Reflecting on the special virtues, and not only the vices, of adultery, prostitution, homosexuality, bisexuality, group sex, sadomasochism, and sex with anonymous strangers is a valuable exercise. Indeed, when we think philosophically about sexuality, it is mandatory to compare these practices with a privileged pattern of relationship in which two adult heterosexuals love each other, are committed and faithful to each other within a formal marriage, and look forward to procreation and family. Some people sincerely strive to attain this pattern, and some live it quite effortlessly. The sexual lives of other people are more complex, even chaotic. It does not matter whether the privileged pattern is actually a widespread form of behavior or a piece of ideology that attempts to influence behavior. Regardless, the contrast between the pattern and the quite different practices mentioned above provides the material for the conceptual and ethical thinking that is the philosophy of sex.

Masturbation, too, violates the spirit and letter of the privileged pattern: it is unpaired and flagrantly nonprocreative sex in which pleasure is relished for its own sake. As we have learned from pundits, masturbation mocks the categories of our sexual discourse: it is sex with someone I care about, to whose satisfaction and welfare I am devoted; it is incestuous; if I'm married, it is sex with someone who is not my spouse and hence adulterous; it is homosexual; it is often pederastic; it is sex we occasionally fall into inadvertently ("if you shake it more than twice, you're playing with it"); and, with a Rousseauvian stretch, it is the promiscuous rape of every man, woman, or beast to whom I take a fancy. No wonder, then, that we advertise our marriages and brag about our affairs, but keep our masturbatory practices and fantasies to ourselves. The masturbatory closet remains shut. The sexual revolution of the 1960s made living together outside matrimony acceptable; it encouraged toleration of homosexuality; it even breathed life into the practices of the daughters and sons of the Marquis de Sade. But to call a man a "jerk off" is still derogatory. Masturbation is the black sheep of the family of sex, scorned, as we shall see, by both the left and the right. Fittingly, masturbation was the straw that broke Joycelyn Elders's back. Masturbation, still taboo in 1996.[1]

This is no joke. When conducting their recent, massive study of sexual behavior in the United States,[2] Edward Laumann and his colleagues gathered their data on masturbatory practices not through oral interviews (which was a technique they used for every other sexual activity studied, including anal), but with a secretive paper-and-pencil instrument. The "interviewers expressed anxiety about asking questions about masturbation" (81); masturbation was "the most sensitive topic of any we discussed, making both respondents and interviewers the most uncomfortable" (69). But sheepishness was not restricted to interviewers and interviewees. "Negative responses" to the masturbation items in the study had been voiced earlier by the "government officials" who reviewed the project in its planning stages; the officials "insisted that questions on masturbation be removed" (81). I'm grateful Laumann and his colleagues didn't cave in; but I continue to be amazed, with them, that "masturbation has the peculiar status of being both highly stigmatized and fairly commonplace" (81).

There is an obvious explanation: masturbation is an act the purpose of which is pure pleasure; it is also an act in which it is easy to engage. So in an Augustinian, sex-negative culture, masturbation will be frequent even though condemned. If we want a more esoteric explanation, try this one, which takes seriously the joke that masturbation is a homosexual act. If X's sexual joy in rubbing X's penis (or clitoris) during masturbation is the hand's pleasure of *touching* a penis (or clitoris), then it is plausible to think that X's act is homosexual (assuming X's gender identity is male [female]); if, on the other hand, X's joy resides mostly in the pleasurable sensations felt in X's genitals, then the act is not homosexual (unless what is significant for the masturbator is that his or her genitals are *being touched by* a same-sex hand). Or consider the difference between self-fellatio done to receive in the mouth the pleasure of sucking a penis and self-fellatio done only to feel pleasure in the penis, an alternative to using a hand; the first case looks homosexual. I suspect that if the pleasure a heterosexual male gets from masturbating decreases if his hand falls asleep during the act (or if it was anaesthetized beforehand), his pleasure is partially homosexual. Suppose, now, that straight men *routinely* discover that when their hands fall asleep, they do not enjoy masturbating as much. At some level of consciousness, then, straight men realize that their masturbation is partially homosexual. Hence the traditional and considerable condemnation of homosexuality would apply, in their minds, also to masturbation—not despite the fact that they do it often, but because they do. The source of the continuing disparagement of masturbation is the continuing disparagement of homosexuality.

The Concept

Conceptual questions about masturbation arise when we critically examine the paradigm case: a person in a private place manually rubs the penis or clitoris and produces an orgasm. The salient features of the paradigm case are conceptually unnecessary. (1) One can openly masturbate in the crowded waiting room of a bus terminal, with erect penis displayed for all to see or with fingers conspicuously rubbing the clitoris or dipping into the vagina. (2) The hands do not have to be employed, as long as the target areas are pressed against a suitably shaped object of comfortable composition—the back of a horse, a bicycle seat, a rug.[3] (3) Orgasm need not be attained, nor need it be the goal. At least for this reason, but also independently, (4) the penis or clitoris need not receive the most, or any, attention. There are other sensitive areas one can touch and press: the anus, nipples, thighs, lips. What remains in the paradigm case does seem indispensable: (5) the person who, by pressing the sensitive areas, causally produces the pleasurable sensations is the person who experiences them; the rubber is the rubbed. Masturbation, the "solitary vice" of "self-abuse," looks logically reflexive.

But *mutual* masturbation would be impossible if masturbation were logically solitary, and we have a paradigm case of mutual masturbation: two persons rubbing each other between the legs. Further, if it is conceptually possible for X and Y to masturbate each other, it must be possible for X to masturbate Y, while Y simply receives this attention, not doing anything to X. "To masturbate" is both transitive and intransitive; like respect and deception, it can take the self or other as object. Reflexivity, then, might be sufficient but it is not necessary for a sexual act to be masturbatory. But it is not easy to explain why mutual masturbation *is* masturbation, and why X's rubbing the labia of Y while Y lies back and relaxes is masturbatory. Saying that these activities are masturbatory just because they involve the hands and genitals is awkward; we end up claiming that all solitary sex acts are masturbatory, even those that do not involve the manual rubbing of the genitals, while paired acts are masturbatory exactly when they do involve the manual rubbing of the genitals. On this view, X's tweaking her own nipples is masturbatory, Y's doing it for X is not masturbatory, yet Y's tweaking X's clitoris is masturbatory.

One way to distinguish masturbatory (solitary or paired) from nonmasturbatory acts is to contrast sexual acts that do not involve any insertion and those that do. The idea is that without the insertion of something, no mixing together of two fleshes occurs, and so the participants remain isolated. Solitary acts of self-pleasuring would be masturbatory for the reason that no insertion occurs (but what about digital anal or vaginal masturbation?); the paradigm case of mutual masturbation also need not involve insertion (but it might, of fingers into vagina); and both male-female coitus and male-male anal coitus would not be masturbatory because they do involve insertion. This view entails that X's fellating Y is not a case of masturbation (which seems correct), it has the plausible implication that coitus between a human male and a female animal (a sheep), or a human female and a male animal (a dog), is not masturbatory (even though each activity involves only one person and is, in that sense, solitary), and it is consistent with the not incredible views that frottage in a crowded subway car is masturbatory and that tribadism can be mutually masturbatory. But to distinguish between masturbatory and nonmasturbatory sexual activity by distinguishing between acts that do not and acts that do involve insertion is inadequate, as my examples have already hinted. Consider others. Cunnilingus might or might not involve insertion, in this case of the tongue or lips or nose; to say it is masturbatory when and only when it does not involve insertion implies that one continuous act of cunnilingus changes from masturbatory to not masturbatory and back again often in a few minutes. And what about a male who punctures a hole in a watermelon to make room for his penis, or a female who reaches for her g-spot with a dildo? These acts are masturbatory yet involve insertion.

Some of these problem examples can be avoided if we were to narrow what counts as "insertion." Masturbation might be characterized more specifically as sexual activity not involving the insertion of a real penis into a hole of a living being. Then all lesbian sexuality is masturbatory, while many sexual acts of male homosexuals would not be. Were we to decide that a male having intercourse with an animal is, after all, masturbating—that is, if we perceive no significant difference between this act and a man's rubbing his penis with a woman's panties—masturbation could be defined more specifically as sexual activity not involving the insertion of a real penis into a hole of a living human being. This refined view is literally phallocentric in characterizing sexual acts with reference to the male organ. As a result, the analysis implies a *conceptual* double standard: fellatio, oral sex done on a male, is not masturbatory, but cunnilingus, oral sex done on a female, always is. And an *evaluative* double standard looms when the usual disparagement of masturbation is added: fellatio is genuine sex, cunnilingus is foolishness. This scholastic view, which is sexist but not heterosexist (its point does not depend on the sex/gender of the fellator), is similar to the claim, which is heterosexist but not necessarily sexist, that the paradigm case of natural sexual activity is male-female genital intercourse. What is conceptually emphasized in such a view—the most specific we can get—is the insertion of a real penis not into just any hole of a living human being, but into a particular hole, the vagina. This suggests that masturbation be understood as any nonprocreative sexual activity, whether solitary or paired, including coitus interruptus—the act that procures but then abdicates the crucial insertion.[4] If so, our sexual lives contain a lot more masturbation than we had thought.

The distinction between solitary and paired sexual activity is apparently clear. But suppose X is having sexual, physical contact with Y, even coitus, and X's arousal is sustained by X's private fantasies. The act is solitary masturbation in the (perhaps only metaphorical) sense that the other person is partially "absent" from X's sexual consciousness. That which would arouse X during solitary masturbation is doing the same thing for X while X rubs X's penis or clitoris on/with Y's body instead of X's hand or on a rug. So the difference between masturbatory and nonmasturbatory sex is, again, not that between solitary and paired sex. Our task is to distinguish paired masturbatory from paired nonmasturbatory sex acts, while preserving the idea that solitary sex acts are masturbatory. But, as the case of fantasizing during coitus suggests, under certain plausible descriptions of sexual activity, no difference exists between the paradigm case of mutual masturbation and two ordinary cases of nonmasturbatory sex: heterosexual genital intercourse and homosexual anal intercourse. Listen to helpful Alexander Portnoy offering his cheating father a redescription of adultery: "What after all does it consist of? You put your dick some place and moved it back and forth and stuff came out the front. So, Jake, what's the big deal?"[5] Adulterous coitus is redescribed, defined "downward," almost as if it were an act of solitary masturbation, which is not as morally threatening as adultery. There is no essential difference between mutual masturbation and genital or anal intercourse, and so every paired sexual act is itself masturbatory, since the mutual rubbing of sensitive areas, the friction of skin against skin, that occurs during mutual masturbation is the same, physically, as the mutual rubbing of skin against skin that occurs during coitus. The only difference, a trivial one, is that different parts of the body or patches of skin are involved in the rubbings; but no one patch or set of patches of skin has any ontological privilege over any other. Further, the only difference between solitary and paired masturbation is the number of people who accomplish these same rubbings; hence no difference remains between solitary masturbation and paired (or group) sex.

A similar conclusion can be reached on Kantian grounds. For Kant, in human sexual interaction, by its nature, a person merely uses another person for the sake of pleasure:

> there is no way in which a human being can be made an Object of indulgence for another except through sexual impulse. . . . Sexual love . . . by itself . . . is nothing more than appetite. Taken by itself it is a degradation of human nature. . . . [A]s an Object of appetite for another a person becomes a thing.[6]

Kant is not asserting the physical indistinguishability of mutual masturbation and coitus. Instead, he is insisting that the intentions involved in both activities—to get pleasure for oneself through the vehicle of the other's body and his or her compliance with one's wishes—are the same. But in portraying all sexual acts as objectifying and instrumental, Kant makes us wonder: is not celibacy required? No:

> The sole condition on which we are free to make use of our sexual desire depends upon the right to dispose over the person as a whole. . . . [I] obtain these rights over the whole person . . . [o]nly by giving that person the same rights over the whole of myself. This happens only in marriage. . . . In this way the two persons become a unity of will. . . . Thus sexuality leads to a union . . . and in that union alone its exercise is possible.[7]

Kant is not claiming, as do humdrum theologians, that the marital pledge assures that even if the spouses are a means to each other's pleasure in the marriage bed, they are not treating each other only as means but also as ends, as persons to whom respect and consideration are due during sex, as well as before and after. Instead, Kant justifies marital sex by abolishing the possibility of instrumentality altogether; he literally unites two persons into one person by marriage.[8] This is to justify all marital sex by reducing or equating it to solitary masturbation, the sex of a single (even if larger or more complex) person.[9]

Kant's notion that the marital union of two people into one cleanses sexuality of its instrumentality apparently has two radical implications: that homosexual marriage would similarly cleanse same-sex sexuality[10] and that solitary masturbation is permissible. Indeed, solitary masturbation should turn out to be morally superior to many paired sexual acts exactly because it avoids using another person as a means. Listen to Bernard Baumrin on coupled sexuality:

> Human sexual interaction is essentially manipulative—physically, psychologically, emotionally, and even intellectually. . . . [E]veryone has spoken to cajole, shifted eyes to charm, acquiesced to trick, clothed to attract, touched to try to thrill, waited for the moment, played on a known weakness, looked for a sign of one's initial success to move the game along. [11]

None of this skulduggery occurs in solitary masturbation. But Kant resists both conclusions, asserting that masturbation and homosexuality are *crimina carnis contra naturam:*

> onanism . . . is abuse of the sexual faculty without any object. . . . By it man sets aside his person and degrades himself below the level of animals. . . . [I]ntercourse between *sexus homogenii* . . . too is contrary to the ends of humanity; for the end of humanity in respect of sexuality is to preserve the species. [12]

Kant caps off his denouncement of these aberrations with a snarl: "He," the masturbator or homosexual, "no longer deserves to be a person." This rejection of both masturbation and homosexuality is suspiciously ad hoc; not content with ruling out as immoral only instrumental sex, in which one person treats another as an object of use, Kant also rules out as "unnatural" any nonprocreative sexual activity that escapes his first net.

Kant has not specifically provided a criterion for distinguishing paired masturbatory sexual activity from paired nonmasturbatory sex—quite the opposite—but Kant's thought suggests a criterion that concedes the physical similarity of mutual masturbation and coitus and focuses instead on a mental or attitudinal difference: sexual activity between two persons, each of whom is concerned not only with her or his own pleasure but also with the pleasure of the other person, is not masturbatory (regardless of what physical acts they engage in), while sexual activity in which a person is concerned solely with her or his own pleasure is masturbatory. Conceiving of another person merely as a means might be a mark of the immoral; here it is being regarded as a mark of the masturbatory as well. This view implies that inconsiderate husbands and rapists are largely the authors of masturbatory acts. It also implies that the physical act we call mutual masturbation is *not* masturbatory if the touchings are meant to produce pleasure not only for the toucher but also, if not mainly, for one's partner.

What we can appreciate in this Kantian approach is this: at the heart of masturbation is the effort to cause sexual pleasure for the self—full stop. It is, however, not part of the core idea that masturbation be solitary; the attempt to produce sexual pleasure for the self can causally involve other people, animals, the whole universe. That masturbation is logically reflexive—X acts to produce sexual pleasure for X—is therefore neither equivalent to nor entails its being solitary. Given the kind of physical creatures we are, attempting to please the self by acting on oneself is easier, even if not always successful or satisfying. Our own bodies, to which we have Pauline access, are handy. Hence we misleadingly associate masturbation entirely with one form of it, the case in which X touches X in order to pleasure X. But the attempt to produce one's own pleasure can involve other people. Solitary and paired sexual acts are masturbatory, then, to the extent that the actor attempts mainly to produce pleasure for the self; paired sex is not masturbatory to the extent that we attempt to produce pleasure for each other. But unlike a strict Kantian criterion, which condemns masturbation, this notion of masturbation is only descriptive, not normative; it neither morally praises nor criticizes masturbation. That the attempt to produce, and the search for, one's own sexual pleasure, either in solitary or paired acts, is selfish or, instead, merely self-interested, or even benevolent (which is possible) is not part of the core idea. Seeking to produce sexual pleasure for the self is that which marks the masturbatory, not these other motivational factors that are more directly relevant to a distinct moral evaluation of sexual acts.

Fulfilling Desire

Three contemporary philosophical accounts of sexuality, proffered by thinkers within a liberal sexual tradition, yield the conclusions that *solitary* masturbation is not a sexual activity at all (Alan Goldman), is perverted sexuality (Thomas Nagel), or is "empty" sexuality (Robert Solomon). These conclusions are surprising, given the sexual pedigree of these philosophers.[13] I propose to take a careful look at them.

Let's begin with Alan Goldman's definitions of "sexual desire" and "sexual activity":[14]

> sexual desire is desire for contact with another person's body and for the pleasure which such contact produces; sexual activity is activity which tends to fulfill such desire of the agent. (74)

On Goldman's view, sexual desire is strictly the desire for the pleasure of physical contact itself, nothing else, and so does not include a component desire for, say, love, communication, or progeny. Goldman thus takes himself to be offering a *liberating* analysis of sexuality that does not tether sex normatively or conceptually to love, the emotions, or procreation. But while advocating the superiority of his notion of "plain sex," Goldman forgot that masturbation needed protection from the same (usually conservative) philosophy that obliged sex to occur within a loving marriage, or to be procreative, in order to be morally proper. On Goldman's analysis, solitary masturbation is not a sexual activity to begin with: it does not "tend to fulfill" sexual desire, namely, the desire for contact with another person's body. Solitary masturbation is unlike mutual masturbation, which does tend to fulfill the desire for contact, since it involves the desired contact and hence is fully sexual. Goldman seems not to be troubled that on his view solitary masturbation is not a sexual act. But he should be, for in response to his claim that "we all know what sex is, at least in obvious cases, and do not need philosophers to tell us" (76), the logical reply is "we all know the obvious, that masturbation *is* sexual, and do not need philosophers to tell us otherwise." It's funny that masturbation is, for Goldman, not sexual, for the conservative philosophy that he rejects would likely reply to his account that by *reducing* sex to the meaningless desire for the pleasure of physical contact apart from love or reproduction, what Goldman has analyzed and promoted is merely a form of masturbation.

The vague "tends to fulfill" in Goldman's analysis of sexual activity presents problems. Goldman intended, I think, a narrow causal reading of this phrase; actually touching another person's body is a sexual act just because by the operation of a simple mechanism the act fulfills the desire for that contact and its pleasure. The qualification "tends to" functions to allow bungled kisses to count as sexual acts, even though they did not do what they were intended to do; kisses tend to fulfill desire in the sense that they normally and effectively produce pleasure, prevented from doing so only by the odd interfering event (the braces get tangled; the hurrying lips land on the chin). It also functions to allow disappointing or bad sex, that which does not bring what anticipation promised, to count as sex. In this sense of "tends to fulfill," solitary masturbation is not sex. Suppose that X desires sex with Y, but Y declines the invitation, and so X masturbates thinking about Y. Goldman's view is not that X's masturbation satisfies X's desire for contact with Y only, or at least, a little bit and hence is a sexual act even if inefficient. This masturbation is not a sexual act at all, despite the sexual pleasure it yields for X, unlike the not pleasurable but still sexual bungled kiss. X's masturbation cannot "tend to fulfill" X's desire for contact with Y, since it excludes that contact.

Suppose we read "tends to fulfill" in a causally broader way. Then giving money to a prostitute—the act of taking bills out of a wallet and handing them to her—might be a sexual act (even if no sexual arousal accompanies it), because doing so causally allows the patron to fulfill his desire for contact with her body. Handing over a hundred-dollar bill would be a *more efficient* sexual act than handing over a ten. But even on this broader reading, solitary masturbation would not be a sexual activity; despite the causal generosity, there is no contact and so masturbation is still precluded from fulfilling sexual desire in Goldman's sense. (For similar reasons, someone masturbating while looking at erotic photographs is not engaged in a sexual act.) Indeed, masturbation will be a "contrasexual" act if the more a person masturbates, the less time, energy, or interest he or she has for fulfilling the desire for contact with someone's body. Only in unusual situations would masturbation be sexual. Suppose X sexually desires Y and Y tells X that Y will sleep with X only if X first masturbates for Y; then X's masturbation is a sexual act, because through a simple mechanism it tends to fulfill X's desire for contact with Y.

Goldman does acknowledge one sense in which masturbation is a sexual activity:

> Voyeurism or viewing a pornographic movie qualifies as a sexual activity, but only as an imaginative substitute for the real thing (otherwise a deviation from the norm as expressed in our definition). The same is true of masturbation as a sexual activity without a partner. (76)

Masturbation done for its own sake, for the specific pleasure it yields, is *not* sexual; masturbation is a sexual act only when done as a substitute for the not available "real thing." But on what grounds could Goldman claim that masturbation's being an "imaginative substitute" for a sexual act makes it a sexual act? In general, being a *substitute for* a certain kind of act or thing does not make something an occurrence of that act-kind or thing. To eat soyburger as a beef substitute is not to eat hamburger, even if it tastes exactly like hamburger. Eating a hamburger as a substitute for the sex I want but cannot have does not make my going to Burger Queen a sexual event, not even if out of frustration I gorge myself on burgers as compensation.

On the other hand, given Goldman's analyses of sexual desire and activity, the claim that masturbation done for its own sake is not sexual makes some sense. If the masturbator desires the pleasure of physical contact, and masturbates trying (in vain) to get that pleasure, the act, by a stretch, is sexual, because it at least involves genuine sexual desire. By contrast, if the masturbator wants only to experience pleasurable clitoral or penile sensations, then the masturbator does not have sexual desire in Goldman's sense, and activity engaged in to fulfill this (on his view, nonsexual) desire is not sexual activity. But now we have a different problem: what are we to call the act of this masturbator? In what category does it belong, if not the sexual? Note that Goldman argues (75–76), along the same lines, that if a parent's desire to cuddle a baby is only the desire to show affection, and not the desire for the pleasure of physical contact itself, then the parent's act is not sexual. Goldman assumes that if the desire that causes or leads to the act is not sexual, neither is the act. Hence, while Bertrand Russell and Victoria Woodhull decimated the reasons that legitimize sexual activity, Goldman decimates the reasons for calling it sex. For example, a woman who performs fellatio on a man for the money she gets from doing so is not, on Goldman's view, performing a sexual act. This fellatio does not fulfill the sexual desire "of the agent," for, like the baby-cuddling parent, the woman has no sexual desire to begin with. Thus the prostitute's contribution to fellatio must be called, instead, a "rent-paying" or "food-gathering" act, since it tends to fulfill her desires to have shelter and eat. This is a neat social constructivist idea, but wrong.

There is, however, a way of understanding masturbation that does construe it as a sexual act, even on Goldman's analysis. The fantasies that accompany solitary masturbation can make it a sexual act, not merely a substitute for a sexual act. Suppose X looks at a photo of Y or conjures up Y in his or her imagination, and in response to this image X desires the pleasure of physical contact with Y. Then X, while masturbating, could tend to fulfill the desire for this pleasure if X were good at imagining touching Y. If X's imagination is powerful, X can experience what X desires at the *sense datum* level of consciousness where little difference exists between experiencing a touch and vividly imagining it. Having smelled and touched Y before would help or enable X to imagine smelling and touching Y now; or if X had never smelled or touched Y, memories of smelling or touching Z could now assist X in imagining smelling or touching Y. Because what X might bring himself or herself to experience, fleetingly and mistily, is the pleasure of the contact X desires, X is engaged in a sexual act. Rousseau's "lively imagination" was accurate.

Note two features of this Goldmanesque view. First, it is not the physical act—the rubbing of the penis or clitoris, for example—that is central to masturbation as a sexual act, but the mental act of imagining contact. Thinking is what causally tends to fulfill the masturbator's desire, since it brings about the experience of pleasurable contact; the rubbing does not do it. The masturbator experiences at least two pleasures: the imaginary sensation and the genital stirring. The first pleasure is the key. Second, masturbation is a sexual act in virtue of the masturbator's ability to produce in the absence of physical contact the very experience of contact. Masturbation is, as a result, bona fide sexual activity for those people who have whatever mental skills are required for creating in fantasy a virtual reality. That seems to be no mean feat.

Completeness

Thomas Nagel's theory of sexuality was designed to distinguish, in human sexuality, between the natural and the perverted.[15] Human sexuality differs from animal sexuality, first, in the role played by intentions: humans respond with arousal to the recognition that another is trying to arouse them with, say, a touch or glance. Second, human sexuality exhibits a spiral phenomenon that depends on self-consciousness. Suppose (1) X looks at Y or hears Y's voice or smells Y's hair—that is, X "senses" Y—and as a result is sexually aroused. Also suppose (2) Y senses X, too, and as a result becomes aroused. X and Y are at the earliest, primitive stage of sexual interaction: the animal level of awareness, response, and arousal. But if (3) X becomes aroused further by noticing (or "sensing") that Y is aroused by looking at X, and (4) Y becomes further aroused by noticing that X is aroused by sensing Y, then X and Y have reached the first level of natural human sexuality. Higher iterations of the pattern are also psychologically characteristic of human sexuality: (5) X is aroused even further by noticing (4). On Nagel's view of human sexuality, when X senses Y at the purely animal stage of sexual interaction, X is in X's own consciousness a subject and only a subject; while Y is for X at this stage only an object of sexual attention. But when X advances to the first distinctively human level of sexuality, and notices that Y is aroused by sensing X, X becomes in X's own consciousness also an object, and so at this level X experiences X-self as both subject and object. If Y, too, is progressing up the spiral, Y's self-consciousness is also composed of feeling Y-self as subject and object. For Nagel, the awareness of oneself as *both subject and object* in a sexual interaction marks it as "complete," that is, psychologically natural for human beings.

Nagel's theory, because it is about natural sex and not the essence of the sexual, does not entail that masturbation is not sexual. However, the judgment that solitary masturbation is perverted seems to follow from Nagel's account. Solitary masturbation, unlike mutual masturbation, does not exhibit the completeness of natural sexuality; it lacks the combination of an awareness of the embodiment of another person and an awareness of being sensed as embodied, in turn, by that person. This is why Nagel claims that "narcissistic practices"—which for him seem to include solitary masturbation—are "stuck at some primitive version of the first stage" (48) of the spiral of arousal; they are sexually perverted because they are "truncated or incomplete versions of the . . . configuration" (47). A world of difference exists between narcissism in some technical sense and masturbation, so even if looking upon one's own body in a mirror with delight is a sexual perversion (must it be?), a theorist of sex should not feel compelled for that reason to judge perverted the prosaic practice of solitary masturbation. Nagel claims that shoe fetishism is perverted (39), because

"intercourse with . . . inanimate objects" is incomplete (48). But just because shoe fetishism might be a perversion that involves masturbation, a
theory of sex need not entail that shoeless masturbation is perverted.

Even if solitary masturbation is incomplete and hence a perverted *act*,
perhaps the masturbator, at least, is not a sexually perverted *actor* or
person (a "pervert"), because, on Nagel's view, the perversions are "sexual
inclinations rather than . . . practices adopted not from inclination but for
other reasons" (39). The "other reason" for masturbating that might
prevent the masturbator from being perverted is, I suppose, frustration.
Masturbating as a substitute for what is really desired is not perverted; a
preference for paired sex implies the absence of a true inclination to
masturbate. But consider a woman who prefers to masturbate (while reading a romance novel), and is content to masturbate with her fantasies, since
doing so is more enjoyable than sex with her incompetent, inconsiderate,
or unattractive husband, and she has no interest in risky extramarital
affairs. It would be wrong to characterize this woman as perverted, even
though she prefers incomplete sex. Nagel claims that incomplete sex is not
necessarily irrational, unpleasurable, or immoral; indeed, incomplete sex
might be very satisfying (50–51). But this is exactly why the woman
prefers masturbation with a novel to sex with her boring husband. Should
we say that this woman *really* prefers that the world were different, say,
that her husband were more competent or physically attractive than he is,
and so she does not have a true inclination to masturbate? Maybe yes,
maybe no. The response might allow the shoe fetishist to escape the charge
of perversion by pleading that because he bemoans whatever happened in
his life that eventually caused his desires, he has no true inclination for
fondling high heels.

The nature of effective sexual fantasy implies that even within Goldman's analysis, masturbation can be sexual; similar thoughts imply that
masturbation can be complete enough to be, within Nagel's analysis, natural. Consider someone who masturbates while looking at erotic photos.
This sexual act avoids incompleteness insofar as the person is aroused not
only by sensing the model's body (the animal level) but by recognizing the
model's intention to arouse or by sensing her real or feigned arousal (the
human level), as much as these things are captured by the camera or read
into the photo by the masturbator.[16] Completeness seems not to require

that X's arousal as a result of X's awareness of Y's arousal occur at the same time as Y's arousal. Nor does it require that X and Y be in the same place: X and Y can arouse each other by talking over the telephone. So, if X masturbates while fantasizing, sans photograph, about another person, X might be aroused by the intentions expressed or arousal experienced by the imagined partner. (Nagel does allow [45] that X might become aroused in response to a "purely imaginary" Y.) A masturbator having a powerful imagination can conjure up these details. If the masturbator is aroused not only by sensing, in imagination, the other's body, but also by noticing (having created the appropriate fantasy) that the other is aroused by sensing X's body, then X can be conscious of X-self as both subject and object, which is the mark of natural sexuality.

Sara Ruddick agrees with Nagel that masturbation is incomplete, but denies that masturbation is for *that* reason perverted; instead, as in Aquinas, masturbation is unnatural sexuality because it is nonprocreative. [17] But note a difference between Aquinas and Ruddick: she does not think that an act's unnaturalness by itself makes it immoral (291). Further, Nagel insists that human perversion be understood psychologically, thereby liberating human sexuality from its association with the merely biological or animal, while Ruddick views sexual perversion physiologically, thereby emphasizing, in this respect, like Aquinas, the biological continuity between the human and the animal. Ruddick also thinks, unlike Nagel, that sex acts that are complete are *morally* superior. She offers three reasons. Complete sex acts

> tend to resolve tensions fundamental to moral life; they are conducive to emotions that . . . are in turn conducive to the virtue of loving; and they involve a preeminently moral virtue—respect for persons. (293–94)

Ruddick is asserting a lot for completeness; I am not convinced.

The tension Ruddick claims is resolved in complete sex is, in her words, that between our "narcissism" and "altruism"; both are "satisfied" in complete acts (294). But if I am aroused by noticing that your looking at or smelling me arouses you, and the same is true of you, it does not follow that we are satisfying or even balancing our self-directed and other-directed motives; both of us could still be wholly self-centered. Similarly, from the fact that we respond with arousal to each other's arousal it does not follow that our interaction includes mutual respect in some morally robust sense; we might be viewing each other merely as means to our respective pleasures.[18] Being caught up in the sexual swirl of Nagelian spirals can even cause us to forget each other's moral personhood. Or suppose X responds with arousal to Y's intention to arouse X; this entails only that X sees that Y is ontologically a person, not that X treats Y as a person in a Kantian moral sense. Ruddick admits that there are "radical differences between respect for persons in the usual moral contexts and respect for persons in sex acts" (296), yet insists that her notion is "no mere play on words." This fudge is just a stubborn refusal on her part to concede that the type of respect exhibited by complete acts, a recognition of ontological personhood, neither constitutes nor contributes to their purported moral superiority. Ruddick also claims that the sexual pleasure experienced in complete sex acts, in particular, is especially favorable for the generation of love-conducive emotions such as gratitude and affection (294). But she provides no reason for thinking that the pleasure of complete sex, as opposed to the pleasure of sex per se, is the important factor. Simply receiving sexual pleasure — say, X performs some favorite act for Y's benefit — might well generate gratitude and affection. If so, then as long as the pleasure of incomplete sex is considerable, it can be love-inducing.

Even granting Ruddick her theses, the moral case against solitary masturbation is weak. We would be objecting to it in terms of its failure to promote or its tendency to impede the virtues achievable through completeness. Although a masturbator is not engaging in an activity that resolves the tension between narcissism and altruism, I do not see how anyone can be faulted for this, unless (which is unlikely) masturbating prevents him from ever appreciably resolving that tension in his life. Further, Ruddick admits that masturbation "only rarely involves disrespect for anyone" (296). Finally, the masturbator can easily be seen as affirming the value of her existence — as loving herself — by producing sexual pleasure for herself.

Since solitary masturbation, when it is the "act of choice," is on Ruddick's view the "paradigmatically incomplete sex act" (286), this sort of masturbation would seem to be the principal object of her moral criticism. Yet Ruddick claims, incongruously, that "the more incomplete [a sexual act] is — the more private, essentially autoerotic, unresponsive, unembodied, passive, or imposed—the more likely it is to be harmful" (297). But her paradigmatic masturbator, by turning away from others, would seem to decrease the chance of doing something harmful to them. Ruddick would be on firmer ground if she meant to criticize a person who engages in paired sex while relentlessly feeding his arousal with private fantasies and who, as a result, ignores his partner's needs. In this "autoerotic" act, there is only selfishness, no seeing the other person as an end; less opportunity exists for gratitude to take root in either direction; and some sort of harm is possible. In this scenario, moral respect is missing, but not exactly because respect in Ruddick's sexual sense is absent; X might respond both to the perceived or imagined arousal of his partner and to his fantasized images, without being especially sensitive to her needs.

Ruddick's basic idea, then, that completeness is a significant moral property, is not obviously right: completeness and morality do not reliably vary together. Unless we want to overturn many of our moral intuitions, we must judge some incomplete sexual acts—not only masturbation, but also incomplete sexual acts in which X tries generously to please Y—to be perfectly morally acceptable. At the same time, some complete sexual acts, even if they encourage respect, are conducive to gratitude, and satisfy both narcissism and altruism, *between* the partners, will also, regarding effects on *others*, encourage a lack of respect, create resentment, and satisfy narcissism at the expense of altruism. Think about the harmful effects on third parties of complete but adulterous sexual acts. The fact that these adulterous acts exhibit all the Ruddickian virtues of completeness, if they do, could not excuse or exonerate them. Further, I doubt that their completeness makes them morally any better than adulterous sexual acts that are incomplete.

This leaves us with the questions of what the sexual role of completeness is and what is wrong, if anything, with incomplete sex. Completeness is not definitive of the sexual; plenty of genuine but incomplete sexual activity occurs. Completeness is not a mark of the natural, as Nagel proposed, since on that criterion we would have to judge perverted too many ordinary sexual behaviors (Nagel partially agrees [47]). There is no equivalence between a sexual act's being pleasurable and its being complete. And completeness is not a measure of morality. Then how does completeness figure in sexuality? Not at all, unless "better sex" means something neither reducible to nor identical with nature, pleasure, or morality. Ruddick does provide another sense. Complete sex is better in the broadly prudential sense of supporting one's mental health; incompleteness, then, is linked to mental pathology. The embodiment that occurs in sexual activity, "the immersion of consciousness in the bodily," Ruddick claims, is "conducive to our psychological well-being" (293). By contrast, "disembodiment" is pathogenic. "To dissociate oneself from one's actual body . . . is to court a variety of ill effects, ranging from self-disgust to diseases of the will . . . and finally to madness." Ruddick concludes from this frightening array of possibilities that complete sex acts are "beneficial." But she has not shown that the embodiment specifically of complete sexual acts, as opposed to the embodiment of sexual acts per se, is what contributes to mental health. Ruddick, at least, is consistent; neither did she give us reason to believe that the pleasure of complete sex acts, and not the pleasure of sex per se, generates affection.

Communication

Robert Solomon, like Nagel, wants to distinguish sharply between animal and human sexuality.[19] On Solomon's view, human sexuality is "primarily a means of communicating with other people" ("SAP," 279). Sensual pleasure is important in sex, but it is not the main point of sexual interaction or its defining characteristic ("SP," 58; "SAP," 277–79). Sexuality is, instead, "first of all language" ("SAP," 281). As "a means of communication, it is . . . *essentially* an activity performed with other people" ("SAP," 279). Could such a view of sexuality be kind to solitary masturbation? Apparently not:

> If sexuality is essentially a language, it follows that masturbation, while not a perversion, is a deviation. . . . Masturbation is not "self-abuse" . . . but it is, in an important sense, self-denial. It represents an inability or a refusal to say what one wants to say. . . . Masturbation is . . . essential as an ultimate retreat, but empty and without content. Masturbation is the sexual equivalent of a Cartesian soliloquy. ("SAP," 283)

If sexuality is communicative, solitary masturbation can *be* sexual; conversing with oneself is not impossible, even if not the paradigm case. The distinctive flaw of masturbation, for Solomon, is that communicative intent, success, or content is missing. Hence solitary masturbation is "empty," a conclusion that seems to follow naturally from the idea that sexuality is "essentially" a way persons communicate with each other.

But denouncing masturbation as a "refusal to say what one wants to say" slights the fact that one might not have, at any given time, something to say (without being dull), or that there might be nothing worthy of being said, and so silence is the appropriate course. Solomon's communication model of sexuality seems to force people to talk to each other, to have empty sex in another sense: to open their mouths when there is nothing interesting or important to be said. Further, even if the masturbator is merely babbling to himself, he enjoys this harmless pastime as much as does the infant who, for the pure joy if it, makes noises having no communicative intent or meaning. For Solomon to call masturbation "self-denial" is therefore wrongheaded, but at least a change from the tedious popular criticism of masturbation as a *failure* of self-denial, a giving in to temptation, an immersing of the self in the hedonistic excesses of self-gratification. [20]

There is no warrant to conclude, within a model that likens sexual behavior to linguistic behavior, that solitary masturbation is inferior. [21] Solomon meant the analogy between masturbation and a "Cartesian soliloquy" to reveal the shallowness of solitary sexuality. But Descartes's philosophical soliloquies are hardly uninteresting, and I suspect that many would be proud to masturbate as well as his *Meditations* does philosophy. Diaries, a kind of masturbatory writing, are not always masterpieces of literature, but that does not make them "empty." Some of the most fruitful discussions one can have are with oneself, not as a last-ditch substitute for dialogue with another person, or as compensation for lacking it, but to explore one's mind or to get one's thoughts straight. This is the stuff of intellectual integrity, not mere preparation for public utterances. In George Steiner's embellishment of the linguistic model of sexuality, coitus is a "dialogue" and

masturbation seems to be correlative with the pulse of monologue or of internalized address. . . . [T]he sexual discharge in male onanism is greater than it is in intercourse. I suspect that the determining factor is articulate-ness, the ability to conceptualize with especial vividness. In the highly articulate individual, the current of verbal-psychic energy flows inward. [22]

This turns Solomon on his head. Warren Beatty should envy Woody Allen, not vice versa, for masturbation is a Neoplatonic virtue, while paired sex is stuck at the level of the crudely physical.

Solomon acknowledges that not only "children, lunatics, and hermits" talk to themselves; "poets and philosophers" do so as well ("SAP," 283). This misleading concession plays on the silly notion that philosophers and poets are a type of lunatic. Where are the bus drivers and cooks? Solomon's abuse of masturbation trades unfairly on the fact that talking to oneself has always received bad publicity—unfair because we all do it, lips moving and heads bouncing, without damning ourselves. Solomon admits, in light of the fact that philosophers and poets speak to themselves—a counterexample to his argument that "sexuality is a language . . . and primarily communicative" and hence masturbation is deviant—that "masturbation might, *in different contexts,* count as wholly different extensions of language" ("SAP," 283; italics added). This important qualification implies that Solomon's negative judgment of masturbation is unjustified. Sometimes we want to converse with another person; sometimes we want to have that conversation sexually. In other contexts—in other moods, with other people, in different settings—we want only the pleasure of touching the other's body or of being touched, and no serious messages are communicated. To turn around one of Solomon's points: sometimes pleasure is precisely the goal of sexual activity, and even though communication might occur, it is not the desired or intended result but only an unremarkable or merely curious side effect. In still other contexts, we will not want to talk with anyone at all, but spend time alone. We might want to avoid intercourse, of both types, with human beings, those hordes from whose noisy prattle we try to escape by running off to Maine—not an "ultimate retreat" but a blessed haven. For Solomon to call masturbation "empty," in the face of such facts about the role of context in human sexuality in its many forms, is to confess that he did not understand the significance of his own qualification.

Solomon's attitude toward masturbation is not innocuous; it leads him to make odd moral judgments. He claims that some solitary masturbation is "potentially . . . pathetic or selfish or self-indulgent" ("SAP," 283). In complaining that solitary masturbation is both "selfish" and "self-denial," Solomon's philosophy is petty and incoherent. Such a grave judgment of a solitary act, as self-indulgent, is a strange overreaction, given how lightly Solomon reprimands "entertaining private fantasies [during paired sex] and neglecting one's real sexual partner," which he calls "an innocent semantic perversion" ("SP," 62). This neglect is not always benign: arousing oneself through one's private fantasies can make one callous or insensitive to the needs of one's partner, and this might be harmful and disrespectful. Of course, privately fantasizing during paired sex is not always a wrong, moral or otherwise. One might have a moral duty to have sex with someone, or one might need to do it for the money, and succeed at the task only by fantasizing. Or one might find oneself fantasizing unintentionally—the mind is a wondrous thing—and then embellish the images. Still, fantasizing during paired sex is morally more dangerous than fantasizing during solitary masturbation, precisely because in the latter one has not undertaken any obligations or created any expectations.

Two Frameworks

Goldman, Nagel, and Solomon, three philosophers unconventional enough to reject traditional, religious, and conservative views about sex, have scorned solitary masturbation. Why? Even as they reject particular conservative or religious judgments about sex, these thinkers still hold the deepest global assumption of their ideological foes. Their accounts of sexuality exemplify a *binary framework:* reference to an interaction between two persons occurs in their accounts of the essence or nature of sexuality or in their description of the best or paradigm kind of sex in a typology or hierarchy of sexual behaviors. They thereby bestow logical, ontological, or normative primacy on paired sex and examine and evaluate the rest of the sexual world from this perspective. The sexually conservative or religious theorist embraces the binary framework either by making much of the Genesis story, in which God created the human pair, or by assimilating human sexuality to the biological sexuality of the animal kingdom, where they find paired sex galore. But there is no obvious reason liberal theorists should also embrace the binary framework. Given that both Solomon and

Nagel want to distinguish sharply between human and animal sexuality, it is disappointing that they construe human sexuality as only a variant of the paired, albeit less sophisticated, sexuality of animals.

The binary framework is clearly exhibited in Goldman's definition of "sexual desire" as the "desire for contact with another person's body" (74). Goldman claims that sexual desire is directed at and hence depends on another *body*. In Nagel, sexual desire is directed at another *person*: "sexual desire is a feeling about other persons"; the sexual "has its own content as a relation between persons" (42). Solomon, too, assumes a binary framework, although for him (*contra* Goldman) sexual desire "is not desire for pleasure" ("SP," 59). Rather, "the end of this desire is interpersonal communication" ("SP," 55); sexuality "is essentially an activity performed with other people" ("SAP," 279). For Solomon, sexual desire is a binary desire to talk with someone; for Goldman, it is a binary desire to touch him.

In Nagel's model of natural sex, two persons experience a spiral of arousal through a reciprocal recognition of their dual status as subject and object; for Solomon, sex is the communication of messages or emotions between two people using the language of the body. As empirical descriptions of what people are doing during sex, these pictures are largely false. This is what Goldman means when he rightly remarks that Nagel and Solomon overintellectualize sex (82). Solomon does this when he claims that shoe fetishism, "certainly" perverted, "is the same as . . . talking to someone else's shoes" ("SP," 61). This interpretation of shoe fetishism as an attempt at paired communication would recommend itself only to someone desperately determined to force every sexual act under the umbrella of a favored theory.[23] But if we understand Nagel and Solomon as speculating about what people are really doing, or trying inchoately to do, when they engage in sexual activity, or what people would be doing were their sexual activity either fully natural or ideal, or were they (contrary to fact) of European descent and college educated, then the technical falsity of their views is tolerable. Nagel and Solomon could be read as trying to illuminate ordinary paired sex by describing an ideal style of paired sex, as chemists employ an ideal gas model to explain the everyday behavior of gases. In this project Nagel and Solomon are partially successful. Solomon's theory, for example, suggests why having sex with the same person gets boring; it's repeating the same conversation. Sex with a stranger or new partner is often good, satisfying sex, because there are new and different things to talk about.

Nagel's view nicely captures what happens when a prostitute pretends to enjoy the sex for which she is paid. To be rid of the customer and conserve time, she wants him to come quickly. She feigns arousal, knowing that when her "arousal" is perceived by the customer this will increase his arousal in a Nagelian spiral: he becomes conscious of himself as both a subject and an object. The customer's mental state is like that of the X who masturbates while fantasizing about a Y who is aroused by sensing X; neither the customer nor the masturbator is "really" both a subject and an object, but only believe or perceive themselves to be. But both activities can be entirely natural, for even when the pair X and Y genuinely progress up the spiral together, it is merely their consciousness of being both a subject and an object, and not the actuality of their being both a subject and an object, that matters.

Nagel's account also provides a nice interpretation of voyeurism. The voyeur fears being an object of another's consciousness, which he avoids, while retaining his status as a subject, by confining his arousal to looking without the object's knowledge. The voyeur who is caught in the act is shocked and flees, having been reduced to the object of someone else's sight, precisely what his maneuvers were designed to prevent. The voyeur does to everyone else what he cannot stand being done to himself; and maybe he busies himself doing it to them to make sure that they are not busying themselves doing it to him. In Nagel's account, for sexuality to be psychologically natural a person must allow himself or herself to be an *object* in the consciousness of another person. Objectification in this sense is not alien to sex but essential to it, as is self-objectification; and this latter part is exactly what the voyeur lacks. Some masturbators are like the voyeur: they hide from their object of attention by fantasizing about instead of approaching her. But a fantasizing masturbator can imagine his object as also a subject, and can imagine himself as also an object for her, so equating the denying strategy of the voyeur and the fantasies of the masturbator (as Goldman does [76]) is inaccurate. A person who is aroused by pornographic images might also be a voyeur, and not want the photographed models to reveal or feign knowledge of his existence; he can then pretend to be peeping. But other masturbators want models to be photographed and shown looking back, smiling, expressing desire, and acknowledging both their existence and the pleasure they cause them to experience.

Accounts of sexuality incorporating a binary framework, despite their successes, will not illuminate the full range of human sexuality. Ordinary, everyday sexuality includes a desire for physical contact with another person (anyone at all or a specific person). And much paired sex occurs. But we should still ask, *why* is paired sexual activity common and desired?[24] In trying to fathom these facts, we formulate a theory of sex. But a binary framework will not help. It is trivial to say that people behave in a paired sexual way because by its essence sexuality is naturally paired, in the same way the dormative power of morphine (in Molière's joke) does not explain why it knocks us out. The theories of Solomon and Nagel are not crudely question-begging. But Goldman's comes close: by defining sexual desire as desire for contact with another's body, Goldman reifies one possible form of sexuality as its essence. This connection between our desires and other persons or their bodies is exactly what needs explanation.

An alternative type of account of sexuality is worth exploring, one that exemplifies a *unitary framework*, in which sexuality is not conceived by its nature as a relation between persons, and in which sexual desire is not assumed to attach necessarily to other persons or their bodies. In a unitary framework, sexual desire is the desire for certain pleasurable sensations; contrary to Goldman (74), sexual desire aims at particular sensations that are both developmentally and analytically "detachable from [their] causal context." Hence the unitary framework does not entail that solitary mas-turbation is logically secondary or peripheral in the domain of sexual acts; indeed, it declares the bona fide sexual nature of solitary masturbation. Moreover, if a theorist of sexuality wanted to distinguish between the instinctual, paired, reproductive sexuality of animals and nearly endlessly varied human sexuality, the unitary framework seems the way to do it. Further, the unitary framework leaves room for interesting explanations of pairing that refer at some point to the desire of persons for pleasurable sensations. The expression of that desire within specific social and cultural contexts would be invoked to explain why people want physical contact with persons of the other biological sex, or the same biological sex, or contact with both, and to explain how the infant's desire for pleasure becomes "perverse" or "normal" adult sexual desire. Part of the value of a unitary framework is that it allows the exploration of the etiology of contingent sexual preferences: whatever it is that we eventually cathect requires explanation. It is a drawback of the binary framework that it tends to obscure these questions.

Nagel notes that if sexual interaction that is complete psychologically is natural to humans, and therefore would be exhibited as a matter of course unless deflected by interfering forces, then to distinguish normal variations in human sexuality from abnormal variations, we would "need an independent criterion for a distorting influence, and we do not have one" (49). The unitary framework, too, must explain the genesis of unusual or infrequent behaviors, but does not conceive of these variants as "deviations" that result from "distorting" influences. The very idea of sexual perversion seems to drop out entirely.[25] Nagel conceives of sexual perversion as an *unnatural preference* (40); but if, as claimed by a unitary framework, the root desire for pleasure latches on to objects only contingently, there are no fully natural preferences (preferences dictated by the desire itself) and hence no sexual perversions. Nagel hints that deriving sexual pleasure from the condom, instead of just wanting to use it contraceptively, would be a sexual perversion. Perhaps he might be willing to say that it would be a *useful* perversion to develop, through re-eroticization. But if we drop the binary framework, we can say, more agreeably, that because anything can be cathected, there are no perversions, and in an age of AIDS and overpopulation, cathecting the condom, being able to get sexual pleasure from it, is a welcome addition to human sexual variety.

Novel Pleasures

Is human sexuality unitary or binary? Does the infant primarily want pleasure and discovers that the mother's breast provides it; or does the infant have a primitive desire for contact with the mother and discovers that this contact yields pleasure?[26] This question is a variant of our earlier question: why *do* so many people seek paired sex? Why do people prefer paired sex to solitary masturbation, if or when they do? Solomon argues, on behalf of his binary communication model, that the point of sex is not the pleasure it undeniably yields ("SP," 60; "SAP," 276). He claims that if persons really were motivated by the promise of pleasure, they would prefer masturbation to paired sex, since masturbation provides the best orgasm and avoids the problems (disease, blows to self-esteem, pregnancy, expenses) that arise in seeking and bedding sexual partners:

> If sex is pure physical enjoyment, why is sexual activity between persons much more satisfying than masturbation, where . . . orgasm is at its highest intensity and the post-coital period is cleansed of its interpersonal hassles and arguments? ("SP," 60)

People do not, according to Solomon, generally prefer solitary masturbation to paired sexuality; therefore, they must not be primarily motivated by anticipated pleasure, and what they seek instead is the point of *paired* sexuality: communication. Here's a variant of the argument: why do heterosexual men pursue coitus with such frenzy, when the vagina is hardly guaranteed to provide the synchronized tightness of one's own hand? Or, as Shere Hite asks, "Why do men rape women? Since orgasm is always available to a man through masturbation, what is the meaning of rape?"[27] The Solomonesque answer is that men desire intercourse, even through rape, in order to communicate, assert, power over women.

Solomon's argument does not establish that a unitary pleasure model is wrong; his conclusion that the prevalence of sexual pairing is best explained in terms of the communicative nature of sex does not follow from his premises. His argument assumes that people know that more pleasure can be gained from masturbation, through its superior orgasm. Yet they still prefer paired sex. So—Solomon's point—people must be seeking something other than pleasure. But what, exactly, do people know about masturbation? Due to the social, medical, and religious prohibition of the act, perhaps people have not fully experienced its pleasures; their joy in masturbation is attenuated by guilt and anxiety produced by the prohibitions. Further, people do know that masturbation, despite its intense and reliable orgasm, fails to furnish other, novel sexual pleasures that paired sex makes possible: the odors, tastes, sounds, and touches of another body. Solomon's argument assumes that people are concerned only with the pleasure of orgasm; but people are not, as he thinks, "obsessed" with orgasm ("SAP," 277) to the detriment of these other pleasures. Or perhaps Solomon assumes, which seems false, that most people find the novel odors and tastes of other bodies largely repulsive rather than attractive and arousing. Hence whether masturbation or paired sex provides the most pleasure for a person, in different contexts, will depend on the relative importance of orgasm and these other sensations in contributing to one's overall pleasure. The explanatory power of a unitary pleasure model has hardly been dealt a death blow.

It is irrelevant to point out, as Solomon does, that "this carnal solipsism [solitary masturbation] is typically accompanied by imaginings and pictures" of other people ("SP," 60). That the masturbator conjures up images of people does not show that sex aims at communication, only that it tends toward pairing, for *whatever* reason. In her fantasy, the masturbator might imagine the sensual delight of embracing the object of her attention, and have that ecstasy securely in mind as the goal of the imagined encounter, without dreaming of communicating anything. To imagine embracing his body is perfectly consistent with a unitary pleasure model. The communication model becomes an empty tautology were it claimed that the masturbator must be desiring some sort of communication, even if she does not realize it. Similarly, that masturbation occurs while reading or viewing pornography—which includes photos or descriptions of other people—in no way supports the contention that people always, "really," or ideally hope to achieve communication, as opposed to sensory pleasure, in sex.

A unitary pleasure model explains a desire for paired sex by referring to the sensations (odors, tastes, sounds, touches, sights) made possible by another person and his or her body. But why do I sometimes want the touch (odor, taste, sound) of the other person instead of my own touch? Why is your rubbing my arm more exciting for me than my rubbing it (*when* it is); why is my rubbing your arm more exciting for me than rubbing my own arm? The answer for touch presumably is similar to the answer for the other sensations: I cannot smell myself or, if I can, the odor is not sharp and lively; I am too familiar with the odor, as I am too familiar with my own voice and the taste of my own body. Pauline access to myself, like Pauline access to a spouse, breeds dullness. The power of the touch of the other, or the allure of touching the other, lies in its novelty. To feel the skin of another against my skin, to taste another's skin or to be tongued, is to sense something different and hence piercing.

The fact that the touch of the other is important for reasons other than communication, and is often desired for the sake of its own novel pleasure, undermines a bit of Solomonesque reasoning by Carole Pateman.[28] Fifteen to 25 percent of the male customers of female prostitutes in Birmingham, England, she tells us, do not purchase coitus but "hand relief"—they want to be masturbated on the penis by the prostitute. These men willingly pay a woman to perform manual masturbation rather than do it to themselves. Pateman finds this fact interesting, because she thinks the men would get the same pleasure either way ("satisfaction of a mere natural appetite does not require a man to have access to a woman's body"). What is her explanation? Not that the men get more pleasure from the newly encountered, pretty, painted, slender fingers of the prostitute than from their own meaty and well-known paws. Instead, Pateman draws the conclusion that the buying of even this noninvasive, noninsertive sex act is an expression of "part of the construction of what it means to be a man." Men pay for *masturbation*, of all things, rather than do it themselves with equal pleasure, because doing so allows them to exercise "their patriarchal right" of "access to a woman." Pateman finds in her Birmingham fact confirmation of this thesis only by ignoring the role of the *fresh* hand in producing sexual pleasure—by narrowly perceiving, in one and the same hand that is both fresh and bought, that the boughtness of the hand instead of its freshness explains why it is also a desired hand. Note that we might have asked a different question about the men buying masturbation: not why they buy it instead of doing it themselves, but why they buy masturbation rather than coitus. The answer could be that the men think being masturbated is safer, less time consuming, and cheaper—virtues of solitary masturbation even Solomon acknowledged. The esoteric patriarchal right of access to her vagina doesn't much move them, in comparison with these mundane benefits.

Janice Moulton, in replying to Solomon's argument,[29] also points out that even though the paired orgasm is not always as intense as the masturbatory orgasm, paired sex can be "more enjoyable" (67) than masturbation because it is more sensually pleasurable:

moderate discrepancies from predicted sensation [are] more pleasurable than sensations that are completely expected. Sensations produced by a sexual partner are not as adequately predicted as autoerotic stimulation. (71)

Novelty undoubtedly plays an important role in sexual pleasure; human beings seek variety in a wide range of activities: the books we read, games we play, routes we take to work—also in the sex acts we perform and with whom we do them. Still, let us not overstate the difference between solitary masturbation and paired sex. Masturbation is not plagued by the boredom of completely expected sensations; men and women are ingenious in devising new methods for masturbating, to produce either new sensations or old sensations in new ways. And paired sex often succumbs to boredom as partners find themselves doing the same thing over and over, or not doing it at all; their sex is the victim of Pauline access. Further, if masturbation repeatedly produced a qualitatively identical pleasure, it might be gratifying exactly for that reason; the completely expected sensations are just the ones enjoyed and desired by the masturbator.

Moulton implicitly recognizes this point when she says, about partners of long standing, that

> sexual satisfaction involves sexual feelings which are increased by the other person's knowledge of one's preferences and sensitivities, the familiarity of their touch or smell or way of moving, and not by the novelty of their sexual interest. (64)

I know myself, hence I know how to please myself and can do so, despite the lack of novelty in touching my own body. Similarly, someone else who knows me well can satisfy me not because her touches are unpredictable, but because she knows what patches of skin to press, when, in what order, and how hard; she can satisfy me because she knows for which predictable touches I yearn. Some women who enjoy having their clitoris licked or manipulated digitally like having it done always in the same correct-for-them way; this presupposes in her partner the knowledge that arises through a constant relationship. Moulton means that X's deep knowledge of Y as an *individual* person, of Y's own particular constellation of sexual likes and dislikes, allows X to please Y. She is not asserting the thoughtless platitude that "women who perform cunnilingus (most often lesbians) are usually more effective in giving pleasure to another woman; that is, a woman knows what feels good to another [*generic*] woman."[30] Moulton thinks that a man who gets to know a woman will be able to please her with cunnilingus, and do so better than another person who is a mere stranger, even if the stranger is a woman; the strange woman would be able to do a decent job only after she, too, has learned the particular likes of her partner. I suspect that when a woman *qua* stranger *is* able to do a superior job, that is due to her prior experience performing the act on other women, not to her being a woman per se. Few women are born cunnilinguists, as few men are born fellators; knowing what feels good when it is done to us does not mean we know, as if by an instinct requiring no instruction, what to do to make others feel good.

Note, however, the logical tension between Moulton's claim that the pleasure of paired sex depends on the knowledge the partners have of each other, and her other claim (mentioned earlier) that paired sex is enjoyable, more so than solitary masturbation, because it involves novel or unpredictable sensations. Her view is still consistent with a pleasure model, but the source of the greater pleasure in paired sex is now the *familiarity* of the other's touch instead of its *newness*.[31] Maybe we can turn this tension to good use, drawing out of it some comprehension of the fact that some people fantasize about perfection: a mate who knows exactly what to do, and when, and who also provides the novelty of a new person.

The function of knowledge in paired sex implies that the touch of the familiar partner who knows what I want is in effect a *self*-touch. In our relationship we might be so psychologically united that at the very moment, during sex, when I want *that* particular touch, you know so and do it, without being told or asked, as if you were reading my mind. The accurately timed and placed touch of my partner is a kind of self-touch I have orchestrated—through communicative sexuality, of course—during the progress of our relationship. To say that I am pleasured by a self-touch, the touch of you *qua* an extension of myself, might not be literally correct. Still, consider a woman who during an embrace moves her partner's hand or face a bit to the right and then settles back to enjoy the rest. He rubs her, to be sure, but she set the rub in motion. Later he will go to the right spot, unprompted. Moulton, then, can be read as proposing a way of grasping or modifying the Kantian idea that in the personal union of love, one comprising reciprocal deep knowledge, paired sexual activity becomes, through broad reflexivity, solitary masturbation.

Moulton must abandon one part of her pleasure model. The original question was why I wanted the touch of the other *instead of* my own touch. One of Moulton's answers—the other knows what to do to produce my pleasure—now can be seen to fail to answer the question, since the touch of *this* other person is just my own touch. Hence, Moulton's earlier thesis is left as the only contender, the explanation that I want to be touched by, and to touch, the other person because I seek novel and sharp sensations. But it could not be only that I want the touch of *that* other person; it must be that I want the touch of *many* others. If the source of the pleasure is the touch's novelty, then touching myself (whether literally in solitary masturbation, or metaphorically in paired sex with someone who sooner or later becomes familiar, that is, with a broadly reflexive self-touch) will get boring. Being touched by or smelling just one other person becomes as undistinguished as touching or smelling myself. When our love matures, "the trouble of desire," as Roger Scruton puts it, comes to "an end." Augustinian perturbations no longer bother us—toward our spouse.[32] Kant, too, although meaning this remark to apply to sibling incest, saw the problem with Pauline access: "too close a connection, too intimate an acquaintance produces sexual indifference and repugnance."[33] So *this* is why married partners do not treat each other selfishly as means to their own sexual satisfaction, and why they can now relax in the calm love into which their previously stormy and youthful relationship has matured: not because mutual ownership combines them into one person, but because they are no longer moved by desire at all. They turn a necessity into a virtue.

Utility

The history of medical, theological, and social opinion about masturbation is fascinating but horrifying reading, especially the descriptions of techniques employed by nineteenth-century medicine to correct or prevent it.[34] Apparently, our recent forebears thought they had good reason for draconian measures: semen/sperm is a valuable fluid the frivolous loss of which could spell only disaster;[35] moreover, masturbation was a grave transgression of natural law (with or without the support of Aquinas) and, as a result, a cause or nasty symptom of severe physical illness or emotional disorder (for example, Ruddick's madness).

Masturbation is still cited as a cause or symptom of medical, moral, or social distress. The problem often perceived with masturbation now is its disutility. For example, even though "masturbation . . . is not physically harmful . . . [and] not a cause of any disease of body or mind," nonetheless "a male who has formed the habit of masturbation . . . may . . . find himself unable to keep up his erection long enough to give [a woman] any satisfaction."[36] One reply is that a boy or man who masturbates can learn about his penis and its cerebral connections and so be able to control ejaculation and maintain an erection; even if he cannot achieve prelapsarian control over getting the erection, at least he can develop some postlapsarian control over losing it too quickly. Once we make the point that masturbation has good effects, however, we are playing by the rules of an irrelevant game: we justify masturbation not by applauding circular pleasure enjoyed for its own sake, but by portraying the activity as useful. Ergo, a Protestant ethic of sexuality: the work of masturbation makes men better (longer) fuckers. A letter to Ann Landers praises masturbation on more mundane grounds: it "eliminates fear, worry, guilt, expense, illness, death and deception." Or masturbation is justifiable, for one Catholic thinker, in terms of being useful for, of all things, the pair—masturbation is instrumentally valuable in "preserving fidelity in marriage when physical separation is a necessity."[37] That's our liberal Paul. *Masturbatio ad remedium concupiscentiae.*

What a shame to restrict the justification of masturbation, or of Greer's re-eroticization of taboo acts and organs, to its usefulness. The point of many of our most enjoyable activities—eating, swimming, dancing, sometimes reading—is the pleasure we get from them directly and not something else that might or does result from doing them. One can diddle oneself for hours just for the sheer enjoyment of it and come repeatedly or never come, or engage in paired sex for hours for its own sake, continuing to come or postponing coming, just for its pleasure. How sad that Solomon extols paired sex in terms of its purported utility, its communicative efficacy. And all the more odd that Goldman criticizes Solomon's view for its narrow logic of sex as a means to an end, and yet Goldman, too, fails to acknowledge the value of the aimless pleasure of masturbation.[38] The idea that masturbation is valuable just because it is useful as a substitute for unavailable paired sex must be rejected. From a condescending and stereotypifying masculinist perspective, masturbation is an act engaged in by inexperienced adolescents and socially inept adults; it is the sex of the deservedly sexless.[39] The image is always of a nerdy guy, never of an awkward woman. This masculinist notion, that paired sex is best and masturbation an inferior substitute, an "ultimate retreat," appeared in all our liberal philosophers, who seem to forget that paired sex is, either by its nature or in virtue of the features, both natural and social, of the partners, often not very good sex. A person engaging in paired sex, despite the lack of pleasure he gets from it, simply because he thinks this is what he should be doing or enjoying, instead of masturbating to a delicious orgasm, receives no helpful advice from our liberals.

But if the horrors of the nineteenth-century medicalization of masturbation have been overcome by enlightened views of its innocuousness, if not its usefulness, staunchly antisexual conservative philosophy is, in the late twentieth century, still very much alive, and continues its tradition of condemning masturbation. Like all active research programs, conservative sexual philosophy has developed its concepts and is abundantly prepared to argue in more urbane ways against the acceptability and wisdom of engaging in masturbation and other outré sexual practices. Its staid Christian-Kantian theological and moral philosophy has been reinterpreted for modern sensibilities and has been combined with recent advances in psychiatry. Why does the conservative consult both philosophy and medicine? For this philosopher, problems of human sexuality are located in the gray area— studiously skirted by the liberal philosophy that accentuates the analytic autonomy of the moral, the prudent, the pleasurable, and the natural—in which it is difficult to separate questions about moral character from issues of mental well-being. In the conservative's world, the morally virtuous personality and the psychologically healthy mind are causally related, and the notions of "sound mind," "sound body," and "sound morality" are conceptually intertwined. In this network, there is no room for masturbation.

Men's Liberation

Soon I examine what the contemporary conservative philosophers John Finnis and Roger Scruton have written about masturbation. One of the conspicuous curiosities of the late twentieth century, however, is that telling the liberal from the conservative is no longer easy. To sense, for example, a profoundly conservative impulse in the opposition of the feminist Catharine MacKinnon to pornography is not dreadfully wide of the mark. Still, I was shocked, when paging through the leftist anthology *Men's Lives* (the book's epigraph, "Isn't it time we destroyed the macho ethic? . . . I don't want to go through life pretending to be James Dean or Marlon Brando," was penned by John Lennon, to whom the volume is dedicated),[40] to find that in six hundred pages covering every aspect of being a man in America, not one of the seventy entries contained a gentle defense of masturbation; none of these heavies in the men's movement thought it worthwhile to get the religious and conservative right off the backs of masturbating men. Indeed, the book's only serious claims about masturbation, in an essay coauthored by one of the book's editors (M. S. Kimmel), show that the radical left, too, is on the backs of masturbating men.

We came across, in Ruddick, the thesis that "disembodied" sexuality involves a "dissociation" inimical to mental health. Another rendering of the thesis, from this essay in *Men's Lives*, itemizes the dangers for young boys of masturbation, their "earliest foray into sexuality":

> Masturbation teaches young men that sexuality is about the detachment of emotions from sex, that sex is important in itself. . . . [It] also teaches men that sexuality is phallocentric, that the penis is the center of the sexual universe. . . . [T]he tools of masturbation, especially sexual fantasy, teach men to objectify the self, to separate the self from the body.[41]

The authors attribute enormous power to masturbation; it is not madness for which masturbation is blamed, but an unhealthy sexual orientation or attitude. (Note how political judgments are being advanced as clinical psychology.) There are three criticisms of masturbation in the passage; I discuss them in turn.

First, the authors warn that masturbation encourages the idea that "sex is important in itself." This criticism is odd, for the culprit in leading men to attribute "increased importance to sex without emotional involvement"[42] has usually been, for sexual conservatives, more specifically pornography. But the reply to the criticism of masturbation and the criticism of pornography, on the grounds that these things play up sexual pleasure for its own sake, is the same. To believe that sex is sometimes if not often "important in itself," a valuable activity even when not particularly communicative or expressive of deep human emotion, is not obviously mistaken. What emotion is masturbation supposed to separate from sex? If they claim that masturbation eliminates affection, or even rudimentary goodwill, from sexuality altogether, and makes paired sex affectless and mechanical, the authors are wrong to attribute such influence to masturbation. If the authors are claiming, instead, that masturbation encourages a separation of sex from weighty emotions such as love, while still permitting a link between sex and affection or at least kindness, masturbation does not deserve to be condemned (maybe it should be praised). Why ignore the implications for men of the feminist insight that young women should be encouraged to learn about sex without being encumbered by thoughts of love, that such freedom is important in exploring sexual orientations and lifestyles? Goldman's "Plain Sex" is starting to look positively refreshing.

Second, the accusation that masturbation teaches young boys that sexuality is phallocentric is ridiculous. One might as well claim that masturbation, in teaching boys that "the penis is the center of the sexual universe," makes them gay. When young boys enter this first "foray" into sexuality, they naturally focus immediately and exclusively on the exquisite and novel sensations in the erect and ejaculating penis. (To encourage girls and women to pay more attention to their clitoris, but play down the glans penis, seems contradictory.) When they get older they can and do learn that stroking other parts of their body, or the bodies of other people, or having these other parts stroked, also brings pleasure. But at first the penis receives the attention deserving an organ that at a certain biological age wakes up and announces to its holder: *I know I'm ugly, but I can do more than piss. I can make you feel some very special things.* Further, the notion that the erect penis is the central actor in heterosexual sexual activity is a notion shared by many women (for better or worse), and *they* did not

come to view sexuality phallocentrically by fastening adolescent masturbatory forays on their penises. Were it true that men's favoring the penis is
instigated by puerile masturbation that focuses on the offending organ,
there is prevention: firmly recommend to young men that they not emphasize the penis when masturbating; advise them that to avoid the narrow
phallocentric sexuality of our culture's notion of masculinity they should
start right away to employ and enjoy the whole body.

Third, the authors claim that masturbatory *fantasies* lead to "separat
[ing] the self from the body." *Au contraire*. What is more likely is that
masturbating *sans* fantasy—quickly eliciting an ejaculation for pleasure or
relief, as if depositing semen into a cup for fertility testing, diagnosis of
disease, or artificial insemination—involves both detaching oneself from
the body and objectifying it, especially the penis. Instead, masturbating
avec fantasy brings together the self and the body: these two ontological
aspects of my existence, body and mind, team up to produce a blend of
bodily, sensual pleasure and a perception of a touch or odor, a mixture that
neither can produce alone. The act demonstrates to me what I cannot
doubt, that I am a unity of body and mind. Masturbation is not only a
Cartesian soliloquy; it is also the answer to Descartes's soliloquy.

This essay, as is the rest of *Men's Lives*, is devoted to demolishing
myths about male sexuality, debunking our cultural standard of male
sexual performance, and exposing, as a disaster for men and women alike,
our cultural definition of masculinity. For example, the authors write that
sex therapists should point out to their patients that this notion of masculinity "command[s men] to be in a constant state of potential sexual
arousal, to achieve and maintain perfectly potent erections on demand"
(478), and therapists should correct such cultural messages by telling
patients that "a real man is strong enough to take risks, eschew stereotypes,
to ask for what he needs sexually from a partner, and, most of all, to
tolerate failure" (480). Despite this sort of good sense, the essay repeats
conservative wisdom about masturbation and echoes the cultural definition
of masculinity that belittles it. That definition says: real men (Marlon
Brando) don't jerk off. The new message is not much different: real men
(John Lennon) don't jerk off. Throughout, the authors generously give
men who suffer sexual performance anxiety permission to fail at heterosexual coitus, but they stingily withhold permission to masturbate. To that

extent, and because they don't abandon the idea of a *real* man, their commitment to an intelligent men's liberation is doubtful.

John Stoltenberg falls into a similar contradiction. He rightly complains about the "cultural imperative" according to which men in our society must "fuck" in order to *be* men (so much for Pateman's nonsense that men can express their masculinity by buying "hand relief"), and he rightly calls "baloney" the notion that "if two people don't have intercourse, they have not had real sex."[43] Stoltenberg also observes that "sometimes men have coital sex . . . not because they particularly feel like it but because they feel they *should* feel like it." But Stoltenberg fails to draw the masturbatory conclusion. Indeed, it is jolting to behold Stoltenberg, in an argument reminiscent of one of the religious objections to contraception (namely, it makes women into sexual objects), laying a guilt trip on men who masturbate with pornography:

> Pay your money and imagine. Pay your money and get real turned on. Pay your money and jerk off. That kind of sex helps . . . support an industry committed to making people with penises believe that people without [penises] are sluts who just want to be ravished and reviled—an industry dedicated to maintaining a sex-class system in which men believe themselves sex machines and men believe women are mindless fuck tubes. (35–36)

This exaggerated ranting has *barely* enough truth in it to induce some people with penises to keep their hands off them for a week.

Given Kant's dismal view of human sexual interaction as essentially instrumental, much can be said on behalf of solitary masturbation, which avoids using other people. Similarly, given the men's movement attack on oppressive cultural definitions of masculinity, which insist that men fuck women, as well as feminist worries about the moral and psychological integrity of sexual activity between unequally empowered men and women, one might have thought that men's masturbation would be praised as a solution to a handful of problems. A man pleasing himself by masturbating is not taking advantage of economically and socially less powerful women; he is not refurbishing the infrastructure of his fragile ego at the expense of womankind; he is not obeying standards of masculinity that instruct him that he must seduce and screw real women to be a man. Yet it is realistic fantasizing and its associated heightened sexual pleasure (44)—

the very things I pointed to in arguing that solitary masturbation is both sexual and natural—that Stoltenberg picks out as constituents of unwelcome and wrongful sexual objectification. He does not condemn just masturbating with pornography (35–36, 42–43, 49–50). Elaborating the idea that fantasy per se is a fault, as in Kimmel, Stoltenberg goes for the throat, condemning men's masturbating while entertaining memories of and passing thoughts about women, even when these fantasies and images are not violent (41–44). According to Stoltenberg, when a man conjures up a mental picture of a woman, her body, or its various parts, he is viewing her as an object, as a thing, as something to be used for his own pleasure.

This mental objectification is, for Stoltenberg, both a cause and a result of our system of "male supremacy" (51, 53–54). Further, mental sexual objectification contributes to violence against women (54–55). Stoltenberg's reason for asserting this claim is flimsy. He supposes that when a man fantasizes sexually about a woman, he reduces her from a person to an object; and that when a man thinks of a woman as a thing, he has given himself carte blanche in his behavior toward her, including violence. Regarding an object, "you can do anything to it you want" (55). Of course the last claim is false; there are innumerable lifeless objects to which I would never lay a hand, either because other people value them, and I value these people, or because I dearly value the objects myself.[44] One can surely cherish objects, even cathect them, without making fetishes of them. Reducing a woman to a thing—or, if we want to describe it more faithfully to men's experiences than does Stoltenberg, emphasizing for a while the beauty of only one aspect of a person's existence—does not mean, either logically or psychologically, that she can or will be tossed around the way a young girl slings her Barbie.

Stoltenberg vastly underestimates the nuances of men's fantasies about women; his phenomenological account of what occurs in the minds of fantasizing men—the purported reduction of persons to things—is crude. One could reply to misgivings about sexual objectification the way Camille Paglia does:

> By focusing on the shapely, by making woman a sex-object, man has struggled to fix and stabilize nature's dreadful flux. Objectification is conceptualization, the highest human faculty. Turning people into sex objects is one of

the specialties of our species. It will never disappear, since it is intertwined
with the art-impulse and may be identical to it.[45]

We can add to this defense of the necessity of objectification a different
point: exactly in virtue of the high human faculty of conceptualization,
objectification is not what it appears to be. Her smile, the way she moves
down the stairs, the bounce of her tush, the sexy thoughts in her own
mind, her lusty yearning for me—these are mere parts of her; but fantasizing or imagining them, making of them a concept while masturbating,
or driving my car, or having coffee, need not amount to, indeed is quite the
opposite of, my reducing her to plastic. These are fantasies about people,
not things. They are fantasies about personality. My fantasy of her (having
a) fantasy of me (or of my [having a] fantasy of her) is structurally too
sophisticated to be called objectification. The fantasizer makes himself in
his consciousness both subject and object and imagines his partner as both
subject and object. Recognizing the imagined person as a person, in an
ontological, nonmoral sense, is hardly a superfluous component of men's—
or women's—fantasies. That Stoltenberg overlooks the complex structure
of men's fantasies about women is not surprising; the crude idea that men
vulgarly reduce women to objects in their fantasies is precisely what would
occur to someone who has already objectified *men*, who has reduced men
from full persons having intricate psychologies to robots with penises.

Stoltenberg has dressed up Augustine's Christianity in the garb of the
philosophy of the men's movement, and he borrows his teacher's trick
from centuries ago: select an act that everyone (over 90 percent) in the
target group does, tell them the act is wicked, exaggerate the nastiness of
which the act is capable, and insist that avoiding it (impossible) is the only
route to salvation. Reading Stoltenberg on how odious and lousy men are
who look at and fantasize about women's bodies is identical to reading
Augustine on how shameful sex is. Stoltenberg thinks the origin of the
objectification of sexual fantasizing is not biological (45); men learn this
"habit," instead, from culture. "Sexual objectifying in people born with
penises is a learned response" (53). But Stoltenberg offers no engaging
advice for how to abstain from the offense, no enticing re-eroticization
technique. Augustine, too, offers no real advice for how to refrain from
having sex just for the pleasure of it. He proffers only the wistful idea that

if men, in a return to Adam's prelapsarian state, could regain voluntary control over erection, so that the propagative act were under the command of the will and had nothing to do with passion, that would be an improvement. So, too, Stoltenberg, whose talk of the ethical implications (46–47, 55–56) of the habit of objectifying in sexual fantasizing implies that men should just cut it out already.[46] Men should control their thoughts the way they should control their dicks, as if both were bits of skeletal muscle.

Stoltenberg's view, that it is wrong for men to look at and think about women's bodies, is not unique to him. The home base of the criticism is feminist views of patriarchal heterosexuality. According to Linda LeMoncheck, for example, a man who silently thinks to himself as he looks at a woman walking by, "that's a nice piece of ass," has committed morally wrongful sexual objectification. He has *treated* the woman "as less than a moral equal, as one less deserving . . . of the rights to well-being and freedom that he enjoys."[47] LeMoncheck packs a lot of meaning and power into a silent thought, or into a thought-and-eyeball-act. She also expands the idea of "treat," so that it covers not only physical and public actions, but also private thoughts. If thoughts are acts, then it makes some sense to say that a silent thought can be a "treatment" and to judge such thoughts to be violations of Kant's Second Formulation. I wonder, though, if LeMoncheck would attenuate her moral verdict if the man were to look at the woman in the same way, yet be pondering, instead, where she bought those enviable pumps. (How could anyone, including the woman he's looking at, know, since his physical movement is the same?) Or if the fellow had thought, instead, "gee, she's pretty," or had glanced shyly, but with adoring desire behind his lashes, for a nanosecond. LeMoncheck should not change her judgment, if she wants to remain faithful to her Augustinian intellectual heritage.[48] "Anyone who looks at a woman lustfully has already committed adultery with her in his heart. If your right eye causes you to sin, gouge it out" (Matthew 5:28–29).

Conjugal Union

Despite the conservative themes in its critique of masturbation, Kimmel's *Men's Lives* is not a sexually conservative treatise; it celebrates, for example, men's being affectionate and erotic with men. In John Finnis,[49] by contrast, we find a conservative negative assessment of masturbation linked conceptually to an equally negative attack on homosexuality—not because masturbation causes one to be gay, or because in much masturbation a man or woman is aroused by touching, respectively, a penis or clitoris, but because both homosexual activity and masturbation are nonconjugal.

Finnis claims that there are morally worthless sexual acts in which "one's body is treated as instrumental for the securing of the experiential satisfaction of the conscious self." Out of context, this might seem to be condemning rape, the use of one person by another for mere "experiential satisfaction." But rape is the farthest thing from Finnis's mind; he means, here, not coerced but fully voluntary sex. When is sex instrumental, and hence worthless, even though consensual? Finnis immediately mentions, creating the impression that these are his primary targets, that "in masturbating, as in being . . . sodomized," one's body is just a tool of satisfaction. As a result of one's body being used as an instrument of pleasure, one undergoes "disintegration": in masturbation and homosexual anal intercourse "one's choosing self [becomes] the quasi-slave of the experiencing self which is demanding gratification." I do not pretend to understand this complex metaphysical psychology; but we should ask—since Finnis sounds remarkably like the Kant who thinks that sex by its nature is instrumental and objectifying—how sexual acts other than sodomy and masturbation avoid this particular problem. Finnis's answer is that they do not; the worthlessness and disintegration attaching to sodomy attach to "all extramarital sexual gratification." The physical character of the act is, then, not the decisive factor; the division between the wholesome and the worthless is between "conjugal activity" and everything else.

So our question becomes this: what is special about the heterosexual conjugal bed that allows marital sex to avoid promoting disintegration? Finnis replies that worthlessness and disintegration attach to masturbation and sodomy in virtue of the fact that in these activities "one's conduct is not the actualizing and experiencing of a real common good," but is only the pursuit of separate satisfactions. Marriage, on the other hand,

with its double blessing—procreation and friendship—is a real common good . . . that can be both actualized and experienced in the orgasmic union of the reproductive organs of a man and a woman united in commitment to that good.

Maybe being married *is* conducive to the worthiness of sexual activity. Even so, what is wrong with sex between two single consenting adults who care about and enjoy pleasing each other in bed? Does not this mutual pleasuring avoid disintegration, shamefulness, and worthlessness? No: the friends might only be seeking pleasure for its own sake, as occurs in sodomy and masturbation. And although Finnis thinks that "pleasure is indeed a good," he qualifies that concession with "when it is the experienced aspect of one's participation in some intelligible good." For Finnis's argument to work, he must claim that pleasure is a good *only when* it is an aspect of the pursuit or achievement of some other good. This is not quite what he says. Perhaps he does not say it because he fears his readers will reject such Thomistic reservations about pleasure, or because he realizes it is false: the pleasure of tasting food is good in itself, regardless of whether the eating is part of the goods of securing nutrition or sharing table. But let's proceed.

What if the friends say that they do have a common good, their friendship, the same way a married couple has the common good that is their marriage? If "their friendship is not marital . . . [then] activation of their reproductive organs cannot be, in reality, an . . . actualization of their friendship's common good." The claim is obscure. Finnis tries to explain, and in doing so reveals the crux of his sexual philosophy:

> the common good of friends who are not and cannot be married (man and man, man and boy, woman and woman) has nothing to do with their having children by each other, and their reproductive organs cannot make them a biological (and therefore a personal) unit.

Finnis began with the Kantian intuition that sexual activity involves treating the body instrumentally, and he concludes with the Kantian intuition that sex in marriage avoids disintegrity since the couple are a (biological) "unit," or insofar as "the orgasmic union of the reproductive organs of husband and wife really unites them biologically." In order for persons to be part of a genuine union, their sexual activity must be both marital and procreative. The psychic falling apart each person would undergo in nonmarital sex is prevented in marital sex by their joining into one; this bolstering of the self against a metaphysical hurricane is gained by the tempestuous orgasm, of all things. At the heart of Finnis's philosophy is a scientific absurdity, and further conversation with him becomes difficult. But the argument, even if it shows the worthlessness of sterile homosexuality and solitary masturbation, has no relevance for heterosexual friends, for those who are not, but could be, married. After all, if marriage has the "double blessing" of procreation and friendship, heterosexual friendship can have the same double blessing. Does Finnis want to claim that if these friends are committed to each other for a lifetime and plan to, or do, have children by each other, they are *married* and hence their sexual interactions are fine? That claim might be true, but Finnis does not and would not assert it. Others in his school make it clear that marriage requires more than an informal agreement to spend lives together; no genuine commitment (or love, or union) exists without a formal compact, since a promise too easily fled is no promise at all. Finnis has not executed his task, to explain the shamefulness of all nonmarital sex. It is fitting that a view intent on condemning masturbation and homosexuality disintegrates over heterosexual friendship.

Transcendental Illusions

Both progressive Kimmel and conservative Finnis are apprehensive about the fate of the self. For Finnis, the self is so fragile metaphysically that sex for the sheer pleasure of it threatens to burst it apart, while the social construction of masculinity, for Kimmel, vanquishes the delicate self, the victim of an oppressive regime it cannot withstand. And for Roger Scruton, another conservative who condemns masturbation, the ephemeral self is in continual danger of being exposed as a fraud: "In my [sexual] desire [for you] I am gripped by the illusion of a transcendental unity behind the opacity of [your] flesh."[50] We are not transcendental selves but material beings; "excretion is the final 'no' to all our transcendental illusions" (151). We are redeemed only through "a metaphysical illusion residing in the heart of sexual desire" (95). Our passions make it *appear* that we are ontologically more than we really are. Sexuality must be treated with kid gloves, then, lest we lose the socially useful and spiritually uplifting reassurance that we are the pride of the universe.

The requirement that sex be approached somberly translates, for Scruton, not only into the ordinary claim that sex must be educated to be the partner of heterosexual love, but also into a number of silly judgments. While discussing the "obscenity" of masturbation, Scruton offers this example:

> Consider the woman who plays with her clitoris during the act of coition. Such a person affronts her lover with the obscene display of her body, and, in perceiving her thus, the lover perceives his own irrelevance. She becomes disgusting to him, and his desire may be extinguished. The woman's desire is satisfied at the expense of her lover's, and no real union can be achieved between them. (319)

Recent feminism has contested the tradition, revived by Scruton, in which the clitoris, the organ of women's masturbation and pleasure and a symbol of their autonomy, is suspicious.[51] Even if in rubbing herself during coitus, a woman asserts independence from her partner, must that be bad? One reply to Scruton, then, is that without masturbation, *her* desire might be extinguished and *his* desire satisfied at the expense of hers, and still there is no union (although a nonunion that is malecentric rather than femalecentric). We could, instead, recommend to the man who "perceives his own irrelevance" that he become more involved in his partner's pleasure by helping her massage her clitoral or some other region or doing the rubbing for her; even when they are linked together coitally, he will find the arms long and the body flexible. But Scruton's claim is false, surely in London or Back Bay but even in Iowa, that most men would perceive a woman's masturbation during coitus as "disgusting." Her doing so can even help the couple attain the very union Scruton hopes for as the way to perpetrate our metaphysical illusion, by letting them experience and recognize the mutual pleasure, perhaps the mutual orgasm, that results.

Why does Scruton judge the woman's masturbation an "obscene display"? One part of his thinking is this. When masturbation is done in public (say, a bus station), it is obscene; it "cannot be witnessed without a sense of obscenity." Scruton then draws the astounding conclusion that *all* masturbation is obscene, even when done privately, on the grounds that "that which cannot be witnessed without obscene perception is itself obscene" (319). Scruton seems not to notice that his argument proves too much; it implies that heterosexual coitus engaged in by a loving, married couple in private is also obscene, if we assume—as I think he would—that this act "cannot be witnessed," in public, "without obscene perception." The fault lies in the major premise of Scruton's syllogism. Whether an act is obscene might turn exactly on whether it is done publicly or privately. Scruton has failed to acknowledge a difference between exposing oneself to anonymous spectators and opening oneself to the gaze of a lover.

All masturbation is obscene, for Scruton, also because it "involves a concentration on the body and its curious pleasures" (319). This theme runs throughout *Sexual Desire*. Obscenity is an "obsession . . . with the organs themselves and with the pleasures of sensation" (154), and even if the acts that focus on the body and its pleasures are paired, they are "masturbatory." (Recall how the conservative criticized Goldman's "plain sex.") "In obscenity, attention is taken away from embodiment towards the body" (32), and there is "a 'depersonalized' perception of human sexuality, in which the body and its sexual function are uppermost in our thoughts" (138). A woman's masturbation during coitus is obscene since it leads the pair to focus too sharply on the physical; she is a depersonalized body instead of a person-in-a-body. Thus, for Scruton, this obscene masturbation cannot sustain—indeed, it threatens—the couple's metaphysical illusion. But if a woman's masturbation during coitus is greeted with delight by a partner, rather than with disgust, and increases the pleasure they realize and recognize in the act together, then, contrary to Scruton, either not all masturbation is obscene (the parties have not been reduced altogether to flesh) or obscenity, all things considered, is not a total sexual, normative, or metaphysical disaster.

Not only is all masturbation—the act—obscene for Scruton, but there is a type of perverted masturbator whose *thoughts* are obscene as well—a conclusion that follows from Scruton's binary framework, in which sexual desire is construed as "essentially" aiming at union with another person (89–90). This is the person for whom masturbation "replaces the human encounter" and thus "simplif[ies] the process . . . of sexual gratification" (317). Fantasies in this case are designed to eliminate "all the dangers and difficulties that surround the sexual encounter" by replacing a "real object" with one that is "obedient to the will" (319; see 344). So much the worse, I guess, for the fact that what we construct in a masturbatory fantasy is frequently the perfect partner—who, in being fantasized, is obedient to our will, even if we attribute all manner of voluntary behavior to him. Solomon sees that the great orgasm of solitary masturbation is safe, inexpensive, and hassle-free, but, unfortunately, empty. For Scruton, masturbation with a hassle-free fantasy aims at bodily pleasure for its own sake and spurns the "human soul" of a real partner, and so is both obscene and perverted.

Scruton condemns masturbation not only for its obscenity and perversion, but also for its pernicious effects. He does not worry that habitual masturbation causes premature ejaculation. Instead, masturbation accompanied by fantasies of a "compliant world" poses the "danger"—both moral and psychological—that when we are in bed with a person, we will become lost in our private fantasies and "orgasm becomes . . . the expenditure of energy on his depersonalized body" (345). To be sure, privately fantasizing during paired sex is morally risky, but Scruton writes as if fantasies—involuntary, fleeting images that are sometimes voluntarily embellished, coursing through (both) our minds during paired sex—were not common in human sexuality. Further, assessing Scruton's causal claim is difficult, and he provides no evidence. At any rate, it contains an ambiguity: is the other person he has in mind an old or new sexual partner? If the former, private fantasies could very well intrude into the sexual act just because the act would otherwise not be arousing enough (or because, as Scruton says, "desire is . . . at an end" [244]); so the presence of fantasies has nothing to do with masturbation. If the latter, it is unlikely, assuming that the new partner is competent and attractive, that even a jaded masturbator would have to rely on fantasies.

In describing his perverted masturbator, Scruton quotes Kant: desire is "unnatural when a man is stimulated not by an actual object but by imagining it, thus creating it himself."[52] But within the context of the rest of the passage, the quoted sentence makes a different point. Kant continues:

For his fancy engenders a desire contrary to an end of nature and indeed contrary to an end more important even than that of the love of life, since it aims only at preserving the individual, while sexual love aims at the preservation of the whole species.

Kant's procreative principle condemns much more than masturbating with fantasies, and the fact that masturbation is accompanied by fantasies is beside the point, since masturbation is not procreative regardless. Kant is probably just repeating his ban against *crimina carnis contra naturam*, but in any event he outdoes Scruton. Scruton claims that normally we do not desire the other's body (the lowest ontological level) but the other person as embodied (the middle level); to desire the body is to descend into perversion. Kant claims that the point of sex is not to benefit the individual person (the middle) but to preserve the species (the top); anything less than *that* is perverted. Scruton knows we are just the body, but insists we need the illusion, generated by sexual passion, that we are more than this; we must not believe that we can, out of ontological necessity, pursue only the body. For Kant, too, if we ever believe that we pursue the other *qua* person, that is an illusion; in reality we pursue neither the other's body nor our own well-being (even though those goals also seem to be the point of our desires), but the well-being of the species.[53] Kant is not very original. We heard plenty of this before from the king of natural law himself, St. Thomas.

Compulsory Pairing

In light of these assaults on masturbation and alternative sexualities, it is lamentable that some ordinarily courageous philosophers, those lesbians who have criticized our culture's "compulsory heterosexuality"—the pressures bearing on women to spend their lives with and for men (rather than, more happily in some cases, with and for women), on pain of numerous psychological, social, economic, and legal punishments and liabilities[54]—nevertheless support the *pairing up* of lesbians. Cheshire Calhoun protests that "within heterosexual society, the experience between lesbian women of sexual fulfillment, of falling in love, of marrying, of creating a home, of starting a family have no social reality," and she wants lesbians to have "access to sexual-romantic-marital-familial relationships."[55] Calhoun's idea is simple: lesbians and gays should be able to couple up, even marry and have families with children, as easily as can heterosexuals. The prevalent (or ideological) pattern with which we began is to be fully democratized across all sexual orientations—precisely the conclusion we drew out of the conservatism of Kant and Finnis.

The masturbator, male or female, thought he or she had an ally, the lesbians, in the critique of Quaylean ideals of family and in rebellion against the traditional condemnation of all sex except that which is marital and procreative. In Calhoun's endorsement of the nuclear lesbian family, I sense a retreat from this battle, for the challenge had been carried out by a union among the orgiast (who does it with more than one), the masturbator (who does it with less than one), the homosexual (who does it with the wrong kind), and the bisexual (the apparent champion of freedom). The masturbator has now been abandoned, left where he should have expected to end up, *alone*. Meanwhile, Calhoun teams up with that great promoter of compulsory pairing, Frank Sinatra ("love and marriage . . . you can't have one without the other"), twisting his tune in a direction he never imagined. Craig Dean is not ashamed to admit it: he *defends* gay marriage on the grounds that it is "pro-family" and "socially conservative because it would strengthen society." [56]

Calhoun's wish that lesbians and gays be able to marry as easily as heterosexuals is insidious in its implication that the pairing up of heterosexuals is eagerly and genuinely desired by those people. To the contrary, heterosexuals (both women and men) are under constant, annoying, enormous pressure to form pairs. So Calhoun wants for gays and lesbians the freedom or power to do what straights are already compelled to do, often against their better judgment. The fact that enormous pressure is brought to bear on people to lead *heterosexual* lives implies that they, left to their own devices, would probably not select that lifestyle often enough to satisfy social needs. [57] That additional pressure is brought to bear on heterosexuals to form stable *pairs* similarly suggests not only that there is social benefit to be gained from pairing, but also that the interests of individuals run counter to those of society and hence individuals must be coerced or gently guided into arrangements they would not select often enough on their own. The ordinarily compulsory nature of pairing ought to make Calhoun leery of the idea that pairing is good for anyone—gays, lesbians, bis, straights. [58] The belief that pairing is usually a happy and beneficial state is merely a bit of fiendish ideology, or popular wishful thinking, that is refuted by experiences and reflections we keep well-closeted for the sake of domestic tranquility. We are often seduced by the packaging into underestimating the hostility and aggression that underlie the family romance.

It is the heterosexual family system that Calhoun objects to as a large part of the source of antigay and antilesbian social prejudice: "if one wants a complete set of regulations that constitute the taboo on lesbianism and homosexuality, one needs to look at all the practices that . . . insure that the family will be built around a male-female pair" (579). Thus, the liberation of gays and lesbians, goes Calhoun's logic, requires that we abolish the exclusive dominance of the male-female pair and expand the institution of the family to include female-female and male-male pairs: Ozzie-and-Harriet-for-homosexuals. But as a matter of logic, a dismantling of the offensive unit, the male-female family pair in which begins antigay and antilesbian prejudice, could also be accomplished by eliminating the *pair* itself. To this alternative possibility Calhoun seems blind. She objects to compulsory heterosexuality, but never dreams of objecting to pairing; like mainstream liberal sexual philosophers, she too embraces the deepest global assumption of her opponents.

Calhoun has bought the ideology of the virtues of pairing hook, line, and sinker, and she purchased it from the same salesman from whom she refused to buy heterosexuality; an otherwise smart shopper fell for the bait-and-switch routine. Her purchase could prove disastrous. Once gay and lesbian marriages are first tolerated and then, in due course, legalized (as of course they should be), and then, eventually, accepted as *normal,* social constraints and pressures will come into play. Gays and lesbians, who will then be just like the rest of society, only different, will be expected to do their part, and their freedom or right to marry will become a duty to do so. Even Christians have begun to promote the idea of homosexual marriage justified by love,[59] so homosexual pairing is well on its way to being "dictated by the laws of God, Nature, Government, and Good Sense all at once."[60] Compulsory pairing will be extended to all. Once lesbians and gays pair up as frequently as straights, those infamously intriguing and exciting role models of the single life will become dinosaurs, absent from our social environment, and resistance to compulsory pairing even among straights will weaken. Of course there would be some good gay and lesbian marriages; but how many? Richard Mohr claims that nonformalized gay marriages, unencumbered by the customary "trappings" of formal hetero-sexual marriage and state regulations, are superior marriages because they are deeper; they "are like the development of a patina on wood."[61] Perhaps. But for how long would gay and lesbian marriages be better than straight ones after the legal formalism is extended democratically? The happiness of the few couples that would benefit from such an arrangement would be attained at the cost of the strengthening of the marriage/family unit, that voracious institutional carnivore that more frequently sucks people up whole and spits out their stripped bones.

Guilt

A common platitude says, "there is not one shred of evidence that mastur-bation is harmful. . . . The only harm that can result from masturbation is if the individual is plagued with feelings of guilt."[62] Thus, in reply to the oft-heard advice that we should not masturbate because doing so will make us feel anxious, depressed, or guilty (and in this sense masturbation might be "unhealthy" sex and hence something to avoid), it is just as often mentioned that only because philosophy, medicine, theology, and popular opinion treat the act in a disparaging way do we run the risk of experienc-ing anxiety or guilt in the first place. That is to some extent true, but to repeat this rejoinder might no longer be sufficient. Maybe we have gone too far in reaction against views critical of masturbation, and it is time for a swing back to traditional intuitions (if not thermoelectrocautery). There are other reasons for the moral criticism of fantasy and masturbation, some of which have emerged from recent trends in feminist thought, especially among those who have continued to press the question of por-nography: if pornography is morally objectionable, seriously degrading to women (an argument we will examine), making heterosexual men feel guilty for masturbating with such horrible stuff might be legitimate. In fact, David Richards thinks it better that feminists fight pornography by making men feel personally guilty about it; use speech against speech, instead of enacting laws.[63] And maybe Rousseau was right, after all, to imply that sexual fantasy, a mental depiction, is little different from rape.

So those who are critical of pornography will have to expound a notion of correct psychic sexuality for a just society. If proponents of this new psychic sexuality were to enlist the aid of the psychiatrists, it could be commended not only as moral but also as healthy. Maybe this is how contemporary Augustinian Christianity will come into its own.

THREE

Analysis

Some kissing is sexual; some is not. Sometimes looking is sexual; sometimes *not* looking is sexual.
> —Janice Moulton, "Sexual Behavior: Another Position"

What is sexual is what gives a man an erection.
> —Catharine MacKinnon, *Toward a Feminist Theory of the State*

Solitary masturbation is a *sexual* act. But why? That's a tough question. "Moulton's Problem," as we might call it, is precisely that: how to tell the difference, conceptually and in practice, between a sexual kiss and a non-sexual kiss. A kiss might be sexual even if it gave no man an erection; but could a kiss give a man an erection yet *not* be sexual?

Adultery

On Michael Wreen's definition of "adultery,"

> X's engaging in sexual intercourse with Y at time t is an act of adultery if and only if either X or Y is married at time t, and X and Y are not married to each other at that time. [1]

This definition seems fine. Examining some specific cases will test whether Wreen has correctly stated the necessary and sufficient conditions for adultery. Doing so will also lead us into interesting philosophical territory concerning the nature of sexual activity.

Suppose that X, who is married to Z, masturbates while thinking about Y. Is this adulterous? Apparently not, according to Wreen's definition. Instead, X is being mildly unfaithful, and what the example shows is that adultery and unfaithfulness are not the same thing. X's masturbation is not adultery for Wreen because, presumably, X's fantasized coitus with Y is not (really) "engaging in sexual intercourse" with Y. True, X is engaging in sex with someone to whom he is not married (X himself); but X is not engaging in sex with someone outside the X-Y marriage. Actually, Wreen's definition is *either* silent about this case: in good binary framework fashion, the definition applies to two-person sex, not one-person sex (if, as Wreen implies, X and Y are different people); *or*, if we replace the variables X and Y with the same constant "John," the definition entails that John's masturbation *is* adulterous, if John is married to Sally and masturbating is "engaging in sexual intercourse" (which, for Wreen, it isn't).

Note that Wreen's definition does not require that *both* persons, X and Y, be married; even if only X is married, the unmarried Y has still committed adultery. Wreen distinguishes here between engaging in "extra-marital" sex, of which only X is guilty, and adulterous sex, of which both are guilty (179).[2] But if *neither* person, X or Y is married, yet at least one is part of an ongoing relationship with Z, is their intercourse adulterous? Wreen's definition entails "no." We might again contrast adultery and unfaithfulness. Even so, little moral difference seems to exist between X's sleeping with Z when X is married to Y and when X is ("only") in a relationship with Y. Nevertheless, adultery *might* be morally worse in virtue of violating the Pauline principle of the mutual ownership of each other's bodies, an ownership possibly absent from committed but nonmarital relationships.

If two people are married to each other, does that really prevent their sex together from being adulterous, as claimed by Wreen's definition? Recall Augustine's pronouncement that if a married X and Z have sex only for pleasure, not for procreation, they are "so to say" committing adultery.[3] I have implicitly touched on the case in which a married X and Z, during coitus with each other, fantasize about other people. Although some Christians label this "mental adultery,"[4] it looks more like mild unfaithfulness. Suppose, instead, that the married X and Z invite an unmarried Y to bed with them, with full consent all around. Is X's or Z's sex with Y adultery? Wreen's definition says yes. If this is right, the example shows that adultery and "cheating" are not the same thing. For the married X and Z who invite Y to share their bed are not deceiving or tricking each other, or secretly engaging in sex with Y alone in a motel room, even though they are willingly adulterous. The question then arises whether noncheating adultery is morally objectionable despite three-way consent. Wreen thinks that X's adultery with a Y who is a sexual therapist is permissible if done to cure X's sexual dysfunction and thereby strengthen the X-Z marriage, and if all parties consent (185). We might worry here about the quality of Z's consent[5] and insist that it be at least Antiochian, given only after much dialogue. But if Z's consent to X's adultery with a therapist Y makes it permissible, an X-Y-Z ménage, done only for pleasure but consensually, also seems permissible.

Indeed, the definition of adultery must mention willing and knowledgeable consent. Suppose X coerces Y, who is married to Z, into coitus—forcibly rapes her. Y's experience (not Y's act, since Y performed no act) was not adulterous, because she didn't have the proper frame of mind: a certain motive was absent, she never intended to commit adultery or engage in intercourse at all. Thus, as Wreen recognizes (186 n. 2), some modification is required in the definition; that the act be freely chosen, not compelled, is a necessary condition. Similarly, suppose an unmarried X didn't know that Y was married, had good reason to think—after Antiochian dialogue—that Y was unmarried; or X believed that X was no longer married, had good evidence that spouse Z died years ago. In these cases, X performs with Y an adulterous act, even if unwittingly and not culpably, unless the definition is modified. Adultery requires more than the physical and legal components of two people, not married to each other, engaging in coitus. It also requires *mens rea*.

But what is the specific motive or intention essential to adultery? That a person engages in the sexual act for its own sake and not as a regimen of therapy? No. That a person does it for the sheer joy of it and not to make some money? No again. It cannot be that coitus is not adulterous as long as a person has a good reason for doing it. Further, the reason for the act, the motive one has, does not figure into whether the act is adultery but only, if anything, into whether the act is wrong. A sexual act can be adulterous no matter what the intentions of the parties are, as long as the act was not coerced or done in ignorance. No particular motive defines adultery. The *mens rea* requirement is a slender one.

Suppose X and Y, attracted to each other but not wanting to get involved (because happily married to others), share one kiss and then bid each other an Arnoldian "adieu!" This suggests a final observation about Wreen's definition: it is silent about whether this kiss is adulterous, because the definition is of adulterous sexual intercourse and not adulterous sex *simpliciter*. (Wreen means "coitus" by "sexual intercourse.") If, for X and Y, the main event is reciprocal oral sex, and they never get around to intercourse, or if they engage in light, safe sadomasochism—X spanks Y to orgasm and neither person removes any clothing—adultery has occurred, if they are married but not to each other. We should make the definition general by replacing "sexual intercourse" with "sexual act." Now the question, Is it adultery? when that turns on the sometimes fine distinction between a sexual embrace and an embrace that is not quite sexual, becomes more difficult. Coitus and oral sex are easy cases, since they are standard sexual acts. But in other cases, not enough touching between X and Y might occur to be sex, or not enough of the right kind of touch. Or not enough sex between X and Y might occur to be adultery, or not enough of the right kind of sex. The kiss might be cheating or unfaithfulness, but not adultery, either because it involved too little contact to be sex or too little sex to be adultery. "No French, no foul."

The vagueness of "sexual act" and "adultery" allows the exoneration of adultery by describing "downward" whatever occurs between X and Y. It was only "fooling around," not the real thing, because, as Roger Angell jokes, "it only took a *minute*" or "it was only with my dorky brother-in-law." [6] Or recall what Alexander Portnoy told his father. But not only those who are lenient on our sexual weaknesses pull this intellectual trick. Conservative theologians who refuse to bend at all with human frailty have often defined adultery "upward." In the spirit of Matthew 5:28, they make a sexual thought sufficient, even in the absence of contact: X commits adultery if X mentally lusts after Y.

Counting Sex

Angell's joke—if the act "only took a minute," it was not really sex—was meant, I think, as sarcastic commentary on a possible gender difference about the scope of "sexual act" noted by Edward Laumann and his colleagues in their survey of sexual behavior:

> men and women may differ in what they consider a sex partner—the men may consider a quick act of sex as counting, while women may not count a brief, inconsequential event. [7]

The authors overlook that a man might discount, for himself and for a survey-taker, quick coitus with a prostitute. For a man whose sense of self or masculinity is linked to sexual performance, counting commercial sex is cheating, like saying you've been to Chicago when all you did was change planes at O'Hare. It's not the real thing. Or a man might not count as a sexual act, or reveal to a survey-taker, any event in which he ejaculated too quickly, before or soon after penetration.

Why do Laumann and his colleagues say that women might discount brief events? They found, as other surveyors have, a disparity between the number of partners men reported having and the number, significantly lower, reported by women. [8] In an attempt to explain in part this result, Laumann and his colleagues suggest that women discount brief events more often than do men. But the explanation is misleading, if we assume that when answering the question, How Many Sexual Partners Have You Had? both men and women sincerely applied to their own behavior the *same* definition of "sexual activity" that Laumann asked them to use. According to this definition, sexual activity is

> mutually voluntary activity with another person that involves genital contact and sexual excitement or arousal, that is, feeling really turned on, even if intercourse or orgasm did not occur. [9]

The definition does not make penis-vagina penetration necessary for an act to be sexual, but requires only manual, oral, or some other kind of contact with someone's genitals. It is plausible, then, that when men apply the definition to their behavior, they would end up reporting having had more sex than they otherwise would have reported, left to their own definitional devices: many heterosexual men conceive of sexual activity more narrowly than Laumann's definition, requiring penis-vagina penetration. By contrast, women's notion of sexuality seems broader, so as to include, *pace* Laumann, acts in which caresses of various kinds predominate. If so, the amount of sex, or number of partners, women reported when using Laumann's definition might have been exactly what they would have reported anyway, on their own definition.

Suppose the men and women subjects had ignored instructions to use Laumann's definition, and used their own. Then Laumann would have found the reverse of what was actually found: women would have reported having had more partners than men, since a man's notion of sex is narrower than Laumann's while a woman's notion is close to it. The fact that the reverse result was not obtained suggests that both men and women honestly attempted to apply Laumann's definition. Hence, the hypothesis that women did not count brief events, and that is in part why they reported fewer partners than men, cannot be quite right, since the proper application of Laumann's definition gives women no leeway for discounting brief events per se.

But Laumann's definition of sexual activity is flawed. It suffers from a conceptual quirk that, when probed, might explain in part the difference between the number of partners reported by men and women. The requirement in the definition that a person be "really turned on" for an event to *be* sexual means that the definition is not exactly of sexual activity per se but, instead, of *good*, arousing, or at least decent sexual activity, in the nonmoral sense, that is, pleasurable sexual activity. According to Laumann's definition, none of the acts of coitus and fellatio performed by a prostitute would be sexual, if he or she was not "turned on" and derived no pleasure from them. Bad sex—boring and sparkless sex, which most of us have experienced, even with loving partners—is still sex, but not acknowledged by the "really turned on" in Laumann's definition. It would have to be a gullible spouse who listened seriously to "I *really* wasn't turned on, not *that* much," so—continues the perverse logic—"it wasn't sex (or only a little) and hence not adultery."

In conflating the difference between sexual acts per se and good sexual acts, Laumann's definition forced his subjects to chomp at the conceptual bit. But they stood up well under the pressure, and in employing his definition disclosed something important about heterosexual relations. The difference in the number of partners reported by men and women can now be seen to be, more specifically, a difference in the number of *good* sexual partners reported by men and women. To explain the discrepancy between their reports, we need not assume that the subjects were lying about their sexual behavior (that men exaggerate and women modestly underestimate) or that they mischievously or inadvertently failed to employ Laumann's definition. Alternatively, we could surmise that regarding one and the same sexual act, men are more likely than women to judge it and hence their partner favorably (as "good"), while women are more likely to judge the event unfavorably.[10] Laumann and his colleagues did find this: 9 percent of the male subjects in the age bracket of eighteen through thirty-four reported that during the preceding twelve months there had been a period in which "sex [was] not pleasurable"; the corresponding figure for women was 26 percent.[11] It would be worth investigating if the sexual activity women did not find pleasurable was unsatisfactory *because* it was too brief, or because they are less quickly aroused than men.

Body Parts

In trying to grasp the essence of sexual activity, let's start with a popular view that is wrong. The basic idea in this beginning analysis is that sexual acts by their nature involve physical contact with the genitals. That these body parts are manipulated is very often a feature of sexual acts, but the genitals hardly exhaust what is interesting sexually about our bodies. X's caressing Y's breasts or tush or elbow or wrist or calf or ankle can surely be sexual, even in the absence of any subsequent contact with the genitals. (Men and women need not disagree about this.) Hence, in the same way that a definition of adultery should refer not just to coitus but to sexual acts in general, an analysis of sexual activity should not be restricted to genital contact. Laumann's definition of sexual activity, because it requires genital contact, is faulty for this reason, too.

   If we state the first analysis in such a way that it acknowledges the variety of erogenous body parts, we arrive at these definitions:

A1. An act's involving physical contact with any sexual part of the body is the distinguishing feature that makes it sexual.

A1–a. Physical contact with any sexual part is necessary for an act to be sexual.

A1–b. Physical contact with any sexual part is sufficient for an act to be sexual.

Even as proper modifications of the original proposal, these definitions will not do. Sexual behavior often involves one's touching the sexual skin of another person or of oneself, but that fact does not yield a convincing analysis. In a medical examination of the genitals, the acts performed are ordinarily not sexual even though sexual parts are touched; contrary to (A1–b), contact is not sufficient. Flirting visually, talking over the phone, and sending e-mail messages can be sexy, and sexual, even though no contact is made with a sexual body part; hence, contrary to (A1–a), contact is not necessary. We can save (A1–a) by saying that looking, speaking, and writing are kinds of physical contact with the other's eyes and ears, which are sexual parts even when not caressed. If we take (A1–a) this way, expanding the notion of "contact," it might be true, but it will not be interesting. (Note that it would be wrong to object to (A1–a) by pointing out that rubbing the sex organs through layers of clothing can be a sexual act even though there is no contact, because there *is* contact here, without unduly stretching that idea.) [12] And we can save (A1–b) by insisting that a gynecological exam *is* a sexual act, albeit not much like other sexual acts, just because it involves genital exposure and contact. That's a desperate, even though tidy, move.

According to (A1), we first identify the sexual parts of the body and then decide whether an act is sexual by observing whether it involves contact with one of those parts; "sexual act" is a concept logically dependent on the idea of a "sexual part." But do we have a clear understanding of what a sexual part is? We might shake hands briefly, without there being anything sexual about the act; or we could warmly press our hands together, and feel a surge of sexual pleasure. So sometimes the hands are used in nonsexual acts and at other times they are used sexually. Are the hands a sexual part? (A1) is silent on this matter. The point is that whether the hands are a sexual part of the body depends on the particular activity in which they are engaged: if the hands are being used nonsexually, the hands at that time are not functioning as sexual parts, but if they are being used sexually, they have become, at that time, sexual parts of the body. Hence, instead of saying, with (A1), that whether an act is sexual depends on the sexual nature of the body part it involves, we should say that whether a part is sexual sometimes depends on the sexual nature of the act in which it is involved. (A1), then, is backwards. We should refute (A1–b) not by saying that a gynecological exam is not a sexual act *despite* the fact that it involves a sexual part of the body; we should argue, instead, that a gynecological exam is not a sexual act because in that context the genitals are not, or are not being treated as, sexual parts. This is why (A1) cannot explain why a medical exam might change *in media res* from being non-sexual to being sexual, or why holding hands might start out as not sexual, move on to being sexual, and return to not being sexual: the same parts are involved at each stage.

Another point should be made about (A1). In one approach to defining pornography, the attempt to fashion a general definition is eschewed. Instead, we begin by making a list of all the sexual acts we can think of; we then divide the list into two categories, the showable (say, kissing) and the unshowable (say, coitus); then we define "pornography" as those items that explicitly depict or portray the unshowable acts. How are we to construct the list? The crudest version of (A1) suggests that any act involving the genitals is sexual. We could improve on this by adding the anus and the mouth, restricting sexual acts to bodily movements of an "insertion" or "intrusion" type. Or we could rely on our sophisticated version of (A1), which yields a much longer list of sexual acts, since it includes acts that use any sexual body part, where that is generously understood, and allows pats, licks, and kisses as well as penetrations. What all these variants of (A1) presuppose is that if we could capture in our analysis the right body parts, or the right combination of body parts and physical motions, we would be able to construct a discrete set of definite bodily movements that comprise the domain of sexual acts. Can we do this?

Figure 1. The Netherlands Post issued this stamp (*Scott 825*) in 1993 to commemorate the hundredth anniversary of Vereniging EHBO (Eerste Hulp Bij Ongevallen, the "First Help with Accidents" organization). In its publicity announcement, the Post says that the stamp portrays "mouth to mouth resuscitation." But the stamp (a duck-rabbit) also or alternatively seems to depict a swooning woman about to be kissed. (Illustration reproduced with the permission of the Netherlands PTT Post.)

Polysemous Behavior

No. Constructing that set is hopeless, for two reasons. First, the variety of bodily movements, in conjunction with the number of volatile or sensitive body parts, is too indefinite to yield a comprehensive catalogue of sexual acts. Annie Sprinkle might be wrong, in the specifics, that we can eroticize air to produce an orgasm by breathing, but her general point remains. Who is to limit in advance what dance, what stroke, what material might be erotic? Maybe we *can* cathect the condom. Catharine MacKinnon continues her account of the sexual (see the epigraph) by reciting a litany of the horrifying things males have been able to cathect: fear, hostility, hatred, helplessness, revulsion, and death.[13] Second, some bodily movements that we would put into the set of sexual acts are, in certain contexts, not sexual at all; so we would still have to search for features of these acts, other than the movements and parts involved, to decide when these acts are sexual. Massaging a breast is sexual if done by lovers, not when done during a cancer exam. Some bodily movements are, as Antioch warns, ambiguous between being sexual and not sexual: looking, touching an arm, a back rub. Hence other features of an act or its context must be called on to do the analytic job that the parts and movements were supposed to do.

Not every bodily movement is ambiguous: the woman who is pawed and pulls her arm away is clearly saying no. We are not likely to fail to categorize coitus, or contact between the mouth and genitals, as sexual, even if we can imagine odd situations in which they are not. But these are easy cases; others are hard, in which one person might see a duck and another a rabbit.[14] There need not be any noticeable physical difference between rubbing soot off someone's arm and a sexual caress, or between sexually holding hands and sharing a friendly clasp, or between the mouth-to-mouth contact of a kiss and the mouth-to-mouth contact of resuscitation (see figure 1). When we are being scoundrels, we might perform an ambiguous act for the sexual pleasure of it and hope it will not be seen for what it is by others. Or a lifeguard might unintentionally feel sexual arousal and pleasure during resuscitation; even though we do not classify the mouth-to-mouth contact of resuscitation as sexual, it can become sexual. Medical touches, despite safeguards, can also become something else. The Magyars have a practice in which friends and relatives greet each other with a kiss to both cheeks. This Magyar cultural practice is not seen by them as sexual, but due to the ambiguity of physical movements and the fact that in many societies kisses are sexual, these pecks—if maybe a nanosecond too long or millimeter too deep—could on occasion be intended or interpreted as sexual. I have often experienced Moulton's Problem in Budapest, Bóly, and New Orleans.

A line of thought naturally arises here that protests that the project of attempting to isolate the essence of sexual acts is mistaken. According to this view, there is no transcultural, ahistorical, and nonsocial common denominator, or essence, that makes sexual acts sexual. All bodily movements in themselves, including the physical movements we have come to associate with sexuality, have no meaning; bodily movements and sounds acquire meaning—as sexual, or as something else—only by existing within a culture that attaches meaning to them. (The physical movement we call "shooting the bird" has no intrinsic meaning; what it communicates is fixed by its home culture.) Individuals cannot mean anything with the motions and sounds they produce unless these connect up with stable social definitions; and individuals cannot mean just anything they want with their movements. Since the social defines our otherwise meaningless physical movements, social signals and context can often be relied on to disambiguate physical acts. They do not altogether succeed. The culture that gives meaning to our movements is not leakproof; the infinity and unpredictability of bodily movements outstrip culture's power to secure their meaning. Once a person has learned from culture how to do or say something, it is a small step to be able to pretend to do it, to do it wrongly on purpose, or to do it in socially unanticipated and undetermined ways. Indeed, we learn from culture how to lie and pretend.

Why think that sexual acts have no transcultural and ahistorical essence? Certain kinds of touches and movements might count as sexual acts in one culture but not in others; the particular body parts, fragrances, mannerisms, and costumes that are sexually attractive and arousing vary among cultures. But these facts do not imply that sexuality has no essence; they imply only that how the details of sexuality are arranged exhibits the beautiful variability of human culture. There is, of course, no language at all without culture, and the language of the ancient Hebrews is not the language of southern California. Still, language is language.

I am therefore reluctant to agree with Robert Padgug's thesis that "the very meaning and content of sexual arousal" varies so much among genders, classes, and cultures that "there is *no* abstract and universal category of 'the erotic' or 'the sexual' applicable without change to *all* societies."[15] Padgug derives this conclusion from Marx's *Grundrisse:* "Hunger is hunger, but the hunger gratified by cooked meat eaten with a knife and fork is a different hunger from that which bolts down raw meat with the aid of hand, nail and tooth."[16] Elaborating, Padgug urges theory to "absorb [biology] into a unity with social reality," because the social transforms the biological "in qualitatively new ways."[17] Padgug's antiessentialism displays a logical oddness. If the sexual radically varies from culture to culture, if no universal feature connects the sexuality of one culture with the sexuality of another, there could be no way to identify acts in different cultures as all of them sexual and hence no way to discover that sexuality has no transcultural essence.[18] Despite his strong antiessentialist claims, Padgug does acknowledge that biology "conditions and limits" sexuality. This concession to a core biological substrate ruins antiessentialism as an ontology of human nature: some nontrivial biological or natural essence does, after all, link Marx's two hungers, just as some nontrivial biology (say, the substrate of sexual pleasure) links the sexualities of the world's cultures; it is this that allows us to identify them all as instances of sexuality. We cannot, then, believe Padgug's talk of "*no* abstract and universal category" of sexuality; nor could culture so transform biology "qualitatively" that sex becomes unrecognizable as sex.[19]

Nancy Hartsock has defended Padgug's antiessentialism. As if rebutting Ellen Willis's view that sexual activity is a "basic human need," Hartsock suggests that

> we should understand sexuality not as an essence or set of properties defining an individual, nor as a set of drives and needs (especially genital) of an individual. Rather, we should understand sexuality as culturally and historically defined and constructed. Anything can become eroticized, and *thus* there can be no "abstract and universal category of 'the erotic' or 'the sexual' applicable without change to all societies."[20]

Hartsock's "anything can become eroticized," which is the premise of her argument, is not Annie Sprinkle's playful jubilance about an open future in which breathing might produce pleasure and orgasms for all. Hartsock, instead, is reporting an ontological fact, one that is in her hands dry and stubborn, and from which we are supposed to conclude that sexuality has no significant essence and everything is determined by culture. But the inference is faulty, as Sprinkle recognizes. "Anything can be eroticized," for Sprinkle, means that under the proper conditions we can cathect air or manure or death or condoms or anything, that is, tie them specifically to sexual arousal and pleasure; so there *is* a universal category of the sort Hartsock denies. Even should it turn out that analyzing such a subjective thing as sexual arousal and pleasure is philosophically vain, that would not be much consolation for antiessentialism; I see no prospect of successfully arguing that sexual pleasure or its experience itself radically varies from culture to culture, or that it, too, has no essence.

Fellatio Insemination

The thesis that sexuality has no transcultural essence, to be credible, would have to be cleverly illustrated. It does the proponent of antiessentialism no good to point out that clucking the tongue is a sexual advance in one culture while only an annoying noise in another. What would call attention to the thesis is a demonstration that some standard sexual act, such as heterosexual coitus, is actually defined or "constructed" in some culture as not sexual, at least when done in certain circumstances that are not unusual for that culture.

The beliefs of the Sambia and Etoro tribes in New Guinea include the following:[21] for adult males the presence in their bodies, in the testicles, of semen is essential for the existence and maintenance of their masculinity; heterosexual intercourse therefore involves the temporary loss of something important (so women are dangerous);[22] the bodies of young boys do not yet internally produce, and so they do not yet have, this ingredient; hence young boys must acquire semen from an external source in order to develop into masculine, adult males. The Sambia and the Etoro have a practice that derives from these beliefs, in which young boys, starting around the age of seven to ten and lasting until puberty, manipulate and fellate older males to orgasm and ingest the ejaculate; this "fellatio insemination" ideally occurs daily. The masculinity of the donors thereby passes to the beneficiaries. Postpubertally, the boys become the men who are sucked and who provide the masculinizing fluid to younger boys; being fellated is the staple of their sexual lives, since they eschew women until marriage.

Laurie Shrage attempts to illustrate antiessentialism with this practice. Having asserted that it is "questionable" that commercial sex in France in the 1600s and in the United States today are "the same practice, . . . prostitution," on the grounds that French commercial sex was governed by different "cultural principles,"[23] Shrage proceeds to make this "point clear" by describing New Guinea fellatio insemination antiessentially:

> From the perspective of our society, the [Sambia/Etoro] practice involves behaviors which are highly stigmatized—incest, sex with children, and homosexuality. Yet, for an anthropologist who is attempting to interpret and translate these behaviors, to assume that the . . . practice is best subsumed under the category of "sex," rather than, for example, "child rearing," would reflect ethnocentrism.[24]

After all, the Sambia consider fellatio insemination akin to breast-feeding; both acts provide nourishment to growing children.[25] Shrage claims that to see this fellatio as a sexual act, rather than as a child-rearing act, is to impose ethnocentrically our particular Western concept of sexuality onto the practices of another culture, practices that are imbued with their own unique social meaning. Indeed, Shrage prefers to call the act "penis-feeding" in order to emphasize its link with breast-feeding, and she puts "fellate" in scare-quotes to indicate to her reader that the act has a "radically different meaning and purpose" in Sambian culture.[26]

This suggestion, that fellatio insemination of young boys by more mature males is not a sexual activity, is provocative but naive.[27] The fact that an ejaculating penis is involved is not exactly the reason; for penises ejaculate, even when flaccid, in lots of nonsexual situations (riding a bike, getting a prostate exam). But the Sambian penis is erect—MacKinnon's criterion—when the young boy fellates it to orgasm, and this fact implies that Sambian men experience the turbulence of sexual arousal and the bliss of sexual pleasure. Why do the boys ingest the semen straight from a fellated, aroused, orgasmic penis, if the mature male's sexual pleasure played no motivating role? The fluid could, instead, be perfunctorily "expressed" by the men into a silver chalice and ingested by the boys after they performed a fanfare of ceremonial songs and dances in its honor; drinking it would, in this case, look much less sexual and more religious. The males who are fellated are still bachelors, and so do not have Pauline access to wives and the pleasure wives provide; but the bachelors have, as socially designed compensation, Pauline access to young boys and daily sexual gratification. The outward form of this sexuality, its official raison d'être, might be child-rearing, and so the men usurp, in genuine patriarchal fashion, women's role as nourisher of children. But at the very least this child-rearing practice is also, for the Sambia, a sexual act, or one aspect of child-rearing is accomplished by a sexual act. There is no contradiction in thinking that the older male's providing semen is both sexually self-serving and altruistic; the man sacrifices, for a while, his energizing semen for the sake of the boy's nourishment.[28] So we do have a fairly good sense of and feel for what the Sambia and Etoro, our cousins under the skin, are doing. No ethnocentric imposition is needed to see that Shrage exaggerated the extent to which the Louisiana bayou and the New Guinea highlands "organize the world differently."[29]

Shrage does grudgingly allow that fellatio insemination might be both a sexual and a child-rearing act: "or . . . the world in which 'penis-feeding' occurs is not one where nurturance and eroticism are opposed."[30] But if nurturing and sex do not exclude each other in fellatio insemination, as they do not exclude each other even in breast-feeding, this ruins the value of the example for antiessentialism. Shrage also mentions that (for "some anthropologists") the "parental nurturing" acts of penis-feeding and breast-feeding both involve "a culturally erotic body part,"[31] which is her attempt, by calling these body parts "culturally erotic," to subsume the dual nurturing and sexual nature of fellatio insemination under antiessentialism. But to claim that the penis and breast are culturally erotic is to deny that they are universally sexual body parts, as if in some cultures they do or could depart from their anatomy and be altogether devoid of erotic appeal and power. The penis and breast are not in all *situations* erotic body parts, as I argued above. But this is not what Shrage means by referring to the breast as culturally erotic; her anthropologists think the breast is sexual only when and because culture determines it to be sexual.

John Stoltenberg expresses a similarly excessive antiessentialism:

> Penises and ejaculate and prostate glands occur in nature, but the notion that
> these anatomical traits comprise a sex . . . is simply that: a notion, an idea.
> The penises exist; the male sex does not. The male sex is socially constructed.
> It is a political entity that flourishes only through acts of force and sexual
> terrorism. [32]

There are good biological and sociological reasons to think that more than
two sexes exist; male and female do not exhaust the field. [33] Some humans
do not fall anatomically, chromosomally, or behaviorally into either category, and are often assigned to one or the other arbitrarily—and unfairly,
if we should be fully acknowledging extra sexes. "Male" and "female"
name categories with rough and flexible borders. This does not mean that
male and female sexes do not exist among humans as they do in other
mammals. The claim that the male sex exists as a sex *only* as the result of
force and terrorism is cut from the same hackneyed if not delusional cloth
as Adrienne Rich's idea that heterosexuality is "a man-made institution"
that is "maintained by force" to "assure male sexual access to women." [34]

Pleasure

From this discussion of Sambian fellatio, we can appreciate the role that
sexual pleasure plays in making an act sexual in an essentialist sense. The
same idea is suggested by the case of a lifeguard who, despite social rules
that he be a detached professional, accidentally gets pleasure from handling
the body of a semiconscious girl and feels, with his mouth on hers, a
tingling feeling in his groin. We arrive, then, at another analysis:

A2. Sexual acts are those acts that produce sexual pleasure.

A2–a. Sexual pleasure is necessary for an act to be sexual.

A2–b. Sexual pleasure is sufficient for an act to be sexual.

This analysis is advanced by Robert Gray. [35] Consider one of his examples,
an X who eats cow manure. X's coprophagia is a sexual perversion, says

Gray, only if it is, to begin with, a sexual act. Fine. But what could make eating cow manure a *sexual* act? If X eats cow manure because X is hungry or enjoys its taste and aroma, there is nothing sexual about eating it. Maybe X is a "food pervert," says Gray, but X is not a sexual pervert: "his motive is hunger, not sex." Eating manure would be a sexual act if X's reasons for doing so were sexual; at least, this example suggests that X's motive is the crucial factor. As Gray says, "the only thing . . . in this example . . . whose change could . . . make it an example of coprophilia in the sexual sense . . . is the motive" (160). But Gray proceeds to argue that the fact, *alone*, that eating manure produces sexual pleasure for X makes it sexual; for Gray, sexual activities are just those that "give rise to sexual pleasure" (160). Indeed, Gray thinks that "we are forced to the conclusion" (163) that producing sexual pleasure is both necessary and sufficient for acts to be sexual: "any activity might become a sexual activity," if sexual pleasure is derived from it (A2–b), and "no activity is a sexual activity unless sexual pleasure is derived from it" (A2–a). I think, however, that although (A2–b) is correct, (A2–a) is untenable, and what Gray says on its behalf is not persuasive.

The view that sexual pleasure is necessary for acts to be sexual has implausible consequences. First, it implies that bungled attempts to obtain sexual pleasure—we wanted to please each other, but the backseat was too cramped—are not sexual acts; (A2–a) entails that our frustrating gyrations, in failing to produce pleasure, also failed to be sexual. Consider, next, the woman whose breast or bottom is grabbed by a passing stranger on the street. She does not experience sexual pleasure; depending on the length of the contact, perhaps neither does he; yet the touch, intended by the stranger to procure a morsel of sexual pleasure, looks like a sexual act. But (A2–a) judges it to be a failed sexual act, and so not sexual at all, because it produced no pleasure. (It is a different kind of failure if the stranger misses his target, grabbing her purse instead.) Third, the prostitute who nightly performs dozens of acts of fellatio, experiencing no sexual pleasure in doing so, could not be said, according to (A2–a), to have engaged in any sexual acts; nor could the woman who submits to unpleasurable coitus because she wants to bear a child; nor could the man who performs cunnilingus for his wife's pleasure but, because his mind wanders to his work, gets none himself. (A2–a), in making pleasure a criterion of the sexual, makes it impossible to use pleasure as a gauge of the quality of sex acts. Consider the couple who have lost sexual interest in each other, and who engage in routine coitus from which they derive no pleasure. (A2–a) forbids us to say about this couple that they engage in sex but it is (nonmorally) bad sex. On Gray's view, we would have to say that they tried to engage in sex, but failed; their dull acts are not sexual at all.

Gray replies only to the last point, that pleasure is a mark of the quality of sex, not a criterion of the sexual. He claims that "if we accept" that sexual acts can be pleasureless, "we are led to the unhappy conclusion that the rape victim has engaged in sexual activity, although, from her point of view, the activity may not have been sexual at all" (162). But why is rape *not* a sexual act for her? Because she agrees with Gray that without sexual pleasure, the act is not sexual? That answer would nearly beg the question, yet Gray does not otherwise explain his refusal to say that rape victims have been forced to engage in sexual activity. Anyway, it seems clumsy, methodologically, to appeal to one uncertain claim—rape is not a sexual act for the victim—to defend another counterintuitive thesis, that the presence of pleasure is necessary for an act to *be* sexual. Note that Gray does assume the act is sexual for the rapist, because the rapist presumably gets sexual pleasure from it; what Gray insists on is that we take seriously the possibility that one and the same act might be sexual for one partici-pant but not for the other. This is why, on his view, the prostitute who performs pleasureless fellatio and the husband who performs oral sex on his wife without any pleasure are *not* engaging in sexual activity, even though their partners *are*. I have no problem with the supposition that an act between X and Y is sexual for X but not for Y; consider the difference between molesting children and sharing sexual experiences with them. But this is an *independent* matter.

Regardless, Gray's argument fails for a very simple reason: as a matter of logic, the claim that unpleasurable sex exists or is possible, which Gray rejects, does not inexorably lead to the additional claim, which he fears, that rape victims have engaged in sex. That some marital, backseat, or commercial sexual acts are not sexually pleasurable does not entail that any other nonpleasurable acts (rapes) are sexual. The "unhappy conclu-sion" *might* be unhappy, but it is not the conclusion. Indeed, Gray's preferred view, that all sexual acts are pleasurable, is itself dangerous; it implies that persons who are raped (if that means forced or coerced to engage in a sexual act) must derive pleasure from it, even if unwillingly.[36]

In asserting that the production or deriving of pleasure is enough for an act to be sexual, (A2–b) entails that a lifeguard's unintentional experience of sexual pleasure makes his actions sexual. This doesn't seem too far-fetched. But consider another example: a man, while driving his car to work, moves his head in paying attention to the pedestrians and catches a glimpse of a walking figure and as a result feels a twinge of sexual pleasure. It would be odd to say that this man performed a sexual act. His body was in motion, and he was the author of this movement; but that it produced sexual pleasure doesn't make the motion sexual. He had a sexual *experience*, even if he didn't perform a sexual act. What would make it clear that he did perform a sexual act would be his continuing to look, even without any further body motion, in an attempt to prolong the pleasure; passively experiencing sexual arousal or pleasure can in this way amount to the performance of a sexual act. Here is Gray's example offered in support of (A2–b): some women operating treadle sewing machines discovered they could masturbate while working (162). There was some point at which the discovery was made, accidentally, that treadling was arousing. For a brief period before this point, then, the women were unintentionally experiencing sexual pleasure and inadvertently masturbating—engaging in a sexual act.

There is just enough reason to judge (A2–b) correct. But note another implication. (A2–b) entails that if a woman or man who is raped experiences by happenstance barely perceptible sensations of sexual pleasure, the rape would be for the victim sexual. Rape might be a sexual act (in addition to everything else it is); I am leery, however, of the idea that *when* it is sexual for the victim, it is sexual *because* the victim experienced pleasure. Of course, if a rape causes the victim to have an unwanted sexual experience, in virtue of the sensations she or he endures, the rape would still not include, just for that reason, any sexual acts the victim performs: she has been forced, she did not act. Further, that an act may cause sexual sensations or pleasure doesn't mean it is enjoyable; Antioch's policy makes sense in supposing that someone might experience pleasure yet not enjoy it and for that reason refuse to proceed. If a rape victim does experience unwanted sexual arousal that she or he senses above the nausea, the acts the victim has been forced into are sexual, but that arousal occurs does not mean it is enjoyed or the victim performs a sexual act.

Intentions

Since we have not yet found a necessary condition for an act to be sexual, and only one sufficient condition, perhaps the right move is to propose an analysis weaker than (A2), one that does not insist on success in producing pleasure for an act to be sexual:

A3. Sexual acts are those acts that are accompanied by or flow from a sexual intention.

A3–a. Sexual intent is necessary for an act to be sexual.

A3–b. Sexual intent is sufficient for an act to be sexual.

What is this "sexual intention" that distinguishes a kiss from resuscitation? Jerome Neu suggests an answer while telling us how to disambiguate physical acts:

> A person who washes his hands fifteen times a day need not be obsessive-compulsive, he may be a surgeon. Similarly, a "golden shower" performed out of sexual interest has a very different significance . . . than one done as an emergency measure to treat a sea urchin wound.[37]

What distinguishes the obsessive person from the surgeon is the reason each has for hand washing. What distinguishes sexual urination from therapeutic urination is that the urination is motivated by "sexual interest," a desire for, or an intention to produce, sexual pleasure. The idea that sexual acts are to be analyzed in terms of this motive occurs in the law; on one legal definition of "sexual contact," it is "any intentional touching of intimate parts of either the victim or the actor or the clothing covering them, if that intentional touching can 'reasonably be construed' as being for the purpose of sexual arousal or gratification."[38] So a sexual intention is an intention to give and/or experience sexual pleasure and often shows itself as a desire to touch and be touched.

We could argue, then, along these lines. The lifeguard is sexually fondling and kissing the swimmer, not only resuscitating her, if and only if he *intends* to get pleasure from contact with her. If the lifeguard just happens to feel sexual pleasure during the resuscitation, that is not enough to make his acts sexual (contrary to [A2–b]); he is merely the passive recipient of sensations he never intended to obtain and that are a distraction from and tangential to what he is deliberately doing, saving her. His experience of pleasure during the movements involved in rescuing her does not condemn his actions as furtively sexual; his acts would still be sexual (contrary to [A2–a]) if he tried to get pleasure from touching her but failed: surrounded by bathers, he can no longer enjoy the feel of her flesh even as contact continues. His touching erotic or attractive areas of her body is not what makes his acts sexual; it is, instead, that he touches them with a particular purpose.

But an intention to produce or experience sexual pleasure might not be either necessary or sufficient for an act to be sexual. A couple engaging in coitus, both parties intending only that fertilization occur and neither concerned with sexual pleasure, are performing a sexual act. They might experience pleasure anyway, but their plan is not that they do. So (A3–a) looks false. Gray's example of the women operating treadle sewing machines was meant to show that an intention to experience sexual pleasure is not necessary: the women inadvertently engaged in sexual activity. Further, an X who knows little about sex, or believes much that is false, might intend to arouse Y with all sorts of signals and caresses that Y does not recognize as sexual. Or X might intend to get Y interested in having sex by flashing some bills at Y; this might both persuade Y to engage in sex and even cause sexual arousal and pleasure in Y; but the act of flashing the bills with the intention of arousing was not a sexual act. So (A3–b) looks false, too.

Maybe we have not found the *right* sexual intention. But if we propose that sexual acts are those done with an intention to procreate, we shall still fail. The intent to procreate cannot be necessary: gays and lesbians experience arousal and desire and engage in sexual acts without any procreative intent. Many acts of heterosexual coitus are not accompanied by an intention to procreate. Solitary masturbation is a sexual act that has no procreative purpose. Nor is procreative intent sufficient. If X and Y believe that kissing and rubbing each other while naked will cause Y to be with child, and *that* is why they do so, their acts are sexual, but not in virtue of the intention they have in performing them. A clinical technician who carries out in vitro fertilization or artificial insemination intends that procreation result from these acts, but that does not make them sexual.

The problem with (A3), however, is not that the intention that is necessary and sufficient for an act to be sexual is elusive, but that intentions are irrelevant in making sexual acts sexual. Suppose X rubs Y's thigh. X might be touching Y's thigh to see what it is like to do so; or in order to win a bet that he could do so; or because X sexually desires Y. Which of these acts are sexual? What makes them sexual, if they are? From Y's viewpoint these questions are strange: Y has been touched on a sensitive part of the body, and no matter why it was done, it registers in Y's consciousness not as some mysterious, inexplicable movement but as at least quasi-sexual. Yet X might protest: X was merely satisfying X's curiosity or winning a bet and did *nothing* sexual. Y can reply, however, that even if X was satisfying X's curiosity or winning a bet, in doing these things X was also, even if not by intention, doing something sexual. Sambian fellatio can be both a nurturing and a sexual act; similarly, X can do, under two different descriptions, two acts at once, so X's intention does not show that what X did was not sexual. Further, X might have bet that X could touch Y's thigh sexually, so that in touching Y sexually X also does another act, winning the bet. This does not mean that X's act was sexual because in Y's consciousness it was sexual; for if Y was asleep or distracted, or deceiving Y-self into not noticing what X was doing, so X's touch did not fully register in Y's mind, X's touch might still be sexual.[39]

Engaging in sex, beyond being intrinsically rewarding, has many uses: to express affection, make money, kill time, avoid the task of grading exams. Annie Sprinkle's list of the benefits of sex multiplies the reasons for engaging in it: "sex can cure a headache, relieve stress and tension, help digestion, strengthen the heart, relieve menstrual cramps, help you sleep, wake you up, clear the mind, open you up to feelings, improve concentration, create life, burn unwanted calories, and cure depression."[40] Given this variety of effects, the motive one has for engaging in sex cannot distinguish sexual from nonsexual acts. For example, rape can be sexual whether the rapist intends to get sexual pleasure from it, or humiliate his victim, or assert his masculinity and dominance (say, in prison).

From the fact that in some rapes the rapist intends to humiliate and degrade his victim, to dominate and assert power over her or him, it does not follow that his act is not sexual. Even if the rapist is not mainly or only concerned with obtaining sexual pleasure, that would not mean the act was not sexual. (This thesis must chagrin the antiessentialist, whose position would have been strengthened by a demonstration that rape is in many cases not sex.) Consider this scenario: a woman who does not enjoy fellatio, or likes it only when the man is her companionate lover, might find it humiliating to be forced by a rapist to perform fellatio on his unwashed and alien penis. She has been compelled to perform an offensive sexual act, and this is why she feels humiliated and ashamed.[41] The victim is degraded exactly by the sexual nature of the act she endures; the rapist has chosen a sexual act on purpose as the way to humiliate her, because he knows she will suffer psychologically as a result of performing this act.[42] The intention to humiliate his victim need not exclude the rapist's having sexual pleasure in the fellatio; nor does it exclude his expecting and obtaining sexual pleasure in response to her humiliation.

Reproductive Form

An intention to procreate is not enough to make an act sexual. But just engaging in a type of physical activity, the biological result of which is sometimes a child, might itself be sufficient to make an act sexual, in the same way that an intention to give or get sexual pleasure is not sufficient, yet the production of pleasure is. This conclusion would not be surprising, for the procreative act is biologically and historically a central case of sexual activity. Consider, then, this final analysis:

A4. Sexual acts are those that are procreative in form.

A4–a. Procreative form is necessary for an act to be sexual.

A4–b. Procreative form is sufficient for an act to be sexual.

Sexual acts are acts that, in virtue of their biological nature, are the kind of act that *could* result in conception (*ceteris paribus*). The principal case of such an act—if not the only case—is heterosexual intercourse. Due to the "could" packed into the "form," (A4) allows that contraceptive coitus and coitus engaged in by infertile persons are sexual acts; these acts would have been open to procreation were the organs working properly or contraceptive devices not employed.

Even if (A4–b) is true, (A4–a) is obviously false. There are many acts we unhesitatingly call sexual that are not procreative in form: kissing, holding hands, fellatio, cunnilingus, anal coitus. (A4–a) ties sexuality and reproduction too tightly. (A4) must be expanded, then, so that it can apply to a wider variety of acts:

A4–exp. Sexual acts are (i) acts that are procreative in form, and (ii) acts that are physiological or psychological precursors or concomitants of acts that are sexual by (i).

So the various activities commonly called "foreplay" fall within the domain of the sexual. Nothing in (A4–exp) excludes their being sexual if done before, during, after, or independently of coitus, when they neither culminate in nor envelop coitus. These acts are sexual because of psychological or physiological links with coitus, but according to (A4–exp) they are sexual even if coitus never occurs. Otherwise, we would have to say that mutual masturbation is sexual when it leads to coitus, but not sexual if the couple are interrupted by a crying baby and never get around to coitus; or that oral sex is sexual if it proceeds to or from coitus, but not if done alone for its own sake. A separate question (on which, see Aquinas) is whether such acts are either natural or moral. Here it is asserted only that they are *sexual.*

(A4–exp) casts a wider net, but not wide enough. No problems arise with (A4–exp)'s stating a sufficient condition for acts to be sexual, but it is troublesome if it states a necessary condition. Solitary masturbation, which is not a procreative act and often, if not ordinarily, not a precursor or concomitant of coitus, is nonsexual according to (A4–exp). Let's add to (A4–exp) another clause:

and (iii), acts that bear an acute structural resemblance to acts that satisfy clauses (i) or (ii).

So, if mutual masturbation between X and Y is sexual, X's rubbing X-self would also be sexual, because it is structurally the same as Y's doing it to X. What about homosexuality? The acts done by two men or two women are not procreative in form; as a result, the kissings and rubbings of these people are not the precursors or concomitants of acts that are procreative in form. To relax the *"could* result in conception," in order to include homosexual acts in the sexual category that includes contraceptive and infertile coitus, is awkward; we would have to say, for example, that homosexual anal intercourse is sexual *because* the act would be open to conception were it done by heterosexuals and the anus eventually replaced by the vagina. If homosexual anal coitus and lesbian cunnilingus are sexual, that would have to be through (iii): both are sufficiently similar in structure to acts that are sexual by clauses (i) or (ii).[43] Clause (iii) might also be invoked to explain why some "perversions" are sexual; copulation with a dog would be sexual in virtue of its structural similarity to coitus. But conceiving of homosexual acts as sexual because they resemble hetero-sexual acts seems wrong: something else is more important—the similar-ity of the pleasure produced by heterosexual and homosexual sexual acts. (Indeed, the family resemblance between homosexual and heterosexual acts, just in terms of the pleasures these acts afford, suggests that distin-guishing between "homosexuality" and "heterosexuality" is both futile and unnecessary.)[44] Further, Gray's example, coprophagia, cannot be han-dled by clause (iii), nor can shoe fetishism, neither of which has the required structure. To insist that ingesting feces and fondling heels are sexual because they *are* sufficiently similar to fellatio, intercourse, or cunnilingus is an unappetizing pansexualism.

Clause (iii) therefore does not help (A4–exp) include within the sexual everything that should be there; moreover, the clause is suspiciously ad hoc and too far removed from the spirit of (A4). But even if we reject (A4–exp) as a complete analysis of the sexual, we can retain it, with clauses (i) and (ii), as stating a sufficient condition. We then have two sufficient conditions for an act to be sexual: that it produces sexual pleasure, *or* that it is procreative in form. The first explains why pleasurable acts are sexual, whether procreative or not (coprophagia; bestiality; talking, flirting, writing; some oral sex; homosexual acts; some rape), while the second explains why procreative acts and their concomitants are sexual, whether pleasurable or not (heterosexual rape; some oral sex). The analytic result is not tidy, but it is enough to ward off antiessentialism: even if we have not found the essence of sex—a necessary condition for acts to be sexual—we know that acts that produce a certain kind of pleasure, or are procreative in the right way, are sexual, both transculturally and ahistorically.

Sexual Reproduction

The person who says in 1996, "we all know what sex is,"[45] and someone who uttered the same words in 1896, or expressed the same thought in 296, in Latin, do not know exactly the same thing. The boundaries of the sexual and of the concept of the sexual change: some of what is accepted, done, believed, and discussed about sex today is different from what was accepted, done, believed, and discussed in 296 or 1896. Changes in sexual behavior and beliefs contribute to and, in turn, are influenced by changes in sexual concepts. One example is the effect of advances in birth control technology on how we perceive and conceive of sexuality. Once the link between reproduction and sex had been effectively undermined, it became possible for someone to ask that fantastically beguiling question, "why species survival, the means of impregnation, and emotional/erotic relationships should ever have become so rigidly identified with each other."[46] How passé the link is between reproduction and sex is exhibited in MacKinnon's view that "the reproductive act" is, in our culture, sexual *because* it is the "forcible violation and defilement of the female." And this "forcible violation of women," according to MacKinnon, is "the essence of sex."[47] Since we no longer link sex and reproduction, MacKinnon thinks she must hunt around for a reason that "the reproductive act" is for us sexual. What she finds is that in our culture what is violent is sexual and what is sexual is violent.[48] Hence the violence of the reproductive act, not its sensations or form, is what makes it sexual.

In very early times, before humans realized that coitus caused pregnancy, the concept of the sexual, if there was any, could not include procreation, but only pleasure. The twentieth century has returned to that ancient time, and congratulates itself for achieving a separation of the pleasurable and the procreative uses of the genitals. What our forebears possessed in ignorance we reappropriate with science. Our sexual concepts reflect our history. Sexual *desire* is not the desire to reproduce: one can desire to touch the other's flesh and to engage in intercourse, without wanting a child to result; one can desire a child fervently without being genitally aroused, and satisfy the desire by artificial insemination or adoption. Sexual *health* and illness are not the same as reproductive health and illness: homosexuals and sterile heterosexuals can have fulfilling sexual lives yet never reproduce. What is distinctive about sexual *perversion*, if anything, is not that it renounces reproduction, but that it sidesteps the natural psychology of human arousal. And sexual *pleasure* is not reproductive pleasure: the pleasure of anal intercourse is not the pleasure of being presented with and contemplating one's newborn child, and the pleasures of the couple during gestation, preparing for the child, are not the pleasures of a bout of mutual oral sex.

These are the lessons of analytic philosophy mirroring the consciousness of our century. "It is obvious," writes Alan Goldman, "that the desire for sex is not necessarily a desire to reproduce." Heterosexual intercourse, then, is both sexual and reproductive in the same way Sambian fellatio is both sexual and nurturing. Goldman continues by acknowledging that history must be given its due: "the psychological manifestation" of sexuality, the desire to experience pleasure, "has become, if it were not always, distinct from its biological roots," sexual activity's procreative capacity.[49] Imagine a world, however, in which the phenomenal desire for sexual pleasure is constantly conjoined with the phenomenal desire to reproduce. We could, or should, still insist that sexuality is analyzable apart from procreation, not just because the two desires are only contingently correlated (in other possible worlds they are not conjoined), but because there are *two* desires, not one, in the imaginary world. However, for the people of this imaginary world, in which procreation is highly eroticized, the concept of the sexual, *their* idea of what sex acts are, would surely include reference to procreation. In order to preserve a link between the sexual and the reproductive for *our* world, one need not take the heroic route and claim that sexual desire is reducible to or ultimately comes from a desire to reproduce, at some suitable level of psyche ordinarily hidden from consciousness. We could, though, easily adjust or readjust our thinking so that we conceive of sex more explicitly in terms of reproduction, since our world is not all that different from the imagined one.

For example, women in our culture who sexually daydream or fantasize about becoming and being pregnant exhibit an emotional, not merely intellectual, link between procreation and sex.[50] Further, to the extent that the masculinity of our culture thinks of sexuality narrowly, focusing on the insertion of the penis in the vagina as the central sex act, or the only one deserving the name, we have implicitly acknowledged a connection between procreation and the sexual. Some Victorian lesbian lovers who engaged in cunnilingus might "have felt themselves perfectly innocent" of the accusation that they were sex partners, because they defined sex in terms of penetration.[51] Some teenage Catholic girls today engage only in anal coitus with their boyfriends, enabling themselves to believe they remain virgins, not having had any *genuine* sex.

Room exists, then, to argue for a link between the sexual and the reproductive, a link that shows it is no accident that both (A2) and (A4) state sufficient conditions for acts to be sexual: some acts, not procreative in form, produce pleasure identical or similar to that normally produced by procreative acts. The similarity of the pleasure, despite the separation achieved by contraception, exhibits the enduring biological tie between sex and procreation. Better: *because* contraception does its separation, the role of a certain kind of pleasure in both sexual and reproductive acts becomes strikingly clear. A family resemblance exists among the pleasures produced by the varieties of sexual activity, a continuum of pleasure that allows us to classify heterosexual acts, homosexual acts, masturbation, talking and writing about sex, and coprophagia, as sexual.

A modification is now required of the notion that sexual pleasure is not reproductive pleasure. Birth and its subsequent activities can be sexual for women in virtue of both the nature of the accompanying pleasures and the structure of the acts. Alice Rossi has no doubt about the dual nature of breast-feeding, as both sexual and nurturing:

> Whether the sucking is by an infant or a lover, oxytocin acts upon the basket cells around the alveoli, causing them to constrict. . . . The interconnection

between sexuality and maternalism makes good evolutionary sense. By providing some erotogenic pleasure to the mother of a newborn baby, there is greater assurance that the child will be nursed. . . . Provide a woman with a rocking chair, and the far-away look of pleasure one often sees among nursing mothers is much closer to the sensual Eve than to the saintly Mary.[52]

This is no mere reactionary antifeminism. Patricia Miller and Martha Fowlkes lamented, in *Signs*, that "female reproductive processes and potential are seen as incidental to or contingent upon sexuality rather than as interactive with a woman's sexual self-concept and responsiveness."[53] The father, too, of the newborn can experience the sexual pleasure that contact with the infant offers; cuddling, clothed or nude, is sensually enjoyable to both cuddler and cuddled and helps cement their bond.[54]

Although sexuality and reproduction are not identical, their distinctness has been magnified by contraception; even so, there remains a biological substrate that keeps them joined. On the horizon, however, are reproductive technologies that go beyond artificial fertilization to extrauterine gestation, in which the embryo-then-fetus lives its prenatal life altogether outside a woman's womb. This technology will continue, but from the other direction, the severing of sex and reproduction. In supplementing sex without reproduction with reproduction without sex, this technology, were it to become pervasive, would put at risk the emotional satisfactions and sensual pleasures for women of carrying a child, giving birth, and breastfeeding. At that time, the connection between sex and reproduction will have become merely historical; people would think about it as often as we contemplate the appendix. Our descendants in that brave new world could, if they wished, rejoin reproduction and sex by so expanding the meaning of "sexual" that the mixing of an egg and sperm by a laboratory technician would be conceived as a sexual act. That conceptual nightmare would be the vindication of the social constructivism of "sex."

Maybe we shouldn't take chances with our conceptual future; maybe, more importantly, we shouldn't take chances with the joys of motherhood. But the biomedico-technological complex, seeing Everest, wants to climb it. The frightening irony is that this male quest to wrest the power of motherhood from women, to remake the womb into a gaudy plastic and shiny metal hydroponic hothouse, has received solace and comfort from those the academic world had once learned to call "radical feminists." In order to save women from the unfairness of compulsory heterosexuality, Ti-Grace Atkinson champions a technology of extrauterine prenatal life.[55] To make sure women never have to depend on men, economically or for protection or to run to the grocery or for getting up the stairs, Shulamith Firestone insists on fully artificial reproduction.[56] And since sexual "intercourse is the pure, sterile, formal expression of men's contempt for women," it is a blessing, a godsend, for Andrea Dworkin, that technology is bringing it about that "intercourse is not necessary to existence anymore."[57] I think it more than coincidental that feminists, in advocating a technologically clean immaculate conception, have given substance to Augustine's prelapsarian ideal, procreation without the sweaty lust and passion of perturbed bodies.[58] Contemporary "unmodified" feminists— not only Dworkin, who thinks men should "give up their precious erections and begin to make love as women do together,"[59] but also MacKinnon and Stoltenberg and others—share a profound distrust of and distaste for the body with Augustine:

> some conclude that women shall not rise [be resurrected] women, but that all shall be men, because God made man only of earth, and woman of the man. For my part . . . both sexes shall rise. For there shall be no lust, which is now the cause of confusion. . . . From those bodies, then, vice shall be withdrawn, while nature shall be preserved. And the sex of woman is not a vice, but nature. It shall then indeed be superior to carnal intercourse and child-bearing.[60]

The sexual use of the female body will be transcended; it will then attain a "new beauty" that does not provoke lust and is "praise to the wisdom" of God. So, too, contemporary feminism: good riddance both to the oppressiveness of heterosexuality and barbaric modes of reproduction. If we are to take proponents of parthenogenesis at their word, good riddance to biological males as well.[61] There is, after all, not much difference among tamed, tidy maleless homosex; tamed, tidy heterosex with a "limp penis"; and tamed, tidy heterosex with a penis controlled by the will like a marionette.

Polymorphosity

The most we have are thoughts about what is sufficient for an act to be sexual, little idea about what is necessary. It would be wrong to conclude that antiessentialism is right; not being able to state the essence of sex is one thing, quite another to think it has no essence. Perhaps we cannot distinguish sexual from nonsexual acts any better than by our two sufficient conditions not because sex has no essence to discover, but because sexuality is so wrapped up with our existence as embodied creatures that it impinges on our lives polymorphously. If the sexual permeates our being, it will be difficult to disentangle sexual threads from nonsexual threads. Body parts, pleasure, intentions, and procreation, even if they individually or collectively fail to provide a comprehensive picture of the ontological essence of sex, are still relevant in another context, that of assessing the moral and nonmoral value of sexual acts. In this domain antiessentialism, or "social constructivism," becomes more attractive; indeed, although antiessentialism seems wrong about the sexual per se, antiessentialism is nearly right about moral and other assessments of sexuality. The idea of "healthy sex" provides fertile soil for the antiessentialist program.

FOUR

Health

> The past few years have seen the development of many new devices, drugs, and surgical procedures to treat erectile dysfunction. . . . Lots of women are indeed benefited by harder and more prolonged erections. . . . But . . . lots of women will be burdened by these erections.
> —Leonore Tiefer, *Sex Is Not a Natural Act*

> When he *assigns* sick-status to a client, the contemporary physician might indeed be acting in some ways similar to the sorcerer or the elder; but in belonging also to a scientific profession that *invents* the categories it assigns . . . the modern physician is totally unlike the healer. Medicine men . . . had no power to invent new devils. Enabling professions in their annual assemblies create the sick-roles they assign.
> —Ivan Illich, *Medical Nemesis*

Alfred Kinsey, Alex Comfort, William Masters, Virginia Johnson, and the rest of contemporary sexology have all done their share to make us more aware of sex. They found a willing audience. We wanted to hear what they had to report, just as we listen to the newspaper and television philosophers of sex who keep us more talkative, even if not always more thoughtful, about sex. These contributors to the sex industry, along with their cousins the pornographers, [1] have helped us evaluate the fine details of our sexual pleasures with the vigilance of the oenophile and inspect our sexual performances with the steady gaze of the shop foreman. Some of this criticism and self-criticism is for the good. We make stupendously exciting erotic discoveries about our tastes, our preferences, our bodies, our selves. Watching and hearing about the sexual feats of others, like their feats in tennis, stimulates and energizes us to be all that we can be. For our own philosophical good, we are compelled to face squarely the late twentieth century's deepest question: not the "To Be or Not to Be?" of Hamlet and Camus, but "To Cheat or Not to Cheat?" And while modern, sexually savvy medicine provides welcome methods for sustaining erections longer and harder, the psychologists soothingly relieve ego-dystonic distress at our not having enough, or too much, span and girth.

The indefatigable search-and-chat also has its down side. We sometimes wonder whether our sexual relationships and acts are troubled or inferior. We might be besieged with envy or disgust, or both, over what we have been led to believe other people are doing and enjoying. The purveyors of sexual knowledge pulled Augustine's trick well: they created the problem, now sell us the cure. For details, catch the next Oprah. Or Peter Gardella:

> Americans today experience pleasure that reaches the limits of physical capacity more often than Americans of 1830, 1880, or 1930. Now there is a need to recover the capacity for sensual celebration that has been forgotten in the quest for a moment of ecstasy. . . . [A] renewed sense of sin might actually facilitate this recovery.[2]

In a sexually liberal culture, opines Gardella, opportunities for endless and free sexual partners and an infinite stream of varied sexual acts have allowed Americans to achieve, as in no other culture, the pinnacle of sexual ecstasy. We should be proud of ourselves. But the Pauline access we have to each other is self-defeating, so "a renewed sense of sin" is just what the doctor ordered to help us reinvigorate or redirect our sex lives. We have here the beginning of a perverse explanation for the rise and popularity of Augustinian feminism: there is nothing like a good dose of Andrea Dworkin to instill the sense of sin we, especially men and collaborating women, so desperately need.[3]

Clean Sex

The concept "healthy sexuality" does not arise naturally in our biographies. We learn at our mother's knee what is right and decent young-gentlemanly or young-ladylike behavior. Mom uses the language of morals and P's and Q's, not the language of health. So there is nothing to be understood. If health is mentioned, we are taught to keep our privates clean, and we are lectured about venereal disease, alongside the unfathomable internal and external anatomy of reproduction. So "healthy sexuality" is easily understood in terms of soap and water and penicillin.

By contrast, "healthy sexuality" is part of the conceptual apparatus of academics. In medical ethics, one central concept is "health," so the natural amalgam "healthy sex" begs to be investigated by philosophers. But the concept is also part of the stock-in-trade of social workers, educators, theologians, psychologists, physicians, and others in the helping professions. These practitioners work with models of healthy sexuality that presuppose rough answers to the ontological and epistemological questions of the philosopher. Is healthy sex an organic state of the body or brain, or is it an autonomously psychological affair? Are judgments about healthy sex normative, or can they flow from a value-free science of sex? If they are normative, grounded in moral or political or religious beliefs, which norms best tell us what healthy sex is? This is why Robert Baker thinks of the "clinician" as a "sexual philosopher"; when providing advice about sex or treating a client's or patient's sexual problem, the helping professional, sometimes unknowingly but ideally self-consciously, discourses about these fundamental matters.[4]

Because we are raised to think about sex morally, and become accustomed to that way of thinking, academic accounts of "healthy sexuality" do not always break free of mom's teachings. Nor could they avoid making normative commitments, no matter how enlightened theoreticians think they have become. As a result, the moral and medical are entangled in our discourse about sex. Children hear lots of reasons, in terms of both morality and health, not to engage in sex. When sexual disease is uncontrollable, moral arguments are buttressed by pointing to nature's retribution. When advances in microbial medicine make arguments based on health unconvincing, deeper psychological or metaphysical health considerations are adduced (for example, the fragility of the self). The balance between moral and medical assessments of sexuality has been changing. In the development of the helping professions over the last hundred years, the moral critique of sex has been increasingly supplemented and then replaced with a no less relentless medical critique; recall the draconian medicalization of masturbation of the 1800s. But the evolving helping professions are not all of a piece, so children and their parents have also been hearing lots of reasons *to* engage in sex, in sex of all kinds, reasons based less on the proven superiority of new, positive moral considerations than on the bankruptcy of the old moralities, and reasons, most importantly, that extol sex itself as a standard of health. To the extent that within the politics of the helping professions sexually liberal attitudes have prevailed, evaluating sexual behavior by a criterion of "healthy sex" is obsolete, superseded by a reverse definition of health in terms of sex. The very first sexual disorder listed in the most recent edition of the *Diagnostic and Statistical Manual of Mental Disorders* (hereafter *DSM-IV*) is "hypoactive sexual desire disorder"; the second is "sexual aversion disorder." There is no specific "hyperactive sexual disorder." [5] Having sex is healthy, not having it is not, and "healthy sexuality" is as redundant as "round circle."

Eryximachus's Dream

In Plato's *Symposium*, an interesting progression occurs, full of prescience, from the speech of Pausanias to that of Eryximachus. Pausanias told the banquet guests about two kinds of love: a "vulgar" eros that promiscuously seeks boys and women alike and wants only the pleasure of the body; and a "heavenly" eros that is attracted to another's intelligence and character and declares itself ready to spend a lifetime with the beloved (180d-181e). The language of morality is thick throughout the speech, so much so that we can hear from the mouth of the pagan Pausanias (except that his heavenly love is homoerotic) the voice of contemporary Christians who condemn the baseness of indiscriminate fucking and applaud the virtues of a chaste, noble, and honorable monogamous marriage of true harmonious minds. But when we listen next to Eryximachus, the doctor, we hear a different voice:

> Health and disease in a body are admittedly different and distinct. . . . [D]esire is one thing in a healthy body, [and] it is another in one diseased. . . . [I]t is fine and even proper to yield to the good and wholesome wants of every body, . . . but it is bad to yield to the noxious and evil desires. . . . For this is

what medicine is, . . . a knowledge of the forces of Love in the body. . . . [A] person who can accurately diagnose whether the noble or the vulgar love is functioning . . . and can interchange them is a master therapist. (186b-d)[6]

Eryximachus's language is not that of Pausanias. He has injected medical concepts into Pausanias's moral account of love in such a way that the medical takes center stage. When the body is sick, it derivatively exhibits vulgar love; when the body is healthy, it exhibits the heavenly. The source of the bad and the good love is not some nebulous "character" or ethereal moral fiber, but tangible bodily components accessible and amenable to the pokings and potions of those who know about bones and sinews and fluids. A good doctor can catch a whiff of a tiny infection of bad love and destroy it before it becomes a stinking sore.

Eryximachus continues, and this is Plato's brilliant dream (or his joke), by outlining the medical science of the future—what Eryximachus took, wrongly, to be his future, but it's ours:

by eliminating one love and replacing it with the other, and knowing when to implant love when it ought to be introduced, and when to extract improper desires when they are present, one may be said to be an able practitioner.

Eryximachus is advocating not the pleasurable re-eroticization of Annie Sprinkle, and not even the utilitarian, contraceptive re-eroticization of Germaine Greer, but hard-core sex therapy of the sort that tries to rescue the rigor and longevity of the dying erections of marriage and, for pedophiles, to prevent erections by de-cathecting the beauty of young boys or girls. In Eryximachus, the medical has not yet ousted the moral; rather, his medicine is needed because the moral is impotent to effect its own mandates. Pausanias might correctly judge promiscuity to be a moral horror, but that pronouncement would not guarantee that anyone afflicted with too much indiscriminate desire would be able to do anything about it. Social and legal threats might sometimes deter one from acting on the desire, but the offending desire would remain. Paul, several centuries later, had the right idea: marriage might cure the sin of promiscuity by repeatedly satisfying our demand, and so repeatedly extinguishing, sexual desire. Eryximachus promotes medicine as the force that will make Pausanias's moral judgment real, by eliminating the base desire itself. In creating treatments that turn us from promiscuous sluts into faithful, monogamous mates, medicine becomes the handmaiden of ethics and religion. In the America of the 1800s, "the promise of medicine [was] to conquer original sin through control of passion."[7] That is the ultimate enlistment of the help of the Eryximachean physician by religion.

But medicine is going beyond this, trying to achieve an autonomy in which it ousts the moral altogether. Schopenhauer, in replying to Kant's moral condemnation of masturbation, wrote this obituary for sexual ethics:

> To combat [masturbation] is much more a matter of diet than ethics; for this reason works against it are written by medical men (such as Tissot and others), and not by moralists. If morality now wishes to take a hand in this matter after dietetics and hygiene have done their part and crushed it with irrefutable arguments, she finds so much already done that there is little left for her to do.[8]

Dr. S. A. D. Tissot took a moral defect and fully medicalized it into insanity, snapping it out of the grip of the priests; but it is no coincidence that exactly what had been regarded as sinful was now seen as sick.[9] More recently, the helping professions have been wresting from the priests the right to apply their techniques to behaviors or dispositions that they would prefer be conceived of as diseases, sexual and otherwise, and not as sins.[10] This would seem to be the best way to interpret, for example, the use of Prozac to treat a case of what one psychiatrist calls "paraphilic coercive disorder," a disease state (not accepted by the DSM-IV) in which the patient has recurrent rape fantasies and either acts on or is distressed by them.[11] A larger study of thirteen patients with sexual troubles reported bleak results in treating, with Prozac, compulsive masturbation and sadomasochistic fantasies.[12] But the doctors are betting that a pharmacological clockwork orange is right around the corner of the next NIMH grant. Does this mean medicine is becoming value-free? A psychiatric corporation in my hometown advertises itself on a billboard with "Because life should be enjoyed, not endured." That might very well be true, but it merely turns upside down, with a Hebrew twist,[13] the values of the Christian religion it seeks to supplant.

Medicine's Dominion

For Eryximachus, a good physician is one who knows the difference between good desire and bad desire and can promote one and crush the other.
This doctor is a good diagnostician and therapist. But she is never called on
to make a moral judgment herself or even to get involved with patients in
such matters; these issues are already decided for her, independently and
objectively, not necessarily by other people (for example, philosophers) but
by a Real World of Value. For Baker, by contrast, the good physician is
well versed in philosophy in order to be able to discuss with patients the
values and metaphysics underlying treatment options. Even if we worry
that a physician, trained for years in science, might not know enough
ethics and philosophy, Baker's view makes sense for the twentieth-century
West, in which normative judgments are no longer conceived as objective
reflections of a Real World of Value. Patients need to have the full array of
possibilities laid out (including the heresies, for the sake of intellectual
honesty) so they can choose for themselves which values and metaphysics
are the most attractive. Eryximachus's doctor knows that bisexual promiscuity is an immorality rooted in bodily disease, as does his patient. Baker's
physician must explain to his promiscuous patient that, on the one hand,
such behavior is judged immoral or physically and psychologically dangerous and destructive by some axiological systems, but, on the other hand, is
either ignored or praised by others. The patient then picks a system from
this menu and the physician helps him achieve the appropriate goals. For
that matter, the patient who complains of having insufficiently spacious
desires will be reminded of exactly the same philosophies.

What can Baker's clinician say on his own about the medicine of healthy
sexuality? If medicine is the science of the functioning, pathology, and
therapy of the body and its parts, then healthy and unhealthy sexuality are
divided organically. Lumiere and Cook's *Healthy Sexuality and Keeping It
That Way: A Complete Guide to Sexual Infections* would reveal most of
medicine's dominion. Healthy is hygienic: clean sex does not transmit
venereal disease; it uses condoms; lovers wash the penis before engaging in
vaginal coitus; fingers are not moved from anus to vagina. Healthy sexuality also includes the absence of trauma, tumors, neuropathology, and toxic
or metabolic disorders, conditions that disturb the effective working of the

sexual parts (for example, some cases of insufficient lubrication) and thereby interfere with sexual pleasure or reproduction. This sense of "healthy sexuality" is modest, respectable, and robust. If there is nothing more to sexual health, sexual philosophy in Baker's clinic is narrow, for no physician should discuss with patients deep matters about the pros and cons of clearing up a prostate discharge. But even within this narrow, creditable domain of sexual medicine, cultural norms lurk that disrupt the value-freedom of sexual science. Consider the values presupposed in deciding whether a sexual organ is "effectively" working.

If the brain as a sex organ is viewed purely organically and medicine attends to the brain's physical and chemical pathology, the dominion of sexual medicine will be larger. This is not a theoretically radical extension of sexual medicine; organic pathology is still its subject matter. However, if the notion of "proper functioning" is extended from the vas deferens to the whole range of brain events—conscious and unconscious thoughts, motives, and desires—and these cannot easily or ever be tightly associated with brain parts, the science of mental functioning becomes an autonomous discipline. If psychiatry is a legitimate branch of medicine, it can make its own contribution to the meaning of "healthy sexuality" and generously expand medicine's dominion. But the notion of "proper functioning," when applied to thoughts and desires, goes beyond physiology and is drenched in philosophy. A complex, supraorganic integration of the sex organs, brain, behavior, consciousness, social situation, and cultural values is now the subject matter. Once this complex integration has been identified as the subject, the study of healthy sexuality spreads irresistibly to psychologists, social workers, religious advisers, secular ethicists, and others in the helping professions, all of whom have their own type of contribution to make.

Institutional medicine is not content with having dominion over the body in only a narrow, organic sense; nor does it enjoy sharing its dominion with other disciplines. The medicine that grabs for control over sexuality also grabs—in collusion with, but also in dire competition with, other helping professions—for control over spouse abuse, narcotics addiction, alcoholism,[14] inner-city violence,[15] attention-deficit toddlers, rebellious teenagers, anorexia, and bulimia.[16] In staking out its piece of the territory, medicine has argued that because it has been empowered to deal with the body, it is empowered to deal with anything concerning the body—which is, after all, the whole of human life. The journal *Medical Aspects of Human Sexuality* therefore includes articles on wives faking orgasm, infidelity in men and women, sex and the work ethic, the definition of a good lover, streaking, sex with and without love, the importance of communication, and the decriminalization of prostitution. The journal thereby suggests, contrary to its title, that there are no nonmedical aspects of sexuality. This medical imperialism is likely concerned about prostitution because some proposals for decriminalization add to physicians' visibility, income, and power by requiring prostitutes (or their clients)[17] to have periodic medical exams. For similar reasons, the birth control movement in the 1920s became "a crusade of a professional medical elite."[18]

The Examination Room

What has medicine been up to, having snatched a chunk of the sex territory away from priests? Here's an example. According to an editorial in a leading medical journal,

> A doctor's special responsibility is to distinguish the healthy from the unhealthy and to teach the facts. And though he must be understandably sensitive about interfering in moral problems he should not shrink from giving guidance on the medical and biological components of them where people's health is concerned.[19]

This sounds reasonable. Yet the subject of the editorial is *pornography.* What can a physician who wants to teach only "the facts" and give biological guidance say about pornography? That masturbating with pornography for five hours can cause blisters or one might catch a disease from a movie theater's seat cushion? That masturbating with pornography yields no genuinely satisfying pleasure and is, in this sense, unhealthy? No. The editorial claims that

> pornography serves to distort the loving and biological expression of the sexual instinct. In so far as it succeeds in doing that it impairs the health and well-being of the people in its thrall.

This passage shows that if clinicians are to be philosophers, they had better be good ones. To claim that pornography distorts the *"loving* expression" of sexuality is one thing. Perhaps those who use pornography come to separate sexual experience and love (or have already done so), but how this is medically interesting is unclear. That pornography might threaten someone's "well-being" is not a medical matter; the Good Life is not exhausted by Health. (When Kathleen Barry complains about pornography that it "introduce[s] movies, books, or pictures as the erotic stimulant between two people, thereby reducing the need for people to relate to *each other,"* she doesn't dress up her disgust in medicalese.)[20] But it is quite another thing to claim that pornography distorts the *"biological* expression" of sexuality. If it does, we might infer correctly that it impairs health in some robust sense. The editorial, however, never tells us what goes wrong biologically when a person is in the "thrall" of pornography. That a vagina lubricates or a penis erects in response to visual or linguistic stimuli is not biologically anomalous; nor does pornography, or the masturbation it induces, destroy the ability of a penis to erect or a vagina to lubricate in the presence of another person. Is the editorial asserting the bold thesis that expressing love is the biological function of sex, so loveless sex is pathological? Or is it rehashing just the political propaganda that pornography threatens stable relationships and the institution of marriage?

The physician Max Levin, writing not in the age of Victoria but as recently as 1973, provides another example:

> oral-genital and other sex acts are healthy and legitimate, provided that both parties enjoy them, and provided they are practiced out of love and devotion . . . and . . . provided they are not more than a part of the foreplay that builds up erotic tension to climax in coitus.[21]

Levin asserts no fewer than three conditions for "healthy" and "legitimate" noncoital sex: the acts are enjoyed by both parties; they are done out of love; and they culminate in coitus. Levin conflates (equates) the healthy and the legitimate deliberately. As Eryximachus did, Levin took his own notion of *morally* decent sex (which is also his society's) and made it the criterion of *healthy* sex, thereby showing how values can crudely influence medical judgments. Levin and the editorial writers are not alone in asserting the healthiness of sexual activity carried out in a context of love. The inspiration of Burt and Meeks's *Toward a Healthy Sexuality* is the thought that healthy sex is informed by love. They write, as if announcing a major theoretical accomplishment, "it was finally the twentieth century that bravely claimed that sex was for pleasure as well as reproduction and that both aspects belonged within a relationship based on love" (8).[22] Equating moral sex and healthy sex, as well as defining both in terms of loving relationships, is the kind of bravery applauded by the authors of "Casti connubii" and "Humanae vitae."

Judd Marmor recites a similar doctrine when he proclaims, "healthy sexuality tends to be discriminating as to partner choice; neurotic patterns tend to be nondiscriminating."[23] Eryximachus borrowed this judgment from the Real World of Value, but this is not Marmor's source. Surely it is more than coincidental that what his Christian culture thinks of as *immoral* he thinks of as *sick*. Levin and Marmor and their peers did not pluck the idea that healthy sex is discriminating or loving sex out of the air; they are repeating in their own form, for their own purpose, with their own gloss, the sex-love justificatory connection that is an embedded value in our culture. The judgment that partner-discrimination is a mark of sexual health is likely, though, to astonish the student of animal sexuality or one who dabbles in evolutionary theories of human male sexuality. That these medical judgments about healthy sexuality follow cultural norms[24] (recall that Tissot rehabilitated masturbation from sin to insanity) is some evidence that antiessentialism, or social constructivism, about healthy sex is on the right track: what is *normal* sex must largely elude transcultural and ahistorical understanding.

Constructivist Health

Given the cultural importance of the sex-love justificatory connection, it is hardly shocking to find Andrew Greeley tickled pink by a mild correlation in men between being adulterous and having mental and physical problems, including the use of alcohol and tobacco.[25] The correlation is a happy one for a traditionalist because it permits the argument that mental illness either contributes to adulterous promiscuity or is its sad result. Medicine shows that adultery cannot win; so, as Schopenhauer urged about the ethics of masturbation, no one should take seriously the subversive ethical and philosophical discussion of adultery. But we could view adultery not as the causal effect of psychic distress; instead, it might be a rational response to stress, an attempt to provide relief from it and to add joy to a troubled life. "There is only one thing wrong with neurotic patients," in the radical vision of Wilhelm Reich: "the lack of full and repeated sexual satisfaction."[26] Whether adulterous sex is judged to be beneficial and hence "healthy" (even if not a complete cure) or, instead, viewed as a festering cause or symptom of psychic disturbance, the influence of values on health judgments is inescapable. Which judgment prevails will be a function of the social construction of "healthy sexuality."

Laurie Shrage, when describing the penis-feeding custom of the Sambia and Etoro, notes that "from the perspective of our society," this practice "involves behaviors which are highly stigmatized—incest, sex with children, and homosexuality," and "we are inclined to see [penis-feeding] as . . . the adult sexual exploitation of children."[27] In Sambian culture, far from being stigmatized or viewed as exploitation, penis-feeding is regarded as essential to the development of boys into men. Shrage thinks that if we see, with the Sambia, this practice not as *sex* but as *child-rearing*, then that change of perspective "clearly . . . will influence our attitude toward" penis-feeding.[28] Once we recognize that for the Sambians the practice is not sexual but nutritional, we are better able to appreciate its role in that culture and could "choose not to condemn" it by standards that apply only to our culture. On Shrage's view, because antiessentialism is right about sex per se, we are not compelled to look down our ethnocentric moral noses at fellatio insemination.

Shrage is too optimistic about the influence of how the act is categorized on subsequent moral judgments. Someone whose philosophy is sex-negative in the Thomist sense will condemn the Sambian practice whether it is classified as a sexual act or an act of child-rearing, while sex-positive liberal philosophy will not condemn the practice even if it is categorized as fully sexual. The Thomist condemns the act because the belief on which it rests—the penis supplies nourishment—is primitive nonsense; nothing in nature justifies feeding semen to young boys by this route, or by any other. Sexual liberals condone the practice both because in Sambian culture it is innocuous and because liberals tend to be tolerant relativists anyway.

Antiessentialism about *sex* is therefore of no consequence. Whereas Shrage claims that how a person classifies the act, as either sex or child rearing, "clearly" influences his or her moral attitude toward it, the relationship, if any, is likely the other way around: how a person evaluates the act influences how he or she decides to classify it.

Shrage is right that penis-feeding is not perceived to be harmful to young boys in Sambian culture, while similar acts of fellatio are often perceived to be damaging in ours. (Recall Frye's qualms about adult-child sex.) But the matter of harm goes deeper than "perception." The spokesman for sex-negativity in our culture would claim that fellatio done on an older man by a young boy in our culture, even one instance, could lead to grievous social, medical, and psychiatric problems for the boy. Further, this spokesman would disagree with the sexual liberal as to whether harm is done to the boys in Sambian culture; the institutional coercion of young boys into performing unnatural acts—in the Thomist worldview—must damage them, even if the scars are not physical and they later lead heterosexual lives. What the Thomist assumes is that a Real World of Value underlies his judgment about the grievous harm, both spiritual and psychological, done by seven years of oral sexual servitude.

The point is not that a Real World of Value exists according to which either the sexual liberal or the Thomist is right. All that Baker's philosophical clinician can do is advise a worried mother that her son's masturbation or homosexuality is either harmful, if she buys into Augustine and Aquinas, or not harmful, if she goes with the liberals. What we should learn, instead, from the example is that "harm" is not a value-free concept. To the extent, then, that we think of unhealthy sexuality as in some way harmful, to either those who engage in such sex or to third parties, our concept of "healthy sex" will be value-laden. This holds whether we are considering liberal claims that orgasm during sleep and masturbation are harmless and hence not unhealthy,[29] or conservative claims that homosexuality is both harmful and unhealthy. The contestability of "harm" contributes to—both allows and encourages—the social construction of "healthy sex"; its meaning, if it has any, is determined by social forces having the power to control what is counted culturally as harm.

Functioning Sex

When thinking about sexual health, one must eventually turn to Masters and Johnson. But *Human Sexual Inadequacy* is a painful book for lovers of conceptual clarity: the authors use "sexual inadequacy" and "sexual dysfunction" interchangeably, and neither concept is in the index. In chapter 1, "Therapy Concepts," the place we expect to find it, no definition of "inadequacy" or "dysfunction" appears. What the authors do, instead, is define each sexual dysfunction (premature ejaculation, insufficient lubrication, etc.), thereby giving only an ostensive definition of the whole category. The most we get as a general definition is the idea that sexual dysfunction involves ineffectiveness, of psychophysiological origin, in the performance of sexual activity.

Still, the idea of sexual dysfunction has caught on. Irving Bieber, for example, observes that "the term 'sexual deviation' is ambiguous, vague, and not useful as a diagnosis or as a nosological category."[30] He proposes to replace "deviation" altogether with "dysfunction":

> Masters and Johnson used criteria that qualified [conditions] as functional and dysfunctional to classify sexual disorders, and they introduced the term "sexual inadequacy." Under this rubric, they included frigidity and sexual impotence.... I suggest homosexuality be characterized as a type of sexual inadequacy since most homosexuals . . . cannot function heterosexually.

I wonder why Bieber thinks "dysfunction" is less ambiguous than "deviation" and hence preferable. After all, in his hands the idea of "inadequacy" is slippery enough to extend to homosexuality, despite the fact that homosexuals have functional and pleasure-producing penises and clitorises galore. My diagnosis is that "dysfunction" sounds more medical and less moralistic than "deviation," presenting an advantage to physicians as they protect their turf from theologians. Bieber's medical judgments as to what to include on a list of sexual dysfunctions will be similar to his moral judgments as to what to put on a list of sexual deviations. The only difference is that the regulation of behavior is located in one province of power and technique rather than another.

Charles Socarides worries that Bieber's proposal, to replace "deviation" by "dysfunction" and then characterize homosexuality as a dysfunction, destroys the powerful condemnation homosexuality, as a disease state, deserves:

> Scientific knowledge is . . . damaged when attempts are made to classify homosexuality simply as "sexual dysfunction," a term regularly applied to loss of erection, premature ejaculation, retarded ejaculation, or total impotence. These impairments constitute disturbances of the standard male-female pattern. . . . Individuals unable to achieve sexual release within the standard pattern . . . turn to modified patterns for orgastic release, and these constitute sexual deviations. Thus the immutable distinctions between sexual deviations and sexual dysfunctions cannot be . . . blurred without incurring formidable scientific chaos.[31]

Socarides does expose a tangle about sexual functioning. In one sense, both heterosexuals and homosexuals can function sexually, that is, engage in sexual activity effectively. But in another sense, the homosexual is different because he or she cannot or does not function heterosexually: they either do not engage in heterosexual activity effectively or have no desire to engage in this activity. (Saying that homosexuals cannot perform heterosexually is too simple. Some people, having tried both, prefer one kind of sex to another, and some people discover that they enjoy both. Also incorrect is the idea that homosexuals generally engage in, or "turn to," their sexual activity because they are incompetent heterosexuals.) But why isn't a heterosexual who cannot function homosexually also to be judged dysfunctional (or deviant)? Bieber, in classifying homosexuality as a dysfunction, assumes that heterosexuality is superior to homosexuality, but at least, for him, they are the same sort of thing, only one is more "effective." Socarides's judgment of superiority is more explicit and brutal, insisting on a Thomistic difference in kind, not only in degree, between inadequately consummated heterosexual relations (say, premature ejaculation) and never-desired heterosexual relations. To his mind, this difference is so stark that another category, "deviance," with its connotation of severe pathology, must be retained so that homosexuality can be properly labeled and condemned. That homosexuality is a difference among a plurality of sexual behaviors, neither morally deviant nor performatively dysfunctional, as healthy as other activities in the sense of yielding pleasure, is an idea that recommends itself neither to Bieber nor to Socarides, who didn't leave their mothers far behind.

Richard Green agrees with Bieber that "dysfunction" is the concept of choice, but disagrees that homosexuality is a sexual dysfunction. On Green's view, "sexual dysfunction"

> would include the heterosexual or the homosexual who finds it difficult to maintain desired object relationships, who compulsively uses sexuality to ward off anxiety or depression, or whose sexuality typically leads to depression or anxiety. . . . With this new classification, psychiatry would have an objective basis for categorizing sexuality that is free of cultural bias. [32]

Green argues that gays and lesbians function quite well sexually, and so as long as (this is Green's proviso) their behavior involves no "ego-dystonic," "psychogenic distress," such as depression and anxiety, their sexuality is not a medical or psychiatric matter.

Michael Levin also recognizes that gays function sexually, but finds fault with them for functioning *too much*. Levin thinks anyone (but he has in mind a gay man) who has had one hundred to five hundred sexual partners exhibits "maladjustment and compulsivity, a chronic inability to find anyone satisfactory." [33] This harsh and psychologically loaded judgment is too quick. Perhaps the promiscuous male finds any *one* sex partner increasingly unsatisfying after having had sexual relations with him a few times. But he does not necessarily find new partners unsatisfying, so he exhibits no chronic failure to achieve satisfaction *simpliciter*. Some people enjoy sex, and variety in sex, more than others do. No longer finding an old partner arousing ("suffering" from impotence) is just the problem of the death of desire—both in and out of marriage. The difference between a gay who is promiscuous and a married straight man is not qualitative. The unattached gay has a way out, which the married heterosexual man pledged to monogamy does not. Given half a chance, straight men unencumbered by the pressure of compulsory marital pairing might find a promiscuous lifestyle fascinating and fulfilling, if only women would accommodate.

Green has his own response to Levin: promiscuity, gay *or* straight, is a psychiatric problem only if it interferes with "*desired* object relationships" and hence causes ego-dystonic distress. Green's notion that a client's condition must produce anguish, cause a person this sort of harm, for it to be a case of unhealthiness, is attractive; indeed, his proviso is by now a central definitional and diagnostic feature of all the "sexual and gender identity disorders" listed in the *DSM-IV*.[34] As I argue below, though, his proviso also gives the lie to Green's belief that his tests for psychiatric disorder are "objective" and "free of cultural bias." In the end, Green's conditions for healthy sexuality are more sophisticated but no less value-laden and contentious than Max Levin's conditions.

Green reserves psychiatric categories and treatment for the person who sincerely wants to be governed by Pausanias's heavenly eros, to live within the warm bounds of an intimate relationship, but is, instead, governed by vulgar eros as if contrary to his will or better judgment. "There was something wrong with me. I was promiscuous with women [even though] I wanted to get married and have children," complained Jeffrey Masson, while explaining why he saw his "promiscuity as an illness" for which he sought psychoanalytic therapy.[35] Marmor would applaud. But Masson is apparently not wringing his hands over what he regards as a moral problem. It is, instead, a psychiatric matter: Masson is unable psychologically to bring himself to do what he really wants, or his better self wants, to do. A married man, an engaged woman, anyone who desires to be chaste and faithful but slides back into promiscuity, is (like the alcoholic) no longer someone with a character defect or one tempted too strongly by Paul's Satan, but the victim of a psychic disturbance, a "sexual dysfunction" to be treated by de-eroticization. The ego-dystonia of backsliding is required for the illness to exist. If Masson had felt no regret about caving in, experienced no depression or anxiety about not achieving fidelity in act or desire, he would have no illness. The very ideas of sexual "backsliding" and of "sexual addiction" would not exist in a less Augustinian culture; and the phenomena would not be recognized. In this case, too, social constructivism is persuasive.

Green claims not only that sexuality is unhealthy when it *causes* depression or anxiety, but also that sexuality employed "compulsively" in the opposite way, *to ward off* depression or anxiety, is unhealthy as well. But if depression and anxiety are evils to be avoided, using sex to decrease their incidence cannot be totally bad. The world we inhabit contains much about which to be depressed and anxious, as do our personal lives, so for Annie Sprinkle to suggest pleasing oneself with sex to deal with depression is neither startling nor a reason to phone a shrink. Similarly odd is Marmor's judgment that sex is pathological when motivated "primarily by needs for reassurance," as if reassurance weren't something most of us, both men and women, needed plenty of.[36] Living well in a hostile and capricious world is the best revenge; warding off life's miseries by soaking oneself in the (safe) pleasures of the flesh is an attractive and rational option. Green might remind us that he is speaking only of "compulsive" sex. But the qualifier "compulsive" is unhelpful. If it means that the person experiences the behavior as not being under voluntary control, we have merely replaced a moral or religious critique of human weakness of will with a conveniently exonerating medical model of addictive sexuality. Or if it means that the behavior, even if originally done for pleasure, after a while brings pain and anxiety,[37] calling compulsive sex unhealthy is not to say anything new, but is only to repeat, with emphasis, that ego-dystonic sexuality is unhealthy.

At any rate, Green's proviso, that sexuality is unhealthy only if ego-dystonic, is dubious, even if blessed by the *DSM-IV*; ego-dystonia and ego-syntonia cannot be employed with much success to do the job Green expects of them, namely, to illumine "objectively" the nature of psycholog-ically healthy sex. Brenda Wiewel's idea that "true sexual liberation will occur when a woman feels . . . comfortable with her sexual response *no matter what* it is"[38] should make us hesitate. Feeling comfortable about or happy with one's desires and preferred acts is not a viable test of health *or* liberation. The rapist or child molester might be content at his desires and feel unhappiness only because or when he cannot more readily satisfy them. His being content with his desires, being satisfied with the constitu-tion of the self, does not tend to support a judgment that he is healthy. To the contrary, it might even bolster the argument that something is psychologically amiss, that he could take such delight at himself. A neces-sary condition for the diagnosis of the sexual disorder "pedophilia," ac-cording to the *DSM-IV* (528), is that "the fantasies, sexual urges, or behaviors cause clinically significant distress or impairment in social, occu-pational or other important areas of functioning." The pedophile who keeps his job and likes his desires escapes the diagnosis. The point is not that pedophilia is psychologically unhealthy. Rather, ego-syntonia and ego-dystonia seem irrelevant to the question.

Furthermore, a person might feel disgust at the thought of doing certain acts, or ego-dystonia when actually doing them, yet should be encouraged to overcome the reluctance this induces; we might, otherwise, all be stuck performing nothing but missionary sex. Being unhappy with one's sexual orientation, homosexual or anything else, is no reliable sign of disorder, just as being happy is no reliable sign that one's sexuality is not disordered. If the claim that our culture makes heterosexuality compulsory has even a small measure of truth, any unhappiness experienced by homosexuals about their sexual orientation loses validity as a sign of psychological disorder. At the same time, the failure of heterosexuals to feel uncomfortable about their orientation does not mean all is well with them. They might be missing out on pleasures and emotions that their bodies otherwise make possible. That looks disordered, like restraining one arm forever. Neither straight nor gay is polymorphous enough.

To insist on a blunt equation between happiness and health is to walk the road of complacency, not the road of the critical Socratic examination of one's sexual life. This attitude entails allegiance to certain values, a picture of The Good (Enough) Life, a vision that is full of the cultural bias Green promised to avoid. Wiewel neglects the fact that feelings can and do change, are often as fragile as Heraclitus's river; they are not a secure foundation for reaching rigorous judgments about sexual health. What Wiewel should say, instead, is this: "consult your sexual feelings as they would have been, or would be, in the ideal world." This counterfactual—healthy sexuality is the sexuality people would feel good doing were they, say, perfectly free and equal—is attractive. But teasing out the implications of this kind of subjunctive has never been easy for political theory. Any attempt to do so involves commitment to an obviously value-laden and culturally variable conception of the ideal world.

Political Science

Even the medical understanding of sexual conditions that are less esoteric than pedophilia and the paraphilias is infected with values and cultural norms. Consider this description of impotence:

> The penis is rubbed and it doesn't get hard. . . . Obviously, something has
> gone wrong, so that the expected response is not produced. . . . When this
> happens, the condition is called a *sexual dysfunction,* which . . . means a
> malfunctioning of the human sexual response system. It means that a person
> hasn't reacted as one would normally expect. . . . [T]he sex organs do not
> respond as they should.[39]

"Healthy sexuality" is supposed to be grasped in terms of the smooth
operation of the penis's mechanical processes. Yet the words "normally"
and "should" imply that an appeal to values is required in the analysis of
"sexual dysfunction." We "normally expect" a rubbed penis to erect; a
rubbed penis that does not erect is not responding "as it should." But how
should penises respond to a touch? To say that a normal penis is one that
responds to a touch with erection is false, since the absence of erection
when one is touched might be due to all sorts of things, like distraction or
boredom, that do not indicate pathology. If what is meant is that a normal
penis erects when touched, *ceteris paribus,* the analysis threatens to be
circular: it will reduce to the claim that a normal penis is one that erects
when touched in normal circumstances. We *can* specify what "normal
circumstances" are—but only by employing our values or cultural norms,
not by doing more biomedical research. Suppose that a penis is touched,
erects, penetrates, but ejaculates in ten seconds. Cultural values, not biomedical science, imply that a normal penis should last longer than this. Or
is this penis disordered if and only if its bearer or its recipient is unhappy
with its performance? Other cultures—or other women, such as Andrea
Dworkin—might prefer and applaud, as Tiefer suggests, the short-lived
erection.

This is not to pick nits, for the way sexual disorders are conceptualized
in the *DSM-IV,* the official handbook of American psychiatry, abundantly
illustrates the point. "Male erectile disorder" is the inability to "attain . . .
or maintain . . . an adequate erection" (502). The qualifier "adequate," if it
has any substantial meaning, must be grounded in cultural standards, and
the medicine of sex must, for good political and economic reasons, embrace
a mainstream conception of "adequate." Or contemplate "female orgasmic
disorder," in which a "woman's orgasmic capacity is less than would be
reasonable for . . . the adequacy of sexual stimulation she receives" (505).
What if she needs, to derive an orgasm from the oral, manual, or penile

manipulation of her erogenous zones, is to hear softly whispered in her ear, at precisely the right moment, "I love you" *or* "there are three more well-hung men waiting in the hallway"? "Adequate stimulation" is either a statistical notion, which will, with its insipid lumpen-values, brand unusual women as being sexually disordered; or "adequate stimulation" has to be tailored to each woman's tastes, in which case no woman can be diagnosed as having this disorder—since we can never be sure, in the absence of orgasm, if we have tried just the right sequence of acts or words "adequate" for her. The *DSM-IV* includes a disclaimer—"notions of deviance, standards of sexual performance . . . can vary from culture to culture" (493)—but does not face squarely the implications. The disclaimer entails that this section of the *DSM-IV*, not being a part of a real medical science of sex, could easily be ripped out, at the same time cleanly abbreviating psychiatry.

We can witness value commitments at work also in the sexual therapy of the men's liberation proponents Jeffrey Fracher and Michael Kimmel. In counseling men for "premature ejaculation, inhibited sexual desire, and erectile dysfunction," they help their clients adopt, as part of *therapy*, a "redefinition of what it means to be a man in contemporary American society."[40] In their hands, re-eroticization occurs through re-definition, a kind of re-education. Their particular redefinition devalues "machismo" and de-emphasizes the importance of male performance. Men should take John Lennon as a role model, not James Dean or John Wayne. Fracher and Kimmel's therapeutic philosophy is at least candidly, if not unabashedly, political, instead of blindly so, as in Max Levin's philosophy of healthy sexuality.

The Masters and Johnson therapeutic regimen for helping "dissatisfied" gay men achieve heterosexuality also includes "cognitive restructuring." This sometimes amounts to exposing a client, who is under the spell of prohibitive Christianity, to "different theological interpretations of the Bible."[41] The diverse interpretative possibilities cannot merely be presented menu-like to the client, as Baker's clinician would, with the hope that the client will on his own select the "right" one. To help the gay man achieve cognitive restructuring, some readings of the Bible (say, Jung and Smith's interpretation, which accepts loving, monogamous gay relationships)[42] must be claimed by the therapist to be better than the others

(Augustine's), just as Fracher and Kimmel stress to their clients the imbecility of machismo. If it seems strange that the Masters and Johnson program involves showing gay clients that the Bible does not damn *homosexuality*, consider the reasoning. The homosexual client suffers guilt feelings from religious teachings, which must be relieved first: "his homosexuality must become ego syntonic ... before he moves to establish a heterosexual life style" (178). Some might say, if the homosexuality is now ego-syntonic, that is cure enough, and do not proceed farther with re-eroticization.

Gender politics play a role in this final example. About his client Anne, the psychiatrist Joseph Glenmullen writes,

> I never cease to be amazed, although I have seen it many times before: Here was a sexually liberated individual, with considerable experience, who reported her current sex life as "great," yet she never had an orgasm during intercourse. Sexual liberation is no guarantee of the freedom to enjoy.[43]

Through a combination of Glenmullen's psychotherapy and Masters-and-Johnson style treatment for sexual dysfunction, Anne was eventually able to have an orgasm during coitus with her lover Jonathan. Should we say that as long as Anne herself wanted to be able to orgasm during coitus, and viewed her ability to experience orgasm (galore) only during oral sex with Jonathan as a problem, then no complaints should be raised? Glenmullen does not restrict himself to this narrow judgment; he universalizes his prescription that a woman, to be fully sexually healthy, to obtain her full share of sexual pleasure, must experience coital orgasm. If she cannot, she needs therapy until she can.[44] At some point Glenmullen had to convince Anne that her sex life was, in the absence of coital orgasm and despite cunnilingual orgasm, not so great after all, or at least he had to plant the idea and hope it would grow. The point is not that Glenmullen is to blame for the fact that values infect his medical judgments. The alternative diagnosis, that Anne's sexuality *was* great (or good enough, thank you) and therefore required no medical intervention, is equally steeped in values. Maybe Anne would have been happier exploring her lesbian potential and eschewing intercourse altogether. Indeed, one physician thinks there are eight different therapies available to the sexually challenged Annes of the world, ranging from Catholicism-inspired therapy to the feminist-inspired.[45] The intersection of politics and sex is distressingly clear, and supports the social constructivism of healthy sex.

Evolutionary Health

Questions about sexual functioning—under what conditions should a woman be able to experience orgasm? how long should a man be able to maintain an erection?—cannot be answered in the absence of an account of our purposes and goals and hence without invoking values. Whether we are talking about the genitals or about the heart or liver, to determine if organs are functioning properly, and hence are healthy, depends in part on what we expect or want our bodies to do.[46] So the core notion of healthy sex is, minimally, the pleasurable sex that is afforded by a healthy body composed of healthy body parts. That's not saying much; but saying more means going beyond, or returning from, biomedical science to ethics.

Christopher Boorse has argued, to the contrary, that health and disease judgments are not evaluative. For Boorse, "the root idea . . . is that the normal is the natural."[47] The healthy, normal functioning of an organ is its natural functioning. For an organ to function in accordance with nature, in turn, is to function in accordance with its evolutionary design. Health is the absence of disease, which interferes with an organ's evolutionary, "species-typical contribution to survival and reproduction."[48] "Disease judgments," therefore, "are value-neutral,"[49] and discovering diseases "is a matter of natural science."[50] To make health judgments we need only ascertain the species design; science can do this for humans as well as it does it for frogs. This is a secular, twentieth-century Thomism.

In applying his theory, Boorse argues that homosexuality is abnormal because it deviates from the species-typical design. As a disease state, homosexuality interferes with a "normal function of sexual desire," namely, "to promote reproduction," and hence is dysfunctional.[51] One way to challenge Boorse's conclusion is to point to recent developments in brain anatomy, endocrinology, and genetics that make it more likely that homosexuality is part of the species design.[52] This rebuttal does not contend that disease should not be analyzed as a deviation from the species design, but only that Boorse has not correctly applied his own concept of disease to homosexuality. A Boorsean, then, can respond in the following way: "Fine. Your claims actually support my analysis of 'health.' Now let the scientists decide empirically whether homosexuality is part of the species design and what mechanisms generate it. As I said, health judgments are a matter for the natural sciences."[53]

But the Boorsean runs into another kind of trouble here. Deciding whether homosexuality is nontrivially genetic in origin and therefore a possible part of the species design, or primarily environmentally caused and hence, on Boorse's view, possibly a disease since it is the result of an external interference with a natural process,[54] might look like a purely scientific question of sorting out the causes and estimating their relative importance. This kind of nature/nurture dispute has never been resolved satisfactorily with respect to any socially or politically significant property. The study, for example, of the origins of racial and gender variations in mental functioning has always been a mess. In principle, scientific solutions might be possible, but they have been elusive in practice. In these areas, psychological factors, broadly construed, influence the kind of solution an individual prefers, and political factors play a large role in determining what solutions are reached and become bits of social knowledge. In today's political climate, some homosexual activists, both gay and lesbian, are attracted to the idea of explaining their sexual orientation biologically.[55] If this preference is caused by Mother Nature, if it is a "genetically immutable trait," homosexual orientation becomes socially easier to justify and to defend legally.[56] One lesbian made the point in a CNN documentary in 1994, faithfully borrowing Aquinas: it was God who made her the way she is. The conservative Thomist will not deny that if God willed it, it is right; he denies only that God willed it. Gay and lesbian politics, then, at least indirectly put pressure on sympathetic scientists to uncover more evidence of the genetic foundation of homosexuality and its biological correlates, to show that God, or nature, did will it. The history of the vicissitudes of the classification of homosexuality within professional psychiatry shows that the homosexual public can affect biomedical conclusions.

The reasoning offered by gay and lesbian activists might be widely persuasive and politically useful, but it is technically fallacious. That a state or condition is immutable because natural or biological in origin does not entail that the state or condition avoids all negative evaluations. Some natural states are disadvantageous, given the rest of our biology or relatively inflexible facts of social life. Being color-blind, deprived of insulin, under 4.5 feet in height, and (sometimes) obese are biologically based yet rarely felicitous. Even though it is logically fallacious to reason from the biological grounding of homosexuality to the conclusion that it is without taint, the alternative position—that homosexuality is a disease state despite being genetic—seems to bear the burden of proof.

If the question of the origin of homosexuality is put aside, Boorse's view can be challenged in other ways. One can maintain plausibly that even if states that interfere with survival are diseases, those that interfere with an individual's reproduction do not interfere with his or her survival and so are not diseases in this narrow sense. Further, even if Boorse is right that homosexual orientation is a disease because it interferes with or fails to sustain reproduction, we could conclude only that homosexuality is a *reproductive* disease, not that it is a *sexual* disease. (It would not even be a reproductive disease for any gay or lesbian who did reproduce, of which there are plenty—another consideration that undermines the conceptual distinction between "heterosexual" and "homosexual.") As soon as we recognize that the sexual body has several distinct functions, including at least reproduction and pleasure production, it becomes possible to claim that with regard to its *important* function—which is determined by values, not science—no disease exists.

Thus, Michael Levin's view, that gay sexual "acts involve the use of the genitals for what they aren't for,"[57] depends on a myopic construal of what the genitals are "for." The penis, given the values that play a role in determining the scope of its functions, is for lots of things: procreating, experiencing pleasure, urinating, waving to strangers during Mardi Gras. For Levin to claim that being inside another man's anus and rectum is not what a man's penis is "for" is incredible.[58] Does masturbation also misuse the penis, or the hand? Does cunnilingus misuse the tongue? Does anilingus misuse *both* the tongue and anus? More relevant to Levin's main accusation, against anal intercourse, is this question: is a finger lodged in the anus a proper use of a digit to produce pleasure when the hole requires scratching, but an improper use when put there for erotic pleasure? If a finger is okay, why not a penis?

So even if, as Boorse claims, "one normal function of sexual desire is to promote reproduction,"[59] other functions attach to human sexuality and its organs, not the least of which is the production of pleasure for the organism that likely makes a contribution to its welfare and, in turn, its survival or longevity. That sexual activity yields pleasure and well-being is part of the species design, and this pleasure can be produced by both heterosexual and homosexual acts. Homosexuality, then, is more like infertility than a sexual deviation, if there are any, such as coprophilia; it is not a malfunctioning of the species-typical sexual desire, arousal, and pleasure system, but at most (if even that) of reproductive capability. If we distinguish between reproductive health and sexual health, and focus on the function of the sexual body to produce pleasure, we can perceive the grain of truth in medical talk of sexual dysfunction: the essential feature of the sexual dysfunctions, the sexually unhealthy states of the body, are those conditions that interfere with attainment of sexual pleasure. On this score, homosexuals, bisexuals, heterosexuals, and anyone else not engaged in reproductive activity by intention or default do not, merely in virtue of being homosexual, bisexual, heterosexual, or sterile, suffer a sexual dysfunction.

Progress

No transcendental criterion tells us which kind of judgment about sexuality (moral/immoral, healthy/unhealthy, criminal/legal), if any, and which discipline (religion, medicine, the courts) should prevail. No algorithm reveals whether narcotics addiction and pedophilia should be in medicine's dominion or handled by the criminal justice system. No value-neutral criterion sorts out everything with an a priori logical neatness. Whether Max Levin's conditions for healthy sex really are, in some impartial sense, medical criteria, or stolen from another discipline (moral philosophy, theology) and disguised as medical is not important. The various disciplines fight for control over domains of discourse and their associated human behaviors.[60] As Joel Kovel puts it, "health, unlike traffic, cannot be defined, or, rather, is the setting of a continual struggle over definition, a struggle arising from the need to gain control over the realm of the . . . body."[61] If medicine is victorious in this struggle, Levin's conditions *are* medical, in a social constructivist sense, and they become the standard of healthy sex. The replacement of moral judgments about sex by value-free medical judgments is often seen as a vital part of the progress made by the humanistic and enlightened modern age, marking the victory of rationality over superstition. This is true only to the extent, and only as long as, the values that inform "healthy sex," underneath the science, are decent.[62] Depending on the interplay between medical ideology and the political climate, Max Levin's sex-love link could be declared to be, and would actually become, the test of healthy sexuality. In 1987, American psychiatry excluded homosexuality altogether from the revised *DSM-III*; but the doctors could democratically reinstall it, and might find support from the Contract with America.

Medicine and the other helping professions did battle with a religious establishment already in disarray, and gained the social right to pass judgments about sexuality. "The opening up of the great medicopsychological domain of [sex] . . . was destined to take over from the old moral categories of debauchery and excess."[63] Medicine justified its sexual judgments in terms of a science of the body, a science that soon bore fruit in the temporal world quite unlike, and suspiciously superior to, the more rarefied fruit served by priests. Sexual problems were to be analyzed, in the case of women for example, as gynecological, as organic diseases. But when this "medico-gynaecological model was invoked in order to explain, diagnose, and treat various aberrant expressions of behavior," according to Susan Edwards, "in the majority of cases, no evidence of organic disease or disorder was present."[64] Another point can be made in addition to Edwards's observation that there were no organic disorders, that the disease of "nymphomania," for example, was not caused by any disease of the gonads. Due to both the flexibility of "organic," which includes any little bump or grind in the body, and the open-ended, Duhemian nature of scientific research, medicine has leeway to defend the heuristic value of believing that, with enough labor, an organic basis can and will be found, even if no specific causal mechanism is currently supported by the data. In this way, medicine can sustain its catalogue of disorders, from obesity and promiscuity to bad temper, even if empirical considerations do not—insert a vague "yet"—provide a full justification. (Or, as in Mary Jane Sherfey, medicine can revise the judgment that a very sexually desirous or active woman has a disease, "nymphomania." Such a woman is, instead, fulfilling her biological potential.)[65]

Medicine frequently only offers a promissory note that an organic cause will be found for a condition, and so doubts can be raised whether medicine has made progress over demon theories. Little difference exists between medicine's creating a disease of masturbatory insanity in the 1800s and the helping professions' increasing, nowadays, the raw numbers of cases of child abuse and rape by employing overly generous identifying criteria.[66] Medicine, however, pays off its promissory notes often enough that we are willing to accept its disease states even in the absence of established causes. Our hopes, our needs for understanding and for cures, lead us into being accomplices. Further, the opportunity for us to avail ourselves of the exonerating power of medicine—if nymphomania is a disease of the internal genitalia, we are not to blame—seduces us into accepting its theories.[67] If alcoholism, obesity, and foul temper are biogenetic diseases involving impulses to drink, eat, and grump that are largely irresistible by the alcoholic, the obese, and the nasty, these victims should not be blamed for their states. Not only the afflicted are exonerated. Dean Hamer tells us about a father who could "forgive himself," whose "sense of relief was overwhelming," when he heard that genes, not his parenting, made his sons gay. Hamer's scientific promissory note is already bearing exculpatory dividends.[68]

Freedom

A provocative, if misleading, thesis is that sexual perversion did not exist before 1840.[69] The medical concept of "sexual perversion" came into being, and along with it sexual perverts as an identifiable disordered group, roughly at the time sexuality was being thought of in terms of an instinct that was separable from its objects and that could therefore latch on to the "wrong" ones.[70] The conceptual isolation of a distinct sexual instinct—an instinct pushing an organism to experience somatic pleasure, not one pushing it to procreate—made it possible to understand sex developmentally and to ask some interesting questions: why some people sexually prefer in other people brown hair to blonde, or large tushes to small (preferences about which we still know little); why some people enjoy sex with persons of the same sex, some with the other sex, some with both, some with animals, some with toys. But the conceptual isolation of the instinct from the various acts and objects that provide somatic pleasure makes it difficult for us to give concrete content to "healthy" and "unhealthy" (or "perverted"). For if the instinct is not tied to any particular object or goal (other than pleasure), the separation of preferences, objects, and acts into the healthy and the perverted appears to lack any foundation. The distinction between social and psychological influences on development that are merely "formative" (say, the influence that creates a preference for brown hair) and influences that are "distorting" (say, an influence that brings about coprophilia) will be hard to make out.[71] Even suggesting the examples is presumptuous, which is why the best route might be to abandon the notion of perversion altogether.

Sexology, however, need not jump ship. One solution is to equate, as Boorse does, the *healthy* development of the sexual instinct with its *natural* development. "Natural" development, however, must be understood in a special way. It cannot *mean* development toward reproductively effective sexual behavior, and it cannot *mean* "heterosexual." That would undermine the research program of providing an explanation for the empirical fact that human sexuality is often, although not always, reproductive and heterosexual. Explaining why the instinct ever latches on to heterosexual objects is impossible if its "natural" expression is assumed to be heterosexual. Hence, a more sophisticated notion of the natural is required: natural sexual development is defined subjunctively as that development persons *would* undergo in the absence of, and thus unimpeded by, social influences on their sexual development. This conception of natural human sexuality derives from liberal state-of-nature political theory, although it can also be found in the noncontractarian social philosophy of John Stuart Mill:

> I consider it presumption in any one to pretend to decide what women are or are not, can or cannot be, by natural constitution. They have always hitherto been kept, as far as regards spontaneous development, in so unnatural a state, that their nature cannot but have been greatly distorted and disguised. ... This will be less and less the case, but it will remain true to a great extent, as long as social institutions do not admit the same free development of ... women which is possible to men.[72]

A strikingly similar passage occurs in Freud:

> Can an anthropologist give the cranial index of a people whose custom it is
> to deform their children's heads by bandaging them round from their earliest
> years? . . . So long as a person's early years are influenced not only by a
> sexual inhibition of thought but also by a religious inhibition and by a loyal
> inhibition derived from this, we cannot really tell what in fact he is like.[73]

The basic idea is that the instinct, if left alone, will develop in a certain
direction, its *own*; if persons are free, if they are not under the thumb
of laws, parental domination, and oppressive religious and educational
institutions, their sexuality will develop according to the instinct's own
inner laws, undistorted, unperverted, and healthy. This notion has almost
become, by now, a standard piece of liberal-professional pop psychology.

We should not overlook the brilliance of this Freudo-Millian conception
of natural human sexuality. The definition does not, by itself, entail that
any given act, object, or preference is unnatural and therefore unhealthy
or perverted. In one sense (intensionally), the definition does tell us what
natural human sexuality is, in the most general terms: the natural is the
free. But in another sense (extensionally), it does not tell us at all what
particular desires or acts are healthy or perverted. That move requires
additional argument, evidence that a behavior is natural because it would
be practiced were there, contrary to fact, no social influences operating on
persons. Because further argument is required, heterosexuality as a standard requires defense and, contrary to Socarides, cannot be assumed. This
makes sexual theorizing intellectually challenging; psychiatry can engage
in Kuhnian puzzle solving. Indeed, the doctrine suggests a neat empirical
methodology: find natural (i.e., free) persons, perhaps "primitives" un-
touched by civilization, and study *their* sexuality. (The Sambia and Etoro?)
Shiploads of European and American anthropologists hoped the Holy Grail
would be found in the South Seas and on the long coast of Brazil and
Argentina. The ships' crews when landing might have presented a more
accurate picture of natural human male sexuality. Who is uncivilized?

But the pride of this approach to discovering healthy sexuality, that
additional argument and investigation are required before we can lay out
the specific details of the healthy, is also its downfall. The difficulty of
showing that any sexual act, object, or desire is natural, that is, would be

preferred or exhibited in complete freedom, partially explains the endless debates theoreticians have had about healthy sexuality. Psychiatry, instead of solving Kuhnian puzzles in a normal-scientific tradition, has been chronically bogged down in a pre-paradigm swamp. Making use of statistical regularities to pinpoint the natural does not help; to take what most people do as a reliable sign of the natural is to assume that people are already as free as they ever could be. The intention was to distinguish between the healthy and the unhealthy in an empirical, nonevaluative way, but the only recourse in the face of this epistemological calamity is to incorporate all kinds of judgments: the moral, the aesthetic, the prudential. Accounts of healthy human sexuality become a masquerade for partisan and contentious views about what sexual behaviors are proper and right, obligatory and permissible, attractive and repulsive, harmful or contrary to society's interests. The *DSM-IV* provides a good illustration in how it conceptualizes sexual perversion. The paraphilias are *pathological* when they "lead to legal complications [or] interfere with social relationships" (525); criminality is of *diagnostic* significance. Paraphilias rise to the level of unhealthiness when they interfere with a kind of lifestyle or life we have judged superior.

We might consider simply ignoring the problems in distinguishing between the healthy and the perverted and rest content with the notion that "healthy sexuality" is just *whatever* sexuality is chosen by free people. From this bare analysis of sexual health it follows, at least, that it would be contradictory to say in any particular instance that an informed and freely chosen sexual act was unhealthy—a forceful idea consistent with an appreciation of the Millian values of individuality and autonomy.[74] In light of such a view of sexual health, perhaps the goal should be to generate as much freedom as possible, to let sex take whatever course it takes under those circumstances, and to be prepared not to tolerate grudgingly, but to celebrate publicly, the plurality of human sexual orientations that might very well emerge. A sexual philosophy of *que será será* can be found in Engels:

> But what will there be new? That will be answered when a new generation has grown up: a generation of men who never in their lives have known what it is to buy a woman's surrender with money or any other social

instrument of power; a generation of women who have never known what it is to give themselves to a man from any other considerations than real love, or to refuse to give themselves to their lover from fear of the economic consequences. When these people are in the world . . . they will make their own practice . . . and that will be the end of it.[75]

What freedom is, unfortunately, is itself a matter of moral and political deliberation: the concept presupposes a view of human nature, its capabilities, and its ideal state. What freedom is to the anarchist is not freedom to the liberal, or the Marxist, or the conservative, and terrible disputes (leading to revolutions, wars, and many dreadful books) have occurred about what conditions are required economically, psychologically, and socially for full human freedom. "Healthy sexuality" turns out to be a notion derived as much from political philosophy as from theology and ethics; it should come as no surprise that various social forces fight to control this concept and its application to our lives.

FIVE

Beauty

The de-eroticization of the world . . . is summed up in debased and
ridiculous fashion when the young women entering Smith College are
told that lookism is included among the currently recognized vices
along with racism, sexism, and homophobia. Yet eros begins, sad but
true, in preferences founded in the first place on what is seen with
the eyes, founded on ideals of bodily beauty. Nobody seriously ever
suggested that this is where it ends, but if this essential beginning is
suppressed, farewell eros. . . . Love of the beautiful may be the last and
finest sacrifice to radical egalitarianism.

—Allan Bloom, *Love and Friendship*

There has been some concern—not only at Smith—about practices, both
personal and institutional, that keep benefits from or assign burdens to
physically unattractive persons and reduce the burdens of or allocate benefits to those who are attractive. The media mention the same moral and
political principles that had been and still are invoked by the black civil
rights movement, the women's movement, the gay/lesbian movement,
even by the "animal rights," "men's rights," and "smokers' rights" movements. We have been hearing, then, about unjust discrimination against
the ugly, the obese, the repulsive.[1] Conservatives see this extension of
moral rights as the *reductio ad absurdum* of the liberal enterprise, which
is how some people respond to the thematically similar demand for legal
protection of the interests of the physically disabled; some Marxists see it
as a case of bourgeois degeneracy, which is how staunch Leninists, in the
not too distant past, viewed (defenses of) homosexuality; other people, of

whatever persuasion, see it as a joke.[2] I intend to take the view seriously, to see how much truth it contains.

The problem is not only that discrimination against, or differential treatment of, the physically unattractive prevents them from obtaining personal and social advantages or makes them suffer. Active discrimination against the ugly harms them; they lose, for example, in the social process that distributes sexual activity and pleasure. But the physically attractive person is sometimes the object of discrimination and suffers as a result. We often discount the intelligence of the attractive; and beauty can be punished, as Lucy Brown recognizes: "she who lives by the pretty face, dies by the pretty face." In general, people who are physically unattractive suffer more often and severely; being attractive is advantageous.[3] Still, the important point is that decisions that affect people's lives are frequently made on the basis of looks; the fundamental issue is whether any use of appearance as a basis for certain decisions is wrong, regardless of whether such judgments work for or against a person's interests.

Relevant Traits

All tasks, roles, and offices require for their performance that the persons charged with them possess certain traits or skills. A moral principle (henceforth, principle D), which can be used to distinguish permissible from impermissible discrimination, asserts that persons should not be excluded from holding an office or performing a task on the grounds that they have or lack traits that are irrelevant to the effective execution of the task or the duties of the office. According to principle D, we must determine whether possessing a property, P, either is necessary for performing the task competently or makes a contribution to the task's competent performance. This is to determine whether P is *relevant* for the task. If P is relevant, we may use a person's possession of P (in conjunction with other traits) as a criterion for selecting persons to perform the task, and relying on this criterion constitutes permissible discrimination against persons who do not possess P. If, however, P is not relevant, then the possession of P should not be used as a criterion for selection, and the use of it to eliminate some candidates from an office constitutes morally wrong discrimination.

But determining the relevance of a property for a task is not always a

purely empirical matter and so is not always easy. Deciding whether a
property is relevant often depends on contentious philosophical claims and
value judgments. Further, the description of the task to be done is often
value-laden. Judgments about the moral permissibility of differential treatment arrived at by the application of principle D are therefore logically
dependent on other judgments of a political, philosophical, or moral nature.
This implies not only that caution is needed in the application of principle
D, but also that it cannot stand on its own.

Principle D can be used, apparently straightforwardly, to resolve questions about sexual and racial discrimination. Both race and gender are
relevant properties for the job of playing Harriet Tubman in a movie, if we
value the kind of authenticity required in a role model. And gender, we
might say, is "logically" relevant for the tasks of wet nurse and sperm
donor.[4] But gender and race are irrelevant for the task of diagnosing and
treating disease; hence discriminating on the basis of gender or race in
medical school admissions is wrong. Yet there are complications. Consider
the college-level teaching of women's studies courses.[5] One view is that
gender is not a qualification; intelligent men having the proper academic
training might well be able to teach women's studies or feminist scholar-
ship and do a good job. Perhaps a man has proven himself by having
studied under a renowned feminist or by publishing in the field. And on a
Kantian view of personhood, in which sex does not play an essential role
in structuring experience, there is room to argue that men *qua* persons can
sufficiently understand women *qua* persons and empathize genuinely with
their experiences, so as to be able to teach women's studies courses competently.

The alternative view is that being a woman (or female) is either necessary for teaching these courses well or contributes enormously to their
success, so that courses taught by men pale beside them. A man teaching
women's studies material to women in particular is suspicious; he might
perpetuate in the classroom the male dominance that the content of these
courses should defuse. Further, men are unable to teach what they do not
understand, and they do not, perhaps cannot, understand many of women's
experiences, for either biological or social reasons. The credibility of a male
professor who purports to grasp the subtle phenomenology of women's
lives will be low and his courses will suffer, because "menstruation, vaginal

penetration, lesbian sexual practices, birthing, nursing, and menopause are bodily experiences men cannot have."[6]

This reminder about biological differences between women and men might entail that men are unable to teach a certain kind of women's studies course, say, one devoted to the psychological meanings of the female body in Western culture. But many women, too, have not had all the experiences in the above list. Anyway, the reminder does not entail that men could not teach, as another example, the moral and political branches of feminist theory, unless being able to experience these things were required for competently understanding the categories of moral and political discourse. But the reminder is problematic. Men by definition cannot experience lesbian sexuality, but from that tautology alone nothing interesting necessarily follows. The question is still left open whether the experiences that men can have in sex (performing oral sex on a woman; being caressed by a woman) are sufficiently similar to the experiences lesbians have during sex (performing oral sex on a woman; being caressed by a woman), so that it will not be far from the truth to assert that men and women understand each other and effectively communicate about the pleasures of sex. Men cannot experience vaginal penetration; but they can experience anal penetration; perhaps the acts are sufficiently alike for men to have enough feel for what women experience during coitus.

Whatever we make of this particular debate, it forces us to recognize that we must take complicating factors into account in determining the relevance of properties for a task. Here is the lesson: depending on the meaning we assign to "adequately understanding" women's experiences and "competence" in teaching, principle D is consistent with the view that men can sufficiently grasp women's experiences and so adequately teach women's studies *and* with the view that men can do neither. But a decision as to what kind of understanding is required by a teacher for a certain level or sort of competence does not rest only on empirical facts about the job of teaching, but also on a comprehensive social philosophy of the purposes and nature of education.

Consider another example. Teaching could be characterized narrowly as the task of the "transmission of knowledge," but we can also describe a teacher's task in a broader way, as the "transmission of knowledge and the providing of a role model." Race and gender are properties that are either relevant or irrelevant under the narrow description of the teacher's task: irrelevant if successful transmission involves only the teacher's speaking and the students' hearing the knowledge, but relevant if transmission implies a higher standard of success—say, were black students to give their full attention, their hearing, more reliably to black teachers. But gender and race are always relevant properties under the broader description of a teacher's task, for a black or a woman cannot avoid, for logical reasons, being a black or a woman role model for black or women students; a white male can be an effective role model of a courageous and smart person, but he could not be a role model of a courageous and smart black woman. How a task is described influences what properties will turn out to be relevant to its performance. And how we *should* describe the task, narrowly or broadly, depends on a variety of considerations, including the purposes of education and the needs or rights, if any, of students for role models. The application of principle D to distinguish between permissible and impermissible differential treatment requires that we be able to articulate and support our views on other, clearly fundamental normative issues.

Receptionists and Models

The angry and disappointed rhinoceros—a big, ugly thing sporting a tiny necktie and a repulsive, malodorous snout—did not get the job. As the personnel director explains to the rhino, matter-of-factly, "The bunny did not get the job because the bunny is cute. The bunny got the job because the bunny knows WordPerfect."[7] Maybe things aren't that simple. The bunny might have been hired because the bunny was sexually provocative and the rhino ugly, while the bunny's knowledge of WordPerfect (whether true or false) was advanced as the publicly acceptable reason for hiring the bunny over the rhino. Principle D might have been violated. Or maybe the bunny did get the job because the bunny knew WordPerfect, but the bunny knew WordPerfect only because at an earlier time the bunny was already cute, and the rhino did not know WordPerfect because the younger rhino was repulsive. When animals were being selected to receive training in WordPerfect, there was a tendency to favor giving training to cute animals; or when the bunny and the rhino were being taught WordPerfect, the sexually pleasing bunny got more attention than the ugly rhino and so came to master that skill more adequately. Impermissible discrimination occurred at that earlier stage: being cute or ugly bears no relevance to the task of learning how to process words. Or maybe the bunny was hired because the bunny apparently knew WordPerfect and the rhino not, but those who judged the applicants' skills ranked the bunny higher than the rhino at least in part under the subliminal influence of the bunny's cuteness or sex appeal. This is wrongful discrimination, too; an evaluation of ability should not be based on cuteness, gender, race, or sexual orientation.

These things happen; not just to rhinos, but to homely humans as well. Elementary school teachers believe that attractive students are smarter and more likely to be academically successful; they then treat the attractive students favorably, making their beliefs self-fulfilling prophecies.[8] Students, for their part, think attractive teachers are better teachers.[9] We often attribute socially desirable personality traits (sincere, safe, sexy, interesting) to those who are physically attractive and believe they lead better, more successful lives (are good marriage partners).[10] We also, however, attribute negative qualities to the attractive as well, including vanity, egoism, and a propensity to engage in extramarital sex.[11] Physically attractive women (men) are more likely to receive help from a stranger than are unattractive women (men), and attractive women are the least solicited for help by both male and female strangers.[12] The writing ability of the attractive is judged superior to that of the unattractive.[13] And, with exceptions, the physically attractive are treated more leniently as defendants when experimental subjects in a mock jury reach verdicts and fix sentences.[14] In the determination, either by a jury or judge, of a punishment to be meted out to a guilty defendant, discrimination on the basis of sex or race is undoubtedly wrong, which is what we expect from a straightforward application of principle D. An equally ordinary application of principle D also entails that discrimination in the severity of punishments on the basis of appearance is wrong.

That discrimination in assigning grades or fixing sentences occurs unintentionally or unconsciously does not mean it is permissible or even excusable. Once we find out, as we all do, the facts about the effects of the physical attractiveness of others on our behavior toward them and acknowledge we have these tendencies, we seem to have an obligation to prevent ourselves from acting on them in sensitive contexts. Yet the interesting question remains: how much more can be said? In what other areas of life might we judge discrimination against the unattractive or, more generally, on the basis of physical attractiveness, to be wrong? On what considerations would these judgments depend?

On L. Duane Willard's view, to assign grades or punishments on the basis of attractiveness is wrongful discrimination, but using attractiveness to pick people to be advertising models, television personalities, flight attendants, and receptionists is okay.[15] Willard bases his judgments about discrimination on principle D: "where these things [looks] have nothing to do with . . . performance of tasks, we recognize the unfairness of using them as decision criteria for selection" (686–87). Willard therefore agrees that most cases of discrimination in employment on the basis of gender, race, and appearance are wrong. Still, Willard believes that principle D does allow discrimination on the basis of attractiveness for these particular jobs. On his view, it would be wrong to exclude blacks *tout court* from the job of airline host or office receptionist, but not wrong to exclude unattractive blacks (or whites). Willard offers no argument for this conclusion beyond the bare assertion that attractiveness *is* required for the job. In light of our analysis of "relevance," this is insufficient.

There is certainly a tendency to prefer to hire physically attractive persons as receptionists. I do not mean that as a matter of fact all employers always prefer to hire attractive receptionists, and not that all receptionists and other office workers (secretaries, typists) are attractive. Still, the applicant pool from which employers select receptionists and other office personnel contains a large number of young women (discrimination has occurred before this stage), and most of these women have been encouraged from their earliest days to care about their appearance. (The pressure women experience to be concerned with appearance has been discussed at great length by contemporary feminists.)[16] An employer, then, would not have to engage in much discrimination to end up with an office full of sexually appealing women. But that the applicant pool contains many young and attractive women is also in part a response to the fact that the hiring of such women for these posts has been a common practice, one having deep social and cultural roots. Is the practice justified?

Suppose we describe the tasks of a receptionist in a narrow way: to answer the telephone, take and relay messages, call out for lunch, keep trouble at bay, and attend to the comfort of office visitors. Physical, sexual attractiveness is not required for, nor does it contribute to, efficiency in doing these things and is therefore not relevant. Similar reasoning applies straightaway to the relevance of physical attractiveness for being a flight attendant or nurse, jobs done in the recent past by young, unmarried, sexually attractive women. The reasoning also applies to the use of attractiveness in the selection of persons to be advertising models or news broadcasters. As much as we enjoy watching attractive men and women try to sell us automobiles or read the news to us (our enjoyment in watching advertisements or news shows with attractive models *is* the prejudice), I cannot discern a rational connection between being attractive and performing these jobs effectively. Attractiveness might, however, be relevant for being a photographer's model in the making of erotic photographs. Because pornography is meant to be sexually arousing, and the ability of pornography to induce arousal depends on the attractiveness of its personnel, then as long as the production of pornography itself is permissible, principle D implies that not hiring unattractive persons is not wrongful discrimination.

One might defend the use of attractiveness as a criterion for the jobs of receptionist and flight attendant by claiming either that cleanliness and neatness are relevant, and attractiveness is a sign of or contributes to these traits, or that having the social skill to be friendly to people, especially strangers, is required in these jobs, and attractiveness is a sign of that ability. In both cases, however, some property other than attractiveness is being used as a selection criterion; and in both cases the nomic connection between attractiveness and the relevant traits is not strong enough to justify using attractiveness by itself as an indicator of competence. I doubt there is a real correlation, as opposed to a stereotypical correlation, between being attractive and being punctual, neat, empathetic, patient, and helpful.[17] Further, to the extent that the attractive are more friendly than the unattractive, this might be due to earlier differential treatment, in the same way that the cute bunny received more stroking from others than did the rhino when they were young. Even if it is permissible to use attractiveness now as a reliable indicator of the truly relevant properties, other discrimination must be attended to.

Principle D, however, would permit discrimination on the basis of attractiveness were we to construe the receptionist's task in a broader way. For example, we could say that the comfort of office visitors includes their pleasure in being in the presence of a physically attractive person. In this case, being attractive is built into the task and so is necessarily a relevant property. (Whether attractiveness in a receptionist is a quality that brings delight is a function of the tastes of the client pool.) Or perhaps the job includes fulfilling the general duty, which all employees have, to do whatever is helpful in maximizing the volume of business, in which case to the extent that clients are influenced, even unconsciously, by front office impressions, attractiveness is relevant. Further, a male employer who hires attractive women to work in his office might have his own comfort in mind, not only that of male office visitors, and would justify his hiring practices in similar terms: how his firm fares depends on how his mood fares, and his mood benefits from being surrounded by beautiful, sexy women.[18] The bunny is hired for her cuteness, although the reason given is that she knows WordPerfect (which might be true).

To assert a general duty of employees to do *anything* that is helpful in promoting business is unconvincing; at least, that claim erases the line between an employee who works for wages under the terms of a contract and a slave. Having a job-related obligation to attend to the needs of office visitors—giving tissues to a sneezing customer—does not mean having a duty to attend to all their needs. Even if part of the job of receptionist is to help promote business, and so to do *more* than simply not chase business away, it does not follow that if doing so maximizes business, a receptionist must sleep with clients or engage in deliberate flirtation. The point is that moral deliberation is required to set or remove limits on the scope and description of the task. Physical attractiveness might be relevant under the various broad descriptions of the task of receptionist we have been considering, and so may be used as a criterion. But justifying this stance entails granting to employers the right to perpetuate, for the sake of business, the institutional sexism that derives from or is constituted by the emphasis we have traditionally placed on attractiveness as an informal, real but unstated, job qualification for women.

If the production of erotic photographs and films, which often involves hiring men and women to engage in sex, is permissible, no further debate is possible about whether the job description should entail that the personnel be willing to engage in sex as a condition of being hired. Refusing to hire people who will not have sex in front of a camera is not wrongful discrimination, since that willingness is a relevant property. The Meese Commission rejected this reasoning, arguing that the making of pornography involved illegal "sex discrimination": hiring people to make pornography involves ordering them to engage in sex to "get or keep" a job.[19] But because in the making of pornography having sex *is* the job, the commission's supplementary concern that the making of pornography involves prostitution is more to the point. The commission ignores the difference between an employer's insistence that a woman sleep with him, on pain of losing her secretarial job, where her engaging in sex with him is not related to her secretarial tasks, and an employer's insistence that a woman sleep with him because she was hired to do exactly that in a pornographic film. If this employer insisted, on pain of her losing *that* job, that she sleep with him apart from her contractual duties, off the set, that would be sex discrimination in the commission's sense. The difference between these cases is that the secretary's sleeping with her boss has no moral, and hence no logical, connection to her job, if it is morally improper to devise a secretary's job description to include that activity; while the model's sleeping with her boss in front of the camera has a logical relation to her job, since devising her job description so that it does not include "sexual activity" is impossible.

Catharine MacKinnon recognizes this point, admitting that women with jobs such as topless dancer might have no or few grounds for complaint if customers come on to them sexually.[20] But a secretary should not have to experience sexual advances, since we do not accept a job description that includes her providing sexual services. As MacKinnon says about the topless dancer, "if the sexual dimension . . . is *properly* job-related, it would be difficult to argue that the employee did not consent to it." Nevertheless, it is still both possible and reasonable to claim it is *not* a logical requirement of topless dancing that a woman allow herself to be the object of sexual advances. A harsh value judgment is required to conclude that being willing to put up with the advances of drunk men is a relevant property for this task and that it is perfectly legitimate not to hire women who would, by their physical appearance or personality, obstruct these advances. Hence the house rule could very well be "look, but don't touch *or* ask."

BEAUTY   185

MacKinnon also mentions the case of a woman who lost her job as waitress in a bar because her breasts were too small.[21] The question of whether having a certain size bosom is relevant for the job of cocktail waitress is similar to the question of whether being attractive is relevant for the job of receptionist. If we describe the job of waitress narrowly, the answer is no; the size of a woman's bosom has no bearing on how well she carries beer and food from here to there. But if we describe the job broadly, to include providing visual pleasure to the male customers of the establishment, then bosom size and attractiveness count. The waitress, according to MacKinnon, asserted to the New York State Human Rights Commission that a breast-size criterion of employment is *both* arbitrary and sexist. Although the waitress believes she is making two separate claims, they are not independent; her belief that the bosom requirement is arbitrary, that is, not related logically to job performance, depends, for its force, on the claim that the practice is offensive or sexist. Someone who denied that preferring waitresses to be sexually appealing is morally objectionable would not judge the bosom requirement arbitrary.

Money

Is it wrong for employers to rely on (or take advantage of) the fact that front office impressions that depend on attractiveness and subliminal sexual messages influence how business fares? Is it wrong to hire attractive waitresses to make heterosexual male customers happy? To believe that attractiveness should not be used as a selection criterion is to look forward to a society in which as many women sit in the clients' waiting room as men, and as many people, or more, who are not moved by looks and sexual appeal as are; a society in which no reason exists to hire sexy women for these jobs, attractive women can find rewarding work elsewhere, no longer ghettoed in the front office, and women do not compete with each other for jobs on the basis of looks. The view that it is not wrong to rely on front office impressions expresses a more relaxed attitude toward the fact that receptionists can be influential with clients this way. Proponents of this view recommend doing nothing to curtail the emphasis society places on the attractiveness of women as members of the workforce. The position might admit that it is crude for a firm to rely on a woman's sexual appearance to promote business, whether in sales or in the front office; yet what matters is whether the parties have freely consented to the arrangement.

The opposition between these two views is reminiscent of debates over different conceptions of economic or property rights. One side fears that failing to hire attractive women, in a social context in which appearance counts, is economic suicide; that factor is taken as providing enough moral reason not to call for or engage in unconventional hirings. The assumption is that the economic rights of today's businesses, and those who depend on their viability, have priority over the welfare rights of future generations of women. The other side assumes either that there are no such economic rights to begin with or that these rights do not always trump the welfare needs of others. Willard sees that discussing wrongful discrimination in employment leads eventually to the question of the scope and content of property rights: he invites us to contemplate what we should conclude about an employer who does not hire an otherwise qualified black person, on the grounds that doing so would hurt business, or one who refuses, on the same grounds, to hire an otherwise qualified homely woman (683 n. 7). This problem can be framed in two ways. A businessman would like to abide by principle D and admits that hiring the qualified black or homely woman would be right in *that* sense, but points out that doing so would conflict with his economic interests if potential customers avoided his store. In this case, the businessman is trying to justify an *exception* to principle D. Alternatively, the conflict can be seen as lying *within* principle D, which is pitted against itself: because how his business fares depends in part on the race of the holder of this job, race is just as relevant as other traits. Regardless of how the problem is framed, the view that discrimination in hiring for jobs on the basis of looks is, or is not, wrongful rests not only on assumptions about not only the effect of attractiveness on efficiency, but also on contentious notions in political theory.

This point is illustrated by another kind of case. Willard claims that a homeowner who has an extra room in his house is guilty of wrongful discrimination if he declines to let the room to a person merely because the would-be tenant is ugly (687). I want to discuss, for now, a weaker claim that is entailed by Willard's, namely, a landlord who declines to let a flat in a separate apartment building to a homely person engages in wrongful discrimination. This claim is more plausible because the landlord doesn't have the excuse that he would, on a daily basis, have to see and associate with the ugly tenant. How does the judgment about the landlord fit with Willard's view that a businessman who hires attractive women as receptionists is *not* acting wrongly? The two judgments are, perhaps, perfectly consistent with each other: in the receptionist case, the employer claims that an unattractive receptionist would chase business away or not help business, so attractiveness is needed for job effectiveness, while in the leasing case the landlord cannot claim that the ugly tenant would hurt business by driving renters away from other units. Furthermore, physical appearance has no connection with an ability to pay the rent. This way of making the two judgments compatible is vulnerable to variations in background conditions; for if other renters did react to the homely tenant as they react to noisy tenants, or if they react to homely tenants the same way office visitors purportedly react to homely receptionists, then not being homely might be a trait landlords have a right to take into account. On the other hand, maybe the two judgments are inconsistent from the start. After all, a landlord is just a businessman. The property rights that allow one businessman to refuse to hire homely women as receptionists are likely extensive enough to permit a landlord to dispose of his units as he sees fit. Whether the potential renters he dislikes are ugly, gay, black, or Jewish, he has the right to exclude from inhabiting his apartments those people he finds viscerally revolting.

A judgment about the moral permissibility of discrimination in the landlord case can be reached only if one has taken some stand on the scope and content of property rights. Proponents of one view of these rights, minimal liberalism, would permit the landlord to dispose of his flats however he wanted, would allow a businessman to refuse to hire blacks if customers would be lost, and would not lose a second's sleep over the fate of the homely receptionist wannabe. For this minimal liberal, discriminatory hiring practices are, at worst, contrary to self-inte.est (if the black who was not hired was competent), but not immoral.[22] Whether the minimal liberal will succeed in convincing the landlord to rent to the ugly or gay person will depend on background conditions; the pressure to lease to gays, for example, might be felt only when many people have left town and the vacancy rate is high. Other conceptions of rights, property and otherwise, would not rank the visceral revulsion of the landlord nearly as high as the needs of people for shelter of their liking, so discrimination against the homely and the gay would be at least morally, even if not everywhere legally, wrong.

Personal Relations

Willard thinks that relying on physical attractiveness as a criterion in selecting people for personal relationships is not wrongful discrimination. Can this common judgment withstand questioning? The medievals sincerely asked, under the influence of Augustine, "whether sexual intercourse with a beautiful wife is a greater sin than with a repulsive one."[23] The trick is to avoid being flippant (sure it's more sinful; with an attractive wife a man thinks more about pleasure than procreation) and to concentrate on the intellectual task: to challenge our confidence in the rightness of allowing attractiveness to play an important role in our personal lives. No one will suggest the Stalinist horror that the knife or drugs of an Eryximachean physician be used on stubborn discriminators to effect a correcting re-eroticization. But perhaps other, milder arrangements would help.

Do not stop the inquiry before it begins by declaring, "there are no ugly women [or men], only lazy ones,"[24] as if to suggest that all the unattractive need to do, in order to be loved or desired, is to make the effort. No discrimination would exist to worry about, because we can all be good-looking (enough). Of course, some guys, drinking beer by the six-pack while watching Monday Night Football, let themselves go to pot, and are to blame for their own repulsiveness. But the advice is disingenuous, meant only to encourage women to buy cosmetics and clothing—that's what not being lazy about one's appearance means in this sexist message. And do not repeat, again to stop the inquiry, that beauty is in the eye of the beholder, and so for a given person, no matter what he or she looks like, at least one other person in the world exists, or plenty more, who finds him or her sufficiently attractive, if not absolutely beautiful, for love or sex or friendship. That dry and dusty chestnut has been refuted countless times by both the grocer on the corner and social psychology; even if what counts as physical attractiveness varies from culture to culture and from person to person in a culture, standards of beauty among people in a culture are not radically subjective but substantially overlap.[25]

Physical attractiveness has been found by social scientists to be an important factor—something that matters, even if not solely determinative—when people choose friends, lovers, and marriage partners.[26] Whether one initiates a relationship with a person partially depends on one's estimate of the likelihood of being warmly received by that person, in which case one does not always approach the most attractive (as John Dryden put it, "None but the brave deserves the fair"). And people who pair off into couples often exhibit similarity in attractiveness, which again implies that people do not always seek the most attractive mate *simpliciter*. Even in this case, however, selection of a partner still occurs at least in part on the basis of attractiveness.[27] The studies indicate that people prefer, value, desire, and seek attractiveness in their intimates—even if, since only a few of us are raving beauties, most of us cannot be fully successful.

There is another qualification: men, more than women, prefer their intimates or mates to be attractive. Even though for both men and women attractiveness is not the most important factor in the selection of intimates (kindness is frequently mentioned as more important, but the experimental subjects might be paying lip service to that ideal), and even though women think attractiveness is important (the distribution curves of men and women for this propensity overlap greatly), the attractiveness of the object of one's attention is regularly found to be more significant for men than women. (This difference also seems to hold between gay men and lesbian women.)[28] Men, it is often said, have attributes other than physical beauty that heterosexual women are concerned with:

> To the extent that men control more power and resources than do women ... men can afford the luxury of picking partners on the basis of their physical appearance. For women of lower power or fewer resources, choices may need a more pragmatic base.[29]

To oversimplify: men select among women, for dating, romantic relations, and marriage, strongly on the basis of their beauty and sexual appeal, or prefer to do so, even if they also look for other traits; while women, even if they, too, keep an eye on the looks of prospective intimates, pick among men on the basis of material resources, wealth, power, prestige, industriousness, and intelligence.[30] As MacKinnon wryly makes the point, women barter their sexuality and beauty for support in getting men to marry them for their looks, or they barter these things for support, instead, at the office, in getting a man to hire them for their looks.[31] Of course, the meaning of the purported fact is open to interpretation: do men prefer beauty in relationships because they are thinking about women as the recipients of their sexual, romantic love, while women are thinking about the reproductive consequences of sexual activity and hence pragmatically about subsequent needs? Or are women as sexually aroused by wealth, power, and so forth, as men are by physical attractiveness? Further, academics have been doing battle over the cause of this apparent gender difference, some theorists citing evolutionary mechanisms, others emphasizing culture and socialization.[32] The latter predict that if women were not so economically dependent on men, if women had their own plentiful resources, then the gender difference in mate selection criteria would decrease, since women, too, would be able to focus on attractiveness[33]— and men would have a reason to focus on the income of women.

Just because we frequently take physical attractiveness into account in selecting persons as intimates does not establish that attractiveness *is* relevant; it establishes only that we treat it as relevant or act as if it were relevant. The issue, then, is whether the attractiveness of a person has any bearing on how well he or she could be a friend, lover, spouse, or sex partner. In order to show that attractiveness is a trait relevant for fulfilling these roles, we must exhibit the way it connects up with the nature and purpose of these relationships. But conceptual analyses and philosophical treatments of "friend" and "spouse," in particular, do not imply that physical attractiveness is required for carrying out these roles or even for fulfilling them in a more than mediocre way. Friends and spouses are persons we confide in, trust, and share experiences or pastimes with, and on whom we depend for companionship, help, support, and solace. Attractiveness has no plausible link with these central functions of personal relationships. Willard's view that attractiveness is properly a basis on which to select people as friends and spouses has this obstacle to overcome.

Willard does not explain how physical attractiveness is a relevant property. But he does provide a reason to think that relying on attractiveness is permissible:

it would seem ... absurd to claim unjust aesthetic discrimination in areas such as friendship, love and/or marriage. ... Certainly justice need not be all that 'blind'; especially if we are to have any reasonable degree of freedom. (685)

Willard might be arguing that because the nature, meaning, and purpose of personal relationships are not fixed or objective, but determined by the individuals having them, there is in principle no limit on what might be a relevant property; people must be free, then, to determine for themselves what traits they wish to treat as relevant. These properties, as a result, *are* relevant, even if only subjectively. Using attractiveness in the selection of persons to be our intimates is, on this reading of Willard's argument, an ordinary application of principle D. But the spirit of the argument seems to be different. Willard is not proposing that physical attractiveness is relevant; instead, he admits that it is *not* relevant. His view is that people may still use it as a criterion, despite its not being relevant, since doing so is warranted by considerations of freedom. That is, Willard sees the use of a physical attractiveness criterion in relationships as a justifiable *exception* to principle D, not as an application of it. Understood this way, Willard's argument acknowledges the point that judgments about the permissibility of discrimination presuppose other moral or political judgments. Here the value defended is a "reasonable" amount of freedom.

Can Willard's argument be extended to the use of sex/gender and race in selecting persons to be our sex partners, friends, and spouses? Race seems clearly irrelevant, in some intrinsic sense, for these roles; but perhaps, *pace* Willard, people should be free to act according to arbitrary racial preferences in their private lives. Sex/gender also seems intrinsically irrelevant for friendship and marriage. But whether it is relevant for sex partners is a more puzzling question. It is a "serious injustice," as Freud said,[34] for society to make it hard for homosexuals (and members of other sexual minorities) to find compatible sex partners; what follows is that persons must in general be free to select sexual partners on the basis of many things, including sex/gender. Whether persons would *want* to do so in an egalitarian future is perplexing.[35] But should we be convinced by Willard's style of argument in the first place? If attractiveness may be used for personal relations, despite its irrelevance, in virtue of the value of freedom, then some of Willard's judgments about other practices are in jeopardy. For example, on some views of how to preserve a "reasonable" amount of freedom, employers who refuse to hire blacks, for whatever reason, are not engaging in wrongful discrimination—their own freedom is otherwise lost. Similarly, the claim that for a landlord not to lease an apartment to an unattractive person is wrongful discrimination is now vulnerable to the rebuttal that if the landlord is to have any "reasonable" freedom, the landlord must be able to lease as he sees fit. The general idea is that Willard has not appreciated all the ways that freedom, if it is to be taken into account, could be taken into account.

Freedom, I suspect, is not the ultimate issue, anyway. What is the value of being able to select on the basis of what suits our fancy? Consider again Willard's example of a homeowner who does not want to lease the extra room in his house to an ugly person. On what grounds is this, as Willard says, wrongful? The freedoms involved in property and economic rights seem to matter little; they do not figure largely into the consciousness or thinking of the homeowner, even if, when pressed, he eventually shouts, "it's my house!" Indeed, a contradiction exists between Willard's judgments that not leasing the room to an ugly person is wrongful, but it is permissible to scorn the ugly by arranging that one's friends be attractive. The reason for thinking that our preferences in relationships may be acted on has something to do with the fact that we spend a good deal of time in the presence of, conversing and sharing space with, the people who are our intimates. This is exactly why we should be lenient, not judgmental, on the homeowner; he does not want to spend his days around someone whose company he will not enjoy.

But why is discrimination in either case okay, since none of what people do with friends depends on their attractiveness, and the ugly renter, we should assume, pays the bills on time? The answer is that being in the presence of beauty, with or without its sexual penumbra, brings people such bodily and spiritual joy, and is such an inspiration to persons to reach, to search, and to attain, that for the sake of gaining this, their own experiential good, they cannot be morally faulted for avoiding or neglecting the unattractive—whose existence, impressed on them by their presence, can only remind them, and confirm the bleakest view they have, of the meanness of the universe. This is why being free to prefer and pursue the physically attractive, as well as the morally and intellectually attractive, is valuable: it allows people to inject the uplifting ecstasy, the rush of splendor, into their otherwise humdrum lives. The problem is whether the value that accrues to persons, as individual seats of experience, from being in the presence of physical, moral, or intellectual beauty is weighty enough to overcome doubts about the morality of discriminatory practices in the whole range of personal relationships. How much ought people to sacrifice of their pleasure in beauty, so that those lacking it do not feel painfully excluded?

Think about a similar issue. Some lesbian sadomasochists derive sexual pleasure from pornographic depictions of their preferred activity, so they oppose censorship, even when proposed by feminists. Here is a reply to these lesbians:

> to the extent that pornography both maintains a normative order that legitimizes the eroticization of violence, and to the extent that it constitutes even a remote cause of violent, nonconsensual, nondesired sex, the "rights" of such adherents to acquire pornographic products important for their sexual gratification must take second place. . . . [S]uch rights to pleasure must surely be subordinated to the more fundamental right to be free from serious harm.[36]

The argument is highly qualified.[37] It doesn't come right out and state that pornography does legitimize violence against women, and it supposes only that pornography might be a remote cause of rape. The authors do claim that "to the extent," even a little bit, these things are true, that would be enough warrant for restricting or censoring pornography. Because the argument is so qualified, deciding which side is more persuasive will not turn on whether we grant to the lesbians a literal "right" to sexual pleasure. Simply recognizing that sexual pleasure, with or without its connection to love, is an important human good will yield the nearly intractable conflict between advancing or protecting the good of some people and advancing or protecting the good of others. At least, the claim in the passage that the lesbians' pleasure "surely" takes a backseat is suspiciously overstated. Many persons would give the pleasure of the lesbians more weight, while acknowledging that choosing between these two goods, if we must, would be agonizing. So whose good—the pleasure of those people who appreciate beauty in their companions; the happiness of those people who are unattractive—should prevail? I don't know. But I would have better thoughts about not sacrificing beauty in relationships if there were ways of making the practice less oppressive. Later I suggest how this might be done.

Arousal

Suppose someone asserted that relying on physical attractiveness as a criterion in personal relationships was justifiable because attractiveness is a reliable sign of the possession of other properties that are relevant. If we focus on friendship, this is a strange claim. It implies that there are traits relevant to the tasks involved in friendship that are both appreciably hidden to an attentive observer yet reliably correlated with physical attractiveness, and hence can be revealed by attractiveness. But that a person is trustworthy and cares about the welfare of others is not inscrutable; trust and concern can and do prove themselves directly. Further, to the extent that genuine, as opposed to opportunistic, concern *is* hidden, we do not verify it by looking for attractiveness; to the contrary, we must get beyond the dazzling attractiveness. Real concern, dependability, and trustworthiness have their own tests, their own proofs, part of which is constancy over time, part of which is rigor in the face of annoyance and aggravation, none of which relies on a link with appearance.

But regarding sexual relationships, physical attractiveness might be a sign of something else, and therefore be epistemically relevant. Consider this evolutionary story. Suppose that reproductive capability per se is a relatively hidden property in that there is no quick, direct test by which we can evaluate a person as "likely to be reproductively successful." Also suppose that people with high reproductive ability also possessed more easily observable traits (call them Q) that are nomically, even genetically, tied with reproductive capability. In concert, Q properties might also contribute to reproductive success, although they do not exhaust its biological foundation. Or perhaps Q both contributes to and is a sign of general health, which itself contributes to and is a sign of reproductive capacity. Suppose, finally, that in contrast to some heterosexuals who were less moved by Q, other heterosexuals were strongly erotically aroused by sensing (seeing, touching, smelling) Q and as a result desired to embrace, and engage in intercourse with, the bearers of Q. Because Q is nomically linked with reproductive capability, persons having a stronger desire-arousal response to Q and its bearers and who accordingly engaged in intercourse with bearers of Q were more reproductively successful than those who responded less powerfully to Q. The link between Q in one person and sexual arousal in another would eventually become predominant in the population.

For this process to work, persons who experience arousal and desire in response to perceiving Q must find the sexual acts and intercourse engaged in with bearers of Q to be more pleasurable and satisfying than intercourse with persons lacking Q. If in response to the desire and arousal created by Q, people were instigated to engage in sex that turned out to be boring, if Q aroused them but led to frustration, they would discover that Q was deceptive and intercourse with bearers of Q would decrease. Any Q that elicited desire and arousal without subsequent pleasure and satisfaction would not be a Q that became widespread in the population. But Q itself might produce pleasure and satisfaction in ways unavailable to those lacking Q. Of course, the desire and arousal in response to Q are themselves pleasurable states. Also, the more powerful the desire and the arousal are in response to Q, the more pleasure there will be when sexual activity does occur. Q is more than a sign of pleasure to come; it is also a cause of that pleasure.

If so, Q (physical attractiveness) would be not only our epistemic handle on reproductive capacity, but also a label of the bearer's ability to provide sexual pleasure; physical attractiveness would be a relevant property for sexual activity. Further, preferences for the attractive in our other personal relationships, including friendship and marriage, might derive psychologically[38] or genetically from a more basic dependence of sexuality on attractiveness. The role of physical attractiveness as directly relevant for sexual activity is causally explained by its link with reproductive advantage. But persons did not initially perceive and judge Q or its bearers to be beautiful or attractive and then in virtue of this judgment were stimulated to have sex with them; instead, persons came to call "beautiful," in retrospect, just those traits Q, whatever they were, that induced desire and arousal and instigated pleasurable sex. What might have been true, phylogenetically, for the species, might also be true, ontogenetically, for the individual: those properties, whatever they turn out to be, that I eventually find myself responding to with desire and arousal, are the properties that I have also come to call "beautiful." Phenomenally, I sexually desire a person because he or she is beautiful; but Q is called "beautiful" because it causes desire.

That sexual arousal and pleasure greatly depend on physical attractiveness is almost a truism. Erotic literature and films, major network television programs, movies galore, and the romance novels that line the walls of bookstores abundantly testify to the connection between sexual pleasure and physical beauty. We asked earlier, Why do we want the touch of the other instead of our own touch? Russell Vannoy answers that question in a way germane to our present concerns:

> I am aroused because I am being touched by someone I find to be quite sexually attractive and whose body I would like to touch in turn. Desire does not escalate . . . unless I first find the flesh of the other to be the embodiment of sexual pleasure.[39]

I think our sexual experiences tend to confirm the connection between attractiveness, arousal, and pleasure, rather than expose Hollywood and Madison Avenue to be perpetrators of ideology or propaganda (in this case, anyway). The direct evidence of our experience sufficiently demonstrates that the attractiveness of our partner is a reliable sign that sex with that person will be pleasurable and that the attractiveness itself contributes to our satisfaction. Exceptions abound, of course. Visual beauty is not always a reliable sign of other sensory beauty; sometimes the taut and tanned body has a bad stench. Further, engaging in sex with those who do not possess much Q is often and strikingly pleasurable. The tendency for there to be a connection between beauty, arousal, and pleasure should not cause us to overlook the full range of rewarding experiences.

The puzzling question is whether this pattern is due to biology or socialization—or to what extent, and in what ways, it is due to one or the other. There are weaknesses in the simple evolutionary explanation of the role of physical attractiveness in sexuality. First, it does not nail down the case that those lacking Q could not provide as much sexual pleasure as bearers of Q, if arousal before sexual activity is not the only or major factor that makes sexual activity pleasurable. For example, recall Janice

Moulton's idea that the knowledge our partner has, of what kind of touch or act we like, matters in our satisfaction. Second, whether someone is aroused by Q will often be a function of that person's sexual state. If I have just engaged in satisfying sex, being in the presence of another instance of Q might have no effect on me; or if I have not engaged in sex for some time, I might find myself aroused by mediocre instances of Q or by those persons lacking Q. As David Hume pointed out centuries ago, the constant conjunction we experience mentally between being in the presence of an attractive person and being aroused works both ways; often, when sensing beauty, we then become aroused, but sometimes in already being aroused (or when horny), we reach the rash judgment that the object of our attention is more beautiful (or intelligent, or funny) than he or she really is.[40] Finally, the evolutionary account does not answer the deepest question, why there should have been, at the beginning, people for whom a connection already existed between Q and their desire-arousal state. If such people existed, they would multiply and become predominant. But the mystery is why they existed at all. Augustine is therefore free to imagine that Adam's prelapsarian sexual intercourse would have been executed by a purely voluntary erection, no matter what Eve looked like.

But alternative accounts of the connection between beauty, arousal, and pleasure as a cultural phenomenon brought about by the various instruments of socialization also seem unable to cast much light on the central puzzle about how physical attractiveness becomes linked to the other items. If standards of attractiveness are produced by historical and political forces and float free of the body, if the components of physical attractiveness, since they are the result primarily of cultural, not biological, processes, have little in common transculturally, then how does beauty, as differentially defined and fashioned in each culture, ever get latched on to such universals as the experiential aspects of desire, arousal, and pleasure? How one constellation of physical components in one society gets eroticized, while in some other society another constellation is eroticized, is a mystery. Hence neither approach answers the central question. If the socialization approach acknowledges even a few transcultural components of attractiveness (say, skin free of sores), this is all the evolutionist needs to get that research program started.[41] The insight of the sociologist is that each culture has its own special array of indicators of beauty; but the evolutionist can see these as embellishments of a set of core biological and hence universal components. The modifications due to culture might be extensive, if the core transcultural components make up only a small set of properties. Or culture could play a large role in establishing the components of attractiveness if the core traits fixed by biology were vague in their content ("skin free of sores" is open-ended).[42] A bit of essentialism survives, but the social constructivists also have their say.

The Beauty Hoax

Our discussion of the role of beauty in sex has been cheerful, even if prosaic and mechanical. But cynical Schopenhauer, for example, thought that the beauty of the object of sexual desire, as well as the excitement it provokes, was nature's way of tricking us. It dupes us into believing that the erotic love we feel for our beautiful beloved and the sexual activity love induces are for our own good as individuals, indeed are our highest good. But sex and love benefit only the species, for the good of which Nature uses us, stripping us clean of worldly possession and self-respect.[43] This God is weird, who resorts to deceptive beauty to enlist the aid of otherwise reluctant humans in His grand project, the ongoing work of creation. For Camille Paglia, sexual "desire is besieged on all sides by anxiety and doubt." Sexual activity, frightening in its sloppy, staining fleshiness and its symbolism of edibility, consumption, and destruction, is something we approach with "apprehension." It is only "beauty, an ecstasy of the eye, [that] drugs us and allows us to act. . . . It allows man to act by enhancing the desirability of what he fears."[44] We are tricked, lured into the fearful event by the power of beauty against which we are defenseless. As two Schopenhauerian moral theologians tell us, "sex pleasure has been ordained by God as an inducement to perform an act which is both disgusting in itself and burdensome in its consequences."[45] The Evil Demon is an ugly bastard.

The idea is intriguing and horrifying, that sexual acts are so intrinsically repugnant or dangerous that the encouragement of beauty and its promise of a moment of bliss to come are required to make sex happen. The puzzle is how something in itself disgusting and revolting could also be so pleasurable as to persuade people to do it. Paglia thinks beauty is a drug that knocks us senseless, makes us less able to appreciate the act's foulness. Or beauty is like Hume's horniness, an aphrodisiac that makes us inflate, overestimate, the merit of the object of desire. What happens when we come across Miss Absolute Beauty herself?

> So beautiful a nymph appears
> But once in twenty thousand years:
> By nature formed with nicest care,
> And, faultless to a single hair.

Of whom it is imagined, since we are under the spell of that most powerful potion, that

> No noisome whiffs, or sweaty streams,
> Before, behind, above, below,
> Could from her taintless body flow. . . .
> You'd swear, that so divine a creature
> Felt no necessities of nature. [46]

Miss Absolute Beauty is no Celia who shits, at least not the first time, or even the second, we have coffee with her.

Men and women know, no matter how much as desiring subject we try to deny it by focusing on the visible beauty of the other, and no matter how much we as desired object try to conceal it by magnifying our visible beauty, that beneath this layer lies the ugliness of the body, its repulsive odors and flavors, its repulsive warts and moles and lines and scars and fat and colored patches and other imperfections too legion to list and too depressing to contemplate much longer. We are all ugly. By our natures, if not by the Fall. Is this why we so desperately seek the sexual touch of another person, to feel beautiful at least momentarily? Not even Vanna White is Vanna White, although she tries hard, she and her staff of thousands in the dressing room.

> This creature on her silly pedestal
> Is not a goddess! All our venuses
> Are well aware of this; so, all the more,
> They try to hide their backstage scenery. [47]

Why is it that Paglia and the moral theologians think that beauty and pleasure conquer revulsion? On the one hand, arousing beauty compels us to the act but, on the other, the backstage body, disgusting and revolting, drives us away—which is to vanquish which? Paglia, who proffers the pessimism that men must be tricked into sex by beauty, optimistically imagines that beauty is sturdy enough to overcome the stench of the pits and crevices of the body. The *visual* beauty of the legs conquers the *olfactory* ugliness of what's between them. Or the visual beauty of the face transforms, by its immense power, the visual ugliness of other body parts into something neutral or even its opposite. But maybe nature's plan is not that beauty triumphs over the ugly, but that ugliness shuns and wards off, and properly so, the approach stimulated by beauty. What could determine whether we think of visual beauty as rightly vanquishing bodily corruption, thereby leading us into happy erotic love, or, instead, think of the body's depravity as rightly making futile the urgings of beauty? Perhaps that we are either sex-positive secular humanists or sex-negative Augustinian Christians.

The battle between visual beauty and olfactory ugliness is one aspect of the entanglement of pleasure and disgust in sex. Desire for a person in virtue of beauty conflicts with fear and revulsion. We can now appreciate that our perceptions of another person, *qua* object of our erotic attention, are fluid enough to slip back and forth between seeing the other as a cute bunny and seeing him or her as a lumpy rhino. The duck-rabbit of our sexual perceptions (recall the kiss or the resuscitation of figure 1) is clearly witnessed in the phenomenology of our visceral responses to the genitals, the anus, the mouth, those parts of the body that evoke both pleasure and nausea. No longer are we talking about the beauty of part A vanquishing, or not, the ugliness of some other part, B; instead, the beauty of A is entangled with the ugliness of A itself. There is a fine line that divides, on the one side, our being pulled by the beauty of the genitals, the anus, the mouth, aroused by them, riveted to them, yearning to merge our flesh with them by kissing and tasting and sensing them fully; and, on the other side, our being deeply disgusted by the sight, by the faintest whiff, by the most fleeting thought of these three dirty, bacteria-infested, slovenly parts of the body. As we walk this fine line, we watch ourselves fall on one side or the other, learning about the features of our lives that push us now one way, now the other.

Freud had a sense of this riddle and provided something of a solution:

> The fundamental processes which produce erotic excitation remain unaltered. The excremental is all too intimately and inseparably bound up with the sexual; the position of the genitals—*inter urinas et faeces*—remains the decisive and unchangeable factor. One might say here, varying a well-known saying of the great Napoleon: 'Anatomy is destiny.'[48]

The anus is both disgusting and pleasurable because: (1) it is disgusting *qua* anus, as the ending of the alimentary canal, but (2) it is pleasurable *qua* sexual part, since its manipulation, as a result of the proximity of the genitals and their neurology, brings pleasure. The answer is incomplete. Why are the genitals themselves both beautiful and disgusting? Freud does not quite permit the question:

> The genitals themselves have not taken part in the development of the human body in the direction of beauty: they have remained animal, and thus love, too, has remained in essence just as animal as it ever was.[49]

> It is worth remarking that the genitals themselves, the sight of which is always exciting, are nevertheless hardly ever judged to be beautiful; the quality of beauty seems, instead, to attach to certain secondary characteristics.[50]

That's false; we often talk about the beauty of the genitals, meaning it seriously when we compliment each other on the shape and dimensions of our penises and vulvae. But the sight and odor of the genitals can be for someone both pleasing and repulsive. How does the duck-rabbit occur here? A background of affection or love is not always or necessarily that which determines what we experience; and whether the other person is familiar to us or a stranger is not decisive. Freud wrongly emphasized the related difference between myself and the other: a person "scarcely finds the smell of *his own* excreta repulsive, but only that of other people."[51] Freud misses that we can experience the same duck-rabbit of pleasure/disgust toward both our own excreta and the excreta of others.

Nor have we begun to illuminate the most perplexing aspect of the entanglement of pleasure and disgust, the fact that disgust can cause pleasure, the repulsive can be beautiful, so that the fence between the ugly and beauty disintegrates, the entire territory becoming both arousing and disgusting. Sallie Tisdale, in response to seeing, in pornography, "a woman going down on a man, sucking his cock . . . , the man pulling away and shooting come across her face, the woman licking the come off her lips," felt, she exclaims, "a heady mix of disgust and excitement."[52] Tisdale has an experience of both disgust and excitement in ambiguous causal relation. The parts and the acts of sex not only become disgusting *because* they are exciting, as in Augustine, but also become exciting *because* they are disgusting, as in Woody Allen.

A fuddy-duddy might reply to this talk of bodily beauty and ugliness, in the manner of Pausanias, that the important matter is not to adjudicate the battle between olfactory ugliness and visual beauty, but to come down on the right side in the battle between the variable and unreliable physical attributes of human beings and their more constant and respectable psychological and ethical character: let's love each other not for our firm tushes, but in spite of our flabby tushes and in virtue of our sterling minds and characters. But this is just a hedge; for the underlying problem can be framed, instead, in terms of the battle between the beauty of character and the ugliness of character—the fly in the ointment is not the backstage body but the backstage mind. Does our moral and intellectual beauty or goodness attract others to us and vanquish their perception of our badness? Have we been able to conceal the bad components of our character well enough, with spiritual perfumes and ethical shoulder pads, so that our mental stench and flab are not too vivid? Make no bones about it; the badness in our characters undoubtedly surpasses the ugliness of our bodies. Our badness is disgusting enough to repel, to keep people from becoming devoted to us. To solve this problem, in turn, we would have to learn to love each other not in virtue of our beautiful souls, but in spite of our having none. But having already risen from loving on the basis of the beautiful body to loving on the basis of the beautiful soul, to what do we rise one more time? Maybe we should give up searching for any kind of beauty in each other, and love each other arbitrarily and without reasons.[53] Or maybe we should just admit, given the corruptness of our souls, that our fleeting, youthful physical beauty is our only beauty, and make the most of it while we can.

Nor will it do to pick on pornography for inducing people to overemphasize beauty. Pornography is *filled* with the physical beauty that resembles the beauty that springs up once in twenty thousand years. In light of this, it has been speculated that the beauty in pornography, together with the beauty that appears in network television, magazine advertisements, Hollywood movies, and pinup calendars, leads men and women to be critical of the appearance of their intimate partners, to be less satisfied with the looks of their mates and lovers.[54] There might be some truth here; depending on whether you live in New York or Bogalusa, it might take as long as a week to four months to come across the amount of beauty concentrated in a ninety-minute videotape. Still, the worry is overblown; enough dissatisfaction and regret of this kind is already generated by mundane features of daily life: the woman or man who lives in the adjoining flat or the person sitting at the next table in a restaurant; family dinners that include your spouse's sister, mother, or brother; picnics with coworkers, colleagues, fellow churchgoers; traveling by train, plane, or ship. All these provide abundant opportunity to make invidious comparisons. For the same reason, a woman's insecurity—"will he be thinking of them [pornography models] ... when he is making love to me?"[55]—results from a shortsighted case of scapegoating. If women really want to worry about the fantasies men are having during (before, after) sex, they can easily worry about the girl or guy next door, on the bus, at work, or the grocer on the corner. Not for nothing, and certainly not because pornography caused a person's eye to wander, did the shrewd author of the Decalogue tack on at the end: Thou shalt not covet thy neighbor's tush or significant other (Exodus 20:17).

The parade of beauty in photographic pornography does have something to teach us. This beauty is perfect visual beauty, unobstructed by every kind of ugliness. The beauty that appeals to the eye prevails, since the ugliness that attacks the nose or tongue is nowhere to be experienced. From the mixture in sex of beauty and disgust, of the arousing and repulsive, pornography screens out the nastiness, leaving the beauty as pure as it ever will be. To be more accurate, what remains is pure visual beauty united with the olfactory and gustatory beauties as imagined by the viewer—or with any ugliness the viewer wishes to imagine. As long as enough room exists in a pornographic depiction for input from the viewer's imagination, the acts are perfect, the personalities of the models are perfect, the odors and tastes are perfect. The appeal of pornography must in part be that it allows the creation of the perfect—the most beautiful or the most ugly—sexual encounters.[56]

Equality

If what we want out of sexual activity is sensual pleasure (not money or fame or revenge), we should probably look for at least two significant properties in potential partners: not just their beauty, although that matters, but also a willingness to do for or with us the sexual things we enjoy. Both traits contribute to our satisfaction, and when present together to a marked degree they make our sexual experiences intense, elegant, and ecstatic. The pundits and poets must decide which is worse: the bewitching exasperation of beauty without versatility and imagination or the cold efficiency of technique without resplendence.

Although he is speaking mostly about the use of the law in the public domain, the spirit of Michael Kinsley's attitude toward the situation of the unattractive is decidedly Tory:

> There are limits. . . . Should we compensate people for being ugly? . . . Should we insure against being unhappy in love? Probably not. Fate is too capricious and imaginative for any society, no matter how generous, to make up for the ways fate can find to make people miserable.[57]

We should not be so complacent about the role of beauty in our personal relationships. Several points can be made about modifications in our institutions and practices, changes that might make them less oppressive.

Elizabeth Rapaport has argued that erotic relationships would be more satisfying and less troublesome—we would not fear the dependency or loss of autonomy that intimate relations often involve—if human personality could develop in a way undistorted by "dysfunctional economic and social relations not just between the sexes but throughout social life."[58] As

a result of these distorting influences, "social status" becomes too important a factor in the formation and maintenance of erotic relationships.
(Some men want trophy wives; some women want only socially successful
lovers.) With the achievement of broader economic and social equality,
Rapaport thinks that

> we could grant our love on some basis other than the supposed absolute pre-
> eminence of the beloved[,] under conditions in which lovers did not seek
> pre-eminence according to social norms of attainment in those they loved.

Then what? If social status is eliminated as a trait influencing whom
we select as partners for erotic relationships, on what basis will such
discriminations be made?

> Love's eye could still seek and find the special qualities that lead to prefer-
> ment, draw affection and nourish the growth of personality in lovers. Human
> differences and variety in sensibility and qualities would still guide and
> motivate love-choices.

The "special qualities" by which we prefer some people over others are not
described by Rapaport. Indeed, given how wordy it is, her answer is empty.
The idea, I guess, is that in conditions of economic and social equality,
when status is no longer relevant, any other human properties would be
acceptable for preferring some persons as lovers. Rapaport's view thus
allows physical attractiveness to play a significant if not dominant role. No
"back to the garden," where looks are irrelevant.

Engels seems to reach the same conclusion. He proposes that whatever
occurs among persons in personal relationships is fine if their choices are
made freely, without coercion, and as long as the economic and political
domination to which Rapaport also objects is absent from their lives.

> Full freedom of marriage can ... only be generally established when the
> abolition of capitalist production and of the property relations created by it
> has removed all the accompanying economic considerations.... For then
> there is no other motive left except mutual inclination.[59]

The idea that personal relationships should be governed only by "mutual
inclination" was a long time coming; social and religious imperatives,

economic and other pragmatic considerations, and the wishes of parents directed the course of marriage. Now the idea is popular, even if we give only lip service to it. [60] Here is Bertrand Russell's version:

> The intrusion of the economic motive into sex is always in a greater or lesser degree disastrous. Sexual relations should be a mutual delight, entered into solely from the spontaneous impulse of both parties. [61]

After pernicious forms of duress have been eliminated, what remains; what is this "mutual inclination" and "spontaneous impulse"? Beauty would seem to persist unabated as a factor swaying people to form personal and erotic relationships here rather than there.

This implication of the views of Rapaport, Engels, and Russell seems plausible. Indeed, eliminating the coercion that infects personal relationships, by establishing more substantial economic, social, and political equality in general and between the sexes, will likely create the conditions in which the use of physical attractiveness to select persons for sexual and other relationships will *blossom*. People will be less useful to each other, because they will have roughly equal resources. As this occurs, the role of other properties, such as attractiveness, expands to fill the vacuum created by the absence of leverage, social status, and the ability to pay as factors influencing choice. As the utility of sex as a route to economic safety or as a vicarious attachment to social status declines, sex will be engaged in for its own sake; as a result, that which pertains to romantic eroticism, beauty in all its forms, becomes more important. Given this background of a deeper and broader social equality, however, the practice of relying on attractiveness for personal relationships will be *less* oppressive, not more.

With increased economic equality between men and women, the difference between men and women in the role of attractiveness should be reduced. As women gain their own political power and economic resources, they will be free, unhindered by a host of constraints that limit them now, to marry and divorce, form and dissolve relationships, as they see fit, according to their own taste and bias. [62] More women will then have what some men have now, the luxury and opportunity to choose partners on the basis of attractiveness, to surround themselves with beauty and the ecstasy it provides. With both men and women eschewing social status as a criterion and placing more emphasis on the role of attractiveness, moving from Aristotelian use-relationships to Aristotelian pleasure-relationships, romanticism will have completed itself by becoming egalitarian.[63] Men will then have as much reason as women have now for watching their weight, for exercising their muscles to keep trim and firm, for not drinking beer during the game, for going more often to the hair salon, for being more self-aware of their bodies and dress in public places. This will possibly make both women and men happy, and it might even be good for them. The advantages and burdens of physical attractiveness, if they exist, will at least be shared equally. But something must be avoided. Listen to Marx:

> What I have thanks to money, what I pay for, i.e., what money can buy, that is what I, the possessor of the money, am myself. . . . I am ugly, but I can buy myself the most beautiful women. Consequently I am not ugly, for the effect of ugliness, its power of repulsion, is annulled by money. . . . Does not my money thus change all my incapacities into their opposite?[64]

Money is power. It entices otherwise repulsed and reluctant men and women into bed or marriage. Marx reminds us to avoid the ugly type of equality in which only a small set of women and men have such appreciable resources that they can buy, and buy again, the beautiful. A more general equality is required beyond gender equality.

Greater equality in economic and political power might alter our institutions so that standards of physical beauty would be more democratically formulated instead of being imposed by political, economic, and biomedical forces. Standards of physical attractiveness could be homegrown, local, pluralistic, flexible and, therefore, broad rather than narrow, inclusive rather than exclusive. Standards of beauty have to be pried loose from the influence of Madison Avenue: the link between the buck and beauty must be severed, and local communities, ethnic and gender subcultures, and members of the various age brackets must be encouraged to elaborate their own indigenous standards. If the oppressiveness to women of the fashion-beauty complex is largely due to "men's institutions and institutional power,"[65] the increased institutional and social power of women, both in the fashion-beauty industry itself and more generally, is necessary. As women become producers of their own pornography, for example, they will exert their own influence over standards of beauty.

There is one more consideration. According to Robert Heilbroner, we do not attach any moral significance to unfairness determined by nature, whereas we do attach such significance to those determined by society. No one considers it *morally* wrong that one person is handsome and another ugly, but everyone holds it to be morally wrong when two persons have incomes which, when compared, offend sensibilities or violate conventions.[66]

Heilbroner too quickly puts attractiveness into the realm of the natural; culture does play a role. Further, and surprisingly, Heilbroner overlooks what is implied by his own thought. If, as he says, income level is not naturally but socially determined, and sometimes offensively, then attractiveness, too, must be to some extent socially determined, and often offensively. Many of the devices of beauty—dentistry and orthodontics; clothing, shoes, cosmetics, and jewelry; hair and skin care; time for engaging in sports and exercising; and, perhaps most importantly, nutrition and the health of the body itself—are distributed according to income. It follows that greater equality would mean more widespread access to the accoutrements of attractiveness.

Future Sex

If society were free of economic inequality and political domination, goes the argument, sexual relations, indeed our lives, would be less troubled. Other than the suggestion that when economic motives have been eliminated from relationships, they will be more satisfying and respectable, what else might be said about the future of sex? Ann Ferguson deems desirable this possible outcome of democratic socialism:

> As for love relationships, with the elimination of sex roles and the disappearance, in an overpopulated world, of any biological need for sex to be associated with reproduction, there would be no reason why such a society could not transcend sexual gender. It would no longer matter what biological sex individuals had. Love relationships, and the sexual relationships developing out of them, would be based on the individual meshing together of androgynous human beings.[67]

This is not a radical vision. To be sure, Ferguson claims that in equality people would be polysexual androgynes; social status, power, money, *and* sexual anatomy and gender would be irrelevant, would make no difference in our selection of intimates. But in Ferguson's vision of the free future of humankind, sex is still tethered to love: first there is the love relationship, then sex develops out of that. *Love* is going to be reconstituted as polysexual and gender-neutral. But no one really supposes that love, either Aristotelian *philia* or Pauline *agape*, has to be heterosexual. If Ferguson wanted to be radical, why did she not bless polymorphous sex outright in terms of its own pleasures, the bodily joys we can achieve in an androgynous future by cavorting with men, women, both, animals? What does love have to do with it?

Ferguson has, however, alerted us to something interesting. From the question, on what basis should we choose sexual partners when economic inequality and political domination are absent (that is, when a certain kind of usefulness of sex is gone), we proceed, under her wing, to this question: when sexual activity has been even more dramatically shorn of its traditional usefulness—its role in the reproduction of human beings—why *then* select some persons rather than others? We arrive at the question, even if we get no answer; Ferguson's phrase "based on the individual meshing together" is as empty as Engels's "mutual inclination." From this, no idea emerges why we would select X instead of Y either for love or for sex. Still, having eliminated a chief biological purpose of sexual acts, we can proceed further, under the wing of Ti-Grace Atkinson, from "whom shall we select?" to "why bother to select anyone at all?"

Atkinson claims that "sexual intercourse is a political construct, reified into an institution."[68] By this she means that people have been engaging in sexual intercourse just because doing so serves a political purpose, not their own individual needs. In particular, sexual intercourse satisfies the social need to keep the species going by replenishing the population (21). In this sense, Atkinson's view of sex is not far removed from Schopenhauer's, who similarly sees the purpose of sex in cosmic terms of the species and not in terms of the person.[69] (Though Schopenhauer is the arch-naturalist and Atkinson the arch-antiessentialist.) People have been groomed by society to perform the act of intercourse, their desire-pleasure system manipulated, indeed created or "constructed," to serve the social purpose of reproduction. Hence, for Atkinson, when the development of reproductive technology eliminates the social function of coitus, individuals' "sexual 'drives' and 'needs' would disappear" as well (20), there not being any reason to keep the grooming in operation. In this Dworkinian-Augustinian vision, the end of biological reproduction is also the end of sex. There would be no reason, any longer, to prefer the beautiful to the ugly.

Atkinson does suppose that the sexual body might have a remainder, a sensuality of simple physical contact itself, skin against skin, that could be the individual's alone, apart from the social function of intercourse (20), and she wonders what this remainder would be like once it existed in its pure state, the reproductive body gone. Atkinson immediately knocks up against a problem we confronted earlier: if the pleasure of the touch would remain, why would it have to be the touch of another person? Why wouldn't the touch of the self suffice (21)? In the future made possible by artificial reproduction, people might not have to choose among sex partners, because masturbation will have come into its own as the primary mode of sexual satisfaction; maybe orgasm will even be "possible from breathing alone, without any touching."[70] The question, why have sex with X rather than Y? is replaced by, why have sex with X rather than masturbate? The answer I gave earlier was that paired or multipersonal sex, be it gay, straight, bi, or polysexual, is an appealing option, given that certain pleasures can be achieved only through other bodies, by the novelty and sharpness of the sensations they provide.

This conclusion is resisted by Atkinson, who takes a Solomonesque path in resolving the difficulty. She argues,

> Since what is being received [through the touch of the other] cannot be a technical or physical improvement on that same auto-experience, any positive external component must be a psychological component. . . . Since neither individual can *add* to the physical experience of the other, it must be that the contribution is a mental one. (22)

The argument fails; its premise, that the body of the other provides nothing additional, is false. Notice where the argument is going. Although Atkinson admits that she is speculating, she supposes that the mental component of paired or multipersonal sex that is its reason for occurring is the "positive" feeling of "approval" transmitted from toucher to touched (23). Once the reproductive function of sex is gone, sexual caresses could finally take on the pure function of expressing caring and supporting emotions. Neither Ferguson nor Atkinson can get beyond this traditional preoccupation. But Atkinson does ask the right question about her proposal: "why would such feelings have to be expressed by touching instead of verbally?" Precisely. If these emotions or attitudes can be expressed some other way than through the erotic body, on her own account sex would serve no purpose at all and would be abandoned.

Nothing about sexual activity, be it straight or gay, is so special as to allow it to function continuously and reliably as a premier expression of approval or support. In a marriage or enduring relationship in which the sexual zip has been zapped, these emotions or attitudes, including love itself, might be expressed better by doing the dishes or washing the car than by offering sexual caresses.[71] For if the excitement and pleasure of the sexual caress become negligible, the caress would seem to be able to express nothing at all, let alone the "mental" stroking Atkinson was hoping for. Engaging in sexual caresses could still express love, exactly when executing the caress has all the character of doing the dishes, that is, when X would prefer not to be caressing Y but does so anyway, out of duty, for Y's sake. But in this case the zip in marital sex must still be there for Y. This is why some say that sex expresses caring in a relationship or marriage only in a negative way: it is by not having sex outside the marriage or relationship, despite the temptation to do so, that we express approval of and support for our partner. But if doing the dishes can express approval and support, and one does the dishes often and well enough, there would seem to be no need to refrain from having sex outside the marriage or relationship in order to express those attitudes. They have already been shown, and being adulterous does not necessarily wipe out that achievement.[72]

Pornographic Beauty

Beauty, especially the beauty of women in all its splendor and variety, saturates heterosexual pornography. Either by nature or artifice, there are few unattractive women in visual pornography. (Only a handful of magazines and videos cater to special tastes, presenting women who are heavy, even obese, or older, in their forties or beyond.) Models are selected for their slender, taut bodies (or for their mildly plumpish bodies), their inviting (small, medium, *or* large) breasts, their appealing faces and (blonde, red, light brown, dark brown, or black) hair, and their curvy (trim *or* big) backsides. Photographic pornography magazines might as well be glossy, illustrated catalogues or Sunday advertising supplements dispatched to the rest of the galaxy, in which humans proudly boast of the beauty, and its variety, that inhabits Earth: this is the best we have, space creatures. Take a nice, long look. And eat your hearts out.

The fact that photographic pornography displays women with many different body types and features makes dubious the common wisdom that pornography "both produces and reproduces *uniform* standards of female beauty."[73] Male consumers of pornography know that the derogatory piece of masculinist philosophy "all cunts are the same" is false. (Others know it to be false from Judy Chicago's "The Dinner Party.") The variety to be found in photographic pornography also makes dubious the thought that "racism . . . pervades pornography" because its "depictions of women . . . are confined" to a "narrow concept of beauty," namely, "very thin, large breasted, blonde women."[74] Pornographic depictions are not "confined" to or even emphasize thin, bosomy blondes; anyone adequately familiar with pornography knows better. Can the charge of racism be maintained anyway, on the grounds that the pornography produced in Europe and the United States presents predominantly white women? A woman who visited and surveyed the merchandise of seven pornography stores in the San Francisco area argues, "White women were featured in most pornography (92% of total) presumably because they fulfill the prevailing racist equation of beauty with whiteness and Caucasian features."[75] Pornography is caught in a catch-22. If it contains no women of color, it is accused of the racism of perpetuating and imposing white standards of beauty; if pornography does contain women of color, it is racist through its coercion of the poor, oppressed, and foreign.[76] A plausible, nonideological explanation for the 92 percent figure is not that this predominance "fulfill[s] a racist equation," but that it reflects the fact that most people in this country are white, which includes not only the models but also the middle-class male consumers of pornography (who prefer white women, but not exclusively).

If pornography is saturated with women's beauty, the men, by contrast, who voraciously consume heterosexual pornography, who yearn for the vicarious contact with the skin and privates of beautiful women that it allows, are themselves, says another piece of standard wisdom, not beautiful, but socially unfit.[77] Apparently, consumer and consumed are perfectly matched, coming together to effect their furtive exchange in that queer dimension made possible by representation. Those who lack beauty desire to touch it, to bring it onto and into themselves. Those who have beauty are locked inside the magazine, paid to expose and display their beauty for those who crave it. Nothing, not even philosophy (*contra* Diotima), shows as well as does pornography, how much we, or men, want and need the inspiration provided by the beautiful. Yet men's interest in pornography is mocked as contributing to, if not constituting, the degradation of women. Could it be that as heterosexual men are worshiping, utterly enraptured, the photographed bodies of beautiful women, they also despoil the very thing that transports their spirit?

Pornography

Could it be conjectured that men's current widespread demand to buy women's bodies to penetrate their mouths is connected to the revitalization of the feminist movement and women's demand to speak?   —Carole Pateman, *The Sexual Contract*

Fellatio has become very popular in pornography, in part because it functions to shut women up.
  —Teresa Hommel, "Images of Women in Pornography and Media"

Wh* l*st*ns t* * w*m*n w*th * p*n*s *n h*r m**th?
      [See Catharine MacKinnon, *Feminism Unmodified*]

In this chapter, I occasionally mention fellatio, *a person's taking a penis into the mouth and then licking and sucking it.* Some readers of that blunt description might feel discomfort; others might respond with arousal, or not be moved at all. Why are some people offended by certain sexual acts, while others welcome them as pleasurable and exciting? This disparity makes it difficult not only to read, and read correctly, the meaning or meanings of a sexual act, but also to discern the messages of representations of sexual acts. We barely know what tank tops mean, let alone Dali's melted clocks and spooky landscapes. Since we are unsure of our readings of sex and its representation, they remain two dark, mysterious, and foreboding continents. No wonder we are perennially tempted to banish both to the gulag.

Oral Sex

A woman is kneeling on the floor, planted on her knees between the spread thighs of a man sitting in a comfortable chair sipping wine and smoking tobacco; she is kissing the head of his erect penis, nuzzling his testicles, squeezing his shaft until it ejaculates; she swallows some of his fluid and smears the rest on her lips and cheeks. According to Catharine MacKinnon and Andrea Dworkin's Model Antipornography Law, trafficking in photographs or videotapes of this event could make one liable to civil suit; actionable pornography includes, among other things, depictions in which "women are presented in postures or positions of sexual submission, servility, or display" (section 2.1.v).[1] I sense some truth in the judgment that the woman is depicted as servile, though I ultimately disagree; if she has "initiated" the act "out of her own genuine affection and desire,"[2] we are not compelled to read the depiction that way. For the Model Law, the woman's posture—her being on her knees, slavishly attending to the man's pleasure—shows her to be submissive. Perhaps. Comprehending indignation about the act and its depiction depends, however, as well, or instead, on recognizing that *all* oral sex is degrading; not posture but the nature of the act is what matters.

The point is not that a woman with a penis in her mouth is, as MacKinnon implies, hilarious: reduced by her sexual task to mumbling and slurping, she is unable to voice her mind on issues political or metaphysical. She wouldn't have any serious opinion to articulate anyway, that's how little we think of women who go around putting penises in their mouths. But oral sex makes fools of everyone this way; who listens to, or could hear, a man with genitalia of any kind in his mouth?[3] If men and women silenced by genital flesh, or by the pizza they are eating, are merely comic, the servility of oral sex must reside elsewhere. Or so a feminist Augustine would reason, in unpacking what is really going on beneath The Law's talk of the servility of posture. Were the man supine, flat on the bed, she on top, her legs cuddling his head and tushie cheeks bouncing on his brow, their faces buried in each other's crotch, her servile posture would be gone, but the servility due to the nature of oral sex remains. Putting your face in someone's crotch, no matter the posture, no matter the language used to name the event, is degrading and humiliating. It takes a humble sense of one's own smallness to do it, whether doing it caringly for the pleasure of the other or selfishly for sensual joy. Your mouth is latched onto an organ, be it penis/foreskin/testicles or labia/clitoris/vagina, that even after bathing and even if powdered and perfumed, within an hour starts to drip and become caked with pungent excretions and fluids; and while your mouth is latched onto that organ, your eyes and nose and lips are located inches, perhaps only a few millimeters, away from the most taboo orifice in the human body, drenched in its own secretions and excretions. Yeats delicately made the point: "Love has pitched his mansion in / The place of excrement."[4] How degrading, this abject immersing of your face into the body's toilet, its cloaca. You'd have to be crazy, either in love or in lust—both, in their own ways, degrading states of mind—to do such a thing. Perhaps this is really why Augustine and Aquinas blessed genital-genital intercourse and condemned oral-genital sex: not because oral contact was nonprocreative and hence unnatural, but because the genitals stink. The saints' ban on oral sex was the Christian version of the Hebrew ban on eating pig, and was just as fanatical.

This portrait of oral sex as degrading is overstated, tinged with too much Augustinian disgust of the body (or reflecting only the rabbit of disgust and not also the duck of pleasure). But something else is less contentiously true of oral sex that can be relied on to make a similar point. Oral sex reifies: when we perform oral sex, we focus on a discrete and distinguished body part that captures our consciousness, taking our awareness away from the person to whom the organ is attached; we concentrate on the distinct features of a complicated piece of flesh and attend to it as an object in its own right. Oral sex, when done well, is scrumptious; how ironic that it is also so impersonal. When receiving the act and savoring its pleasure, we drift off into our own world of free associations and fantasy, since we are not locked into any interpersonal space, or fixed in one sexual place, by the look of the other, whose face and hence personhood has disappeared between our thighs. Giving and taking the genital kiss lacks the humaneness of the facial kiss, during which we gaze into each other's eyes, into the seat of our souls. In the facial kiss we grasp in one experience both the taste and the eyes of the other, the sensual pleasure and the soul wrapped into one. But in oral sex we get the taste by itself, no face, no eyes, no soul. We kiss not a living countenance but an organ, the sign of life of which is not a pupil opening, but expansion, its being passively filled with blood, its engorgement. Aroused genitals, male and female, exhibit the dumb life of a balloon.

The only eye we see during the genital kiss, if any, is a mute brown eye. If only it were a real eye, the soul it reveals would save oral sex from its fate; it would make the genital kiss a facial kiss, human and darling. Look at René Magritte's painting *Le viol* (figure 2): a face encircled by wavy hair, whose eyes are embodied as two breasts, whose nose is now a belly button, whose mouth is a pubic triangle. Were you to perform oral sex on this woman, your lips would envelop her labia, one by one, as you looked into her open eyes. You could caress her cheeks and her neck, smooth her hair and press it against her head, run your fingers around her eyes and gaze into them, recognizing and confirming her humanity, precisely while you are licking her clitoris and bringing her to orgasm. Given the facts of human anatomy, the sexual acts that do not reify the body are those that occur face-to-face with the eyes open or faces pressed together.[5] Were we built, instead, as imagined by Magritte, we could have oral sex as if having exactly this contact. The surreal anatomical rearrangement turns oral sex into something humanized and alive. When her face and body exist separately, she is spirit without body, if we concentrate on her face, or she appears as body without spirit, if we focus on her genitals. But after Magritte welds together her face and body, she achieves a tangible union of body and mind, flesh and spirit, as the lower sources of life, breasts and womb, merge with the higher residence of personality. When, in this fantasy, you enjoy her body parts, by kiss or look or embrace, you also automatically kiss or see or embrace her soul. Surreal glasses that append a floppy, rubber penis to the nose make fellatio humane the way *Le viol* humanizes cunnilingus.

When I inspect *Le viol*, I am charmed by the thought that Magritte has sliced through the stubborn reification problem by imagining that a less evil God or less careless nature would have put the genitals in close proximity to where the soul shines. I detect the parts from the lower regions of the body imbued with spirit, dereified by being raised upwards to, located on, made equivalent to the face. Susan Gubar finds something else in *Le viol*; she supposes that "none of Magritte's portraits more shockingly fragments the female by turning her into a sexual body than

Figure 2. René Magritte, *Le viol* (The rape), 1934. This face/body can be seen as "one of the most graphic subordinations of a woman to an object, for it reduces her to genitalia" (T. Gracyk, "Pornography as Representation," 125). But it can also be seen another way: the sexual parts from the lower regions of the body have been imbued with spirit by being raised upwards to and located on her face. (The Menil Collection, Houston. © 1996 C. Herscovici, Brussels/Artists Rights Society [ARS], New York.)

Le viol.[6] Instead of perceiving the sexual body elevated to the physical and hence metaphysical level of the face, she is impressed that "the female face is erased by the female torso imposed upon it" and so becomes "sightless, senseless, and dumb" (50). A woman is silenced, not by having a penis in her mouth, but by becoming her own genitals. "The articulation of the woman as genital organ makes her inarticulate," says Gubar, rephrasing for the aesthetic domain MacKinnon's claim that the pornographic free speech of men silences the speech of women.[7] Gubar finds in *Le viol* another lesson that would please unmodified feminists: its "image of mindless physicality justifies rape" (52). Magritte is the pornographer of women's submission and servility.

In *Le viol*, I see a body transformed into a face and filled thereby with spirit, while Gubar sees a face demoted to the body: "the face that was supposed to be a window to the soul embodies a sexuality that is less related to pleasure and more to dominance over the woman who is 'nothing but' a body" (52). The point is not to do battle with Gubar about the "real" meaning or message of *Le viol*. If we take into account not only the work's title but also its relation to other works of Magritte, if not its next of kin in Surrealism,[8] Gubar's reading might win by a nose; these additional bits of information help fix *Le viol*'s meaning. But framing devices and external cues are effectively unavailable and irrelevant when we are trying to understand representations of sexual acts, that is, commercially produced pornographic depictions. The titles of videos and the captions attached to photographs are absurd and so either flatly ignored by the consumer or replaced mentally by his own caption; or the captions themselves are polysemous. Further, consumers who use the material for sexual arousal do not bother to relate the video or photographs to other works by the same artist or place the composition in its history. Only academics being overly cerebral about pornography take titles, captions, and art-historical context seriously. External cues aside, then, the duck-rabbit we discover in Magritte's wonderfully polysemous *Le viol* is characteristic of depictions in general, including the sexual. If we can flick back and forth between perceiving the face of *Le viol* as a body and perceiving the body of *Le viol* as a face; if we can alternate between seeing a passionate kiss and resuscitation on the Dutch stamp (figure 1); if we can visually or olfactorally sense the anus and genitals as either beautiful or repulsive; if "no" can mean "no" or "yes," and "yes" can mean "yes" or "no"; if a boy can look like a girl or a boy, and a girl look like a boy or girl; then we should be able to shift back and forth as easily among various readings of both the act of someone's licking an erect penis and depictions of her or him doing so.

The Beaver

Helen Longino, in an essay widely reprinted since its first appearance in 1980, presents several arguments meant to justify curtailing the production, distribution, and consumption of pornography. Longino defines pornography as verbal or pictorial representations of sexual behavior that recommend or endorse the degradation of people (especially women, in pornography made for heterosexual men).[9] According to one of Longino's arguments, pornography is libelous; it defames women by telling lies about their sexuality.[10] Pornography claims that women derive pleasure from catering to the sexual needs of men, ignoring their own needs in the process; that women enjoy being sexually degraded and abused; that women are "wanton, depraved, and made for the sexual use of men" (39–40). Further, as endorsement of what it depicts, pornography approves the demeaning, abusive treatment of women and thereby promotes the degradation of women, contributing causally to acts harming women (39–41). Thus pornography, for Longino, is not only "immoral" (35); it also forfeits First Amendment protection (42–45).

The notion of degrading a person in sex acts and depictions is essential both to Longino's definition of pornography and to her arguments. According to Longino, a person is degraded by actions that violate or do not acknowledge or respect the person's "basic human dignity" (36). This idea is vague. The most exact Longino gets in explaining its meaning is to say that "mutual respect" requires that "the desires and experiences of each participant [be] regarded by the other[s] as having a validity . . . equal to" their own (36). How a depiction of a sexual act shows that X does or does not *regard* the desires of Y as being equally valid to X's is not clarified, except by Longino's mentioning examples of abusive coercion and brutality that are clearly degrading in this way (36–38). Otherwise, Longino repeats that in pornography women are degraded by being treated in a manner "beneath their [human] dignity" (36, 38). Whatever her notion of degradation is, it is complex, for Longino won't accept a woman's *choosing* an activity as evidence against its being degrading (37). But unless the meaning of failing to respect someone's "basic human dignity" in sex acts (other than coercive beatings) is articulated, arguments meant to have legal impact are weak. It is remarkable, then, that Susan Dwyer, who cannot decide whether on Longino's view *Playboy* and *Penthouse* are pornographic, contends that "this indeterminacy is not a fault of Longino's definition, but rather is indicative of our uncertainty about what is degrading."[11] Nonsense. "Our uncertainty" is not to blame for any deficiency; it was Longino's own choice to use in a legal argument, of all places, the vague and moralistic concept "degradation."[12]

Longino claims that her arguments do not turn on the fact that pornography is sexual: "what is wrong with pornography . . . is its degrading and dehumanizing portrayal of women (and *not* its sexual content)" (39). If this claim is false, Longino's view would support politically and sexually conservative positions, with the result that sexual material and acts of which Longino approves would be in danger. Since, on Longino's definition, pornography is sexual and degrading, she must assert that it is not degrading just because it is sexual. Does this commit her to the thesis that no sexual act is degrading just because it is sexual? But sadomasochistic sexual acts—spanking someone to orgasm accompanied by verbal humiliation— look degrading because sexual. Could we argue that when an act or its depiction is degrading because sexual, the fault is only the degradation, not the sex? Contrast an act that is degrading and sexual, but not degrading because sexual (a woman's being brutally coerced into cunnilingus by another woman) and an act that is degrading and sexual, and degrading because sexual (verbal humiliation). In the first example, the degradation can be removed but the act remains, cleansed of degradation and now permissible (mutually respectful oral sex). But in the second case, the degradation cannot be eliminated without eliminating the act (nondegrading verbal humiliation is not verbal humiliation). Perhaps Longino agrees that some sex acts are degrading at least in part because sexual. Then her view would be that pornography is material that depicts degradation and sex together, whether the degradation is separable from the sex act or is necessarily attached to it. But now the conservative has all he or she needs to claim that many more acts than originally countenanced by Longino are degrading, beneath "human dignity," just in virtue of being sexual—for example, lesbian cunnilingus—and therefore are "immoral" and forfeit, when depicted, First Amendment protection.

This point applies to Longino's treatment of *Playboy*-style photographs of undressed women, "beaver" photographs. The content of a typical beaver photograph is a woman exhibiting her body, spreading her legs to expose her privates, perhaps using her hands in some helpful manner. Longino thinks that this kind of photograph *is* pornographic:

> The pornographic view of women is thoroughly entrenched . . . reaching and affecting . . . those of us who are forced into an awareness of it as we peruse magazines at newsstands . . . or even as we approach a counter to pay for groceries. . . . No longer confined within plain brown wrappers, it jumps out . . . from magazine covers displaying a woman's genital area being spread open to the viewer by her own fingers. (39)

Longino is not complaining about a forced, public encounter with any old, obnoxious photograph; she protests being forced to encounter pornography, in particular. But what feature of this photograph makes it exhibit the "pornographic view" of women?[13] Perhaps Longino presumes that the photograph endorses the idea that women are "made for the sexual use of men" or tells the lie about women that "our pleasure consists in pleasing men and not ourselves." But I am unable to perceive in this beaver, or any beaver, or a whole magazine or warehouse of beavers, anything like this. If the model is masturbating, she is being portrayed as pleasing herself and not (only) the men who view her; just because she is masturbating, that does not mean she is "wanton, depraved." If the model is only displaying her privates, the photograph carries no implication she was "made" (created, fated, born, socialized) for the sexual pleasure of men or of anyone else; nor does the photograph say or imply or mean or hint that the only thing she is good for or adept at is parading her privates for anonymous strangers. Is this photo degrading only because it is sexual?

The principal clue Longino provides is in her description of an unobjectionable photograph: "a representation of a nude human body (in whole or in part) in such a manner that the person shown maintains self-respect—e.g., is not portrayed in a degrading position" (36). The "basic human dignity" of the nude person must be acknowledged; the model must maintain her self-respect. Fine. But the claim that the beaver is objectionable on these grounds—the position undermines self-respect because it is degrading—is unconvincing. I am unable to perceive any loss of self-respect in the beaver, no matter in what posture a model displays her body. Further, to claim that the beaver degrades in virtue of the model's position, her legs spread and genitals and perhaps anus exposed, implies that the beaver is degrading *because* it is sexual. Eliminating the degradation in the beaver, if it is there, is impossible without eliminating the sexual act itself of spreading and displaying. To ask the model to retain her self-respect by keeping her legs closed destroys the beaver. That's what the conservative, concerned about the purity of women, would encourage the model to do, shut her legs, maintain her honor, and eliminate the genre.

Dworkin and MacKinnon condemn the beaver more explicitly than Longino. Recall section 2.1.v of their Law: pornography includes depictions in which "women are presented in postures or positions of sexual submission, servility, or display." Beavers are one of the items they have in mind: *Playboy* presents women in "postures of submission and sexual servility." The poses in this magazine are meant to provide male viewers with "constant access" to all the holes of a woman's body.[14] In beaver material like *Playboy*, women are "sexually accessible, have-able, . . . wanting to be taken and used."[15] Of course, men who look at beavers do not really have access to anyone; it's fake, a sham, a phony Pauline access to the mouth or anus that lasts not a lifetime but until they turn the page. Men looking at a beaver create a pleasurable sexual fantasy, a fantasy elicited by the photograph's content interacting with their thoughts and desires. This is why it is stunningly one-dimensional for Dworkin and MacKinnon to claim that the purpose of the beaver is to give men "constant access" to a woman's holes. They could have said, if they had wanted to describe the phenomenon fairly, that beavers allow a man to satisfy his curiosity (not dominance); to imagine touching (not owning) her blessed vulva, as Michelangelo's Adam touched God; to conjure up, in an act of admiration (not abuse), her odor and taste; to dream of performing oral sex on her for her sake (not for his); to wonder what it would be like being married to her and living in the suburbs (not stringing her up and slicing her); or to whisper to her his love and yearning (not hate and disgust). Where is the man's seeing her as wanting to be taken and used, and his using her?

Where is her submission? To maintain their point, Dworkin and MacKinnon could say that access to a woman still exists in these fantasized scenarios. But this access is innocuous; it is not the access characteristic of the master-slave relationship or patriarchal gender relations.

Another clause of the Model Law also applies to the beaver: pornography includes depictions in which "women's body parts . . . are exhibited such that women are reduced to those parts" (sec. 2.1.vi).[16] The Law is dead silent about what it *is* for a photo to reduce a woman to her parts; it expects us, or a jury, to fill in the details. Perhaps we can employ Gubar's interpretation of *Le viol*, that the painting demotes a woman to "nothing but" her body.[17] This view suggests that a photograph of a whole, naked woman, followed or surrounded by photos of her body parts—face alone, face and breasts together, bottom alone, genitals alone, face and tush together, and so forth—asserts (or, more weakly, implies) that she is "nothing but" these parts, individually or collectively. We can stuff a bit of metaphysical or metaphorical truth into such a view; some sexual conservatives even insist on its literal truth. But the photos could just as easily assert, if anything, that if we look closely and in more detail at this beautiful woman, we will see yet other beauties—in the same way that microscopic examination of cells reveals other beauties. I doubt that anyone knows enough about the thoughts of men who enjoy beavers to declare, with authority, what men are thinking. Are men supposed to be imagining either the absurdity that "this woman *is* her bottom" or the antitheological notion that "if you put together breasts, bottom, and genitals, and nothing else (no soul is needed), this is what you get, her"? To attribute a normative (instead of ontological) assertion to the photos is equally implausible; for example, "the *only* or *most* important thing about this woman (or any woman) is her chest." The photos do not assert (or even imply) that, although I can understand that a sensitive, young, or tender mind or a personality prone to sensationalism, exaggeration, paranoia, or political manipulation might read them uncharitably.

When we pay attention to body parts, during sexual activity or in pornography, reification occurs. The genitals, for example, are reified during oral sex, or when someone gazes at a photo of genitals and dreams about doing so. The bearer of the genitals, however, even if photographed, has not been identified with the genitals or reduced to anything less than a person. A recipient of oral sex has simply been left behind, not demoted; and the one performing the act is still a person, one that has vanished to the black hole of the space between our legs. When the act has been completed, we pull ourselves up from below back to her or his face, and utter the "hi" that means "I'm back" or hear the "hi" that means "thanks, and I'm glad to see you again." We kiss. The separating voyage is over.

Polysemous Pornography

Consider a photograph of a nude woman sitting in a chair with her legs spread: she might be seen as prepared to be used for sex, a vulnerable object; or as demanding prolonged oral attention; or as watching television and rehearsing the *Cogito*. Or consider an equally simple photograph of a woman licking an erect penis. She is in control, she is responsible for his pleasure, she can stop inconsiderately, or nibble the wrong way or cause distraction by coughing, she has the choice and the power to prolong or end his pleasure, and he is grateful. Or he is in control, he is taking all the pleasure he can get from her lips and tongue, he is using her mouth. Or the scenario is an experiment, she is curious about the taste and feel of a penis, he is curious about the warmth and wetness of a woman's mouth. For both photos, multiple interpretations are possible that are not fixed by their content. Here is another example. A nude woman is bound immobile with rope. She can be perceived as an unwilling (or willing) victim of slavery, as waiting to be sold in an auction to the highest bidder, then to be used sexually by her master. In another, not necessarily incompatible, reading, being bound symbolizes safety, trust, the lifeline of the umbilical cord, a pleasant, temporary escape from the duties of freedom. This inter-pretation is not far-fetched, since it is how some men and women describe their experiences with bondage. Sometimes unusual readings strike us as silly, but often we can learn something from them. Richard Mohr, for example, perceives an anal fistfuck photograph, *Helmut and Brooks* by Robert Mapplethorpe, as a marriage portrait. "In keeping with the genre, the image consists of two people and a chair. . . . [A] hand in the ass replaces the traditionally passive hand on the shoulder." [18] This reading is a stretch, to be sure, but one that allows us to perceive the photo, and Mohr's or Mapplethorpe's world, in a new way.

The cover of the June 1978 *Hustler* is grist for this mill. It depicts female legs and bottom sticking out from a manual meat grinder; the head and torso have already been ground into raw burger. Eva Kittay, while explaining ostensively the meaning of "pornography," includes this cover in a list of items that she could have lifted from a WAP slide show: depictions of a gun in a woman's mouth, whippings, handcuffs, rape, bondage, bondage, and yet more bondage.[19] Look, yells an outraged Kittay, *Hustler* endorses the brutalization of women for men's sexual pleasure. This interpretation of the cover is the least promising; Kittay fell head over heels into Larry Flynt's trap by reacting with anger and disgust and adding this obvious piece of bad taste to the list of horrors perpetrated by pornography against women. At the very least, we should go one step beyond this crude reading: *Hustler* was admitting that, in displaying in its pages women's bodies for the pleasure of men, it treats women as hunks of meat. No, more than admitting, proclaiming and celebrating it, as if to reply "in your face" to feminist criticism of pornography. Hence Flynt's announcement on the cover, "We will no longer hang women up like pieces of meat" means "better, we shall grind them." As soon as we see a political statement in the cover, other readings are possible. For example: the cover is sarcastic, mocking what feminists claim about pornography.[20] *You* say we treat women like meat; well, *this* is treating women as meat; look inside, we don't do this. Or—a fishing expedition—the cover "refers to a male desire to eliminate 'the female head' . . . and just be left with the sex," and so it "play[s] on men's *fear* of thinking women."[21] (But the rump, the sex, is about to be ground too, no?) Finally, don't overlook the phallic shape of the woman's body and the dreadful implication that this is the head of the viewer's penis being ground into burger. Flynt's announcement on the cover is becoming Magritte's "Ceci n'est pas une pipe."

Does the *Hustler* cover run afoul of the MacKinnon/Dworkin Law? See section 2.1.iv: pornography includes depictions in which "women are presented as sexual objects tied up or cut up or mutilated or bruised or physically hurt."[22] The choice is between seeing the cover as a paradigm case of woman-hating propaganda that bluntly depicts a woman being ground, or seeing it as a clever piece of masculinist self-parody in which the manifest image must be viewed in a more tolerant way. The Model Law, perhaps any law, is not subtle enough to reflect this difference. If we focus on the cover's explicit image, it apparently falls within the category defined by section 2.1.iv, since the cover shows mutilation; but if so, The Law is in danger of making too many items actionable, in particular items whose deep meaning is vastly more important than their manifest content. That attempts to circumscribe a class of actionable pornography would fail for this sort of reason is one thing to learn from the debate about the "real" meaning of the *Hustler* cover.

Maybe the cover does not violate section 2.1.iv after all, because the photograph is not "sexually explicit" or is not a sexual item to begin with, so that the woman being ground into burger is not a *sexual* object. That the remaining part of the woman is nude does not necessarily make the photograph sexual or her a sexual object. On the other hand, remember that, for MacKinnon, "what is sexual is what gives a man an erection."[23] Some men, while looking at the *Hustler* cover, do get at least a partial erection. But from what, exactly? From the perception or idea of grinding a woman (or their own penis) into burger? MacKinnon has no doubt that "hostility," "hatred," and "death" provoke the "penis [to] shudder and stiffen,"[24] that men masturbate to and get pleasure from the destruction and death of women.[25] It is not obvious, however, that the *grinding* leads to any erections; at least, MacKinnon doesn't really know that it does. My suspicion is that some men feel twinges of arousal when they visually fasten, exclusively, on the adorable, upraised tush on the cover, and that they deliberately ignore the rest. Even if the cover is sexual by inducing pleasure, then, it doesn't induce pleasure through mutilation, so it might not be sexual in a way required to fall within section 2.1.iv of The Law. We have learned again not to look with literal eyes at pornographic depictions; for some men, a bound woman arouses not because she is bound, but because her tush is nicely posed.[26]

Other Animals

Pornography also includes, according to the Model Law, depictions of "women . . . presented dehumanized as sexual objects" (2.1.i). I have already argued that the accusation that the beaver makes women into "sex objects" in two senses is weak: these photographs do not clearly present women as "wanting to be taken and used," nor do they imply that women's sexuality is the only or most important thing about them. The accusation has another meaning, though, the gist of which is dramatically expressed in one of Dworkin's descriptions of pornography:

> It is women turned into subhumans, beaver, pussy, body parts, genitals exposed, buttocks, breasts, mouths opened and throats penetrated, covered in semen, pissed on, shitted on, hung from light fixtures, tortured, maimed, bleeding, disemboweled, killed.[27]

Dworkin might be predicting that if men start with light stuff, the beaver, they will not stop until they kill women; or perhaps she is arguing that slicing and grinding are already included, embryonically or metaphorically, in photographs of isolated body parts. But it is impossible not to be revolted by this list of purported atrocities; this is why Dworkin's tactic of mentioning, in the same breath, not only the beaver and body part photo but also maiming and killing is unfair.

Dworkin does claim that the beaver and the body part photo make women subhuman; the beaver dehumanizes by displaying women as, or suggesting that women are, animals, while body part photos dehumanize by reducing a whole, human woman to nonhuman, animal parts. Dehumanization, in the sense of conceiving of or treating a person as an animal, is severely wrong. The truth here must be expressed carefully, for to condemn too vigorously the animality of sex is to embrace an Augustinian sexual worldview. Sexuality focuses on the vegetative, autonomic, and reflexive parts of the body; we rut in the slop, the smell, the sweat; we become our bodies in sex as much as we do during strenuous manual labor or full-court basketball. These facts about sex provide reason, for some, to reject the whole enterprise; or reason to purify sex by inviting God into bed or supplementing sex with the sweetness of love, the commitment of marriage, or the wholesomeness of motherhood. These maneuvers are antisexual, anti-animal flights from the body that deny that sexual pleasure can be its own bottom.

Complaints about the animality of sex are nothing new. In a passage that nicely illustrates how distress about the animality of human sexual activity can be linked with worries about the servility of sexual posture (two themes in the MacKinnon/Dworkin Law), Burchard of Worms issued this ecclesiastical judgment: "Have you had intercourse with your wife or any other woman from behind, in dog-like fashion? If you have, you should do penance for ten days on bread and water."[28] People screwing as dogs screw must be sinful; it reduces oneself to an animal and treats a woman (or oneself) as a bitch in heat. But the animality that is essential to sex ("basic" animality) is different from imposed animality ("surplus" animality). Consider these two scenarios: compelling, under threat of execution, a woman to work in the fields as an ox, to eat slop with the pigs, as she also sexually services you, her master, and your buddies; or taking advantage of a woman's poverty, paying her peanuts to clean your house, wash your clothes, wipe your ass, and keep herself sexually accessible. The repulsion and wrongfulness that attach to these cases of treating a woman as an animal, or as no better than an animal, are undeniable. But they do not attach to the beaver or the body part photo, or even to orgiastic hardcore pornography in which nothing happens except coarse and steamy animalistic sex. The allure of the beaver and the body part photo, of the grit and reeking fleshiness of the pornographic orgy, is closer to basic animality than to what sex becomes under blatant oppression.

MacKinnon and Dworkin's willingness to lump together all sexual descents into the animal as unscrupulous dehumanization leads them to include, as another type of actionable pornography, depictions in which "women are presented being penetrated by objects or animals" (section 2.1.viii). Soon after providing her catalogue of atrocities, Dworkin adds that pornography is "a woman being fucked by dogs, horses, snakes." The reasoning here is that nothing reduces a woman to an animal more effectively than her having sex with an animal. I confess I do not find the thought of humans frolicking with animals to be intrinsically disgusting or demeaning, to the human or the animal. Surprisingly, neither does Diana Russell, an ally and supporter of MacKinnon's attack on pornography. Russell notes, as one criticism of pornography, that it abuses animals; but her solution is not to exclude animals altogether. "Erotica," her acceptable sexually arousing material, is "free of sexism, racism, and homophobia" and "respectful of all human beings and animals portrayed."[29] For Russell, then, someone could engage in sex with an animal in a fashion that brought mutual delight to the human and the animal while showing respect for the basic dignity of all sentient creatures involved. As long as we are willing to treat animals with kindness and respect, as if they were human, nothing could be wrong, in turn, with treating humans as animals.

MacKinnon and Dworkin have been castigated enough already for including, in this section of The Law, the depiction of objects penetrating women. Many people think nothing is wrong with the use of dildos, vibrators, and cucumbers in paired sex or masturbation. "There are even lesbians who relish going down on dildos," Gayle Rubin relates. "Embedded in [MacKinnon's] idea of porn as a documentary of abuse is a very narrow conception of human sexuality, one lacking even elementary notions of sexual diversity."[30] Still, a question remains: why are both objects and animals mentioned in one section of The Law? Penetration by an object (orally, vaginally, or anally) and penetration by an animal have in common that sex occurs outside contact with another human, so perhaps both are dehumanizing, in a bloated sense. But the woman who discovers delirious pleasure impaling herself with the rubber of a solid dildo need not be seen as degraded by the act or by the camera that records it.[31] She might be a glutton; but when it comes to our own private sexual pleasures most of us have the embarrassing ability to be gluttonous at the drop of a hat. Given MacKinnon's and Dworkin's relentless disapproval of heterosexual coitus, maybe they should applaud the independence, the refusal to collaborate, of women who pleasure themselves with dildos (or dogs?), for they have renounced the raping, brutal penetration of a man's penis.

One other thing objects and animals have in common might explain why they were included together in section 2.1.viii of The Law. Both resemble and symbolize penetration of a woman by a man's penis. Hence, if penetration by a man's penis subordinates and degrades, so does penetration by a dildo or dog. Further, women depicted as desiring and enjoying the pleasure of being penetrated by objects and animals are women who love being penetrated by a man's penis. They love it so much that if they cannot get the real thing, they will grab any nearby phallic object and pound themselves silly with it, that's how hungry for a man's penis they are. This is close to how Margaret Baldwin describes "the substance of pornography":

> women live to be fucked, men inevitably fuck. Women especially love to be fucked by animals, dildoes, fists, and penises, especially while being bound, beaten, cut, mutilated and killed.[32]

MacKinnon, too: in the world of pornography, "women's desire to be fucked ... is equal to men's desire to fuck"; women "desperately want to be bound, battered, tortured, humiliated, and killed."[33] These grossly exaggerated accounts of pornography's content probably underlie The Law's inclusion of the dildo photo in section 2.1.viii. But to interpret the dildo photo this way is to read it with blinders. Men are sometimes horny for the touch, the closeness, of a woman; sometimes they are so hungry for a woman and her sex, they seek photos that help put to sleep their yearning desires. The whole world knows this and humiliates men, embarrasses them, makes them feel guilty. Some of these photos might imply that some women, for their part, love and yearn for a man and his sex as much as some men love and yearn for a woman and her sex. These photos, then, are not the degradation of women; they are reassurance, for men, that the universe is ultimately not inimical to their needs and desires. Admitting that the photos are reassuring, but tacking on that they reassure men *by* maligning women, is unpersuasive. Nothing in some women's hunger for a man and some men's hunger for a woman is worth complaining about. We are all hungry for something.

Fantasy

The claim is often made that pornography lies about women. What lie does it tell? When Longino inspects pornography, she finds women portrayed as existing for the pleasure of men; "to the extent that women's sexual pleasure is represented at all, it is subordinated to that of men and is never an end in itself."[34] Pornography, in depicting women as subservient to men, not deeming their own pleasure to be intrinsically valuable, "is the vehicle for the dissemination of a deep and vicious lie about women" (41). Susan Griffin finds the same message:

> the pornographer's idea of his object's pleasure is to please him. She exists for no other purpose. . . . Throughout pornography, this image of a penis in a woman's mouth is among the most popular of images. And under the image we hear the pornographic voice whisper, "*She* exists for *his* pleasure."[35]

"In much pornography," Ann Garry concurs, "the women's purpose is to cater to male desires, to service the man or men. Her own pleasure is rarely emphasized for its own sake."[36] Garry proposes that acceptable, egalitarian pornography would "treat men and women as equal sex partners. The man would not control the circumstances in which the partners had sex or the choice of positions or acts; the woman's preference would be counted equally" (138). Or, as Longino puts it, "the desires and experiences of each participant [would be] regarded by the other[s] as having a validity ... equal to" their own (36). These proposals are odd; most heterosexual, orgiastic pornography, in creating a fantasy of an ideal sexual world, rarely shows men and women quibbling about positions and acts. In pornographic fantasy, because the parties spontaneously want the same thing, women's preferences and desires are automatically given their due.

Furthermore, women are not usually depicted in pornography as servile to men's desires, and women's pleasure is not usually depicted as subordinate to men's pleasure. Longino, Garry, and Griffin do not merely exaggerate, they get it backwards, for women's pleasure for its own sake is ordinarily the center of heterosexual pornography. Women moan and cry with desire, grind and squirm in delight, not because they passively attend to men's needs but because they are active seekers of their own sexual pleasure.[37] Indeed, conservatives criticize pornography as demeaning on the grounds that it depicts women as too eagerly performing unconventional and promiscuous sexual acts for their own pleasure outside the proper context of love and marriage.[38] Pornography tells *this* vicious lie, instead, about women. But feminists also raise this objection; for example, Susan Griffin:

> we see her beg for this pleasure, as if it were *hers alone.* One sees this image over and over in pornography—a woman driven to the point of madness out of the desire to put a man's penis in her mouth.[39]

Griffin, who denounces pornography for depicting women as slaves to men's sexual pleasure, now denounces it for depicting women as slaves to their own sexual pleasure. Women in pornography are slandered because, like Augustine's postlapsarian Adam, they are animals lacking control over their passions. While making the accusation that pornography "blithely lies ... about the nature of women" by implying that they are "mindless, masochistic nymphomaniacs," Judith Hill believes it necessary to remind us that pornography's view "is false. Most women are *not* mindless, masochistic nymphomaniacs."[40] They do *not* lose control like animals, or men.

What lie does pornography tell? I don't think it matters. We should abandon tedious, interminable debates about the meanings of polysemous pornography and instead pay more attention to why pornography is consumed. The fundamental function of pornography is to provide sexual pleasure. Pornography does this by showing a phantasmagoria of sexual activity, a cornucopia of varied sexual acts, attractive bodies *ad libitum*, and adventurous women and men *ad infinitum*. These images do not fix the actual thoughts that induce and accompany arousal; instead, the variety of images provides raw material from which individual consumers select their own point of focus or construct their own story.[41] (In some ways, beavers and silent eight-millimeter films, in omitting the voice or mannerisms of models, allow viewers more freedom to fantasize about personality than videotapes do; more complex photographic sequences and videotapes, on their side, supply more varied raw material.) Since the perceptions—what part of the photo or scene the user concentrates on—and the fantasies that trigger arousal are not determined by the pornographic image, any thesis about the propositional content of pornography does not grapple with what is central to the phenomenon. Pornography does not cause pleasure by advancing arguments or developing a logic of Woman; it is not consumed for any arguments or logic it accidentally contains. Pornography lays down the physical basis enabling a consumer to imagine whatever he wishes to imagine in creating a world more varied and much less violent than imagined by MacKinnon and Dworkin.

Further, the pornographic depiction of the world, in laying a thick and varied foundation for creative fantasizing, goes beyond the merely factually false to the unrealistic, in the way that science fiction is *pure* fantasy. Pornography does not depict the actual nature of women or their sexuality, granted. But all pure fantasy depictions fail to correspond with reality in this trivial sense. Pornography as fantasy never purports to be telling the truth in the first place; it is false, but not in a way that permits anyone to conclude it promulgates lies about women (or about men). Fantasy material is not false in the same way that nonfantasy material, say, a scientific theory or a piece of journalism, might be false. Similarly, the reading of romance novels by women (which rivals in quantity the use of pornography by men) is motivated by the enjoyment, frequently sexual, of contemplating a fantasy world in which everlasting loves, or masculine lovers, are plentiful. Romances hardly depict men with documentary accuracy, yet no one worries that they are defamatory or demeaning, and with good reason: we know that romances are pure fantasy. For romances and pornography to engage in wild pretense is not to spread lies.

Pornography's airy and fanciful propositional content therefore need not be taken seriously. As a facilitator of sexual fantasy, pornography is more a technological widget like contraceptive foam (both contribute to pleasure) than a religious pamphlet. Or it is more like a vibrator, a "sex aid," than a supermarket tabloid. Frederick Schauer similarly claims that pornography is "a sexual surrogate" like a "rubber product."[42] Because pornography is first a generator of sensual experiences and only marginally a conveyor of ideas, it loses, for Schauer, First Amendment protection. But Schauer suggests that even if pornography is not speech, the values of privacy and choice "may argue against regulation" (184). The same constitutional considerations that protect a woman's right to have an abortion, the right of interracial couples to marry, the right to purchase contraceptive devices—all the considerations that should have led the Supreme Court to find in favor of Michael Hardwick, thereby protecting consensual homosexual activity—could be used to protect pornography.

Academic Lies

That pornography is more like a dildo than a pamphlet is also part of Elizabeth Wolgast's argument that pornography forfeits First Amendment protection. Pornography, on her view, should be restricted when and because its insinuations about women are "demeaning." She asks, though, whether philosophical works, those written by Aristotle, Schopenhauer, or Nietzsche, and similar treatises in the biological and social sciences should be regulated. Don't these claim that women are inferior, that human society is naturally patriarchal, and that women enjoy subservient or abusive sex? Wolgast answers that philosophical and scientific works make *assertions* about women and so can be criticized and, in principle, refuted by other speech. But pornography is among those "materials that say nothing" and hence are "beyond this risk of refutation." So sexist academic texts, for Wolgast, but not sexist pornography, retain First Amendment protection.[43] MacKinnon is not as tolerant as Wolgast of academic lies.

Pornography, in the Model Law, includes depictions in which "women are presented as whores by nature" (sec. 2.1.vii).[44] In their writings, both Dworkin and MacKinnon claim that women are for reasons of social structure "whores." Women are compelled by their situation to barter sex or sex appeal for money or support, to a (potential) husband, a male employer offering her a job, a john in prostitution.[45] The phrase "by nature" in The Law is therefore crucial. Apparently, it would be okay for a pornographic movie to present women as whores "by social pressure"—if conveying that message were possible. Indeed, how could pornography convey the message that women are whores *by nature*, that they exchange sex for support in virtue of, say, evolutionary biology? Dworkin and MacKinnon do not clarify, but they give an example:

> Underlying all of *Playboy*'s pictorials is the basic theme of all pornography: that all women are whores by nature, born wanting to be sexually accessible to all men at all times. *Playboy* particularly centers on sexual display as what women naturally do to demonstrate this nature.[46]

I find the claim puzzling that the beavers of *Playboy* convey the message that women are "born" as whores and "naturally" display themselves. MacKinnon and Dworkin, however, do not say the photos explicitly assert that message; rather, the theme "underlies" the photographs. The question, then—how could pornography depict women as whores "by nature"?—is moot, for the "by nature" has been forced into the photos. Reading them this way looks like a scoundrel's trick, but reason exists for taking it seriously: if pornography is radically polysemous, reading the beaver as loosely as Dworkin and MacKinnon do is of course possible. But to utilize gaping semiotic holes in the meaning of simple photographic pornography—to do exactly what the consumer of pornography does in constructing a fantasy from the groundwork of the image—in making this point about the beaver is strange. Attributing an underlying "real" meaning to the photos, and disregarding their surface content, conflicts with MacKinnon's implicit claim that she can read the content of men's minds, their attitudes and desires, their loving death, straight from the manifest content of pornography. MacKinnon's strategy here also permits us to maintain, with even more confidence, all the "nonaccess" ways of looking at the beaver I mentioned above.

The depictions referred to by Dworkin and MacKinnon in section 2.1.vii might not, however, be of women exchanging sex for support, but of women as active seekers of sexual pleasure. "Whores" in The Law is an inaccurate term; MacKinnon and Dworkin likely meant "presented as promiscuous sluts by nature." Then the depictions are being condemned because they say of women that by birth ("born") or, perhaps, by character, they are promiscuous; women would perform these acts even if not paid or coerced to do so. These depictions might be offensive, then, not just because they portray women in an unflattering moral light, as unable to obey Augustine's demand for self-control. In addition, they show women in an unflattering pragmatic light, as eager and willing to engage in sex without obtaining or expecting the job, marriage, or money they are entitled to receive in return. Given their social situation as described by MacKinnon and Dworkin, sexually active women, both in life and in pornography, have abandoned their rights. [47]

This offensive theme, that women are whores or sluts by nature, can be found explicitly in relatively less polysemous scholarly treatises. For example, the sociobiology of the academics David Buss and Donald Symons asserts that access to women's bodies for sexual purposes is, by evolutionary design, a service or favor women grant to men in exchange for material support. [48] And the physician-researcher Mary Jane Sherfey asserts as clearly as anyone could, in her scholarly text, that women's sexuality is biologically insatiable, that women require multiple male partners in orgies for complete satisfaction. [49] If so, women are and will likely always be whores or sluts by nature, in these senses. Wolgast would protect these books because, unlike pornography, they could be refuted by speech. But MacKinnon repudiates the distinction between pornography and scholarly texts. Pornography is both an act—it orders "get her"—and speech. [50] More accurately, for MacKinnon no difference exists between these categories: "Speech acts. . . . Acts speak." [51] Pornography is in a constitutional sense speech, not conduct, but even as speech pornography is an act that forfeits First Amendment protection, like libel, verbal bribery, antiunion speech, discriminatory advertisements, and sexually harassing talk. [52] What follows is that if pornography should be regulated by legal and social methods to protect women, then so, too, should scholarly treatises containing the same message ("get her"). Even if *Playboy* is off the hook, because the allegation that it conveys the idea that women are naturally whores is undermined by the polysemousness of its photos, sociobiological textbooks written in clear English do not have that defense. It is odd, then, that MacKinnon doesn't emphasize that scholarly texts, which assert their messages relatively unambiguously, present scientific evidence for their claims, and have behind them the authority of the academy, might have more cognitive impact than polysemous photographs. Indeed, MacKinnon seems to deny it: on her view, the power of rational argument pales beside the power of the pornographically produced masturbatory orgasm.[53]

In explaining her position on scholarly texts, MacKinnon offers this pregnant analogy:

> The current legal distinction between screaming "go kill that nigger" and advocating the view that African-Americans should be eliminated from parts of the United States needs to be seriously reconsidered, if real equality is ever to be achieved.[54]

Similarly, the legal distinction between pornography (screaming "get her") and the assertion in a scholarly text that men's rape of women is biological or that women are whores by nature must be abandoned for the sake of achieving gender equality. MacKinnon is not (here, yet) calling for censorship of scholarly texts; rather, she wants to prevent the "imposition" on students and others of texts demeaning to women:

> No teacher should be forced to teach falsehoods as if they must be considered provisionally true, just because bigots who have managed to get published have made their lies part of a debate.[55]

In the abstract, the principle sounds reasonable. But I can hear this sentence spoken by a defender of creationism: "no one should be forced to teach or listen to the falsehoods of evolution just because godless bigots have published their lies in fashionable textbooks that have dominated the market and the debate." On the other hand, I can also hear the sentence spoken by a proponent of evolution: "no one should be forced to teach or hear the nonsense of religious bigots just because their stuff has been published in third-rate journals (that *they* finance) and has become part of

the popular debate." Loyal fans of MacKinnon are supposed to fill in the
sentence: "no one should be forced to teach or hear falsehoods about
women—for example, that they are whores by nature—just because academic bigots like Symons have published their crap far and wide (Oxford
University Press, big deal) and are worshiped by other spineless parties in
the debate."

  A classic danger of advocating censorship, and a risk also of advocating
milder legal and social methods to exert control over offensive texts, is that
the proponent of control might herself be silenced by those policies. I can
hear, then, one more, tiny voice: "no one should be forced to pay attention
to lies about men just because some bigot has managed to get published by
Yale and Harvard (*mutatis mutandis,* big deal) and has inundated the
debate by publishing the same essays, the same paragraphs, the same
footnotes, and the same old 1970s statistics, over and over again, with
different titles." MacKinnon might be seen as another kind of gender bigot,
one who, like Symons and Buss, has dressed up her narrow vision in the
garb of university imprints. What might someone protest as MacKinnon's
own "lies"? Recall, for now, her versions of "men love death."

Brutality

"Pornography tells lies about women," insists John Stoltenberg. "But
pornography tells the truth about men."[56] What is this truth? Ignoring
the arguments that one cannot read the thoughts, desires, and fantasies in
a man's mind from the pornographic image he looks at,[57] MacKinnon
defiantly asserts that pornography reveals both the way men view the
world and what they want from and in it. For MacKinnon, "men want . . .
women bound, . . . battered, . . . tortured, . . . humiliated, . . . degraded and
defiled, . . . killed."[58] About whom is she talking? What men? Maybe this
is how some men see the world; maybe some few men want women killed
for sexual pleasure. So why doesn't MacKinnon write, "some men want
women killed"? Carelessness? Perhaps, but probably not. As demeaning
and as false as it is, this is MacKinnon's view of *men.* Besides, to write a
boring truth, that only a few rare men want women killed for sexual
pleasure, would create for MacKinnon no audience. But to slander men as
a class (isn't that what she and Dworkin are doing?),[59] like David Duke's

slander of Jews as a class, and blacks, guarantees success. MacKinnon is not embarrassed to have published this accusation, for she repeats the smear in *Only Words* (17): "men masturbate to women being exposed, humiliated, violated, degraded, mutilated, dismembered, bound, gagged, tortured, and killed." Not "some" or "a few," but *men*. Generic.[60] Lots of men masturbate to exposed women in beavers. *Maybe* some men exist who masturbate to a depiction of a woman being killed.[61] But not in the vast numbers implied by MacKinnon's "men masturbate."[62]

Since MacKinnon claims that men masturbate to depictions of women being killed, it is fitting, despite the fact she must know that no decent evidence exists of any genuine snuff film,[63] that she says over and over again that women *and* children are tortured and killed in the making of pornography.[64] In part, this is why she asserts that the message of pornography is "get her" (that is, women), which she likens to ordering a pit bull to kill.[65] In exaggerating the brutality in pornography, MacKinnon and Dworkin play on and take advantage of the fears of women. Sexually inexperienced women are often frightened by the perceived bizarreness of the male and female sexuality presented by pornography. The realization that the ideology they learned as children is false—sex is not, after all, always connected with love and monogamous marriage; men and women happily engage in taboo sexual activities, from anal intercourse to the Sadean perversions—can be shocking. An eighteen-year-old female student who has never seen an erotic magazine, and is perhaps a virgin, must be amazed when viewing orgiastic pornography. Worse, showing this freshman the most violent pornography, slide after slide after slide packed into an hour of continuous visual brutality, or assigning (imposing?) *Only Words* for her to read in a course, must make her reel with disgust and fear. Fear also comes from the suspicion that pornography is a mirror of the reality of male desire *and* behavior, that pornography, in particular the killing kind that MacKinnon insists exists, is a transparent window into the minds of men. Talk about brutality. Like Augustine, MacKinnon and Dworkin churn up the fear, whip it raw, then offer a solution, the salvation of *their* Law.

Over the last twenty years, while doing the research for my book *Pornography* and several essays on the subject, I browsed in a hundred pornography stores, in half the states of the continental United States and a half-dozen European countries; I waded inside stacks of magazines and videos; I inspected a virtual stream of catalogues.[66] Genuine brutality in photographic pornography has been and still is almost impossible to come across. The brutality depicted—bondage, spankings, humiliation, maid service, and the like—is obviously staged, fake, pretended. Material depicting this sex makes up between 10 and 15 percent of the material available in the heterosexual stock of a typical pornography store (counting by titles) and is split about equally between men dominating women and women dominating men.[67] Children are as scarce as hens' teeth in the United States, somewhat more available in Europe. The depiction of a woman barely fellating a horse or not quite being penetrated by a dog is slightly more common, but not very. A few magazines and videos show urination and defecation, some of which is genuine; a woman dumping something on a man or woman is somewhat more likely than a man relieving or evacuating himself on a woman. On the one hand, critics of pornography complain about the brutal and degrading treatment of women in pornography; on the other hand, most pornography is uncomplicated, orgiastic, heterosexual oral sex, coitus, and anal sex. The only way to make sense of this incongruity is to assume the critics seriously judge orgiastic heterosexual pornography to be degrading or brutal; but then their opposition to pornography is opposition to sexuality, or heterosexuality, itself. That surely captures the conservative or Augustinian critics; it also captures some of the feminists.

Reading Dworkin and MacKinnon, I find it difficult to resist this conclusion.[68] Dworkin claims that heterosexual coitus per se, and not merely depictions of women having sex with animals and objects, is the subordination of women. In intercourse, "female is bottom, stigmatized." The biology of sexual intercourse makes "a woman inferior: communicating to her cell by cell her own inferior status, impressing it on her, burning it into her by shoving it into her, over and over, pushing and thrusting until she gives in." Sexual intercourse "is the pure, sterile, formal expression of men's contempt for women."[69] When MacKinnon is explaining how the sexual activity depicted by pornography is not "simulated," she says that men's erect penises are photographed "ramming up" repeatedly into women; the photographs show this "ramming up" because "ramming up" really happened.[70] To make the elementary point that the sexual activity in pornography is genuine, one need say only *that*. To make the point by describing coitus as "ramming up," to take "ramming up" as paradigmatic of coitus, and to use "ramming up" as an example of what really occurs in the making of pornography is hatred, pure and simple, for coitus and the male coital role. MacKinnon's promiscuous use of "fuck" in her writings also expresses it. Heterosexual copulation, without more, is, for Dworkin and MacKinnon, violent brutality.

MacKinnon's forcing us to read about ramming penises—who had a real choice? who was adequately warned?—is itself a kind of aggressive priapic weapon. MacKinnon is the pushy writer who compels captured readers to suffer an unwelcome sexual experience, for her unsolicited sexual talk is, as she knows, an unsolicited sexual act.[71] No wonder Mac-Kinnon's prose seems to hammer and pound, to reproduce the pornographic words/acts she condemns with those very words. In an attempt, I suppose, to make the reality of women's oppression in pornography and sexuality clear, MacKinnon, through her style, subjects her readers to what she believes women experience daily. This is particularly true in her attitude toward men. The implied foulness in her words "men masturbate," her belittling criticism of men's most secret act, violates men. She shouts at them, "you are all perverted killers," the same way pornography supposedly shouts at women, "you are all mindless sluts." *Only Words* is Mac-Kinnon's tit-for-tat, returning brutal, slanderous pornography for what she perceives as brutal, slanderous pornography.[72]

Reality

Leaving the theater after watching Cowboy Bob in *Big Guns on the Pampas*, Dennis the Menace says to his friend, "He didn't *really* kiss her. ... They got stuntmen for that kinda stuff." But Dennis knows that even if Cowboy Bob escaped that fate, someone had to kiss her, poor guy. While this poor guy's expression of delight during the kiss was feigned, the pressing of his lips against hers was real, not feigned. Cowboy Bob, the rich and famous star, could weasel out of it; a young, aspiring actor, or a has-been, was bribed by the studio to do it for him.

Pornography is often objected to on the grounds that the sexual acts constituting the content of pornography are really done:

For any picture to be taken of a woman being fucked, beaten, tied and hung from rafters, shaved and spread, an actual woman had to be fucked, beaten, tied and hung from rafters, shaved and spread.[73]

MacKinnon, too, claims that in the making of pornography, women and children are "bound, battered, tortured, humiliated, and killed."[74] These claims contain some truth, although not nearly as much as asserted; most orgiastic pornography is monotonous in its making, momentous only in its killing the personnel with boredom. But consider a film of coitus between a thirty-year-old man and a ten-year-old girl. The film might symbolize the Soviet Union's invasion of Hungary; the perennial confrontation between the generations; or one aspect of Freud's theory of the family. But no matter how polysemous depictions are, the events as they occurred, recorded by the film (unless it has magnificently tricked us), are unerasable by flights into metaphor. This film does not contain the fake violence of commercial sadomasochistic pornography that MacKinnon turns into real brutality. We are encountering a documentation, perhaps homemade or amateur, of a morally horrible act. The fault lies in the very content of the film, not its message or meaning or what the raw material enables a viewer to fantasize. If we judge this sex morally wrong, the film is condemned by its content even if we can construct reasonable and illuminating deep readings of its meaning. The issue of meaning is quite secondary. The brute content prevails in our consciousness and judgments about the film because the film's content is inseparable from the film's production. We need not rely on adult-child coitus to make the point. Even if no man or woman is depicted in pornography *as* a whore, the personnel, the models, are prostitutes *in* the making of pornography. If or when prostitution is wrong, objectionable, or repugnant, the making of pornography will be wrong, too. No one should be compelled to make it, or to carry out any other activity, by material deprivation.

One of MacKinnon's major accusations against pornography focuses on the way it is produced: women are coerced, manipulated, wheedled, and preyed on by pornographers to pose for pornography.[75] The Model Law, appropriately, is directed at the coercion of persons into making pornography: "Section 3.1. *Coercion into pornography:* It shall be sex discrimination to coerce, intimidate, or fraudulently induce . . . any person . . . into performing for pornography."[76] The proposal to legitimize civil suit for coercing someone into making pornography (that is, for *rape*) seems fine. "Coercion," however, is as contestable a concept as has ever existed in political theory. How "coercion" and its sibling "consent" are understood is crucial if we are to evaluate the production of pornography, yet arriving at anything near a consensus about their meaning is difficult. Indeed, what the Model Law proceeds to say about "coercion" has elicited strong criticism. The Law characterizes coercion negatively: "proof of one or more of the following shall not, without more, negate a finding of coercion"—at which point The Law lists thirteen conditions that, if proven to obtain (singly or together) by a defendant accused of coercing someone into the making of pornography, would *not* prevent a court or jury from deciding that coercion of the complainant had occurred.

According to some of these clauses, that the woman is or has been a prostitute outside the making of this particular item of pornography is irrelevant for the decision of whether coercion took place. The historical fact of earlier or concurrent prostitution cannot be used as evidence by the defendant that participation in the making of pornography was entered into by the woman's free consent. Here the MacKinnon/Dworkin Law is as sensible as the Antioch policy, which makes history irrelevant; the policy does not allow sexual partners to assume, even though consent had been given to previous sexual acts, that they may proceed with sexual activity in the absence of new consent. Several other clauses in the Model Law have similar rationales. That a woman is connected by blood or marriage to, or has had sexual relations with, anyone involved in the making of the pornography, or that she has made pornography before does not negate a finding of coercion. These clauses, like Antioch's policy, sensibly insist that a woman's sexual history bears no relevance to her claim that she has been raped.

The clauses of The Law that have drawn critical attention are these:

> Proof of one or more of the following shall not, without more, negate a finding of coercion: . . . (xi) that the person signed a contract, or made statements affirming a willingness to cooperate in the production of pornography; or (xii) that no physical force, threats, or weapons were used in the making of the pornography; or (xiii) that the person was paid or otherwise compensated.

Because a signed contract, the absence of force in the content of the pornography, and a check deposited by the woman do not, not even together, imply that she consented to the sex in which she took part in making pornography, The Law apparently "creates a strong presumption" that women who make pornography are coerced to do so.[77] By voiding these things, especially when combined, as sufficient evidence of consent, The Law apparently puts the burden on the accused to show that he did not coerce anyone into making pornography. Since a contract, the absence of force, and a check made out to a woman do "not, without more, negate a finding of coercion," one might scratch one's skull wondering what "more" a defendant in a civil suit could do to exonerate himself. While insisting that "no" means "no," The Law (like Antioch's policy) refuses to take a woman's "yes" seriously.

On this reading of The Law, it resembles Lois Pineau's treatment of rape. For Pineau, we can reasonably presume that a woman would not consent to certain sexual acts. She means, in particular, aggressive, non-communicative, and unpleasurable sex: the man is pushy; silence replaces discussion about what will occur; she feels no desire for him. If a woman does engage in this unattractive sex, the presumption of nonconsent means that the man, to defend himself against the charge of rape, must show that she did consent.[78] Gayle Rubin finds this theme in The Law:

> Dworkin and MacKinnon appear to think that certain sexual activities are so . . . distasteful that no one would do them willingly, and therefore the models . . . must have been forced to participate.[79]

The argument that group fellatio and anal intercourse are so universally repugnant that no woman would freely participate in them is a flop, of course; so, too, is the weaker claim that they create a presumption that women who participate have been coerced to do so. Dworkin's and MacKinnon's harsh words about heterosexual coitus and puritanical descriptions of pornographic depictions suggest that this is indeed their argument. MacKinnon does claim that no woman today participates freely in the making of pornography, but she offers a second and more powerful argument, one that turns not on "distaste" but primarily on economic considerations.

MacKinnon and Dworkin's claim that the items mentioned in clauses xi-xiii should not *automatically* rule out a judgment of coercion seems right. The facts that a check was written and cashed, she signed a contract, and no force is visible in the film do not make it impossible that she was forced into the whole affair. If she can display wounds or bruises, for example, some reason exists to be at least suspicious of a signed contract. Hence we can understand why Dworkin and MacKinnon claim with deliberate exaggeration that models in pornography are physically abused: if all pornography involves abuse of its personnel, all pornography becomes dubious. When explaining this part of the Model Law, MacKinnon begins by claiming that Linda Marchiano (Lovelace) was "systematically beaten" and "kept under constant psychological intimidation and duress."[80] Clauses xi-xiii of The Law were designed to thwart this chicanery.

After mentioning the occurrence of physical and mental abuse as one reason for the "coercion into pornography" section of The Law, MacKinnon goes on to say,

> The further fact that prostitution and modeling are structurally women's best economic options should give pause to those who would consider women's presence there a true act of free choice.[81]

So an additional reason for the "coercion" section is that women are economically coerced into making pornography. But MacKinnon does not restrict economic coercion to the influence of poverty. The sentence just above implies that *no* woman participating in pornography does so freely; if she is not physically or psychologically abused into it, she is coerced by the lure of good money, better money than she would get at Burger Queen. Hence every sex act done in the making of pornography is rape. The clause in The Law according to which payment does not negate a finding of coercion is therefore misleading; the payment *proves* coercion. A payment cannot ever negate a finding of coercion because the payment *is* the coercion.

A defender of MacKinnon might reply that the sentence does not say *that*, literally; it says only "should give pause."[82] Then consider this, which comes a few lines later:

> I will leave you wondering, with me, why it is that when a woman spreads her legs for a camera, she is assumed to be exercising free will.

What's to wonder? The answer is that we usually assume, for both adult women and men, that what they agree contractually and are paid to do, they do freely, unless special conditions indicate otherwise—poverty, a gun at the head, bruises. MacKinnon does not accept this answer, else she would not have rhetorically wondered. Her point can be only that when women spread their legs for cameras, they don't do so freely. Elsewhere MacKinnon makes exactly the same point in almost exactly the same language, again not literally, but with sarcasm. [83]

Rosemarie Tong interprets MacKinnon as claiming that "all (or almost all) sexual intercourse is rape unless proven otherwise." [84] This interpretation, given what MacKinnon wrote in defense of clauses xi–xiii, seems justified, at least about sex in pornography. What about more generally? MacKinnon replies to Tong, "were this my view, I would have taken the occasion of my rather extensive work on the subject to express it," [85] and she chastises Tong (among other critics) for distorting her meaning by not having quoted the passages in which this thesis—that all heterosex is rape unless shown otherwise—was supposed to reside. "Nothing is in my own words," MacKinnon complained about Tong's review essay. So contemplate, to start, MacKinnon's *Sexual Harassment of Working Women*. While criticizing Susan Brownmiller's treatment of rape in *Against Our Will*, MacKinnon writes that Brownmiller failed to ask

> whether, under conditions of male supremacy, the notion of consent has any real meaning for women. . . . Consent is not scrutinized to see whether it is a structural fiction to legitimize the real coercion built into the normal social definitions of heterosexual intercourse. . . . [Readers] need never confront whether women have a chance, structurally speaking and as a normal matter, even to consider whether they want to have sex or not. (298 n. 8)

And now *Toward a Feminist Theory of the State:*

> the *major* distinction between intercourse (normal) and rape (abnormal) is that the normal happens so often that one cannot get anyone to see anything wrong with it. (146, italics added)

> The law of rape presents consent as free exercise of sexual choice under conditions of equality of power without exposing the underlying structure of constraint and disparity. . . . Exercise of women's so-called power presupposes more fundamental social powerlessness. (175)

women are socialized to passive receptivity; may have or perceive no alternative to acquiescence; may prefer it to the escalated risk of injury and the
humiliation of a lost fight; submit to survive. . . . If sex is normally something men do to women, the issue is less whether there was force than
whether consent is a meaningful concept. (177–78)

To this, MacKinnon attaches a footnote, quoting Carole Pateman with
approval, whose thesis is that in contemporary patriarchy, we cannot speak
meaningfully of the consent of women to sex.[86] One reason for this
conclusion, as applied to sex in pornography in particular, is, for MacKinnon, that

empirically, all pornography is made under conditions of inequality based on
sex, overwhelmingly by poor, desperate, homeless, pimped women who were
sexually abused as children.[87]

If true, this fact might well justify clauses xi-xiii of The Law; the poverty,
misery, and abuse suffered by all the women who make pornography
would override contracts and payments. At this crucial place in her argument, however, MacKinnon's use of the word "empirically" is a bluff. The
academic lawyer, who stuffs her books with endnotes sending readers to
sources galore to substantiate her claims, appends no footnote or endnote
to this pivotal assertion. The needed substantiation is glaring by its absence.[88] "Overwhelmingly" is not a conclusion to be reached merely on
the basis of the self-selected women who gave testimony at various pro-
ceedings over the last dozen years.[89]

Romanticism

Despite MacKinnon's pounding message that women are brutalized by
men, sex, pornography, and the law, and that in patriarchal society no
difference exists between rape and intercourse, a few of her words display
a romantic side to her sexual philosophy.

In *Only Words*, for example, MacKinnon reveals her idea of what sex
should be: "shared intimacy" (27). Pornography lies, says a MacKinnon
who sounds like John Paul II, because genuine sex is shared intimacy, while
pornography is the sexual domination of women by men. MacKinnon is
speaking normatively: the best sex, the only sex worthy of the name, is

sex that occurs within, or expresses, shared intimacy. The cold, loveless fucking of pornography and of everyday life is dehumanizing, beneath human dignity. Prostitution, whether of a housewife, employee, or call girl, is especially repugnant. Nothing is colder than a bought fuck.

Elsewhere, MacKinnon writes that "consent in sex . . . is supposed to mean freedom of desire expressed, not compensation for services rendered."[90] Consent *in sex* is supposed to mean "freedom of desire expressed," not compensation (say, payment) for actions. Forcing a woman into sex at gunpoint is wrong, and offering her money is also coercive and wrong—not through the nature of coercion, but through the nature of sex and what sex is "supposed" to be. Therefore, consent in prostitution is a kind of category mistake, a conceptual impossibility. Consent is also necessarily absent from pornography, since the making of pornography involves commercial sex. Hence, as Dworkin says, in the pornography industry "ten billion dollars a year now is being spent on watching [women] being raped for fun."[91] But why does MacKinnon assume that sex for money excludes "freedom of desire," that a "freedom of desire" for money itself is offensive (assuming poverty has been eliminated)? The motives for sex are legion. Where is the freedom of desire in having sex in order to get a good night's sleep, have a child, make someone happy? No nonarbitrary way exists to exclude, as incompatible with the nature of sex, a desire for compensation of some sort or another, including money but maybe just reciprocal body- and ego-stroking. MacKinnon has placed a busybody's limit on respectable reasons to have sex, demanding the perfectly loving world that her God who does not exist promised her.

MacKinnon's romanticism seeps out once more, at the end of *Only Words*, where she imagines that in a truly egalitarian society, men will find pornographic depictions of women a "turn-off" (110). There is no "men masturbate" in our egalitarian future. But MacKinnon has not laid any theoretical foundation for this bit of feminine (not necessarily feminist) wishful thinking. How would gender equality, or equality in general, destroy the erotic power of photographs or the masturbatory urge in response to a Bronzino? MacKinnon does not merely claim that with equality, women will have no economic incentive to participate in making pornography, that equality will abolish its *supply* (unless some women decide, anyway and freely, to spread their legs for the camera). That feminist vision is reasonable and follows from her worries about the economic coercion of women into the making of pornography. But Mac-Kinnon, like a romanticizing masturbator, escapes into fantasy: in equality, the nature of men will have changed so dramatically that men will find the beaver, and masturbating to it, not merely boring but a turn-off. The *demand* for pornography will be dead, regardless of the health of its supply. Equality creates men who, to the same extent as women, think of cold sex without shared intimacy as beneath human dignity. But given MacKinnon's relentless condemnation of men for masturbating to pictures of women being mutilated and killed, one must wonder about the magical power of equality to change men into these lovable and loving Christian/feminine creatures. These are the sweet words of hope unmodified feminism has for the future of men, for the men of the future.

Notes to Chapter One

1. *The Limits of Love*, 47.

2. "Sexuality," in *The Examined Life*, 67.

3. More precisely, Judeo-Christian. For a recent defense of the Judaic part (against homosexuality), see Dennis Prager, "Homosexuality, the Bible, and Us." Recall what the Lord said to Moses at Leviticus 20:13.

4. Susan Farr, "The Art of Discipline," 184.

5. Diane Vera, "Temporary Consensual 'Slave Contract,' " 76.

6. Karol Wojtyla, *Love and Responsibility*, 126, 129.

7. *Being and Nothingness*, pt. 3, chap. 3, sect. 2, 404.

8. "On Affectionate Relationships," 209.

9. Ben Jonson's translation of the first two lines of "Foeda est in coitu voluptas," 83. Petronius's point in the rest, after he had condemned the *doing* (coitus), is that sex is best when lovers snuggle, lick, and probe *ad libitum*, not concerned to make Marvel's sun run.

10. *Sexual Desire*, 338.

11. "Prostitution, Exploitation and Taboo," 533–34.

12. *Summa theologiae*, 2a2ae, q. 154, a. 2, 213; see *Summa contra gentiles*, bk. 3, pt. 2, chap. 122, 144–46.

13. *On Marriage and Concupiscence*, bk. 1, chap. 1, 99, 106–7.

14. *Contra Julianum*, 3, 14; quoted in Elaine Pagels, *Adam, Eve, and the Serpent*, 140–41.

15. *The City of God*, bk. 14, no. 18, 466.

16. *On Marriage*, bk. 1, chap. 8, 106.

17. *City of God*, bk. 14, no. 16, 464–65; no. 24, 473.

18. *City of God*, bk. 14, no. 10, 457; no. 26, 474–75. See Pierre J. Payer, *The Bridling of Desire*, 23–25, 39–40, 203 n. 67.

19. *On Marriage*, bk. 1, chap. 9, 107; see chap. 13, 112; and chap. 16, 115.

20. *On Marriage*, bk. 1, chap. 16, 115.

21. See Pagels, *Adam, Eve, and the Serpent*, 110–11, 140–41. Payer argues that because, for Augustine ("so often the whipping boy for what are perceived to be incorrect views about sex"), there would eventually have been sexual intercourse in Paradise had Adam and Eve not fallen, Augustine acknowledged "the natural goodness" of sex (*Bridling of Desire*, 24). I am not convinced. There would have

been sexual intercourse, but no bodily arousal, concupiscence, or rushes of desire, so Augustine ends up acknowledging as good and natural nothing we would take to be sexually valuable. He still deserves the whipping.

22. W. M. Alexander, "Sex and Philosophy in Augustine," 208; *On Marriage*, bk. 1, chap. 14, 113.

23. "That Not All Sexual Intercourse Is Sinful," in *Summa contra gentiles*, bk. 3, pt. 2, chap. 126, 155–56.

24. This is the King James. The New International is more explicit: [3]The husband should fulfill his marital duty to his wife, and likewise the wife to her husband. [4]The wife's body does not belong to her alone but also to her husband. In the same way, the husband's body does not belong to him alone but also to his wife. [5]Do not deprive each other except by mutual consent and for a time, so that you may devote yourselves to prayer. Then come together again so that Satan will not tempt you because of your lack of self-control.

25. Socrates: "one does not desire what one does not lack" (Plato, *Symposium* 200b; Hamilton, 76). John Paul II's innocence is amusing: "Marital continence is so much more difficult than continence outside marriage, because the spouses grow accustomed to intercourse. . . . Once they begin to have sexual intercourse as a habit, and a constant inclination is created, a mutual need for intercourse comes into being" (*Love and Responsibility*, 237).

26. "On the Connection of Sex to Reproduction," 40.

27. Margaret A. Farley ends her essay "Sexual Ethics" with the sermonizing, triumphant statement that "more and more theorists are coming to the conclusion that sexual desire without interpersonal love leads to disappointment and . . . meaninglessness" (1587). At last someone is catching up with those theorists who have concluded that sexual desire *with* love leads to disappointment and meaninglessness.

28. This was my argument over breakfast in "A Catholic Defense of Pornography," Saint John's University and College of St. Benedict, December 4–5, 1985.

29. Contrast the egalitarian 1 Corinthians 7:4 with the patriarchal Ephesians 5:22–33.

30. *Lectures on Ethics*, 166–67.

31. C. H. Whiteley and Winifred N. Whiteley, *Sex and Morals*, 80; see H. Tristram Engelhardt, Jr., "Having Sex and Making Love," 64 n. 2. Susan T. Nicholson writes that Aquinas "does not shrink from drawing the conclusion that rape (in which semen is deposited) is a lesser sin than 'unnatural' sex with one's spouse" (*Abortion and the Roman Catholic Church*, 8).

32. Adultery is mentioned here (q. 154, a. 1) by Aquinas as morally wrong not because it is unnatural but because it violates relations among men. But if monog-

amy is part of the natural design, then will not adultery be unnatural and thus morally wrong on both counts? Indeed, adultery could be morally wrong on *three* counts, as when X and Y are both married to others and engage in homosexual acts. By contrast, an unmarried man who engages in heterosexual coitus with a married woman is committing only one wrong—he offends the husband. She, however, is committing two—she offends her husband *and* nature. Were they to engage in anal intercourse, his immorality count would jump to two and hers to three.

Because there are different types of adultery, it is not clear that Aquinas contradicts himself (as claimed by John Boswell, *Christianity, Social Tolerance, and Homosexuality*, 324) when he says, on the one hand, that sexually monogamous marriage is part of the natural design (and hence adulterous fornication is unnatural and a mortal sin; *Summa theologiae*, 2a2ae, q. 154, a. 2, 213) and, on the other, that adultery is only a violation of proper relations among men (and, being natural, is only a venial sin). For Aquinas, that is, there might be a difference between a married man's adultery *before* he has any children with his wife (a venial sin that violates relations among men) and *after* he has children with her (add on the mortal sin of violating the naturalness of a monogamy divinely designed for the sake of the children).

33. On "bestiality" and "bestial" in Aquinas, see John T. Noonan, *Contraception*, 225, 241; and Boswell, *Christianity, Social Tolerance, and Homosexuality*, 323 n. 69.

34. *On Marriage*, bk. 1, chap. 17, 116.

35. *Summa contra gentiles*, bk. 3, pt. 2, chap. 122, 144.

36. Vern L. Bullough and Bonnie Bullough, *Sexual Attitudes*, 128.

37. Nicholson thinks Aquinas extended his analysis of sterile sex to contraception: both are permissible (*Abortion*, 8–9); Farley claims Aquinas "opposed contraception . . . because it was in intention nonprocreative" ("Sexual Ethics," 1580); Paul Simmons thinks contraception is, for Aquinas, not unnatural but still wrong, since it falls into the same category of evil as incest and rape ("Theological Approaches to Sexuality," 202); Noonan relies on the *Summa contra gentiles* passage I quote in the text to argue that, for Aquinas, contraceptive sex is unnatural (*Contraception*, 242).

38. "Humanae vitae," in Baker and Elliston, eds., *Philosophy and Sex*, 2d ed., 172–73.

39. Joseph Glenmullen's patient David went soft whenever putting on a condom, "because," said David, "that would expose the carnality of it" (*The Pornographer's Grief*, 77). His problem is a variant of the woman's who is reluctant to carry condoms in her bag.

40. *Love and Responsibility,* 239; see 228, 235–36.

41. *Love and Responsibility,* 235. For a similar view, see Robert Solomon, "Sexual Paradigms," in Soble, ed., *Philosophy of Sex,* 2d ed., 55, 58.

42. *On Marriage,* bk. 1, chap. 17, 116. Noonan calls this "fundamental" passage "vehement" (*Contraception,* 120).

43. See Noonan, *Contraception,* 120, 447.

44. "On Christian Marriage," 37, 39.

45. *Love and Responsibility,* 283.

46. *Sex and Reason,* 269.

47. This comparison suggests that a couple might employ periodic abstinence to put the zip back into sex by thwarting Pauline access. Was the rhythm method really proposed as a solution to Paul's dilemma?

48. *Love and Responsibility,* 241; see 242. Before presenting this solution, John Paul acknowledged the objections I have mentioned to other formulations (235, 240).

49. In his 1995 encyclical "Evangelium vitae," John Paul ignores the candid (even brilliant) solution presented in *Love and Responsibility* and reverts to an untenable account of "natural methods of regulating fertility." He now praises medical science for making it possible for husband and wife to know with more accuracy when in her cycle they can engage in intercourse without risking pregnancy (722).

50. Philip Roth's adulterers Drenka and Mickey "could eroticize anything . . . except their spouses" ("The Ultimatum," 126).

51. Sylvère Lotringer, *Overexposed,* 88–89, 122. For conditioning techniques employed to create arousal to previously unarousing acts or things (for example, black knee-length women's boots), see Edward C. Nelson, "Pornography and Sexual Aggression," 183–87; Dolf Zillmann, *Connections between Sex and Aggression,* 183. For techniques to help "dissatisfied" gays achieve heterosexuality, see Mark F. Schwartz and William H. Masters, "The Masters and Johnson Treatment Program."

52. "Beyond Bisexual," 512 (italics omitted). Guy Sircello's "orgy in Pasadena" rivals Sprinkle's exuberance ("Beauty and Sex," in Soble, ed., *Philosophy of Sex,* 2d ed., 117–18). (A tantalizing photograph of Ms. Sprinkle is in Kate Ellis et al., eds., *Caught Looking,* 93.) For a pluralistic sexual philosophy, see Irving Singer, *The Goals of Human Sexuality.*

53. *Sex and Destiny,* 140–47.

54. Joseph A. Diorio, "Sex, Love, and Justice," in Soble, ed., *Eros, Agape and Philia,* 276. Two recent Christian sexual treatises that take love this seriously, and so end up blessing loving homosexual unions, are Patricia Jung and Ralph Smith, *Heterosexism;* and Christine E. Gudorf, *Body, Sex, and Pleasure.*

55. Craig R. Dean, "Fighting for Same Sex Marriage," 276. In idem, "Gay Marriage," the economic benefits of marriage seem to be more important than the "love right" (113).

56. *Gays/Justice*, 113.

57. "Sexual Behavior," in Soble, ed., *Philosophy of Sex*, 2d ed., 70.

58. Below I discuss Robin Morgan and Robin West on coercion. For an extreme position, see Charlene L. Muehlenhard and Jennifer L. Schrag, "Nonviolent Sexual Coercion," in which the authors describe ways "women are coerced into having unwanted sexual intercourse" that are "more subtle" than violent rape (115). Among these are compulsory heterosexuality (116–17), status (119), verbal pressure (122–23), and "discrimination against lesbians" (121).

59. "Abortion: Is a Woman a Person?" in *Beginning to See the Light*, 209. In the revision of this essay that appears in Ann Snitow et al., eds., *Powers of Desire*, "In 1979" is replaced by "One hundred and fifty years after Freud" (474). That's wrong; Freud lived from 1856 to 1939, so 150 years after Freud covers 2006 to 2089. The mistake is repeated in Janet A. Kourany et al., eds., *Feminist Philosophies*, 85.

60. Sidney Callahan, "Abortion and the Sexual Agenda," 238.

61. *Feminism Unmodified*, 144–45; see *Toward a Feminist Theory of the State*, 190, and "Liberalism and the Death of Feminism," 6–7. Andrea Dworkin sympathetically reports that conservative women think that abortion "reduce[s] women to the fuck" (*Right-Wing Women*, 103).

62. "Abortion and the Sexual Agenda," 237–38.

63. Russell Vannoy, *Sex without Love*.

64. *Marriage and Morals*, 227–28.

65. Brownmiller, however, speaks of rape both as violence and as sex; see *Against Our Will*, chap. 12.

66. *Feminism Unmodified*, 233; see *Toward a Feminist Theory*, 132, 286 n. 63. But MacKinnon claims that contrasting sex and violence is also misleading: doing so obscures the violence and coerciveness of "normal" sexuality in patriarchy (*Sexual Harassment of Working Women*, 218–19; *Feminism Unmodified*, 160; *Toward a Feminist Theory*, 127, 137, 140, 150, 172–74, 211). The distinction between rape and consensual intercourse is "difficult to sustain" (*Toward a Feminist Theory*, 146).

67. John Stoltenberg agrees with MacKinnon, adding a twist: "It is the fashion nowadays to presume that an act is more or less outside the pale of ethical examination if at any point along the course of it there is an erection or an ejaculation" (*Refusing to Be a Man*, 47), that is, if male sexual pleasure in particular is involved.

68. Alfred Kinsey et al., *Sexual Behavior in the Human Male,* in Martin S. Weinberg, ed., *Sex Research,* 75.

69. *Symposium,* 183a-b; Hamilton, 49.

70. "Adultery," in Soble, ed., *Philosophy of Sex,* 2d ed., 192.

71. In Miriam Allott and Robert H. Super, eds., *Matthew Arnold,* 132.

72. "The Principles of Social Freedom," 17.

73. Bk. 3, pt. 2, chap. 122, 142.

74. J. F. M. Hunter, *Thinking about Sex and Love,* 28, 111–12.

75. *Lectures on Ethics,* 169–71.

76. *Summa theologiae,* q. 154, a. 12, 248.

77. *City of God,* bk. 15, no. 16, 500–501. See Jerome Neu, "What Is Wrong with Incest?"

78. See Timo Airaksinen, "The Style of Sade."

79. *The Nature and Evolution of Female Sexuality,* 137–39.

80. Simon LeVay, *The Sexual Brain,* 105–30; Dean Hamer and Peter Copeland, *The Science of Desire;* Chandler Burr, "Homosexuality and Biology"; David Nimmons, "Sex and the Brain"; *Scientific American* (May 1994); see also the notes to chapter 4, below; and Edward Stein, "The Relevance of Scientific Research about Sexual Orientation to Lesbian and Gay Rights" (which argues that it has none).

81. *Body, Sex, and Pleasure,* 65. But a genuinely good God, according to the writer of *Deep Throat,* would have put it elsewhere.

82. "A Philosophical Analysis of Sexual Ethics," 9–10. Belliotti repeats this in *Good Sex,* 233–42.

83. *On the Basis of Morality,* 60.

84. "Adult-Child Sex."

85. "A Thorny Issue," 20.

86. *Sexual Democracy,* 233; see my review.

87. "Critique," 454; "Not-Knowing," 48.

88. See Jeffrey Weeks's sensitive discussion of adult-child sex, *Sexuality and Its Discontents,* 223–31. The self-proclaimed "postmodern" and "pragmatic" treatment of Steven Seidman (*Embattled Eros,* 200–205) is pompous and pedestrian.

89. "What's Wrong with Prostitution?"

90. *Marriage and Morals,* 122.

91. *Sex and Reason,* 389.

92. *Going Too Far,* 166. In 1874 Victoria Woodhull had written, "Night after night . . . millions of poor, heart-broken, suffering wives are compelled to minister to the lechery of insatiable husbands, when every instinct of body and sentiment of soul revolts in loathing and disgust" ("Tried as by Fire," 8).

93. Sandra Harding, *Whose Science? Whose Knowledge?* 126.

94. Alison Jaggar, "Prostitution," in Soble, ed., *Philosophy of Sex*, 2d ed., 272; Kathleen Barry, *The Prostitution of Sexuality*, 37.

95. *The Second Sex*, 525. See MacKinnon, *Feminism Unmodified*, 180.

96. Hilda Hein thinks degradation is wrong even if it is consensual ("Sadomasochism and the Liberal Tradition," 87):

> To degrade someone, even with that person's . . . consent, is to *endorse* the degradation of persons. It is to affirm that the abuse of persons is *acceptable*. For if some people may be humiliated . . . all may be. . . . To voluntarily make a victim of oneself is to endorse the state of victimization implicitly for others.

If consensual degradation does endorse, what exactly is endorsed? Consensual kissing does not endorse nonconsensual kissing, so consensual degradation endorses only consensual degradation. Further, consensual degradation might endorse nothing at all. Two people can engage in consensual degradation without endorsing it to anyone, since merely doing something does not necessarily recommend that others do it. I can chew a pencil without recommending that act to others and without endorsing your shoving unrequested pencils into someone else's mouth.

97. *Going Too Far*, 168.

98. "The Harms of Consensual Sex."

99. "Plain Sex," in Soble, ed., *Philosophy of Sex*, 2d ed., 87. See similar principles in Robert Nozick, *Anarchy, State and Utopia*, 31; and Bernard Baumrin, "Sexual Immorality Delineated," in Baker and Elliston, eds., *Philosophy and Sex*, 2d ed., 303–4.

100. Michael Ruse, *Homosexuality*, 185.

101. *Lesbian Choices*, 221.

102. *Love and Responsibility*, 30; see 84.

103. See Alan Soble, "Union, Autonomy, and Concern."

104. "Between Consenting Adults," 269–70.

105. Woodhull, "Principles of Social Freedom"; and idem, "Tried as by Fire."

106. "A Philosophical Analysis," 11.

107. *Toward a Feminist Theory*, 183; see 181.

108. See Timothy Perper and David L. Weis, "Proceptive and Rejective Strategies," 462.

109. Belliotti repeats his "when in doubt, ask" advice in *Good Sex*, 106–7.

110. *Real Rape*, 97–98.

111. I'm not sure these examples capture what Estrich's remark, that some women who say yes would say no *if they could*, means. She makes the point elsewhere: "many women who say 'yes' are not in fact choosing freely but are

submitting because they feel a lack of power to say 'no' " ("Rape," 177). Stephen J. Schulhofer ("The Gender Question," 308–9) discusses cases in which "yes" does not mean "yes": the man obtains consent through fraud or deception. Estrich seems not to have these cases in mind.

112. "Do Women Sometimes Say No When They Mean Yes?" 872. See Neil Gilbert, "Realities and Mythologies of Rape," 9.

113. "Coercion and Rape," 365.

114. Carole Pateman ("Women and Consent," 162) turns this around, arguing that if men do not take "no" as "no," they have no right to take "yes" as "yes."

115. Muehlenhard and Hollabaugh, "Do Women Sometimes Say No," 878.

116. I quote from a copy of the "Sexual Offense Policy" and its introduction sent to me in 1994 from the office of the president, Antioch University. The numbering and arrangement of the clauses are my own. The policy is intended to be gender-neutral, allowing the possibility of homosexual acquaintance rape and the rape of a man by a woman.

117. Jacqueline D. Goodchilds and Gail L. Zellman, "Sexual Signaling," 236. "Males have a more sexualized view of the world than females, attributing more sexual meaning to a wide range of behaviors" (239). See Antonio Abbey, "Sex Differences in Attributions."

118. At least seven times in the policy and its introductory passages, it is stated that consent to sexual activity must be verbal. Only once does the policy depart from this formula: "the person with whom sexual contact/conduct is initiated is responsible to express verbally and/or physically her/his willingness or lack of willingness when reasonably possible." Because the bulk of the policy insists that consent be verbal, I discount this one awkward and possibly contradictory sentence. Further, the use of "reasonably" here nearly destroys the power of the policy to solve our problems *about* reasonableness.

The policy also says, "If sexual contact . . . is *not* mutually and simultaneously initiated, then the person who initiates sexual contact . . . is responsible for getting the verbal consent of the other individual(s) involved" (italics added). From the statement that when mutual and simultaneous initiation is absent, verbal consent is required, it does not follow (nor does the policy ever assert) that when mutual and simultaneous initiation is present, verbal consent can be dispensed with. To claim otherwise—that is, to deny on *this* basis that the Antioch policy always requires verbal consent—is to commit an elementary logical fallacy. Anyway, if we are to construe the Antioch policy as an interesting and novel approach to the problems we are discussing, we should not read it as asserting that such a thing as "mutual and simultaneous initiation" can cancel the need for verbal consent. The person who subjectively has no doubt that the other person is consenting, but is mistaken about that, is the person who assumes that his initiation is reciprocated mutually and simultaneously by the other person, but is similarly mistaken. Thus the good intentions of the Antioch policy would fall prey to the same psychological and moral delusions that undermined Belliotti's principle, "when in doubt, ask." Indeed, the Antioch policy would merely reduce to the uninteresting silliness of that old and tired advice.

119. Perper and Weis, "Proceptive and Rejective Strategies," 476.

120. "Date Rape," 239.

121. Is badgering "coercion"? Morgan would say yes, West no. Mary Koss's category "sexually coercive men" includes those who obtain sex "after continual discussions" or by false avowals of love (Mary P. Koss and Kenneth E. Leonard, "Sexually Aggressive Men," 216; see Gilbert, "Realities and Mythologies," 7).

122. See Patrick D. Hopkins, "Rethinking Sadomasochism."

123. "Good Sex."

124. Antioch does little to make specific (A4)'s "specific," so the policy is vulnerable to wisecracks:

X: May I kiss you?
Y: Of course.
[Y makes Y's mouth available; X slides X's tongue deeply into Y's oral cavity.
    Y pulls sharply away.]
Y: I didn't say you could *French* kiss me!

Another one, the epigraph to chapter 9 of Susan Haack, *Evidence and Inquiry* (182), is an exchange between Jane Russell and Fred Astaire:

She: For the last time, do you love me or don't you?
He: I DON'T!
She: Quit stalling, I want a *direct* answer.

Professor Haack thanks David Stove for this.

125. So claims the policy: "consent must be clear and verbal (i.e., saying: yes, I want to kiss you also)."

126. Jennifer Wolf, "Sex by the Rules," 258.

127. "Sex and Reference," 42.

128. Pateman, "Women and Consent," 150.

129. Some teenagers (both sexes) think male anger and assault are justified if a girl reneges on a sexual deal (Goodchilds and Zellman, "Sexual Signaling," 237, 241–42).

130. Carolyn M. Shafer and Marilyn Frye, "Rape and Respect," 342.

131. George Bataille, *Story of the Eye*, 8.

Notes to Chapter Two

1. J. M. Cameron ("Sex in the Head," 19) and Jeffrey Weeks (*Sexuality and Its Discontents*, 23) think that the sex studies of Masters and Johnson gave masturbation a boost during the "sexual revolution" of the 1960s and beyond. I think that masturbation might have been boosted in the academy, but it remained in the popular doghouse. Shere Hite *(The Hite Report on Male Sexuality)* found that only 1 percent of her subjects had never masturbated (486), yet "most men felt guilty and inadequate about masturbating" (487).

2. *The Social Organization of Sexuality.*

3. Many dictionaries claim that "masturbation" comes from the Latin *manus*, hand. For example, *The Oxford Dictionary of English Etymology*, ed. C. T. Onions (561): the word is "of unkn. origin, but commonly held to be alt. of *man(u)stuprare*, 'defile with the hand.' " I prefer Werner A. Krenkel's etymology (in his "Masturbation in der Antike," a paper sent to me by the late classicist John Sullivan of the University of California, Santa Barbara): *mas* (male) and *turbatio* (disturbance). The *Oxford English Dictionary* agrees. Vern L. Bullough and Bonnie Bullough say that for "a new generation of scholars," the word is a hybrid of the Greek *mezea* (genitals) and the Latin *turbare* (*Sexual Attitudes*, 67).

4. "But Onan knew that the offspring would not be his; so whenever he lay with his brother's wife, he spilled his semen on the ground to keep from producing offspring for his brother. What he did was wicked in the Lord's sight, so He put him to death also" (Genesis 38:9–10). According to Pius XI, God killed Onan for engaging in Greerian *contraceptive* sex ("On Christian Marriage," 38). John Noonan argues persuasively against this reading (*Contraception*, 34–36).

5. Philip Roth, *Portnoy's Complaint*, 88.

6. *Lectures on Ethics*, 162–71, at 163. Also see idem, *The Metaphysical Principles of Virtue:* "the allowed bodily union . . . of the two sexes in marriage" is "in itself . . . only animal union" (86).

7. *Lectures on Ethics*, 166–67. See *Metaphysical Principles of Virtue*, 85.

8. "If a fusion of one and the other truly exists, . . . the very possibility of using an *other* as a means no longer exists" (Robert Baker and Frederick Elliston, eds., *Philosophy and Sex*, 1st ed., 18; 2d ed., 26–27). Kantian fusion seems to make rape in marriage (a kind of use) logically impossible.

9. "Masturbation" is the answer to Barbara Herman's question, "sex would then be what?" if Kant were right that (in her words) "we become parts of a new self that has two bodies" ("Could It Be Worth Thinking about Kant," 61).

10. Herman, "Could It Be Worth Thinking," 66 n. 22.

11. "Sexual Immorality Delineated," in Baker and Elliston, eds., *Philosophy and Sex*, 1st ed., 116, 118; 2d ed., 300, 301.

12. *Lectures on Ethics*, 170.

13. A notable contrast is Russell Vannoy's "humanist" treatment of masturbation, *Sex without Love*, 111–17. See also David Goff, "Masturbation: Touching Oneself Anew," in Franklin Abbott, ed., *Men and Intimacy*, 210–14.

14. "Plain Sex," in Soble, ed., *Philosophy of Sex*, 2d ed., 73–92.

15. "Sexual Perversion," in Soble, ed., *Philosophy of Sex*, 2d ed., 39–51.

16. See Alan Soble, *Pornography*, 156–57.

17. "Better Sex," in Baker and Elliston, eds., *Philosophy and Sex*, 2d ed., 280–99.

18. See Goldman, "Plain Sex," 87.

19. "Sexual Paradigms," in Soble, ed., *Philosophy of Sex*, 2d ed., 53–62 (page references to this essay are preceded by "SP"); "Sex and Perversion," in Baker and Elliston, eds., *Philosophy and Sex*, 1st ed., 268–87 (references preceded by "SAP").

20. See Fred R. Berger, "Pornography, Sex and Censorship."

21. Hugh Wilder, "The Language of Sex and the Sex of Language"; Goldman, "Plain Sex," 80–83.

22. *After Babel*, 39.

23. James Giles defines, in good binary fashion, sexual desire as "just the desire for mutual baring and caressing of bodies." He recognizes that fetishism does not obviously fall within this definition. To make room for it, Giles sees the fetish object as a "fantasized body" or a body "extension" ("A Theory of Love and Sexual Desire," 353). This is also desperate.

24. Heterosexuality, likewise, is as much in need of explanation as homosexuality: "from the point of view of psycho-analysis the exclusive sexual interest felt by men for women is also a problem that needs elucidating and is not a self-evident fact based upon an attraction that is ultimately of a chemical nature" (Sigmund Freud, *Three Essays on the Theory of Sexuality*, in *Standard Edition*, vol. 7, 146). Sarah Kofman goes farther, claiming that on Freud's view of the intensity of the male's castration anxiety experienced in response to the recognition that the mother lacks a penis, it is principally male heterosexuality that requires explanation: "It seems . . . that in the face of this horror," there are "only two solutions, homosexuality or fetishism; far from being 'pathological,' either one, under these conditions, would be the *normal* destiny of the masculine libido. Under these conditions, what becomes *abnormal* is heterosexuality. We then have the problem of understanding how" men "overcome their horror and even experience pleasure in sexual relations with a woman" (*The Enigma of Woman*, 84).

25. See Jerome Neu, "Freud and Perversion."

26. See Nancy Chodorow, *The Reproduction of Mothering*, 64–67.

27. *Hite Report on Male Sexuality*, 757.

28. *The Sexual Contract*, 199.

29. "Sexual Behavior," in Soble, ed., *Philosophy of Sex*, 2d ed., 63–71.

30. James D. Haynes, "Oral-Genital Sex," 427. Consider also Edward Vacek's opinion that homosexuals engage in sex "more humanely" than heterosexuals, "largely because they are better able empathetically to feel what their partner is feeling" ("A Christian Homosexuality?" 683).

31. In another essay, Moulton plays down her pleasure model, explaining the superiority of paired sex to masturbation in a different way: the "psychological aspects [of sex] are important. They are the *whole* reason for engaging in interpersonal sexual activity rather than masturbation" ("Sex and Reference," in Baker and Elliston, eds., *Philosophy and Sex*, 1st ed., 42, italics added). This view is as cramped as Solomon's view that the whole point of sex is communication. Both leave no room for people who are interested primarily in pleasure some of the time and for promiscuous singles (men, women, straight, gay, bi) who seek pleasure most of the time.

32. *Sexual Desire*, 244. Scruton does mention that the "trouble" of desire is, in another sense, just beginning: "how to prevent the calm love of nuptial union from being shattered by the turbulence of a new desire" for a third party.

33. *Lectures on Ethics*, 168.

34. See Vern L. Bullough and Bonnie Bullough, *Sin, Sickness, and Sanity*, 55–73; and idem, *Sexual Attitudes*, 67–84; H. Tristram Engelhardt, Jr., "The Disease of Masturbation"; and Thomas Szasz, *The Manufacture of Madness*, 180–206.

35. In the West and elsewhere; see my discussion of the Sambia and Etoro, chapter 3. But retaining semen is also dangerous; see Jeanne Schroeder, "Feminism Historicized," 1197 n. 242.

36. C. H. Whiteley and Winifred N. Whiteley, *Sex and Morals*, 87–88. See also Freud: "I cannot rule out a permanent reduction in potency as one among the results of masturbation" ("Contributions to a Discussion on Masturbation," in *Standard Edition*, vol. 12, 252).

37. James J. McCartney, "Contemporary Controversies in Sexual Ethics," 224–25. A defense of masturbation in terms of its contribution to the health and maintenance of the pair is the major theme of Suzanne Sarnoff and Irving Sarnoff, *Sexual Excitement/Sexual Peace: The Place of Masturbation in Adult Relationships*. Their inability to envision the playfulness of masturbation is nicely noted by Leonore Tiefer in her review: "In their world there'll be no more idle jerking off. Every masturbatory episode will provide an opportunity for self-analysis."

38. "Plain Sex," 74, 81.

39. The fact seems to be, however, that "higher levels of autoeroticism are associated with higher levels of partnered sexual activity" (Laumann et al., *Social Organization*, 137; see 80, 83, 86).

40. Michael S. Kimmel and Michael A. Messner, eds., *Men's Lives*, which anthology the editors describe as "a product of the profeminist men's movement" (vi). What Lennon had to mean in the epigraph was "I don't want to emulate the *image* of James Dean; I don't want to be his public persona." The private James Dean is irrelevant (for example, that he might have been gay). For the same reason, the editors should have dedicated their book to the image of Lennon, not to Lennon himself; to what they imagined he was, not to "the kind of man he was"—unless Lennon, despite being a media star, was absolutely transparent.

41. Jeffrey Fracher and Michael Kimmel, "Hard Issues and Soft Spots," in *Men's Lives*, 476. Kimmel repeats this passage, on his own, in his introduction to *Men Confront Pornography*, 9.

42. Dolf Zillmann and Jennings Bryant, "Pornography's Impact on Sexual Satisfaction," 438; see 450.

43. *Refusing to Be a Man*, 39.

44. Pauline Bart quips, "It is not true that we are treated like property. We should be so lucky!" ("Unexceptional Violence," 11).

45. *Sexual Personae*, 30.

46. Men should "prevent the images . . . from intruding into their minds. To tackle this, men need to meet together to . . . examine their feelings" (Peter Baker, "Maintaining Male Power," 143).

47. *Dehumanizing Women*, 7, 28. Robert Nozick asks the question in *Anarchy, State and Utopia* (32): "In getting pleasure from seeing an attractive person go by, does one use the other solely as a means? Does someone so use an object of sexual fantasies?"

48. See Augustine, *City of God*, bk. 14, no. 17, 465; and Genesis 3:7.

49. John Finnis and Martha Nussbaum, "Is Homosexual Conduct Wrong? A Philosophical Exchange," 12–13. Finnis's argument is essentially the same in idem, "Law, Morality, and 'Sexual Orientation' " (see 1065–68).

50. *Sexual Desire*, 130. For critiques of Scruton, see Edward Johnson, "Inscrutable Desires"; and J. Martin Stafford, "Love and Lust Revisited."

51. See Shere Hite, *The Hite Report: A Nationwide Study on Female Sexuality*, passim.

52. *Metaphysical Principles of Virtue*, 86.

53. See Arthur Schopenhauer, *The World as Will and Representation*, 538.

54. Adrienne Rich, "Compulsory Heterosexuality and Lesbian Existence," in

Blood, Bread, and Poetry, 23–75. Rich asserts that compulsory heterosexuality is a "man-made institution" (34) "designed to keep women within a male sexual purlieu" (49), and that heterosexuality is "forcibly and subliminally imposed on women" (57).

55. "Separating Lesbian Theory from Feminist Theory," 581.

56. "Gay Marriage," 114.

57. Rich, sounding like Kofman's Freud, thinks what needs explaining is why *women* ever become heterosexual. "If women are the earliest sources of emotional caring and physical nurture for both female and male children, it would seem logical . . . to pose the following questions: whether the search for love and tenderness in both sexes does not originally lead toward women; *why in fact women would ever redirect that search*" ("Compulsory Heterosexuality," 35).

58. Ruth Colker belabors the "power," the "pull," and the "pressures" of compulsory heterosexual marriage that she feels "everywhere," yet incongruously complains that gays do not have "the privilege that [straights] enjoy" ("Feminism, Sexuality and Authenticity," 144–45). I also find incredible, and distrust, her remark, "I am often surprised that my straight friends are not really aware that gay people cannot get married" (145). Colker is an academic lawyer; who are her friends, who don't know such a thing?

59. See Patricia Jung and Ralph Smith, *Heterosexism.*

60. John McMurtry, "Monogamy: A Critique," in Baker and Elliston, eds., *Philosophy and Sex,* 2d ed., 107.

61. *Gays/Justice,* 18, 105 n. 22; *A More Perfect Union,* 46.

62. James D. Haynes, "Masturbation," 384.

63. "Panel Discussion," 237.

Notes to Chapter Three

1. "What's Really Wrong With Adultery," in Soble, ed., *Philosophy of Sex,* 2d ed., 180.

2. Wreen meant his distinction between "extramarital" and "adulterous" sex to be an alternative to Richard Wasserstrom's definition of adultery as "any case of extramarital sex" ("Is Adultery Immoral?" in Baker and Elliston, eds., *Philosophy and Sex,* 1st ed., 208; 2d ed., 94).

3. See Pierre J. Payer, *The Bridling of Desire,* 120–23, for a history of this idea in various medieval texts.

4. For example, St. Alphonsus Liguori; see Peter Gardella, *Innocent Ecstasy,* 21.

5. Kathleen Marie Higgins, "How Do I Love Thee?" 108–9.

6. "Bedtime: The Sequel." All joking aside, Ann Manning reported about her

adultery with Newt Gingrich, "We had oral sex. . . . He prefers that modus operandi because then he can say, 'I never slept with her' " (W. Speers, "Newsmakers").

7. *The Social Organization of Sexuality*, 185.

8. For example, "over half the men but only about 30 percent of the women report having had five or more sex partners since turning eighteen" (*Social Organization*, 184). On the discrepancy, see *Social Organization*, 184–85; and Dorothy Einon, "Are Men More Promiscuous than Women?" For discussion of Laumann's results, see R. C. Lewontin, "Sex, Lies, and Social Science" and letters in *New York Review of Books* (Laumann et al. and Lewontin, May 25, 1995; Lewontin, June 8, 1995).

9. *Social Organization*, 176. The inclusion of "voluntary" in the definition indicates that Laumann and his colleagues were trying to ascertain the amount of nonrape sex.

10. Lewontin mentions something like this solution, but does not take it seriously, due to a lack of evidence for it (or for any other solution); see his letter, *New York Review of Books*, June 8, 1995.

11. *Social Organization*, tables 10.8A and 10.8B, pp. 360–61.

12. In Moon's Unification Church, there is an "indemnity ceremony" in which "the wife-to-be bends over, and her prospective husband beats her on the buttocks three times with [a] paddle. Then he bends over and she returns the favor. This is not a bizarre sex ritual: all participants are fully clothed" (K. Gordon Neufeld, "Jim Jones"). That the betrothed are clothed could not be the reason the activity is not sexual; and if this prenuptial smacking really were a religious ceremony, their being naked wouldn't by itself make it sexual.

13. *Toward a Feminist Theory of the State*, 137. There is enough reason in this dismal slander against men to keep us out of bed with them for a long time. As Susanne Kappeler (*The Pornography of Representation*, 214) puts it, "With lovers like men, who needs torturers?" Or Andrea Dworkin: one of the most difficult things for a woman to find is a lover who is not a Nazi (*Intercourse*, 141).

14. Ludwig Wittgenstein, *Philosophical Investigations*, 194e (IIxi); Norwood Russell Hanson, *Patterns of Discovery*, 13–14.

15. "Sexual Matters," 53–54 (italics added).

16. "Sexual Matters," 53.

17. "Sexual Matters," 51.

18. Joseph A. Diorio, "Feminist-Constructionist Theories of Sexuality," 25.

19. A view similar to Padgug's appears in Milton Fisk, *Ethics and Society*. Fisk claims that the needs for food, sex, support, and deliberation are basic, universal, and natural (98); but later he fudges:

We cannot . . . say that a Detroit autoworker and an Indian peasant have a common nature because the four survival needs are common to them. . . . Being prepared to join a walkout when the assembly line is sped up . . . might be natural to the autoworker, but it is not among the tendencies of the peasant. . . . There is then a distinction between having a common feature naturally and having a common nature. Humans have the universal needs naturally without thereby having a common nature. (101–2)

Oh? Timothy F. Murphy's antiessentialist treatment of sexuality in "Homosex/ Ethics" (10–12) also fudges.

20. *Money, Sex, and Power,* 156 (italics added). Hartsock is quoting Padgug.

21. For the Sambia, see Gilbert H. Herdt, *Guardians of the Flute* (1–4 and passim); Robert J. Stoller and Gilbert Herdt, "Theories of Origins of Male Homosexuality." For the Etoro, see Raymond C. Kelly, "Witchcraft and Sexual Relations," 45–46; idem, *Constructing Inequality,* 156–57.

22. Maybe the Sambia are on to something. Sex "really is a . . . drain of male energy by female fullness. Physical and spiritual castration is the danger every man runs in intercourse with a woman. Love is the spell by which he puts his fear to sleep" (Camille Paglia, *Sexual Personae,* 13).

23. "Should Feminists Oppose Prostitution?" 350. I do not trust Shrage as an observer of French culture, or of ours, for in her later 1992 paper on prostitution she writes, "in our own culture we define a woman's participation in sexual activity for a motive other than love as prostitution" ("Is Sexual Desire Raced?" 49). *We? Our* culture? In 1874, Victoria Woodhull *proposed,* as the most accurate "scientific" definition of prostitution, "all sexual commerce that has not a proper basis in love and desire" ("Tried as by Fire," 19; see 35).

24. "Should Feminists Oppose Prostitution?" 351.

25. Herdt, *Guardians,* 234–35.

26. *Moral Dilemmas of Feminism,* 126, 206 n. 8.

27. Herdt, who did fieldwork among the Sambia, never doubts that the practice is sexual for donor and beneficiary (*Guardians,* xv, 2, 11, 233, 237, 239; Stoller and Herdt, "Theories of Origins," 131–32). Herdt also thinks that the fellatio is homosexual behavior, but not a sign or part of homosexual "identity" or orientation (3–4, 8). What has received the most attention is not the question whether homosexual acts in different cultures are sexual, but whether homosexuality (or heterosexuality) has an essence. See Richard Mohr's discussion of social constructivism in *Gay Ideas* (221–42); John Boswell, *Christianity, Social Tolerance, and Homosexuality,* chap. 2; and Edward Stein, ed., *Forms of Desire.*

28. Germaine Greer, *Sex and Destiny*, 142; Stoller and Herdt, "Theories of Origins," 109.

29. *Moral Dilemmas*, 126.

30. Ibid.

31. "Should Feminists Oppose Prostitution?" 351 n. 9.

32. *Refusing to Be a Man*, 30. Larry May and Robert Strikwerda say about the final two sentences that they are "one of the book's most powerful moments" (*Rethinking Masculinity*, xiii). Ridiculous.

33. See Anne Fausto-Sterling, "The Five Sexes"; Gilbert H. Herdt, ed., *Third Sex, Third Gender*.

34. "Compulsory Heterosexuality and Lesbian Existence," in *Blood, Bread, and Poetry*, 34, 50, 43. The idea comes from Ti-Grace Atkinson (1968): "the concept of sexual intercourse is a political construct, reified into an institution" that exploits women ("The Institution of Sexual Intercourse," in *Amazon Odyssey*, 13; see 14, 17–19).

35. "Sex and Sexual Perversion," in Soble, ed., *Philosophy of Sex*, 1st ed.

36. According to MacKinnon, rape is prevalent, not rare, because there is not much, if any, difference between rape and "normal" intercourse (*Toward a Feminist Theory*, 146, 174). If so, it is more likely than we supposed that some rapes involve sexual pleasure for women. Women have accommodated to, have eroticized, the dominance expressed by men in the forceful, "normal" sex that they never think of as rape (*Toward a Feminist Theory*, 177). On Andrea Dworkin's view, much sex women engage in with men involves surrender to their power; even in "normal" intercourse, women are possessed by a man who owns her, and women experience this possession as "deeply erotic." This is "collaboration," against their interests as women, with their oppressors. "The act itself, without more, is the possession" (*Intercourse*, 63; see 64–67, 134–37, 141–42). Eva Feder Kittay agrees: women "fantasize scenes of rape, humiliation, and submission to pain and brutality. That women have such fantasies is a sign of how deeply the 'internal colonization' of women has taken hold" ("Pornography and the Erotics of Domination," 170).

37. "Freud and Perversion," 207–8.

38. Susan Estrich, *Real Rape*, 83; she is paraphrasing, not quoting. The law might not be defining "sexual contact" but "culpable sexual contact."

39. Jerome Shaffer ("Sexual Desire," 186–87) asks a different question here: what are the features of X's desire that make it *sexual* desire? What is the difference between a curiosity desire or win-the-bet desire to touch Y's thigh and a sexual desire to do so? His answer is that X's sexual desire, as it is leading X to touch Y's thigh, but not curiosity desire, as it is leading to the same act, is

accompanied by sexual excitement and arousal. We can ask, in turn, what sexual arousal is, as opposed to the excitement X felt while touching the thigh to win the bet. Shaffer answers that sexual arousal is "directly sexual in that it involves the sexual parts, viz., the genital areas." I see.

40. "Beyond Bisexual," 511.

41. Pamela Foa, "What's Wrong with Rape," 351–53.

42. See Pauline Bart, "Unexceptional Violence," 13:

> That rape may be violent makes it more, not less, sexual, since domination and subordination . . . are so eroticized in this society. . . . [A] victim say[s], "He made me do such terrible things. He made me lick his whole body and he made me lick his rectal area. He knocked me around and knocked me out. . . ." If that wasn't about sex, then . . . [w]hy didn't he just beat her up?

Bart attributes the point to MacKinnon.

43. Dolf Zillmann counts homosexual activity as sexual on the grounds that it is an "emulation" of heterosexual activity (*Connections between Sex and Aggression*, 19).

44. Thus, to tear down this barrier we need not resort to the Meilaender-Nozick syrup school of thought: "Homosex . . . like heterosex . . . is a rich and fertile language for discovering and articulating the meanings of human life" (Murphy, "Homosex/Ethics," 10).

45. Goldman, "Plain Sex," 76.

46. Rich, "Compulsory Heterosexuality," 35.

47. *Toward a Feminist Theory*, 140.

48. *Toward a Feminist Theory*, 179. MacKinnon equates assault by a fist and assault by a penis; both are both violent and sexual (*Feminism Unmodified*, 92; *Toward a Feminist Theory*, 178). Hence MacKinnon says that violent sexual acts done to women are "doubly sexy" (*Toward a Feminist Theory*, 179).

49. "Plain Sex," 77.

50. Geoffrey Gorer, *The Danger of Equality*, 175–76.

51. Karla Jay, "School for Scandal," 9.

52. "A Biosocial Perspective on Parenting," 17, 29; see Niles Newton, *Maternal Emotions*, 85–94.

53. "Social and Behavioral Constructions of Female Sexuality," 791.

54. Anthony Graybosch, "Parents, Children, and Friendship," 313.

55. *Amazon Odyssey*, 19–20.

56. *The Dialectic of Sex*, 8–12, 225–28, 233–34.

57. *Intercourse*, 138.

58. *City of God*, bk. 14, no. 16, 464–65. See Gardella on Mary Baker Eddy's

"Christian Science" ideal of sexless, spiritual reproduction (*Innocent Ecstasy,* 54, 110); and Jeanne Schroeder's analogy between MacKinnon's feminism and medieval sexology ("Feminism Historicized").

59. *Our Blood,* 13. But—see epigraph—no erection, no sex.

60. *City of God,* bk. 22, no. 17, 839.

61. For example, Valerie Solanas, *Scum Manifesto.*

Notes to Chapter Four

1. For another, more graphic statement of this analogy, see Catharine MacKinnon, *Feminism Unmodified,* 143.

2. *Innocent Ecstasy,* 161.

3. A good example is her testimony for the Meese Commission (*Final Report,* pt. 3, chap. 16, "Victim Testimony," 198–99).

4. "The Clinician as Sexual Philosopher," 88, 107.

5. American Psychiatric Association, *Diagnostic and Statistical Manual of Mental Disorders,* 4th ed., 496, 499.

6. Groden's translation, 56.

7. Gardella, *Innocent Ecstasy,* 54.

8. *On the Basis of Morality,* 60.

9. See Vern L. Bullough and Bonnie Bullough, *Sexual Attitudes,* 71.

10. "Suicide was made the property of medics [rather than clerics] only at the beginning of the nineteenth century, and a major fight it was" (Ian Hacking, "Making Up People," 85).

11. Martin P. Kafka, "Successful Treatment of Paraphilic Coercive Disorder (a Rapist) with Fluoxetine Hydrochloride." The title of the paper is misleading. The patient once attempted to rape his mother. He did, however, masturbate one to four times a day accompanied by fantasies of forced heterosexual sex. Prozac cut his masturbation to once or twice a week accompanied by *nonparaphilic* fantasies. This is the "successful treatment," as announced by the paper's title; but it is not specifically the "successful treatment" of a man *qua* rapist.

12. Dan J. Stein et al., "Serotonergic Medications for Sexual Obsessions, Sexual Addictions, and Paraphilias."

13. "The Jew is made for joy and joy for the Jew" (Sigmund Freud, letter to Martha Bernays, July 23, 1882, in *Letters,* 21).

14. See Herbert Fingarette's dissent, "Alcoholism: The Mythical Disease." Fingarette thinks that Alcoholics Anonymous, the National Council on Alcoholism, and the American Medical Association have political and financial reasons for supporting the medical/disease model of alcoholism (8–9, 21).

15. See Robert Wright, "The Biology of Violence."

16. See Susan Bordo, *Unbearable Weight*, 53.

17. Victoria Woodhull's 1874 idea ("Tried as by Fire," 22).

18. Ann Snitow et al., eds., *Powers of Desire*, 18.

19. "The Porn Industry."

20. *Female Sexual Slavery*, 181.

21. "Pornography and Redeeming Social Values," 624.

22. Victoria Woodhull, slightly before the twentieth century, said as much, but added the biomedical ("stirpicultural") gem that only the progeny of coitus motivated by love and mutual desire would turn out healthy ("Tried as by Fire," 36–39).

23. "What Distinguishes 'Healthy' from 'Sick' Sexual Behavior?" 67.

24. See Frederick Suppe, "The Diagnostic and Statistical Manual of the American Psychiatric Association," 112, 132; idem, "Explaining Homosexuality," 259.

25. "Marital Infidelity," 12.

26. *The Function of the Orgasm*, 73 (italics omitted).

27. "Should Feminists Oppose Prostitution?" 351; *Moral Dilemmas of Feminism*, 126.

28. "Should Feminists Oppose Prostitution?" 351.

29. Dwight Dixon and Joan K. Dixon, "Autoeroticism," 54, 55.

30. In Robert Stoller et al., "A Symposium," 1210.

31. Stoller, "A Symposium," 1213.

32. Stoller, "A Symposium," 1214.

33. "Why Homosexuality Is Abnormal," 277.

34. The stock phrase is that the condition causes "marked distress or interpersonal difficulty." It occurs two dozen times at 496–538; see 784.

35. Jane Gross, "In New Yorker Libel Trial the Analyst Is Examined."

36. "What Distinguishes 'Healthy' from 'Sick,' " 67.

37. Both senses of "compulsive" are employed by Eli Coleman in "Sexual Compulsivity."

38. Letter (italics added).

39. F. Philip Rice, *Sexual Problems in Marriage*, 22–23.

40. "Hard Issues and Soft Spots," 472, 481.

41. Mark F. Schwartz and William H. Masters, "The Masters and Johnson Treatment Program," 178.

42. *Heterosexism*, chap. 3 (being gay is like being left-handed, "part of God's original blessing," 23); see John Boswell, *Christianity, Social Tolerance, and Homosexuality*, chap. 4; and Ronald Green, "The Irrelevance of Theology," 258.

43. *The Pornographer's Grief,* 44.

44. What Meryl Altman says about David Reuben is relevant: "The situation is always the same: a woman is unhappy. . . . [S]he cries in the office of the understanding male therapist; he takes care of her; she undergoes treatment; she makes a successful adjustment. . . . This is propaganda for psychiatry. . . . [F]emale sexuality is represented in terms of disease for which proper re-socialization is the cure" ("Everything They Always Wanted You to Know," 120).

45. Peter Robert Breggin, "Sex and Love," 244–46.

46. Joel Feinberg, *Doing and Deserving,* 253–55.

47. "On the Distinction between Disease and Illness," 57; "Health as a Theoretical Concept," 554.

48. "On the Distinction," 57; "Health as a Theoretical Concept," 555.

49. "Health as a Theoretical Concept," 542.

50. "Health as a Theoretical Concept," 543; "On the Distinction," 59.

51. "On the Distinction," 62. Even though homosexuality is a disease, it is not necessarily, for Boorse, also an illness—a disbeneficial disease (61).

52. In "Are There Gay Genes?" Michael Ruse outlines possible sociobiological mechanisms for the existence of gay genes; see idem, *Homosexuality,* 203–35. For reviews of more recent biological studies, see Simon LeVay, *The Sexual Brain,* 105–30; Dean Hamer and Peter Copeland, *The Science of Desire;* Simon LeVay and Dean H. Hamer, "Evidence for a Biological Influence in Male Homosexuality"; Chandler Burr, "Homosexuality and Biology"; David Nimmons, "Sex and the Brain." Five noteworthy original research reports are J. Michael Bailey and Richard C. Pillard, "A Genetic Study of Male Sexual Orientation"; J. Michael Bailey et al., "Heritable Factors Influence Sexual Orientation in Women"; Dean H. Hamer et al., "A Linkage between DNA Markers on the X Chromosome and Male Sexual Orientation"; Stella Hu et al., "Linkage between Sexual Orientation and Chromosome Xq28 in Males but Not in Females"; and Simon LeVay, "A Difference in Hypothalamic Structure between Heterosexual and Homosexual Men." For criticism of biological explanations of homosexuality, see William Byne and Bruce Parsons, "Human Sexual Orientation"; William Byne, "The Biological Evidence Challenged." On Ruse, see Lee Rice and Steven Barbone, "Hatching Your Genes Before They're Counted."

53. See Robert Gray, "Sex and Sexual Perversion," 166.

54. "On the Distinction," 59; "Health as a Theoretical Concept," 566.

55. In "Women versus the Biologists," his 1994 review of a half-dozen books written or edited by Ruth Hubbard, the recent work in the genetic understanding of homosexuality is deftly ignored by R. C. Lewontin, who politically sympathizes

with and intellectually supports feminist antigeneticism (see R. C. Lewontin et al., *Not in Our Genes*, 131–63). The fact that feminists generally oppose genetic explanations of gender differences while some gays and lesbians look on the work of LeVay and others favorably points to a philosophical and rhetorical gap between the women's and the gay/lesbian movement. (Consider, as another example, the defense of consensual sadomasochism among gays and lesbians, but its repudiation by much of feminism.)

Lewontin's failure to mention, in his 1994 "Women versus the Biologists," the research that suggests homosexual orientation has a nontrivial genetic basis is odd for another reason. In his 1992 *Biology as Ideology* (which includes his 1992 essay "The Dream of the Human Genome"), Lewontin had criticized human genetics research, expressing his disdain for the science and politics of the "genome project." Yet in March 1993, he not only knew about the early results of Dean Hamer's research, but thought the research was "scientifically sound" (so says Hamer, at least; *Science of Desire*, 132; see 129–32); and by mid-1993 he had seen Hamer's research report in *Science*. So why the silence, in the 1994 review, about this piece of genetics? (Too hot a political potato?)

Lewontin reviewing the work of Hubbard, his colleague in Cambridge, is like Engels reviewing the life work of Marx. As we worry about the politics of medicine, we should also worry about the politics of publishing.

56. Rochelle Diamond, letter to *Science*, 1258; she identified herself as "Chair, National Organization of Gay and Lesbian Scientists and Technical Professionals, Inc." See Natalie Angier, "Study Suggests Strong Genetic Role in Lesbianism"; Paul Recer, "Study: Male Homosexual Gene Pattern Is Found"; Daniel J. Kevles, "The X Factor," 85. Because people who believe that homosexuals are "born that way" hold more tolerant, positive attitudes about homosexuality than those who believe that homosexuality is learned or chosen (Kurt E. Ernulf et al., "Biological Explanation, Psychological Explanation, and Tolerance of Homosexuals"), these hopes might be viable. Christian S. Crandall has found ("Prejudice against Fat People," 886–87) that Republican, conservative students more so than Democratic, liberal students hold prejudicial attitudes about fat people *and* believe that fat people are responsible for their size. Crandall also provides evidence that getting persons to change their minds about responsibility for fatness, coming to accept that being fat is a genetic or biological condition (a medically diagnosable disease state), attenuates prejudice against fat people (883, 887–88).

57. "Why Homosexuality Is Abnormal," 253.

58. See Ruse, *Homosexuality*, 190–91; Edward Stein, "The Relevance of Scientific Research," 285; and, on Levin generally, Timothy F. Murphy, "Homosexuality and Nature."

59. "On the Distinction," 62.

60. In this competition, the philosopher Susan Bordo stacks the deck in her own favor by appealing to an extreme antiessentialism (*Unbearable Weight*, 69):

To acknowledge . . . that meaning is continually being produced at all levels—by the culture, by the subject, by the clinician as well—and that in a fundamental sense there *is* no body that passively awaits the objective deciphering of trained experts, is to question the presuppositions on which much of modern science is built. . . . [I]t is to suggest that the study of the disordered body is as much the proper province of cultural critics . . . as it is of the "experts."

Her conclusion is self-serving; if there is, in some "fundamental" sense, no purely biological body, then academic disciplines other than medicine—for example, conveniently, philosophy as cultural criticism—have a job to do.

61. *The Age of Desire*, 171.

62. Suppe, "Diagnostic and Statistical Manual," 118.

63. Michel Foucault, *The History of Sexuality*, 118. See Susan Edwards, *Female Sexuality and the Law*, 80–81.

64. *Female Sexuality*, 75. See Thomas Laqueur, *Making Sex*; and my review.

65. *The Nature and Evolution of Female Sexuality*, 110, 134.

66. Charles Krauthammer, "Defining Deviancy Up," 22.

67. See Leonore Tiefer, "The Allure of Medicalized Sexuality," in *Sex Is Not a Natural Act*, 151ff.

68. *Science of Desire*, 19. Fuzzy thinking exists everywhere. Parents who give birth to biogenetic monstrosities often blame themselves because of their own defective genetic material.

69. See Arnold Davidson, "Sex and the Emergence of Sexuality."

70. Foucault, *History of Sexuality*, 117–18.

71. Thomas Nagel, "Sexual Perversion," in Soble, ed., *Philosophy of Sex*, 2d ed., 48, 50.

72. *The Subjection of Women*, 190, 153.

73. *The Future of an Illusion*, in *Standard Edition*, vol. 21, 47–48. See " 'Civilized' Sexual Morality and Modern Nervous Illness," in *Standard Edition*, vol. 9, 199.

74. *On Liberty*, chap. 3.

75. *The Origin of the Family, Private Property and the State*, 96. For discussion, see Alan Soble, *Pornography*, chap. 3.

Notes to Chapter Five

1. An early example (1972) is "Equality for Uglies." More recent examples include Margaret Carlson, "And Now, Obesity Rights," which mentions the "look-ism" ridiculed by Bloom; Andrea Lee, "Sit on It"; and David Galef's venomous letter criticizing this lighthearted essay.

2. See Bruce McCall, "Ethnicity, Genetics, and Cuteness."

3. See Elaine Hatfield and Susan Sprecher, *Mirror, Mirror*; Robert A. Baron and Donn E. Byrne, *Social Psychology*, 200–207, 521–23; Donn E. Byrne, *The Attraction Paradigm*, 127–34, 234–35, 389–90; Ted L. Huston and George Levinger, "Interpersonal Attraction and Relationships," 121–23.

4. These two examples are mentioned by Catharine MacKinnon, *Sexual Harassment of Working Women*, 137.

5. Thomas Attig, "Why Are You, a Man, Teaching This Course on the Philosophy of Feminism?"; Alison Jaggar, "Male Instructors, Feminists and Women's Studies"; T. Michael McNulty, "Teaching Feminism: A Response to Jaggar."

6. Sandra Harding, "The Instability of the Analytic Categories of Feminist Theory," 300. Harding wants "to know the implications for social relations and *intellectual life* of [this] different embodiment" (italics added).

7. Cartoon by Charles Barsotti, *New Yorker*, February 21, 1994, 101.

8. Hatfield and Sprecher, *Mirror, Mirror*, 46–50; Margaret M. Clifford and Elaine Walster, "The Effect of Physical Attractiveness on Teacher Expectations"; William Goldman and Philip Lewis, "Beautiful Is Good"; Robert Rosenthal and Lenore Jacobson, *Pygmalion in the Classroom*.

9. Hatfield and Sprecher, *Mirror, Mirror*, 53.

10. Karen Dion et al., "What Is Beautiful Is Good."

11. Marshall D. Dermer and Darrel T. Thiel, "When Beauty May Fail"; Michael R. Cunningham, "Measuring the Physical."

12. Hatfield and Sprecher, *Mirror, Mirror*, 96–100; Arie Nadler et al., "Good Looks May Help."

13. David Landy and Harold Sigall, "Beauty Is Talent."

14. Baron and Byrne, *Social Psychology*, 521–23; M. Efran, "The Effect of Physical Appearance on the Judgment of Guilt"; Harold Sigall and Nancy Ostrove, "Beautiful but Dangerous" (the physically attractive woman gets a lighter sentence than the unattractive woman for burglary, but a heavier sentence for swindle); Richard Izzett and Leslie Fishman, "Defendant Sentences as a Function of Attractiveness" (physically attractive persons get a lighter sentence than the unattractive when both have excuses, but a heavier sentence without); Marsha B. Jacobson, "Effects of Victim's and Defendant's Physical Attractiveness" (physically attractive

male rape defendant is less likely than the unattractive to be judged guilty and receives a lighter sentence; the accused rapist of an unattractive female victim is less likely to be judged guilty than the accused rapist of an attractive victim).

15. "Aesthetic Discrimination against Persons," 678, 685 (but see 683 n. 7, where Willard recognizes problems with the view).

16. Rita Freedman, *Beauty Bound*; Susan Bordo, *Unbearable Weight*; Naomi Wolf, on the "professional beauty qualification," *The Beauty Myth*, 25ff.; Sandra Lee Bartky, on the "fashion-beauty complex," *Femininity and Domination*, 39–42. Earlier feminists knew it, too: "Taught from their infancy that beauty is woman's sceptre, the mind shapes itself to the body, and roaming around its gilt cage, only seeks to adore its prison" (Mary Wollstonecraft, *A Vindication of the Rights of Women*, 53).

17. The data of Dion et al. ("What Is Beautiful Is Good," 287–88) indicate that even though people do attribute being friendly, warm, sociable, and sensitive more to the attractive than to the unattractive, there is not a great deal of difference between them.

18. See MacKinnon, *Sexual Harassment*, 18–23.

19. *Final Report*, chap. 17, 244–45.

20. *Sexual Harassment*, 209.

21. *Sexual Harassment*, 296–97.

22. A classic statement is Milton Friedman, *Capitalism and Freedom*, 109–10. Andrew Sullivan, a kind of neoconservative who is gay, defends the right of landlords to lease according to their ethnic and sex/gender preferences (or prejudices). See *Virtually Normal*, 137, 142–45, 161–62.

23. W. M. Alexander, "Sex and Philosophy in Augustine," 197 (quoting Michael Müller).

24. Attributed to Helena Rubinstein by Bartky (*Femininity and Domination*, 40, 126; citing *The Freewoman*, September-October 1978). Is the quote apocryphal?

25. See Alan Soble, *Pornography*: beauty's "being in the eye of the beholder means neither that these judgments vary widely nor that they are subjective, if the eyes of beholders have been influenced by similar background conditions" (111). Compare this with David M. Buss: "Beauty may be in the eyes of the beholder, but those eyes and the minds behind the eyes have been shaped by millions of years of human evolution" (*The Evolution of Desire*, 53).

26. Baron and Byrne, *Social Psychology*, 200–207; Dennis Krebs and Aileen A. Adinolfi, "Physical Attractiveness, Social Relations, and Personality Style"; Bernard I. Murstein, "Physical Attractiveness and Marital Choice"; Bernard I. Murstein and Patricia Christy, "Physical Attractiveness and Marriage Adjustment."

27. Ellen Berscheid and Karen Dion, "Physical Attractiveness and Dating

Choice"; James S. Shanteau and Geraldine F. Nagy, "Probability of Acceptance in Dating Choice."

28. Buss, *Evolution of Desire*, 60–63.

29. William G. Graziano et al., "Social Influence, Sex Differences, and Judgments of Beauty," 530.

30. Alan Feingold, "Gender Differences in Effects of Physical Attractiveness on Romantic Attraction"; Devendra Singh, "Adaptive Significance of Female Physical Attractiveness"; Donald Symons, *The Evolution of Human Sexuality*, 166–205; David M. Buss, "Sex Differences in Human Mate Preferences" (which includes Buss's original research report, twenty-seven commentaries, and Buss's reply).

31. *Sexual Harassment*, 175; see 23.

32. Buss, who defends the evolutionary explanation, and his commentators cover the ground in "Sex Differences in Human Mate Preferences."

33. Kim Wallen, in Buss, "Sex Differences in Human Mate Preferences," 37. Buss replies that "women who make *more* money tend to value monetary and professional status of mates *more* than those who make less money" (41).

34. *Civilization and Its Discontents*, in *Standard Edition*, vol. 21, 104.

35. See Richard Wasserstrom, "Racism, Sexism, and Preferential Treatment," 604–6.

36. Mary Fainsod Katzenstein and David D. Laitin, "Politics, Feminism, and the Ethics of Caring," 274.

37. The authors at least offer an argument. By contrast, Kathleen Barry chooses simply to call these women names; her own type of "radical feminism more and more was directing its energies to the struggle against pornography, challenging sexual liberals and just plain liberals for their promotion of sexual abuse and exploitation. This brought out the 'sexual outlaws'; lesbian sadomasochists and heterosexual women hiding behind their private pornographic sexual lives joined forces to form the 'Feminist' Anti-Censorship Task Force" (*The Prostitution of Sexuality*, 3). Is this not incredibly abusive of Nan Hunter and Sylvia Law? MacKinnon, too, is abusive, accusing women lawyers who defend pornography of "thundering ignorance" and of "procuring women for men" (*Feminism Unmodified*, 205, 14); she also says FACT is the Uncle Tom of the women's movement ("Liberalism and the Death of Feminism," 12).

38. "All that seems certain is [beauty's] derivation from the field of sexual feeling. The love of beauty seems a perfect example of an impulse inhibited in its aim. 'Beauty' and 'attraction' are originally attributes of the sexual object" (Freud, *Civilization and Its Discontents*, 83).

39. "Philosophy and Sex," 448.

40. "One, who is inflam'd with lust, feels at least a momentary kindness

towards the object of it, and at the same time fancies her more beautiful than ordinary" (*A Treatise of Human Nature*, bk. 2, pt. 2, sect. 11, 395). See Hatfield and Sprecher, *Mirror, Mirror*, 172–77; Dolf Zillmann, *Connections between Sex and Aggression*, 145–46.

41. See Buss, *Evolution of Desire*, 53–54, on such apparent universals of beauty as cleanliness and clear skin; and Singh on the waist-to-hip ratio ("Adaptive Significance of Female Physical Attractiveness"). Cross-cultural agreement in evaluations of facial attractiveness has been found by D. I. Perrett, K. A. May, and S. Yoshikawa ("Facial Shape and Judgements of Female Attractiveness"): both Caucasian (living in the United Kingdom) and Japanese (living in Japan) male and female subjects preferred the same Caucasian and the same Japanese female faces. For a summary, see "Beauty Transcends Culture."

42. Calvin once asked Hobbes, "What do you find attractive in women?" Hobbes replied, "Well, I've always been partial to redheads . . . with green eyes. I like green eyes . . . and whiskers! Long whiskers."

43. *The World as Will and Representation*, 538–40.

44. *Sexual Personae*, 16, 32. For Freud, "probably no male human being is spared the terrifying shock of threatened castration at the sight of the female genitals" ("Fetishism," in *Standard Edition*, vol. 21, 154). This is one way in which the female genitals might be revolting. Freud took it seriously:

> We know, too, to what a degree depreciation of women, horror of women, and a disposition to homosexuality are derived from the final conviction that women have no penis. ("The Infantile Genital Organization," in *Standard Edition*, vol. 19, 144)
>
> One thing that is left over in men from the influence of the Oedipus complex is a certain amount of disparagement in their attitude towards women, whom they regard as being castrated. In extreme cases this gives rise to an inhibition in their choice of object, and, if it is supported by organic factors, to exclusive homosexuality. ("Female Sexuality," in *Standard Edition*, vol. 21, 229)

In working out Freud's logic, Sarah Kofman suggests that the *penis envy* men attribute to women explains how men "overcome their horror and even experience pleasure in sexual relations with a woman." Thus "woman's genital organs arouse an inseparable blend of horror and pleasure; they at once awaken and appease castration anxiety" (*The Enigma of Woman*, 84–85).

45. John McHugh and Charles Callan, *Moral Theology*, vol. 2, point 2492; quoted in Peter Gardella, *Innocent Ecstasy*, 38, 167.

46. Jonathan Swift, "Strephon and Chloe," in *The Complete Poems,* 455.

47. Lucretius, *The Way Things Are,* 154.

48. "On the Universal Tendency to Debasement in the Sphere of Love," in *Standard Edition,* vol. 11, 189. See also two long footnotes in chap. 4 of *Civilization and Its Discontents,* 99–100 and 105–7. *Nota bene:* Freud's most notorious dictum, "Anatomy is destiny," appears in his corpus *right here,* and obviously has nothing to do with a woman's anatomy dictating her destiny.

49. "On the Universal Tendency to Debasement," 189.

50. *Civilization and Its Discontents,* 83.

51. The first footnote in chap. 4 of *Civilization and Its Discontents,* 100.

52. "Talk Dirty to Me," 42.

53. For discussion, see Alan Soble, *The Structure of Love.*

54. Dolf Zillmann and Jennings Bryant, "Pornography's Impact on Sexual Satisfaction," 450–51.

55. This is Alice Walker imagining the fears a black woman has when her lover looks at pornography containing white women ("Coming Apart," 96), but the point applies regardless of race. Paula Caplan also mentions this fear (*The Myth of Women's Masochism,* 138).

56. This is why Freud worried about masturbation: "in the phantasies that accompany satisfaction the sexual object is raised to a degree of excellence which is not easily found again in reality" (" 'Civilized' Sexual Morality and Modern Nervous Illness," in *Standard Edition,* vol. 9, 200).

57. "Fate and Lawsuits," 25.

58. "On the Future of Love," in Soble, ed., *Philosophy of Sex,* 1st ed., 387.

59. Frederick Engels, *The Origin of the Family, Private Property and the State,* 94–95. See Engels on beauty, 88.

60. Jeffrey Weeks, *Sexuality and Its Discontents,* 27.

61. *Marriage and Morals,* 121.

62. Jane Sjogren, "Income and Marriage."

63. "Romanticism develops in proportion to the liberation of women from their biology" (Shulamith Firestone, *The Dialectic of Sex,* 165; italics omitted). It also develops in proportion to women's liberation from economic dependence on men. Buss reports that the importance of physical attractiveness as a selection criterion has been increasing since 1930. However, the gap between the sexes has remained constant (*Evolution of Desire,* 58).

64. *Economic and Philosophical Manuscripts,* in David McLellan, ed., *Karl Marx: Selected Writings,* 109.

65. Wolf, *Beauty Myth,* 12–13.

66. "The Road to Selfdom," 8.

67. *Sexual Democracy,* 207.

68. *Amazon Odyssey,* 13.

69. See Carol Caraway, "Romantic Love: A Patchwork," 89–90.

70. Annie Sprinkle, "Beyond Bisexual," 512.

71. Janice Moulton, "Sexual Behavior," 68–69; Alan Goldman, "Plain Sex," 78–80 (both in Soble, ed., *Philosophy of Sex,* 2d ed.).

72. So reasons Richard D. Mohr (*A More Perfect Union,* 50), who claims that this is one lesson straight marriages can learn from gay relationships. But straights have known it for centuries.

73. Harry Brod, "Pornography and the Alienation of Male Sexuality," in Soble, ed., *Philosophy of Sex,* 287 (italics added).

74. Diana E. H. Russell, "Introduction," in Russell, ed., *Making Violence Sexy,* 3.

75. Alice Mayall and Diana E. H. Russell, "Racism in Pornography," in Russell, ed., *Making Violence Sexy,* 168 (see 167).

76. Russell, "Introduction," 2.

77. Barry W. Lynn condescendingly opines that "a complex interaction of factors such as poverty, loneliness, our cultural definition of attractiveness, and despair probably drives many to these stores" (" 'Civil Rights' Ordinances," 120).

Notes to Chapter Six

1. "Symposium on Pornography," 759–60. Rosemarie Tong says that according to the MacKinnon/Dworkin Law, "any woman could have secured an injunction against [trafficking] . . . without a showing of harm" ("Brief Encounter," 8; idem, "Women, Pornography, and the Law," in Soble, ed., *Philosophy of Sex,* 306, 307–8). Barry W. Lynn reads The Law similarly: "all pretense of locating specific harm is dropped" (" 'Civil Rights' Ordinances," 104). (See also Nadine Strossen, *Defending Pornography,* 76.) MacKinnon replies to Tong (letter, *Women's Review of Books,* 5) that the trafficking clauses *do* require a showing of harm; the Model Law "make[s] this most unambiguous." And she reprimands Tong for not quoting it. Here, then, is the relevant passage ("Symposium," 760, sect. 3):

> 2. *Trafficking in pornography:* It shall be sex discrimination to produce, sell, exhibit, or distribute pornography. . . . (iii) Any woman has a claim hereunder as a woman acting against the subordination of women. Any man, child, or transsexual who alleges injury by pornography in the way women are injured by it also has a claim.

Apparently, no proof of harm is required, only that a woman be "acting against subordination." This is not the "most unambiguous" language we are entitled to from a professional lawyer drafting a significant piece of legislation. MacKinnon is right, but only in the sense that on her view, and in the Model Law, pornography is the subordination of women and hence *is* harm, so that to show that someone trafficked in pornography is to show automatically that he or she engaged in harmful activity. No *additional* harm need be shown. For my purposes—what is, according to the Model Law, objectionable sexual material?—the issue need not be settled.

2. Robin Morgan's principle of acceptable sex (*Going Too Far*, 165).

3. "Apparently grasping for any objection he could find" to oral sex, the evangelical Christian Ed Wheat "concluded his discussion by pointing out that 'oral-genital sex definitely limits the amount of loving verbal communication the husband and wife can have as they make love' " (Peter Gardella, *Innocent Ecstasy*, 157; quoting Ed and Gaye Wheat, *Intended for Pleasure*, 217–18). This was not meant as the joke it appears to be. And do not, as I once did, quickly read "grasping" as "gasping."

4. "Crazy Jane Talks with the Bishop," in *Collected Poems*, 259–60.

5. And acts accompanied by a judicious use of mirrors, so that the partners can look into each other's eyes, regardless of position.

6. "Representing Pornography," 49.

7. See *Toward a Feminist Theory of the State*, 247, 205; *Feminism Unmodified*, 193–95; *Only Words*, 6–7, 40–41, 72–73. One example, I suppose, is the fact, according to MacKinnon, that she would not be permitted to say, as part of a Dan Rather news broadcast, that pornography turns women into "cunts" (*Feminism Unmodified*, 224). True, but neither would Al Goldstein be allowed to say on the national news that women *are* "cunts." Andrea Dworkin has expressed, on the talk shows, what MacKinnon wants to say on the news—not with those words, but she had a larger and more credulous audience than Ted Koppel gets.

Two of MacKinnon's explicators, Rae Langton ("Speech Acts and Unspeakable Acts," 324–25) and Jennifer Hornsby ("Speech Acts and Pornography," 226–28), point to men's failure to take a woman's "no" as "no" as an example of MacKinnon's thesis that pornography silences women (see *Toward a Feminist Theory*, 139, 182–83, 197). Langton supposes that because women in some pornography never say no, men who learn "the rules of the game" from this material don't learn to recognize refusals for what they are (324). Do some people learn about sex only from pornography? Susan Dwyer is pretty confident, although she supplies not a shred of research data: "It is at least plausible that pornography represents, for many young men, the[ir] only detailed information" about sex (*The Problem of Pornography*, 201). Where does she live? What makes her suppose such a thing?

Peter Baker ("Maintaining Male Power," 138) surmises that consumers of pornography "assume that because women are depicted as enjoying these activities, that all women really enjoy them even when they say the opposite." Baker's proposed mechanism attributes stupendous stupidity to users of pornography; they are supposed to reason, "women enjoy eating pizza, *ergo* they enjoy and want pizza even when they say no to it." These writers slight the fact that boys discover that "no" does not always mean "no" when they are young, that is, pre-pornographically. Boys detect the maneuver in some girls who say no but soon show that they do not mean it; these girls say no only because they have been pushed by their mothers to say no, even though pushed by their mothers, without complete success, to mean it. (See also Charles L. Muehlenhard and Lisa C. Hollabaugh, "Do Women Sometimes Say No When They Mean Yes?" Thirty-nine percent sometimes do.) Hornsby nearly concedes the point when she admits that she cannot estimate the "relative influences of different sorts of cultural products" (228) on this phenomenon. Langton qualifies the thesis when she points out that pornography could have this effect only if its viewers regard it as "authoritative" speech (311–13). MacKinnon is sure that pornography is authoritative; she speaks of pornography as "the ruling ideology" (*Toward a Feminist Theory*, 205). I am not convinced; many different voices try to impress us with their sexual philosophies, and pornography—the realm of pure fantasy—is not a big winner. Langton remarks that whether pornography is authoritative cannot "be settled from the philosopher's armchair" (312). She tries anyway, relying on Robin Warshaw, *I Never Called It Rape* and Naomi Wolf, *The Beauty Myth*, instead of going to the original research literature in social psychology (312 n. 40). (Plan to spend about an hour straightening out the mistakes in Langton's references to Warshaw and Wolf.)

8. Magritte complicates matters in *La connaissance naturelle*, in which the woman's body is the face/body of *Le viol*. Also inspect Paul Delvaux's *Le récitant*.

9. "Pornography, Oppression, and Freedom," in Dwyer, ed., *Problem of Pornography*, 35–36.

10. See Judith M. Hill, "Pornography and Degradation"; Rosemarie Tong, "Feminism, Pornography, and Censorship."

11. "Characterizing Pornography," in Dwyer, ed., *Problem of Pornography*, 26.

12. Nan D. Hunter and Sylvia A. Law, "Brief *Amici Curiae*," 470–72; Thelma McCormack, "If Pornography Is the Theory," 308; David Ward, "Should Pornography Be Censored?" 510.

13. Instead of explaining, Longino recounts the harm done to women by their being forced to look at pornography at the cashier. Women "are crippled by internalizing as self-images those that are presented to us by pornographers.

Isolated from one another and with no source of support for an alternative view of female sexuality, we may not always find the strength to resist a message that dominates the common cultural media" (39). This is the art of victimology at its best.

14. Andrea Dworkin and Catharine MacKinnon, "Questions and Answers," 79.

15. *Toward a Feminist Theory*, 138; see *Feminism Unmodified*, 138, 172, 199.

16. "Symposium on Pornography," 759–60.

17. Strossen thinks that Magritte's *Le viol* would be "damned" under The Law because the painting "shows a woman 'reduced to' her body parts" (caption to *Le viol* in *Defending Pornography*, n.p.).

18. *Gay Ideas*, 188.

19. "Pornography and the Erotics of Domination," 146–47.

20. Avedon Carol, "Snuff: Believing the Worst," 126–27.

21. Susan Barrowclough, review of "Not a Love Story," 29. Or, as suggested to me by Kathrin Koslicki, the cover depicts F. Jeffrey Pelletier's "universal grinder," changing the count noun "woman" into the mass noun "woman."

22. "Symposium on Pornography," 759.

23. *Toward a Feminist Theory*, 137.

24. Ibid.

25. *Feminism Unmodified*, 160, 172, 199; *Toward a Feminist Theory*, 136–38, 140, 211; *Only Words*, 17. MacKinnon learned well from Dworkin: "Men love death" ("Why So-Called Radical Men," 148).

26. Lynn, " 'Civil Rights' Ordinances," 85.

27. "Against the Male Flood," 454.

28. Quoted in Pierre J. Payer, *The Bridling of Desire*, 220 n. 74.

29. "Introduction," in Russell, ed., *Making Violence Sexy*, 3 (italics deleted).

30. "Misguided, Dangerous and Wrong," 32.

31. "A clitoral orgasm with a full cunt is nicer than a clitoral orgasm with an empty one," opines Germaine Greer, "as far as I can tell at least" (*The Female Eunuch*, 305).

32. "The Sexuality of Inequality," 632. Baldwin's essay is pure MacKinnon, front to back; MacKinnon was faculty adviser of the journal that published it.

33. *Feminism Unmodified*, 171–72; see 148, 199.

34. "Pornography, Oppression, and Freedom," 36.

35. *Pornography and Silence*, 38.

36. "Pornography and Respect for Women," in Bishop and Weinzweig, eds., *Philosophy and Women*, 137.

37. So much for Paula Caplan's claim: "the message of hard-core porn is that,

because women are passive, they need to be raped" (*The Myth of Women's Masochism*, 137).

38. For something like this view, see Karol Wojtyla, *Love and Responsibility*, 192–93.

39. *Pornography and Silence*, 61 (italics added). For the idea that some women do love or crave fellatio, see the poem by Sharon Olds, "The Sisters of Sexual Treasure" (in Vance, ed., *Pleasure and Danger*, 427).

40. "Pornography and Degradation," 48–49. So some are?

41. The role of the viewer is widely recognized. Two perceptive examples: Barrowclough, review of "Not a Love Story," 32, 35–36; I. C. Jarvie, *Thinking about Society*, 469 n. 63.

42. *Free Speech*, 181, 182. Lynn criticizes Schauer in " 'Civil Rights' Ordinances," 56ff. For Schauer, the pornography that loses First Amendment protection has "nothing else" but its physical effect (182); Lynn denies that any pornography totally lacks propositional content (60).

43. *The Grammar of Justice*, 122–23. For criticism of the idea that "eroticizing a value is an unfair or dirty trick that bypasses reason" (this might be what Wolgast fears and tries to prevent by denying pornography First Amendment protection), see Robert Skipper, "Mill and Pornography," 728. See also Mark R. Wicclair, "Feminism, Pornography, and Censorship," 286–87.

44. "Symposium on Pornography," 760.

45. *Intercourse*, 127–28; *Sexual Harassment of Working Women*, 175–76.

46. "Questions and Answers," 79.

47. Pornography "portrays women with their negotiating or bargaining power removed . . . by the woman's raging sexual passion" (Ira L. Reiss, *Journey into Sexuality*, 193).

48. Donald Symons, *The Evolution of Human Sexuality*; David M. Buss, *The Evolution of Desire*.

49. *The Nature and Evolution of Female Sexuality*, 108–14, 134–40.

50. *Only Words*, 21.

51. *Only Words*, 30. See 11–12, 21–22, 29–30, 121 n. 31.

52. *Toward a Feminist Theory*, 311 n. 45.

53. *Only Words*, 17. See also her claim (21) that pornography's message is "addressed directly" to a man's penis (that is, not his brain—unless she thinks that his penis *is* his brain).

54. *Only Words*, 108.

55. *Only Words*, 107.

56. *Refusing to Be a Man*, 121.

57. Lynne Segal, "Sweet Sorrows," 66, 71.

58. *Toward a Feminist Theory*, 138.

59. See Fred R. Berger, "Pornography, Feminism, and Censorship," 339.

60. See MacKinnon's crisp sentence "Men" in *Feminism Unmodified* (10).

61. MacKinnon mentions only one user of "snuff films," Thomas Schiro, a man who raped a woman, killed her, had anal intercourse with her corpse, and chewed her dead body. MacKinnon approvingly quotes this man's statement that pornography caused his acts (*Only Words*, 18–19). To cite the words of such a man as supporting evidence is desperate; it is also weird coming from someone who demands that we listen preferentially to the voices of the *victims* of sexual assault and who thinks that their testimony is the epistemological foundation of feminism (see *Feminism Unmodified*, 5). On Schiro, see Ronald Dworkin, "Women and Pornography," 38; MacKinnon's letter to the *New York Review of Books* and Dworkin's reply; Diana E. H. Russell, "The Experts Cop Out," in Russell, ed., *Making Violence Sexy*, 165–66; and Strossen, *Defending Pornography*, 270–72.

62. MacKinnon is sloppy elsewhere. (1) She says a dozen times throughout her books, reporting results from Diana Russell's studies done in the late 1970s, that "only 7.8 percent" of U.S. women have never been assaulted or harassed sexually over the course of their lives (e.g., *Feminism Unmodified*, 6, 171; *Toward a Feminist Theory*, 127). What is the assault or harassment that Russell found 92.2 percent of women have experienced (at least once in their lives; but maybe only once)? In two footnotes (*Feminism Unmodified*, 233 n. 18; *Toward a Feminist Theory*, 279 n. 5), MacKinnon lists: "all the forms of rape or other sexual abuse or harassment surveyed, noncontact as well as contact, from gang rape by strangers to obscene phone calls, unwanted sexual advances on the street, unwelcome requests to pose for pornography, and subjection to peeping Toms and sexual exhibitionists." Counting unwanted advances on the street and requests to pose for pornography as assault or harassment, in producing the 92.2 percent figure, is not the way to convince reasonable people while remaining respectful of their intelligence. I'm surprised that including "unwanted advances" did not make the figure 100 percent. (This is the beginning of a reply to MacKinnon's outraged astonishment that few people believe the 7.8 percent figure; see *Feminism Unmodified*, 171.)

(2) In *Feminism Unmodified*, MacKinnon says that "a third of all men *predict* that they *would* rape" if they knew they would not be caught (187; italics added); in *Toward a Feminist Theory*, "one-third of all men say they would rape a woman if they knew they would not get caught" (145). In both cases, she refers to Neil Malamuth's studies, but this is a wrong, and very misleading, way to describe his findings (see also *Only Words*, 19). Only in one footnote (*Feminism Unmodified*,

297 n. 120) does MacKinnon get it right: these men "reported some likelihood" they would rape (not "would" rape). The most accurate way to describe Mala- muth's data is this: x percent of the subjects "do not rule out the possibility" or "might be inclined to rape" *if* they would not be caught and punished (Neil M. Malamuth et al., "Testing Hypotheses regarding Rape," 134). Others make this mistake. See Warshaw: "Malamuth reported that 30 percent of the men he ques- tioned said they would commit rape if they knew there was no chance of being caught" (*I Never Called It Rape*, 97; for almost identical wrong wording, see Wolf, *Beauty Myth*, 165); Karen R. Rapaport and C. Dale Posey, who on one page slide from "might be likely" to rape to "would be likely" to rape and "being likely" ("Sexually Coercive College Males," 218); and Diana E. H. Russell, who commits an intellectual crime by speaking of these men as "willing to consider rape as a plausible act for them to commit" ("Pornography and Rape," in Russell, ed., *Making Violence Sexy*, 147). MacKinnon also claims that exposure to pornography *increases* men's self-reported predictions that they would commit rape (*Feminism Unmodified*, 187, 265 n. 9; *Toward a Feminist Theory*, 304 n. 6). Edward Don- nerstein et al. deny this (*The Question of Pornography*, 101–2); see also the negative findings of Neil M. Malamuth and Joseph Ceniti, "Repeated Exposure to Violent and Nonviolent Pornography." MacKinnon ignores the negative results, as does Russell, in both the original 1988 version of her "Pornography and Rape" and its revised 1993 version. Langton, who also claims that men exposed to pornogra- phy are "more likely to say that they . . . would rape if they could get away with it," cites the book by Donnerstein et al. *as the source* for her claim ("Speech Acts," 306), even though they clearly deny it. In going through the social scientific literature, be careful to keep distinct (1) an increase in a man's report about how likely *he* would be to rape, after being exposed to pornography, and (2) a higher likelihood of raping self-reported by a group of men exposed to pornography in comparison with another group of men not so exposed.

63. Carol, "Snuff."

64. See *Only Words*, 15, 22, 23, 26, and a dozen other places; *Feminism Un- modified*, 180, 199, 200. Her evidence is in *Feminism Unmodified*, 272 n. 56, 285 n. 61, and *Toward a Feminist Theory*, 312 n. 52. See also Morgan, *Going Too Far*, 167; Dorchen Leidholdt's contribution to "Pornography: Love or Death?" 38; Dworkin's testimony in *Final Report*, 198–99; and Russell, "The Experts Cop Out," in *Making Violence Sexy*, 166. Noteworthy is the hysteria of Susanne Kappeler: "In the case of snuff films, increasingly popular as videos in the American home, the woman does not get paid and dismissed. She is . . . dead" ("Pornography: The Representation of Power," 97).

65. *Only Words,* 21, 12; *Feminism Unmodified,* 156. Hunter and Law, like Hill, remind us of the obvious: "Men are not attack dogs but responsible human beings" ("Brief *Amici Curiae,*" 474).

66. For the short, accurate course, see Kate Ellis et al., eds., *Caught Looking.* The essays are good, too.

67. I reported 7 percent female-submissive and 9 percent male-submissive (*Pornography,* 19 n. 32). In repeating my offhand data, never meant to be examined statistically, F. M. Christensen shows how to manipulate numbers to prove one's favorite thesis: "one researcher found roughly 30 percent more submissive males than submissive females" (*Pornography: The Other Side,* 80).

68. See Strossen, *Defending Pornography,* 107–11.

69. *Intercourse,* 137, 138; see 128–29; and *Our Blood,* 108. Contrast Susan Brownmiller: "I have no basic quarrel with the procedure" (*Against Our Will,* 4).

70. *Only Words,* 27; see 23–24.

71. *Only Words,* 30, 33, 46, 58, 67–68.

72. See Carlin Romano, "Between the Motion and the Act"; and Walter Berns, "Dirty Words." Note the acronym of *Feminism Unmodified.*

73. Baldwin, "Sexuality of Inequality," 637.

74. *Feminism Unmodified,* 199.

75. *Only Words,* 15.

76. "Symposium on Pornography," 760.

77. Hunter and Law, "Brief *Amici Curiae,*" 475.

78. "Date Rape," 224, 233, 243. But for Pineau, by contrast, a man accused of rape could defend himself by showing that the woman accepted "some pay-off for her stoic endurance, money perhaps, or tickets to the opera" (224).

79. "Misguided," 32. See Lynn, " 'Civil Rights' Ordinances," 100; Donna Turley, "The Feminist Debate," 90.

80. *Feminism Unmodified,* 180.

81. Ibid. Carole Pateman glosses this claim as "economic coercion is involved since the sex industry pays better wages than most occupations open to women" ("Sex and Power," 406).

82. Mariana Valverde notes that MacKinnon plays fast and loose with language ("Beyond Gender Dangers," 182).

83. See *Feminism Unmodified,* 136.

84. "Brief Encounter," 8. See also Jeanne Schroeder, "Feminism Historicized," 1202 n. 259, and Adrienne Rich, *Blood, Bread, and Poetry,* 42.

85. Letter, *Women's Review of Books,* 5. I have already mentioned several passages in MacKinnon's corpus that support Tong's reading; see chap. 1, n. 66 and chap. 3, n. 36.

86. *Toward a Feminist Theory,* 298 n. 25; see 174, 181, 183.

87. *Only Words,* 20.

88. See Laura Antoniou, "Defending Pornography," 21.

89. In *Feminism Unmodified* (181), MacKinnon claims that the movie *Deep Throat* inspired men to demand deep-throat fellatio from women, by which act men caused "the death of some women." This strong assertion, that men have killed women with what Dworkin calls "throat rape" (*Final Report,* 198), requires strong evidence. But have a look (*Feminism Unmodified,* 286 n. 65).

90. *Feminism Unmodified,* 11.

91. "Woman-Hating Right and Left," 39.

Abbey, Antonio. "Sex Differences in Attributions for Friendly Behavior: Do Males Misperceive Females' Friendliness?" *Journal of Personality and Social Psychology* 42, no. 5 (1982): 830–38.

Abbott, Franklin, ed., *Men and Intimacy.* Freedom, Calif.: Crossing Press, 1990.

Airaksinen, Timo. "The Style of Sade: Sex, Text, and Cruelty." In Soble, ed., *Sex, Love, and Friendship,* 527–35.

Alexander, W. M. "Sex and Philosophy in Augustine." *Augustinian Studies* 5 (1974): 197–208.

Allott, Miriam, and Robert H. Super, eds. *Matthew Arnold.* Oxford: Oxford University Press, 1986.

Altman, Meryl. "Everything They Always Wanted You to Know: The Ideology of Popular Sex Literature." In Vance, ed., *Pleasure and Danger,* 115–30.

American Psychiatric Association. *Diagnostic and Statistical Manual of Mental Disorders.* 4th ed. Washington, D.C.: American Psychiatric Association, 1994.

Angell, Roger. "Bedtime: The Sequel." *New Yorker,* November 28, 1994, 162.

Angier, Natalie. "Study Suggests Strong Genetic Role in Lesbianism." *New York Times,* March 12, 1993, A8.

Antoniou, Laura. "Defending Pornography (For Real This Time)." *Harvard Gay and Lesbian Review* (summer 1995): 21–22.

Assiter, Alison, and Avedon Carol, eds. *Bad Girls and Dirty Pictures.* London: Pluto Press, 1993.

Atkinson, Ti-Grace. *Amazon Odyssey.* New York: Links, 1974.

Attig, Thomas. "Why Are You, a Man, Teaching This Course on the Philosophy of Feminism?" *Metaphilosophy* 7 (1976): 155–66.

Augustine. *The City of God.* New York: Modern Library, 1950.

———. *On Marriage and Concupiscence.* In *Works,* vol. 12. Edinburgh: T. & T. Clark, 1874.

Bailey, J. Michael, and Richard C. Pillard. "A Genetic Study of Male Sexual Orientation." *Archives of General Psychiatry* 48 (1991): 1089–96.

Bailey, J. Michael, Richard C. Pillard, Michael C. Neale, and Yvonne Agyei. "Heritable Factors Influence Sexual Orientation in Women." *Archives of General Psychiatry* 50 (1993): 217–33.

Baker, Peter. "Maintaining Male Power: Why Heterosexual Men Use Pornography." In Itzin, ed., *Pornography,* 124–44.

Baker, Robert. "The Clinician as Sexual Philosopher." In Shelp, ed., *Sexuality and Medicine*, vol. 2, 87–109.

Baker, Robert, and Frederick Elliston, eds. *Philosophy and Sex*. 1st ed. Buffalo: Prometheus, 1975; 2d ed. 1984.

Baldwin, Margaret. "The Sexuality of Inequality: The Minneapolis Pornography Ordinance." *Law and Inequality* 2, no. 2 (1984): 629–53.

Baron, Robert A., and Donn E. Byrne. *Social Psychology*. 3d ed. Boston: Allyn and Bacon, 1981.

Barrowclough, Susan. Review of "Not a Love Story." *Screen* 23, no. 5 (1982): 26–36.

Barry, Kathleen. *Female Sexual Slavery*. Englewood Cliffs, N.J.: Prentice-Hall, 1979.

———. *The Prostitution of Sexuality*. New York: New York University Press, 1995.

Barsotti, Charles. Cartoon. *New Yorker*, February 21, 1994, 101.

Bart, Pauline. "Unexceptional Violence." *Women's Review of Books* 4, no. 3 (1986): 11–13.

Bartky, Sandra Lee. *Femininity and Domination*. New York: Routledge, 1990.

Bataille, Georges. *Story of the Eye*, trans. Joachim Neugroschel. New York: Urizen Books, 1977.

Baumrin, Bernard. "Sexual Immorality Delineated." In Baker and Elliston, eds., *Philosophy and Sex*, 1st ed., 116–28; 2d ed., 300–311.

"Beauty Transcends Culture." *Society*, July-August 1994, 3.

Beauvoir, Simone de. *The Second Sex*. New York: Bantam, 1961.

Belliotti, Raymond. "A Philosophical Analysis of Sexual Ethics." *Journal of Social Philosophy* 10, no. 3 (1979): 8–11.

———. *Good Sex: Perspectives on Sexual Ethics*. Lawrence: University Press of Kansas, 1993.

Berger, Fred R. "Pornography, Feminism, and Censorship." In Baker and Elliston, eds., *Philosophy and Sex*, 2d ed., 327–51.

———. "Pornography, Sex and Censorship." *Social Theory and Practice* 4, no. 2 (1977): 183–209. Reprinted in Soble, ed., *Philosophy of Sex*, 1st ed., 322–47.

Berns, Walter. "Dirty Words." *Public Interest*, no. 114 (winter 1994): 119–25.

Berscheid, Ellen, and Karen Dion. "Physical Attractiveness and Dating Choice: A Test of the Matching Hypothesis." *Journal of Experimental Social Psychology* 7 (1971): 173–89.

Bloom, Allan. *Love and Friendship*. New York: Simon and Schuster, 1993.

Boorse, Christopher. "Health as a Theoretical Concept." *Philosophy of Science* 44, no. 4 (1977): 542–73.

————. "On the Distinction between Disease and Illness." *Philosophy and Public Affairs* 5, no. 1 (1975): 49–68.

Bordo, Susan. *Unbearable Weight: Feminism, Western Culture, and the Body.* Berkeley: University of California Press, 1993.

Boswell, John. *Christianity, Social Tolerance, and Homosexuality.* Chicago: University of Chicago Press, 1980.

Bowers v. Hardwick. 106 S. Ct. 2841 (1986); 487 U.S. 186 (1986).

Breggin, Peter Robert. "Sex and Love: Sexual Dysfunction as a Spiritual Disorder." In Shelp, ed., *Sexuality and Medicine,* vol. 1, 243–66.

Brod, Harry. "Pornography and the Alienation of Male Sexuality." *Social Theory and Practice* 14, no. 3 (1988): 265–84. Reprinted in Soble, ed., *Philosophy of Sex,* 2d ed., 281–99.

Brownmiller, Susan. *Against Our Will: Men, Women, and Rape.* New York: Bantam, 1976.

Bullough, Vern L., and Bonnie Bullough. *Sexual Attitudes: Myths and Realities.* Buffalo: Prometheus, 1995.

————. *Sin, Sickness, and Sanity.* New York: New American Library, 1977.

————, eds. *Human Sexuality: An Encyclopedia.* New York: Garland, 1994.

Burr, Chandler. "Homosexuality and Biology." *Atlantic Monthly,* March 1993, 47–65.

Burt, John J., and Linda B. Meeks. *Toward a Healthy Sexuality.* Philadelphia: Saunders, 1973.

Buss, David M. "Sex Differences in Human Mate Preferences: Evolutionary Hypotheses Tested in Thirty-seven Cultures." *Behavioral and Brain Sciences* 12 (1989): 1–49.

————. *The Evolution of Desire.* New York: Basic Books, 1994.

Byne, William. "The Biological Evidence Challenged." *Scientific American,* May 1994, 50–55.

Byne, William, and Bruce Parsons. "Human Sexual Orientation." *Archives of General Psychiatry* 50 (1993): 228–39.

Byrne, Donn E. *The Attraction Paradigm.* New York: Academic Press, 1971.

Cahill, Lisa Sowle. "On the Connection of Sex to Reproduction." In Shelp, ed., *Sexuality and Medicine,* vol. 2, 39–50.

Calhoun, Cheshire. "Separating Lesbian Theory from Feminist Theory." *Ethics* 104, no. 3 (1994): 558–81.

Califia, Pat. "A Thorny Issue Splits a Movement." *Advocate* (San Francisco), October 30, 1980, 17–24, 45.

Callahan, Sidney. "Abortion and the Sexual Agenda." *Commonweal,* April 25, 1986, 232–38.

Cameron, J. M. "Sex in the Head." *New York Review of Books,* May 13, 1976, 19–28.

Caplan, Paula. *The Myth of Women's Masochism.* 2d ed. Toronto: University of Toronto Press, 1993.

Caraway, Carol. "Romantic Love: A Patchwork." *Philosophy and Theology* 2, no. 1 (1987), 76–96. Reprinted in Soble, ed., *Sex, Love, and Friendship,* 403–19.

Card, Claudia. *Lesbian Choices.* New York: Columbia University Press, 1995.

Carlson, Margaret. "And Now, Obesity Rights." *Time,* December 6, 1993, 96.

Carol, Avedon. "Snuff: Believing the Worst." In Assiter and Carol, eds., *Bad Girls and Dirty Pictures,* 126–30.

Chodorow, Nancy. *The Reproduction of Mothering.* Berkeley: University of California Press, 1978.

Christensen, F. M. *Pornography: The Other Side.* New York: Praeger, 1990.

Clifford, Margaret M., and Elaine Walster. "The Effect of Physical Attractiveness on Teacher Expectations." *Sociology of Education* 46 (1973): 248–58.

Coleman, Eli. "Sexual Compulsivity: Definition, Etiology, and Treatment Considerations." In E. Coleman, ed., *Chemical Dependency and Intimacy Dysfunction,* 189–204. New York: Haworth Press, 1988.

Colker, Ruth. "Feminism, Sexuality and Authenticity." In Martha A. Fineman and Nancy S. Thomadsen, eds., *At the Boundaries of Law,* 135–47. New York: Routledge, 1991.

"*Colloquium.* Violent Pornography: Degradation of Women versus Right of Free Speech." *New York University Review of Law and Social Change* 8, no. 2 (1978–79): 181–308.

Crandall, Christian S. "Prejudice against Fat People: Ideology and Self-Interest." *Journal of Personality and Social Psychology* 66, no. 5 (1994): 882–94.

Cunningham, Michael R. "Measuring the Physical in Physical Attractiveness: Quasi-Experiments on the Sociobiology of Female Facial Beauty." *Journal of Personality and Social Psychology* 50, no. 5 (1986): 925–35.

Curley, E. M. "Excusing Rape." *Philosophy and Public Affairs* 5, no. 4 (1976): 325–60.

Davidson, Arnold. "Sex and the Emergence of Sexuality." *Critical Inquiry* 14, no. 1 (1987): 16–48. Reprinted in Stein, ed., *Forms of Desire,* 89–132.

Dean, Craig R. "Fighting for Same Sex Marriage." In Anne Minas, ed., *Gender Basics,* 275–77. Belmont, Calif.: Wadsworth, 1993.

———. "Gay Marriage: A Civil Right." In Murphy, ed., *Gay Ethics,* 111–15.

Dermer, Marshall D., and Darrel T. Thiel. "When Beauty May Fail." *Journal of Personality and Social Psychology* 31, no. 6 (1975): 1168–76.

Diamond, Rochelle. Letter. *Science* 261 (1993): 1258–59.

Dion, Karen, Ellen Berscheid, and Elaine Walster. "What Is Beautiful Is Good." *Journal of Personality and Social Psychology* 24 (1972): 285–90.

Diorio, Joseph A. "Feminist-Constructionist Theories of Sexuality and the Definition of Sex Education." *Educational Philosophy and Theory* 21, no. 2 (1989): 23–31.

———. "Sex, Love, and Justice: A Problem in Moral Education." *Educational Theory* 31, nos. 3–4 (1982): 225–35. Reprinted in Soble, ed., *Eros, Agape, and Philia,* 273–88.

Dixon, Dwight, and Joan K. Dixon. "Autoeroticism." In Bullough and Bullough, eds., *Human Sexuality,* 53–55.

Donnerstein, Edward, Daniel Linz, and Steven Penrod. *The Question of Pornography.* New York: Free Press, 1987.

Dworkin, Andrea. "Against the Male Flood: Censorship, Pornography, and Equality." In Smith, ed., *Feminist Jurisprudence,* 449–66.

———. "Why So-Called Radical Men Love and Need Pornography." In Lederer, ed., *Take Back the Night,* 148–54.

———. "Woman-Hating Right and Left." In Leidholdt and Raymond, eds., *The Sexual Liberals,* 28–40.

———. *Intercourse.* New York: Free Press, 1987.

———. *Our Blood.* New York: Harper and Row, 1976.

———. *Right-Wing Women.* New York: Perigee, 1983.

Dworkin, Andrea, and Catharine MacKinnon. "Questions and Answers." In Russell, ed., *Making Violence Sexy,* 78–96.

Dworkin, Ronald. Reply to letter. *New York Review of Books,* March 3, 1994, 48–49.

———. "Women and Pornography." *New York Review of Books,* October 21, 1993, 36–42.

Dwyer, Susan, ed. *The Problem of Pornography.* Belmont, Calif.: Wadsworth, 1995.

Edwards, Susan. *Female Sexuality and the Law.* Oxford: Martin Robertson, 1981.

Efran, M. "The Effect of Physical Appearance on the Judgment of Guilt, Interpersonal Attraction, and Severity of Recommended Punishment in a Simulated Jury Task." *Journal of Research on Personality* 8 (1974): 45–54.

Ehman, Robert. "Adult-Child Sex." In Baker and Elliston, eds., *Philosophy and Sex,* 2d ed., 431–46.

Einon, Dorothy. "Are Men More Promiscuous Than Women?" *Ethology and Sociobiology* 15 (1994): 131–43.

Ellis, Kate, Beth Jaker, Nan D. Hunter, Barbara O'Dair, and Abby Tallmer, eds. *Caught Looking.* East Haven, Conn.: LongRiver Books, 1992.

Engelhardt, H. Tristram, Jr. "The Disease of Masturbation: Values and the Concept of Disease." *Bulletin of the History of Medicine* 48 (summer 1974): 234–48. Reprinted in Tom L. Beauchamp and LeRoy Walters, eds., *Contemporary Issues in Bioethics,* 109–13. Encino, Calif.: Dickenson, 1978.

―――. "Having Sex and Making Love: The Search for Morality in Eros." In Shelp, ed., *Sexuality and Medicine,* vol. 2, 51–66.

Engels, Frederick. *The Origin of the Family, Private Property and the State.* Peking: Foreign Language Press, 1978.

"Equality for Uglies." *Time,* February 21, 1972, 8; see also letters, *Time,* March 13, 1972, S1.

Ernulf, Kurt E., Sune M. Innala, and Frederick L. Whitam. "Biological Explanation, Psychological Explanation, and Tolerance of Homosexuals: A Cross-National Analysis of Beliefs and Attitudes." *Psychological Reports* 65 (1989): 1003–10.

Estrich, Susan. "Rape." In Smith, ed., *Feminist Jurisprudence,* 158–87.

―――. *Real Rape.* Cambridge: Harvard University Press, 1987.

Farley, Margaret A. "Sexual Ethics." In Warren Reich, ed., *Encyclopedia of Bioethics,* vol. 4, 1575–89. New York: Free Press, 1978.

Farr, Susan. "The Art of Discipline." In Samois, ed., *Coming to Power,* 181–89. Palo Alto, Calif.: Up Press, 1981.

Fausto-Sterling, Anne. "The Five Sexes." *Sciences,* March-April 1993, 20–24.

Feinberg, Joel. *Doing and Deserving.* Princeton: Princeton University Press, 1970.

Feingold, Alan. "Gender Differences in Effects of Physical Attractiveness on Romantic Attraction: A Comparison across Five Research Paradigms." *Journal of Personality and Social Psychology* 59, no. 5 (1990): 981–93.

Ferguson, Ann. *Sexual Democracy.* Boulder: Westview, 1991.

Final Report of the Attorney General's Commission on Pornography. Nashville: Rutledge Hill Press, 1986.

Fingarette, Herbert. "Alcoholism: The Mythical Disease." *Public Interest,* no. 91 (spring 1988): 3–22.

Finnis, John M. "Law, Morality, and 'Sexual Orientation.'" *Notre Dame Law Review* 69, no. 5 (1994): 1049–76.

Finnis, John, and Martha Nussbaum. "Is Homosexual Conduct Wrong? A Philosophical Exchange." *New Republic,* November 15, 1993, 12–13.

Firestone, Shulamith. *The Dialectic of Sex.* New York: Morrow, 1970.

Fisk, Milton. *Ethics and Society: A Marxist Interpretation of Value.* New York: New York University Press, 1980.

Foa, Pamela. "What's Wrong with Rape." In Vetterling-Braggin et al., eds., *Feminism and Philosophy,* 347–59.

Foucault, Michel. *The History of Sexuality.* Vol. 1, *An Introduction.* New York: Vintage, 1976.

Fracher, Jeffrey, and Michael S. Kimmel. "Hard Issues and Soft Spots: Counseling Men about Sexuality." In Kimmel and Messner, eds., *Men's Lives*, 471–82.

Freedman, Rita. *Beauty Bound*. Lexington, Mass.: D. C. Heath, 1986.

Freud, Ernst L., ed. *The Letters of Sigmund Freud*. New York: Basic Books, 1975.

Freud, Sigmund. *The Standard Edition of the Complete Psychological Works of Sigmund Freud*, ed. and trans. James Strachey. London: Hogarth Press, 1953–74.

Friedman, Milton. *Capitalism and Freedom*. Chicago: University of Chicago Press, 1962.

Frye, Marilyn. "Critique" [of Ehman]. In Baker and Elliston, eds., *Philosophy and Sex*, 2d ed., 447–55. Rev. ed., "Not-Knowing about Sex and Power." In *Willful Virgin*, 39–50. Freedom, Calif.: Crossing Press, 1992.

Galef, David. "Ugly Americans?" [letter]. *New Yorker*, December 13, 1993, 10.

Gardella, Peter. *Innocent Ecstasy*. New York: Oxford University Press, 1985.

Garry, Ann. "Pornography and Respect for Women." *Social Theory and Practice* 4 (1978): 395–421. Reprinted in Sharon Bishop and Marjorie Weinzweig, eds., *Philosophy and Women*, 128–39. Belmont, Calif.: Wadsworth, 1979.

Gilbert, Neil. "Realities and Mythologies of Rape." *Society*, May-June 1992, 4–10.

Giles, James. "A Theory of Love and Sexual Desire." *Journal for the Theory of Social Behavior* 24, no. 4 (1994): 339–57.

Glenmullen, Joseph. *The Pornographer's Grief and Other Tales of Human Sexuality*. New York: HarperCollins, 1993.

Goldman, Alan. "Plain Sex." *Philosophy and Public Affairs* 6 (1977): 267–87. Reprinted in Soble, ed., *Philosophy of Sex*, 1st ed., 119–38; 2d ed., 73–92.

Goldman, William, and Philip Lewis. "Beautiful Is Good: Evidence That the Physically Attractive Are More Socially Skillful." *Journal of Experimental Social Psychology* 13, no. 2 (1977): 125–30.

Goodchilds, Jacqueline D., and Gail L. Zellman. "Sexual Signaling and Sexual Aggression in Adolescent Relationships." In Malamuth and Donnerstein, eds., *Pornography and Sexual Aggression*, 233–43.

Gorer, Geoffrey. *The Danger of Equality*. New York: Weybright and Talley, 1966.

Gracyk, Theodore A. "Pornography as Representation: Aesthetic Considerations." In Robert M. Baird and Stuart E. Rosenblum, eds., *Pornography: Private Right or Public Menace?* 117–37. Buffalo: Prometheus, 1991.

Gray, Robert. "Sex and Sexual Perversion." *Journal of Philosophy* 75, no. 4 (1978): 189–99. Reprinted in Soble, ed., *Philosophy of Sex*, 1st ed., 158–68.

Graybosch, Anthony. "Parents, Children, and Friendship." In Robert M. Stewart, ed., *Philosophical Perspectives on Sex and Love*, 313–21. New York: Oxford University Press, 1995.

Graziano, William G., Lauri A. Jensen-Campbell, Laura J. Shebilske, and Sharon R. Lundgren. "Social Influence, Sex Differences, and Judgments of Beauty: Putting the *Interpersonal* Back in Interpersonal Attraction." *Journal of Personality and Social Psychology* 65, no. 3 (1993): 522–31.

Greeley, Andrew. "Marital Infidelity." *Society*, May-June 1994, 9–13.

Green, Karen. "Prostitution, Exploitation and Taboo." *Philosophy* 64 (1989): 525–34.

Green, Ronald. "The Irrelevance of Theology for Sexual Ethics." In Shelp, ed., *Sexuality and Medicine*, vol. 2, 249–70.

Greer, Germaine. *The Female Eunuch.* New York: McGraw-Hill, 1971.

———. *Sex and Destiny: The Politics of Human Fertility.* New York: Harper and Row, 1984.

Griffin, Susan. *Pornography and Silence.* New York: Harper and Row, 1979.

Gross, Jane. "In New Yorker Libel Trial the Analyst Is Examined." *New York Times*, May 11, 1993, A7.

Gubar, Susan. "Representing Pornography." In Susan Gubar and Joan Hoff, eds., *For Adult Users Only: The Dilemma of Violent Pornography*, 47–67. Bloomington: Indiana University Press, 1989.

Gudorf, Christine E. *Body, Sex, and Pleasure: Reconstructing Christian Sexual Ethics.* Cleveland: Pilgrim Press, 1994.

Haack, Susan. *Evidence and Inquiry.* Oxford: Blackwell, 1993.

Hacking, Ian. "Making Up People." In Stein, ed., *Forms of Desire*, 69–88.

Hamer, Dean, and Peter Copeland. *The Science of Desire.* New York: Simon and Schuster, 1994.

Hamer, Dean H., Stella Hu, Victoria L. Magnuson, Nan Hu, and Angela M. L. Pattatucci. "A Linkage between DNA Markers on the X Chromosome and Male Sexual Orientation." *Science* 261 (1993): 321–27.

Hanson, Norwood Russell. *Patterns of Discovery.* Cambridge: Cambridge University Press, 1958.

Harding, Sandra. "The Instability of the Analytic Categories of Feminist Theory." In Sandra Harding and Jean F. O'Barr, eds., *Sex and Scientific Inquiry*, 283–302. Chicago: University of Chicago Press, 1987.

———. *Whose Science? Whose Knowledge?* Ithaca: Cornell University Press, 1991.

Hartsock, Nancy C. M. *Money, Sex, and Power: Toward a Feminist Historical Materialism.* New York: Longman, 1983.

Hatfield, Elaine, and Susan Sprecher. *Mirror, Mirror . . . The Importance of Looks in Everyday Life.* Albany: State University of New York Press, 1986.

Haynes, James D. "Masturbation," and "Oral-Genital Sex." In Bullough and Bullough, eds., *Human Sexuality*, 381–85 and 426–28.

Heilbroner, Robert. "The Road to Selfdom." *New York Review of Books*, April 17, 1980, 3–8.

Hein, Hilda. "Sadomasochism and the Liberal Tradition." In Robin Ruth Linden, Darlene R. Pagano, Diana E. H. Russell, and Susan Leigh Star, eds., *Against Sadomasochism: A Radical Feminist Analysis*, 83–89. East Palo Alto, Calif.: Frog in the Well, 1982.

Herdt, Gilbert H. *Guardians of the Flute*. New York: McGraw-Hill, 1981.

———, ed. *Third Sex, Third Gender*. New York: Zone Books, 1994.

Herman, Barbara. "Could It Be Worth Thinking about Kant on Sex and Marriage?" In Louise M. Antony and Charlotte Witt, eds., *A Mind of One's Own*, 49–67. Boulder: Westview, 1993.

Higgins, Kathleen Marie. "How Do I Love Thee? Let's Redefine a Term." *Journal of Social Philosophy* 24, no. 3 (1993): 105–11.

Hill, Judith M. "Pornography and Degradation." *Hypatia* 2, no. 2 (1987): 39–54.

Hite, Shere. *The Hite Report: A Nationwide Study on Female Sexuality*. New York: Dell, 1976.

———. *The Hite Report on Male Sexuality*. New York: Knopf, 1981.

Hommel, Teresa. "Images of Women in Pornography and Media." In *"Colloquium. Violent Pornography."* 207–14.

Hopkins, Patrick D. "Rethinking Sadomasochism: Feminism, Interpretation, and Simulation." *Hypatia* 9, no. 1 (1994): 116–41.

Hornsby, Jennifer. "Speech Acts and Pornography." In Dwyer, ed., *The Problem of Pornography*, 220–32.

Hu, Stella, Angela M. L. Pattatucci, Chavis Patterson, Lin Li, David W. Fulker, Stacey S. Cherny, Leonid Kruglyak, and Dean H. Hamer. "Linkage between Sexual Orientation and Chromosome Xq28 in Males but Not in Females." *Nature Genetics* 11 (1995): 248–56.

Hume, David. *A Treatise of Human Nature*, ed. L. A. Selby-Bigge. Oxford: Clarendon Press, 1986.

Hunter, J. F. M. *Thinking About Sex and Love*. New York: St. Martin's, 1980.

Hunter, Nan D., and Sylvia A. Law. "Brief *Amici Curiae* of Feminist Anticensorship Task Force et al., in *American Booksellers Association v. Hudnut*." In Smith, ed., *Feminist Jurisprudence*, 467–81.

Huston, Ted L., and George Levinger. "Interpersonal Attraction and Relationships." *Annual Review of Psychology* 29 (1978): 115–56.

Illich, Ivan. *Medical Nemesis*. New York: Pantheon, 1976.

Itzin, Catherine, ed. *Pornography: Women, Violence and Civil Liberties*. Oxford: Oxford University Press, 1992.

Izzett, Richard, and Leslie Fishman. "Defendant Sentences as a Function of Attractiveness and Justification for Actions." *Journal of Social Psychology* 100 (1976): 285–90.

Jacobson, Marsha B. "Effects of Victim's and Defendant's Physical Attractiveness on Subjects' Judgments in a Rape Case." *Sex Roles* 7 (1981): 247–55.

Jaggar, Alison. "Male Instructors, Feminists and Women's Studies." *Teaching Philosophy* 2, nos. 3–4 (1979): 247–56.

———. "Prostitution." In Soble, ed., *Philosophy of Sex*, 1st ed., 348–68; 2d ed., 259–80.

Jarvie, I. C. *Thinking about Society: Theory and Practice.* Dordrecht: D. Reidel, 1986.

Jay, Karla. "School for Scandal." *Women's Review of Books* 1, no. 3 (1983): 9–10.

John Paul II [Pope]. "Evangelium vitae." *Origins* 24, no. 42 (April 6, 1995): 689–727.

Johnson, Edward. "Inscrutable Desires." *Philosophy of the Social Sciences* 20, no. 2 (1990): 208–21.

Jung, Patricia, and Ralph Smith. *Heterosexism: An Ethical Challenge.* Albany: State University of New York Press, 1993.

Kafka, Martin P. "Successful Treatment of Paraphilic Coercive Disorder (a Rapist) with Fluoxetine Hydrochloride." *British Journal of Psychiatry* 158 (1991): 844–47.

Kant, Immanuel. *Lectures on Ethics,* trans. Louis Infield. New York: Harper and Row, 1963.

———. *The Metaphysical Principles of Virtue,* trans. James Ellington. Indianapolis: Bobbs-Merrill, 1964.

Kappeler, Susanne. "Pornography: The Representation of Power." In Itzin, ed., *Pornography,* 88–101.

———. *The Pornography of Representation.* Minneapolis: University of Minnesota Press, 1986.

Katzenstein, Mary Fainsod, and David D. Laitin. "Politics, Feminism, and the Ethics of Caring." In Eva F. Kittay and Diana T. Meyers, eds., *Women and Moral Theory,* 261–81. Totowa, N.J.: Rowman and Littlefield, 1987.

Kelly, Raymond C. "Witchcraft and Sexual Relations." In Paula Brown and Georgeda Buchbinder, eds., *Man and Woman in the New Guinea Highlands,* 36–53. Washington, D.C.: American Anthropological Association, 1976.

———. *Constructing Inequality.* Ann Arbor: University of Michigan Press, 1993.

Kevles, Daniel J. "The X Factor." *New Yorker,* April 3, 1995, 85–90.

Kimmel, Michael S., ed. *Men Confront Pornography.* New York: Crown, 1990.

Kimmel, Michael S., and Michael A. Messner, eds. *Men's Lives.* New York: Macmillan, 1989.

Kinsley, Michael. "Fate and Lawsuits." *New Republic*, June 14, 1980, 20–25.

Kittay, Eva Feder. "Pornography and the Erotics of Domination." In Carol C. Gould, ed., *Beyond Domination*, 145–74. Totowa, N.J.: Rowman and Allanheld, 1984.

Kofman, Sarah. *The Enigma of Woman: Woman in Freud's Writings*, trans. Catharine Porter. Ithaca: Cornell University Press, 1985.

Koss, Mary P., and Kenneth E. Leonard. "Sexually Aggressive Men: Empirical Findings and Theoretical Implications." In Malamuth and Donnerstein, eds., *Pornography and Sexual Aggression*, 213–32.

Kourany, Janet A., James P. Sterba, and Rosemarie Tong, eds. *Feminist Philosophies*. Englewood Cliffs, N.J.: Prentice Hall, 1992.

Kovel, Joel. *The Age of Desire*. New York: Pantheon, 1982.

Krauthammer, Charles. "Defining Deviancy Up." *New Republic*, November 22, 1993, 20–25.

Krebs, Dennis, and Aleen A. Adinolfi. "Physical Attractiveness, Social Relations, and Personality Style." *Journal of Personality and Social Psychology* 31 (1975): 245–53.

Kundera, Milan. *The Unbearable Lightness of Being*. New York: Harper and Row, 1984.

Landy, David, and Harold Sigall. "Beauty Is Talent: Task Evaluation as a Function of the Performer's Physical Attractiveness." *Journal of Personality and Social Psychology* 29 (1974): 299–304.

Langton, Rae. "Speech Acts and Unspeakable Acts." *Philosophy and Public Affairs* 22, no. 4 (1993): 293–330.

Laqueur, Thomas. *Making Sex*. Cambridge: Harvard University Press, 1990.

Laumann, Edward O., John H. Gagnon, Robert T. Michael, and Stuart Michaels. Letter. *New York Review of Books*, May 25, 1995, 43.

———. *The Social Organization of Sexuality: Sexual Practices in the United States*. Chicago: University of Chicago Press, 1994.

Lederer, Laura, ed. *Take Back the Night*. New York: William Morrow, 1980.

Lee, Andrea. "Sit on It." *New Yorker*, November 8, 1993, 76–77.

Leidholdt, Dorchen, and Janice G. Raymond, eds. *The Sexual Liberals and the Attack on Feminism*. New York: Teachers College Press, 1990.

LeMoncheck, Linda. *Dehumanizing Women: Treating Persons as Sex Objects*. Totowa, N.J.: Rowman and Allanheld, 1984.

LeVay, Simon. "A Difference in Hypothalamic Structure between Heterosexual and Homosexual Men." *Science* 253 (1991): 1034–37.

———. *The Sexual Brain*. Cambridge: MIT Press, 1993.

LeVay, Simon, and Dean H. Hamer. "Evidence for a Biological Influence in Male Homosexuality." *Scientific American*, May 1994, 44–49.

Levin, Max. "Pornography and Redeeming Social Values." *Current Medical Dialogue* 40 (1973): 621, 624.

Levin, Michael. "Why Homosexuality Is Abnormal." *Monist* 67, no. 2 (1984): 251–83.

Lewontin, R. C. "The Dream of the Human Genome." *New York Review of Books,* May 28, 1992, 31–40.

———. Replies to letters. *New York Review of Books,* May 25, 1995, 43–44; June 8, 1995, 69.

———. "Sex, Lies, and Social Science." *New York Review of Books,* April 20, 1995, 24–29.

———. "Women versus the Biologists." *New York Review of Books,* April 7, 1994, 31–35.

———. *Biology as Ideology: The Doctrine of DNA.* New York: HarperPerennial, 1992.

Lewontin, R. C., Steven Rose, and Leon J. Kamin. *Not in Our Genes: Biology, Ideology, and Human Nature.* New York: Pantheon, 1984.

Longino, Helen. "Pornography, Oppression, and Freedom: A Closer Look." In Lederer, ed., *Take Back the Night,* 40–54; in Dwyer, ed., *The Problem of Pornography,* 34–47.

Lotringer, Sylvère. *Overexposed: Treating Sexual Perversion in America.* New York: Pantheon, 1988.

Lucretius. *The Way Things Are,* trans. Rolfe Humphries. Bloomington: Indiana University Press, 1968.

Lumiere, Richard, and Stephani Cook. *Healthy Sexuality and Keeping It That Way.* New York: Simon and Schuster, 1983.

Lynn, Barry W. " 'Civil Rights' Ordinances and the Attorney General's Commission: New Developments in Pornography Regulation." *Harvard Civil Rights-Civil Liberties Law Review* 21, no. 1 (1986): 27–125.

MacKinnon, Catharine A. Letter. *New York Review of Books,* March 3, 1994, 47–48.

———. Letter. *Women's Review of Books* 3, no. 11 (1986): 5.

———. "Liberalism and the Death of Feminism." In Leidholdt and Raymond, eds., *The Sexual Liberals,* 3–13.

———. *Feminism Unmodified.* Cambridge: Harvard University Press, 1987.

———. *Only Words.* Cambridge: Harvard University Press, 1993.

———. *Sexual Harassment of Working Women.* New Haven: Yale University Press, 1979.

———. *Toward a Feminist Theory of the State.* Cambridge: Harvard University Press, 1989.

Malamuth, Neil M., and Joseph Ceniti. "Repeated Exposure to Violent and Nonviolent Pornography: Likelihood of Raping Ratings and Laboratory Aggression against Women." *Aggressive Behavior* 12, no. 2 (1986): 129–37.

Malamuth, Neil M., and Edward Donnerstein, eds. *Pornography and Sexual Aggression*. Orlando: Academic Press, 1984.

Malamuth, Neil M., Scott Haber, and Seymour Feshbach. "Testing Hypotheses regarding Rape: Exposure to Sexual Violence, Sex Differences, and the 'Normality' of Rapists." *Journal of Research in Personality* 14, no. 1 (1980): 121–37.

Marmor, Judd. "What Distinguishes 'Healthy' from 'Sick' Sexual Behavior?" *Medical Aspects of Human Sexuality* 11 (October 1977): 67.

Masters, William H., and Virginia E. Johnson. *Human Sexual Inadequacy*. Boston: Little, Brown, 1970.

May, Larry, and Robert Strikwerda, eds. *Rethinking Masculinity*. Lanham, Md.: Rowman and Littlefield, 1992.

Mayall, Alice, and Diana E. H. Russell. "Racism in Pornography." In Russell, ed., *Making Violence Sexy*, 167–77.

McCall, Bruce. "Ethnicity, Genetics, and Cuteness." *New Yorker*, December 5, 1994, 152.

McCartney, James J. "Contemporary Controversies in Sexual Ethics: A Case Study in Post-Vatican II Moral Theology." In Shelp, ed., *Sexuality and Medicine*, vol. 2, 219–32.

McCormack, Thelma. "If Pornography Is the Theory, Is Inequality the Practice? *Philosophy of the Social Sciences* 23, no. 3 (1993): 298–326.

McLellan, David, ed. *Karl Marx: Selected Writings*. Oxford: Oxford University Press, 1977.

McMurtry, John. "Monogamy: A Critique." *Monist* 56, no. 4 (1972): 587–99. Reprinted in Baker and Elliston, eds., *Philosophy and Sex*, 1st ed., 166–77; 2d ed., 107–18.

McNulty, T. Michael. "Teaching Feminism: A Response to Jaggar." *Teaching Philosophy* 3, no. 1 (1979): 93–95.

Meilaender, Gilbert. *The Limits of Love: Some Theological Explorations*. University Park: Pennsylvania State University Press, 1987.

Mill, John Stuart. *On Liberty*. Indianapolis: Hackett, 1978.

———. *The Subjection of Women*. In Alice Rossi, ed., *Essays on Sex Equality*, 123–242. Chicago: University of Chicago Press, 1970.

Miller, Patricia Y., and Martha R. Fowlkes. "Social and Behavioral Constructions of Female Sexuality." *Signs* 5, no. 4 (1980): 783–800.

Milligan, Don. *Sex-Life: A Critical Commentary on the History of Sexuality*. London: Pluto Press, 1993.

Mohr, Richard D. *Gay Ideas*. Boston: Beacon Press, 1992.

———. *Gays/Justice*. New York: Columbia University Press, 1988.

———. *A More Perfect Union*. Boston: Beacon Press, 1994.

Montaigne, Michel de. "On Affectionate Relationships." In M. A. Screech, ed. and trans., *The Essays of Michel de Montaigne*, 205–19. London: Penguin, 1991.

Morgan, Robin. *Going Too Far*. New York: Random House, 1977.

Moulton, Janice. "Sex and Reference." In Baker and Elliston, eds., *Philosophy and Sex*, 1st ed., 34–44.

———. "Sexual Behavior: Another Position." *Journal of Philosophy* 73, no. 16 (1976): 537–46. Reprinted in Soble, ed., *Philosophy of Sex*, 1st ed., 110–18; 2d ed., 63–71.

Muehlenhard, Charlene L., and Lisa C. Hollabaugh. "Do Women Sometimes Say No When They Mean Yes? The Prevalence and Correlates of Token Resistance to Sex." *Journal of Personality and Social Psychology* 54, no. 5 (1988): 872–79.

Muehlenhard, Charlene L., and Jennifer L. Schrag. "Nonviolent Sexual Coercion." In Parrot and Bechhofer, eds., *Acquaintance Rape*, 115–28.

Murphy, Timothy F. "Homosex/Ethics." In Murphy, ed., *Gay Ethics*, 9–25.

———. "Homosexuality and Nature: Happiness and the Law at Stake." *Journal of Applied Philosophy* 4, no. 2 (1987): 195–204.

———, ed. *Gay Ethics: Controversies in Outing, Civil Rights, and Sexual Science*. Binghamton, N.Y.: Haworth, 1994.

Murstein, Bernard I. "Physical Attractiveness and Marital Choice." *Journal of Personality and Social Psychology* 22 (1972): 8–12.

Murstein, Bernard I., and Patricia Christy. "Physical Attractiveness and Marriage Adjustment in Middle-Aged Couples." *Journal of Personality and Social Psychology* 34, no. 4 (1976): 537–42.

Nadler, Arie, Rina Shapira, and Shulamit Ben-Itzhak. "Good Looks May Help: Effects of Helper's Physical Attractiveness and Sex of Helper on Males' and Females' Help-Seeking Behavior." *Journal of Personality and Social Psychology* 42, no. 1 (1982): 90–99.

Nagel, Thomas. "Sexual Perversion." *Journal of Philosophy* 66 (1969): 5–17. Reprinted in Soble, ed., *Philosophy of Sex*, 1st ed., 76–88. Rev. version in Thomas Nagel, *Mortal Questions*, 39–52. Cambridge: Cambridge University Press, 1979. Reprinted in Soble, ed., *Philosophy of Sex*, 2d ed., 39–51.

Nelson, Edward C. "Pornography and Sexual Aggression." In Maurice Jaffé and Edward C. Nelson, eds., *The Influence of Pornography on Behaviour*, 171–248. London: Academic Press, 1982.

Neu, Jerome. "Freud and Perversion." In J. Neu, ed., *The Cambridge Companion to Freud*, 175–208. Cambridge: Cambridge University Press, 1991.

————. "What Is Wrong with Incest?" *Inquiry* 19, no. 1 (1976): 27–39.

Neufeld, K. Gordon. "Jim Jones" [letter]. *New Yorker,* December 27, 1993 and January 3, 1994, 14.

Newton, Niles. *Maternal Emotions.* New York: Hoeber, 1955.

Nicholson, Susan T. *Abortion and the Roman Catholic Church.* Knoxville, Tenn.: Religious Ethics, 1978.

Nimmons, David. "Sex and the Brain." *Discover,* March 1994, 64–71.

Noonan, John T. *Contraception: A History of Its Treatment by the Catholic Theologians and Canonists.* Enlarged ed. Cambridge: Harvard University Press, 1986.

Nozick, Robert. *Anarchy, State and Utopia.* New York: Basic Books, 1974.

————. *The Examined Life.* New York: Simon and Schuster, 1989.

Olds, Sharon. "The Sisters of Sexual Treasure." In Vance, ed., *Pleasure and Danger,* 427.

O'Neill, Onora. "Between Consenting Adults." *Philosophy and Public Affairs* 14, no. 3 (1985): 252–77.

Onions, C. T., ed. *The Oxford Dictionary of English Etymology.* Oxford: Clarendon Press, 1966.

Padgug, Robert. "Sexual Matters: On Conceptualizing Sexuality in History." In Stein, ed., *Forms of Desire,* 43–67.

Pagels, Elaine. *Adam, Eve, and the Serpent.* New York: Vintage Books, 1988.

Paglia, Camille. *Sexual Personae.* New Haven: Yale University Press, 1990.

Parrot, Andrea, and Laurie Bechhofer, eds. *Acquaintance Rape: The Hidden Crime.* New York: John Wiley, 1991.

Pateman, Carole. "Sex and Power." *Ethics* 100, no. 2 (1990): 398–407.

————. "Women and Consent." *Political Theory* 8, no. 2 (1980): 149–68.

————. *The Sexual Contract.* Stanford: Stanford University Press, 1988.

Paul VI [Pope]. "Humanae vitae." *Catholic Mind* 66 (September 1968): 35–48. Reprinted in Baker and Elliston, eds., *Philosophy and Sex,* 1st ed., 131–49; 2d ed., 167–83.

Payer, Pierre J. *The Bridling of Desire: Views of Sex in the Later Middle Ages.* Toronto: University of Toronto Press, 1993.

Perper, Timothy, and David L. Weis. "Proceptive and Rejective Strategies of U.S. and Canadian College Women." *Journal of Sex Research* 23, no. 4 (1987): 455–80.

Perrett, D. I., K. A. May, and S. Yoshikawa. "Facial Shape and Judgements of Female Attractiveness." *Nature* 368 (March 17, 1994): 239–42.

Peterson, Susan Rae. "Coercion and Rape: The State as a Male Protection Racket." In Vetterling-Braggin et al., eds., *Feminism and Philosophy,* 360–71.

Petronius. "Foeda est in coitu voluptas." *Arion* 2, no. 1 (1963): 82–84.

Pineau, Lois. "Date Rape: A Feminist Analysis." *Law and Philosophy* 8 (1989): 217–43.

Pius XI [Pope]. "On Christian Marriage." *Catholic Mind* 29, no. 2 (1931): 21–64.

Plato. *Symposium,* trans. Suzy Q Groden. Amherst: University of Massachusetts Press, 1970. Trans. Walter Hamilton. London: Penguin, 1951.

"The Porn Industry" [editorial]. *British Medical Journal,* no. 5830, September 30, 1972, 779.

"Pornography: Love or Death?" *Film Comment* 20, no. 6 (1984): 29–49.

Posner, Richard A. *Sex and Reason.* Cambridge: Harvard University Press, 1992.

Prager, Dennis. "Homosexuality, the Bible, and Us—A Jewish Perspective." *Public Interest,* no. 112 (summer 1993): 60–83.

Primoratz, Igor. "What's Wrong with Prostitution?" *Philosophy* 68, no. 264 (April 1993): 159–82.

Rapaport, Elizabeth. "On the Future of Love: Rousseau and the Radical Feminists." *Philosophical Forum* 5, nos. 1–2 (1973–74): 185–205. Reprinted in Soble, ed., *Philosophy of Sex,* 1st ed., 369–88.

Rapaport, Karen R., and C. Dale Posey. "Sexually Coercive College Males." In Parrot and Bechhofer, eds., *Acquaintance Rape,* 217–28.

Recer, Paul. "Study: Male Homosexual Gene Pattern Is Found." *Times•Picayune* (New Orleans), July 17, 1993, G20.

Reich, Wilhelm. *The Function of the Orgasm.* New York: Noonday Press, 1961.

Reidhead, Julia A. "Good Sex" [letter]. *New Yorker,* January 10, 1994, 8.

Reiss, Ira L. *Journey into Sexuality: An Exploratory Voyage.* Englewood Cliffs, N.J.: Prentice-Hall, 1986.

Rice, F. Philip. *Sexual Problems in Marriage.* Philadelphia: Westminster, 1978.

Rice, Lee, and Steven Barbone. "Hatching Your Genes before They're Counted." In Soble, ed., *Sex, Love, and Friendship,* 89–98.

Rich, Adrienne. *Blood, Bread, and Poetry.* New York: Norton, 1986.

Richards, David A. J. Contribution to "Panel Discussion: Effects of Violent Pornography." In *"Colloquium.* Violent Pornography," 235–37.

Romano, Carlin. "Between the Motion and the Act." *Nation,* November 15, 1993, 563–70.

Rosenthal, Robert, and Lenore Jacobson. *Pygmalion in the Classroom.* New York: Holt, Rinehart, and Winston, 1968.

Rossi, Alice. "A Biosocial Perspective on Parenting." *Daedalus* 106, no. 2 (1977): 1–31.

Roth, Philip. "Drenka's Men." *New Yorker,* July 10, 1995, 56–66.

———. "The Ultimatum." *New Yorker,* June 26 and July 3, 1995, 114–27.

———. *Portnoy's Complaint.* New York: Random House, 1969.

Rousseau, Jean-Jacques. *Confessions,* trans J. M. Cohen. New York: Penguin, 1979.

Rubin, Gayle. "Misguided, Dangerous and Wrong: An Analysis of Anti-Pornography Politics." In Assiter and Carol, eds., *Bad Girls and Dirty Pictures,* 18–40.

Ruddick, Sara. "Better Sex." In Baker and Elliston, eds., *Philosophy and Sex,* 1st ed., 83–104; 2d ed., 280–99.

Ruse, Michael. "Are There Gay Genes? Sociobiology and Homosexuality." *Journal of Homosexuality* 6, no. 4 (1981): 5–34.

———. *Homosexuality: A Philosophical Inquiry.* New York: Blackwell, 1988.

Russell, Bertrand. *Marriage and Morals.* London: George Allen and Unwin, 1929.

Russell, Diana E. H. "Pornography and Rape: A Causal Model." *Political Psychology* 9, no. 1 (1988): 41–73. Rev. version in Russell, ed., *Making Violence Sexy,* 120–50.

———, ed. *Making Violence Sexy: Feminist Views on Pornography.* New York: Teachers College Press, 1993.

Sarnoff, Suzanne, and Irving Sarnoff. *Sexual Excitement/Sexual Peace: The Place of Masturbation in Adult Relationships.* New York: M. Evans, 1979.

Sartre, Jean-Paul. *Being and Nothingness,* trans. Hazel E. Barnes. New York: Philosophical Library, 1956.

Schauer, Frederick. *Free Speech: A Philosophical Enquiry.* Cambridge: Cambridge University Press, 1982.

Schopenhauer, Arthur. *On the Basis of Morality,* trans. E. F. J. Payne. Indianapolis: Bobbs-Merrill, 1965.

———. *The World as Will and Representation.* Vol. 2, trans. E. F. J. Payne. Indian Hills, Colo.: Falcon's Wing Press, 1958.

Schroeder, Jeanne L. "Feminism Historicized: Medieval Misogynist Stereotypes in Contemporary Feminist Jurisprudence." *Iowa Law Review* 75 (1990): 1135–1217.

Schulhofer, Stephen J. "The Gender Question in Criminal Law." In Jeffrie G. Murphy, ed., *Punishment and Rehabilitation,* 3d ed., 274–311. Belmont, Calif.: Wadsworth, 1995.

Schwartz, Mark F., and William H. Masters. "The Masters and Johnson Treatment Program for Dissatisfied Homosexual Men." *American Journal of Psychiatry* 141, no. 2 (1984): 173–81.

Scruton, Roger. *Sexual Desire: A Moral Philosophy of the Erotic.* New York: Free Press, 1986.

Segal, Lynne. "Sweet Sorrows, Painful Pleasures." In Lynne Segal and Mary McIntosh, eds., *Sex Exposed: Sexuality and the Pornography Debate,* 65–91. New Brunswick: Rutgers University Press, 1993.

Seidman, Steven. *Embattled Eros.* New York: Routledge, 1992.

Shafer, Carolyn M., and Marilyn Frye. "Rape and Respect." In Vetterling-Braggin et al., eds., *Feminism and Philosophy*, 333–46.

Shaffer, Jerome. "Sexual Desire." *Journal of Philosophy* 75, no. 4 (1978): 175–89. Reprinted in Soble, ed., *Sex, Love, and Friendship*, 1–12.

Shanteau, James S., and Geraldine F. Nagy. "Probability of Acceptance in Dating Choice." *Journal of Personality and Social Psychology* 37, no. 4 (1979): 522–33.

Shelp, Earl E., ed. *Sexuality and Medicine*. Vols. 1 and 2. Dordrecht: D. Reidel, 1987.

Sherfey, Mary Jane. *The Nature and Evolution of Female Sexuality*. New York: Vintage, 1973.

Shrage, Laurie. "Is Sexual Desire Raced? The Social Meaning of Interracial Prostitution." *Journal of Social Philosophy* 23, no. 1 (1992): 42–51.

——. "Should Feminists Oppose Prostitution?" *Ethics* 99, no. 2 (1989): 347–61.

——. *Moral Dilemmas of Feminism*. New York: Routledge, 1994.

Sigall, Harold, and Nancy Ostrove. "Beautiful but Dangerous: Effects of Offender Attractiveness and Nature of the Crime on Juridic Judgment." *Journal of Personality and Social Psychology* 31 (1975): 410–14.

Simmons, Paul. "Theological Approaches to Sexuality." In Shelp, ed., *Sexuality and Medicine*, vol. 2, 199–217.

Singer, Irving. *The Goals of Human Sexuality*. New York: Schocken Books, 1974.

Singh, Devendra. "Adaptive Significance of Female Physical Attractiveness: Role of Waist-to-Hip Ratio." *Journal of Personality and Social Psychology* 65, no. 2 (1993): 293–307.

Sircello, Guy. "Beauty and Sex." In D. F. Gustafson and B. L. Tapscott, eds., *Body, Mind, and Method*, 225–39. Dordrecht: D. Reidel, 1979. Reprinted in Soble, ed., *Philosophy of Sex*, 2d ed., 117–32.

Sjogren, Jane. "Income and Marriage" [letter]. *New York Times*, November 13, 1994, E14.

Skipper, Robert. "Mill and Pornography." *Ethics* 103, no. 4 (1993): 726–30.

Smith, Patricia, ed. *Feminist Jurisprudence*. New York: Oxford University Press, 1993.

Snitow, Ann, Christine Stansell, and Sharon Thompson, eds. *Powers of Desire*. New York: Monthly Review Press, 1983.

Soble, Alan. Review of *Making Sex*, by Thomas Laqueur. *Teaching Philosophy* 14, no. 3 (1991): 339–42.

——. Review of *The Pornography of Representation*, by Susanne Kappeler. *Philosophy of the Social Sciences* 19, no. 1 (1989): 128–31.

——. Review of *Sexual Democracy*, by Ann Ferguson. *Journal of Value Inquiry* 27 (1993): 261–70.

————. "Union, Autonomy, and Concern." In Roger Lamb, ed., *Love Analyzed.* Boulder: Westview, 1996.

————. *Pornography: Marxism, Feminism and the Future of Sexuality.* New Haven: Yale University Press, 1986.

————. *The Structure of Love.* New Haven: Yale University Press, 1990.

————, ed. *Eros, Agape and Philia.* New York: Paragon House, 1989.

————, ed. *Philosophy of Sex.* 1st ed. Totowa, N.J.: Rowman and Littlefield, 1980; 2d ed. Savage, Md., 1991.

————, ed. *Sex, Love, and Friendship.* Amsterdam: Editions Rodopi, 1996.

Solanas, Valerie. *Scum Manifesto.* London: Phoenix Press, 1991.

Solomon, Robert. "Sex and Perversion." In Baker and Elliston, eds., *Philosophy and Sex,* 1st ed., 268–87.

————. "Sexual Paradigms." *Journal of Philosophy* 71 (1974): 336–45. Reprinted in Soble, ed., *Philosophy of Sex,* 1st ed., 89–98; 2d ed., 53–62.

Speers, W. "Newsmakers." *Philadelphia Inquirer,* August 10, 1995, F2.

Sprinkle, Annie. "Beyond Bisexual." In Alison M. Jaggar, ed., *Living with Contradictions,* 510–12. Boulder: Westview, 1994.

Stafford, J. Martin. "Love and Lust Revisited: Intentionality, Homosexuality and Moral Education." *Journal of Applied Philosophy* 5, no. 1 (1988): 87–100.

Stein, Dan J., Eric Hollander, Donna T. Anthony, Franklin R. Schneier, Brian A. Fallon, Michael R. Liebowitz, and Donald F. Klein. "Serotonergic Medications for Sexual Obsessions, Sexual Addictions, and Paraphilias." *Journal of Clinical Psychiatry* 53 (1992): 267–71.

Stein, Edward. "The Relevance of Scientific Research about Sexual Orientation to Lesbian and Gay Rights." *Journal of Homosexuality* 27, nos. 3–4 (1994): 269–308. Reprinted in Murphy, ed., *Gay Ethics,* 269–308.

————, ed. *Forms of Desire.* New York: Routledge, 1992.

Steinbock, Bonnie. "Adultery." *QQ: Report from the Center for Philosophy and Public Policy* 6, no. 1 (1986): 12–14. Reprinted in Soble, ed., *Philosophy of Sex,* 2d ed., 187–92.

Steiner, George. *After Babel.* London: Oxford University Press, 1975.

Stoller, Robert J., and Gilbert Herdt. "Theories of Origins of Male Homosexuality: A Cross-Cultural Look." In Robert Stoller, *Observing the Erotic Imagination,* 104–34. New Haven: Yale University Press, 1985.

Stoller, Robert, Judd Marmor, Irving Bieber, Ronald Gold, Charles W. Socarides, Richard Green, and Robert L. Spitzer. "A Symposium: Should Homosexuality Be in the APA Nomenclature?" *American Journal of Psychiatry* 130, no. 11 (1973): 1207–16.

Stoltenberg, John. *Refusing to Be a Man.* Portland, Ore.: Breitenbush Books, 1989.

Strossen, Nadine. *Defending Pornography.* New York: Scribner, 1995.

Sullivan, Andrew. *Virtually Normal: An Argument about Homosexuality.* New York: Knopf, 1995.

Suppe, Frederick. "The Diagnostic and Statistical Manual of the American Psychiatric Association." In Shelp, ed., *Sexuality and Medicine,* vol. 2, 111–35.

———. "Explaining Homosexuality: Philosophical Issues, and Who Cares Anyhow?" In Murphy, ed., *Gay Ethics,* 223–68.

Swift, Jonathan. *The Complete Poems,* ed. Pat Rogers. New Haven: Yale University Press, 1983.

Symons, Donald. *The Evolution of Human Sexuality.* New York: Oxford University Press, 1979.

"Symposium on Pornography: Appendix." *New England Law Review* 20, no. 4 (1984–85): 759–77.

Szasz, Thomas. *The Manufacture of Madness.* New York: Harper and Row, 1970.

Taylor, Richard. *Having Love Affairs.* Buffalo: Prometheus, 1982.

Thomas Aquinas. *Summa contra gentiles* [Bk. III, Part II, *On the Truth of the Catholic Faith*], trans. Vernon J. Bourke. Garden City, N.Y.: Image Books, 1956.

———. *Summa theologiae.* Blackfriars: 1964–76.

Thornton, M. T. "Rape and Mens Rea." *Canadian Journal of Philosophy,* supp. vol. 8 (1982): 119–46. (Kai Nielsen and Steven C. Patten, eds., *New Essays in Ethics and Public Policy.* Guelph: Canadian Association for Publishing in Philosophy, 1982.)

Tiefer, Leonore. Review of *Sexual Excitement/Sexual Peace,* by Suzanne Sarnoff and Irving Sarnoff. *Psychology of Women Quarterly* 8, no. 1 (1983): 107–9.

———. *Sex Is Not a Natural Act and Other Essays.* Boulder: Westview, 1995.

Tisdale, Sallie. "Talk Dirty to Me." *Harper's Magazine,* February 1992, 37–46.

Tong, Rosemarie. "Brief Encounter." *Women's Review of Books* 3, no. 8 (1986): 7–9.

———. "Feminism, Pornography, and Censorship." *Social Theory and Practice* 8 (1982): 1–17.

———. "Women, Pornography, and the Law." *Academe* 73, no. 5 (1987): 14–22. Reprinted in Soble, ed., *Philosophy of Sex,* 2d ed., 301–16.

Turley, Donna. "The Feminist Debate on Pornography: An Unorthodox Interpretation." *Socialist Review* 16, nos. 3–4 (1986): 81–96.

Vacek, Edward. "A Christian Homosexuality?" *Commonweal,* December 5, 1980, 681–84.

Valverde, Mariana. "Beyond Gender Dangers and Private Pleasures: Theory and Ethics in the Sex Debates." In Dwyer, ed., *The Problem of Pornography,* 177–91.

Vance, Carole S., ed. *Pleasure and Danger: Exploring Female Sexuality.* Boston: Routledge and Kegan Paul, 1984.

Vannoy, Russell. "Philosophy and Sex." In Bullough and Bullough, eds., *Human Sexuality,* 442–49.

———. *Sex without Love.* Buffalo: Prometheus, 1980.

Vera, Diane. "Temporary Consensual 'Slave Contract.' " In Pat Califia, ed., *The Lesbian S/M Safety Manual,* 75–76. Boston: Alyson Publications, 1988.

Vetterling-Braggin, Mary, Frederick A. Elliston, and Jane English, eds. *Feminism and Philosophy.* Totowa, N.J.: Littlefield, Adams, 1977.

Walker, Alice. "Coming Apart." In Lederer, ed., *Take Back the Night,* 95–104.

Ward, David. "Should Pornography Be Censored?" In James A. Gould, ed., *Classic Philosophical Questions,* 504–12. New York: Prentice Hall, 1995.

Warshaw, Robin. *I Never Called It Rape.* New York: Harper and Row, 1988.

Wasserstrom, Richard. "Is Adultery Immoral?" In Baker and Elliston, eds., *Philosophy and Sex,* 1st ed., 207–21; 2d ed., 93–106.

———. "Racism, Sexism, and Preferential Treatment: An Approach to the Topics." *UCLA Law Review* 24 (1977): 581–622.

Weeks, Jeffrey. *Sexuality and Its Discontents.* London: Routledge and Kegan Paul, 1985.

Weinberg, Martin S., ed. *Sex Research: Studies from the Kinsey Institute.* New York: Oxford University Press, 1976.

West, Robin. "The Harms of Consensual Sex." *American Philosophical Association Newsletters* 94, no. 2 (1995): 52–55.

Whiteley, C. H., and Winifred N. Whiteley. *Sex and Morals.* New York: Basic Books, 1967.

Wicclair, Mark R. "Feminism, Pornography, and Censorship." In Thomas A. Mappes and Jane S. Zembaty, eds., *Social Ethics,* 4th ed., 282–88. New York: McGraw-Hill, 1992.

Wiewel, Brenda. Letter. *Ms.,* March 1981, 7.

Wilder, Hugh. "The Language of Sex and the Sex of Language." In Soble, ed., *Philosophy of Sex,* 1st ed., 99–109. Reprinted in Soble, ed., *Sex, Love, and Friendship,* 23–31.

Willard, L. Duane. "Aesthetic Discrimination against Persons." *Dialogue* (Canada) 16 (1977): 676–92.

Willis, Ellen. *Beginning to See the Light.* New York: Knopf, 1981.

Wittgenstein, Ludwig. *Philosophical Investigations,* trans. G. E. M. Anscombe. Oxford: Basil Blackwell, 1968.

Wojtyla, Karol [Pope John Paul II]. *Love and Responsibility.* New York: Farrar, Straus and Giroux, 1981.

Wolf, Jennifer. "Sex by the Rules." *Glamour*, May 1994, 256–59, 290.

Wolf, Naomi. *The Beauty Myth*. New York: Anchor Books, 1992.

Wolgast, Elizabeth H. *The Grammar of Justice*. Ithaca: Cornell University Press, 1987.

Wollstonecraft, Mary. *A Vindication of the Rights of Women*. Buffalo: Prometheus, 1989.

Woodhull, Victoria C. "The Principles of Social Freedom," and "Tried as by Fire." In Madeleine B. Stern, ed., *The Victoria Woodhull Reader*. Weston, Mass.: M & S Press, 1974.

Wreen, Michael J. "What's Really Wrong with Adultery." *International Journal of Applied Philosophy* 3, no. 2 (1986): 45–49. Reprinted, revised, in Soble, ed., *Philosophy of Sex*, 2d ed., 179–86.

Wright, Robert. "The Biology of Violence." *New Yorker*, March 13, 1995, 68–77.

Yeats, William Butler. *The Collected Poems of W. B. Yeats*, ed. Richard J. Finneran. New York: Macmillan, 1989.

Zillmann, Dolf. *Connections between Sex and Aggression*. Hillsdale, N.J.: Erlbaum, 1984.

Zillmann, Dolf, and Jennings Bryant. "Pornography's Impact on Sexual Satisfaction." *Journal of Applied Social Psychology* 18, no. 5 (1988): 438–53.

Abortion: and sexual freedom, 21–22

Absolute Beauty, Miss: never defecates, 199

Abstinence, 6, 14–15, 17, 65, 254 n. 47. *See also* Natural family planning

Adult-child sex, 31–32, 124–26, 154–55, 160–61

Adultery, 4, 76, 144, 252 n. 32, 262 n. 32; definition, 111–14, 264 n. 2; and health, 113, 153–54; in masturbation, 60, 64, 112; mental (in thought), 99, 112, 114; morality of, 8, 11, 13, 26–27, 113, 211

Affection: in sex, 23, 75, 94, 201. *See also* Gratitude; Love

Allen, Woody, 79; sex arousing because disgusting, 202

Angell, Roger: on Edward Laumann (et al.), 114

Antiessentialism, 265 n. 19, 273 n. 60; regarding "sexuality," 122–27, 134, 140, 154–55, 209–10. *See also* Social constructivism

Antioch University's "Sexual Offense Policy," 47–53, 55–58, 113, 121, 130, 243–44

Aristotelian friendship, 19, 207, 209

Aristotelian mean: in sexuality, 6, 8, 15, 16

Aristotle, 234

Arnold, Matthew ("Faded Leaves"), 26–27, 114

Artificial insemination: as sex, 133, 140

Atkinson, Ti-Grace: reproduction without sex, 141, 209–10; sex and love (a Solomonesque argument), 210–11; social constructivism of sexuality, 209–10, 267 n. 34

Augustine (Saint), 25, 29, 112, 188, 251 n. 21; body and sex as disgusting, 5–6, 9, 32, 202, 216; contraception, 12–13; passion and will in sex, 24, 51, 98–99, 141, 197, 228, 232, 236

Augustine's trick, 98, 144, 239

Augustinian feminism, 98–99, 141, 144,

210, 215–16, 240, 268 n. 58

Autonomy, 38, 204; and Antioch's policy, 49, 53, 244; as ethical value, 28, 39, 173

Baker, Robert: clinician as philosopher, 145, 149, 155, 163

Baldwin, Margaret: women killed in pornography, 230, 242

Barry, Kathleen: effect of pornography on relationships, 152; lesbian sadomasochists and FACT, 276 n. 37

Bart, Pauline: women as things, 263 n. 44

Bartky, Sandra: fashion-beauty complex, 275 n. 16

Basic human need: sex as, 20–21, 23–24, 123. *See also* Duty; Right, moral

Baumrin, Bernard: manipulation in sex, 66

Beauty, 19, 141, 175, 202, 219; as aphrodisiac or drug, 198–200; causes sexual arousal and pleasure, 182, 194–98, 204; irrelevant in Eden, 5, 197, 205; means more for men, 189, 206–7; mixed with ugliness, 196, 200–202; in pornography, 203–4, 211–13

Beauty hoax, 198–204

Beauty Myth (Naomi Wolf), 280 n. 7, 284 n. 62

Beauvoir, Simone de: on prostitution, 36

Beaver photograph, 222–24, 227–29, 235–36, 249. *See also* Pornography

Belliotti, Raymond: necrophilia, 30–31; sexual contracts and promises, 43–45, 49, 57, 258 n. 118

Bestiality, 10, 136–37; in pornography, 229–31, 240

Bieber, Irving: homosexuality as illness, 156–58

Bloom, Allan *(Love and Friendship):* beauty in eros, 175

Boorse, Christopher: sexual health, 165–68

Bordo, Susan: antiessentialism of the body, 273 n. 60

Boring sex, 50, 195, 252 n. 27; from familiarity or in marriage, 6–9, 27, 81–82,
86, 88–90, 105, 144, 147, 158, 211,
254 n. 47; as natural, 116, 129; as therapy, 16. *See also* Pauline access
Boswell, John: adultery in Aquinas, 252 n.
32
Bowers v. Hardwick, 19, 234
Brando, Marlon: masculine role model,
93, 95
Breast feeding: both sexual and nurturing, 125–26, 139–40
Brown, Lucy: the pain of beauty, 176
Brownmiller, Susan *(Against Our Will)*,
246; rape, 25, 255 n. 65
Bunny and rhino, 179–80, 182, 183, 200
Burchard of Worms: coitus a tergo, 228–
29
Buss, David: beauty, 275 n. 25, 277 n. 41;
women's sexuality, 236

Cahill, Lisa: sex and reproduction, 7, 29
Calhoun, Cheshire: homosexual marriage
and family, 106–8
Califia, Pat: adult-child sex, 32
Callahan, Sidney: conservative-feminist
sexuality, 22
Calvin, 277 n. 42
Camus, Albert, 144
Caplan, Paula: pornography says women
need to be raped, 282 n. 37
Card, Claudia: consent in lesbian sadomas-
ochism, 41
Celibacy. *See* Abstinence
Chicago, Judy ("The Dinner Party"), 212
Child-adult sex. *See* Adult-child sex
Christensen, F. M.: manipulating statis-
tics, 286 n. 67
Coercion, 20, 38, 251 n. 111, 255 n. 58,
286 n. 81; in Catharine MacKinnon,
242–43, 245–48; verbal forms of, 49,
259 n. 121. *See also* Consent; Money;
Prostitution; Rape
Coitus interruptus: as contraception, 12,
17; as masturbation, 64
Colker, Ruth: compulsory heterosexual
marriage, 264 n. 57
Completeness, sexual, 71–77, 81–82
Compulsive sex, 148, 159–60
Compulsory heterosexuality, 106–8, 141,
161, 255 n. 58, 263 n. 54, 267 n. 34

Compulsory pairing, 107–8, 158, 264 n.
57
Condom: carry in bag, 253 n. 39; cathect,
16, 84, 121
Consent, 33, 43, 184–85, 248, 258 n. 114;
into the future, 30–31, 50, 56–57; justifies sex, 8, 9, 27–28, 40–41, 113; relationship to degradation, 34, 36, 221,
257 n. 96. *See also* Coercion; Libertarian ethics; Metaconsent; Money; West,
Robin
Contraception, 7, 24, 96; Catholic views
of, 11–15; by re-eroticization, 17, 21.
See also Natural family planning; Reproduction
Coprophilia: as perverted, 168, 171; as sexual, 127–28, 136, 137, 139. *See also* Excrement

Dean, Craig: gay marriage, 107, 255 n. 55
Dean, James: masculine role model, 93,
95, 163
Deep Throat, 256 n. 81, 286 n. 89
Degradation, sexual, 215–17; in pornogra-
phy, 213, 220–23, 230–31; relationship
to consent, 34, 36, 221, 257 n. 96. *See
also* Dehumanization; Objectification
Dehumanization, sexual, 8, 97, 227–30.
See also Degradation; Objectification
Dennis the Menace: on kissing, 241
*Diagnostic and Statistical Manual of
Mental Disorders*, 148; sexual disor-
ders, 146, 159, 160, 162–63, 169; "sex-
ual health" as evaluative in, 163, 173
Dryden, John ("Alexander's Feast"): who
deserves the fair, 189
Duck-rabbit: of a kiss, 120–21; of the genitals and sex, 200–202, 214, 217; of
René Magritte's *Le viol*, 219. *See also*
Polysemousness
Duty: sex as, 9, 57, 80, 211. *See also* Basic
human need; Pauline access; Right,
moral
Dworkin, Andrea, 144, 210, 255 n. 61;
heterosexuality as oppressive brutality,
141, 240–41, 265 n. 13, 267 n. 36; sex
sans erections, 141, 162. *See also*
Model Antipornography Law (MacKinnon-Dworkin)
Dwyer, Susan: degradation in pornography, 221; pornography teaches, 280 n. 7

Eddy, Mary Baker: reproduction without sex, 268 n. 58
Edwards, Susan: nymphomania as disease, 169
Ehman, Robert: adult-child sex, 32
Elders, Joycelyn: masturbation, 60
Engels, Frederick, 271 n. 55; money motive in sex, 173–74, 205–6
Erectile dysfunction, 143, 152, 158, 162–63. See Sexual health
Erect penis: accomplished by act of will, 5, 91, 99, 141; justifies sex, 255 n. 67; as mark of the sexual, 111, 125, 227, 269 n. 59; in pornography, 240–41; sex best if absent, 141, 162. See also Penis
Eryximachus. See Symposium (Plato)
Estrich, Susan, 52; rape, 45–47, 257 n. 111
Etoro: fellatio insemination, 124–26, 154–55
Euthanasia, 35
Evil Demon, 198
Excrement: Sigmund Freud, 201; in pornography, 228, 240; W. B. Yeats, 216. See also Coprophilia
Exoneration: by medicine, 160, 170; of sexual behavior, 24–27, 55, 114, 255 n. 67
Explaining: heterosexuality, 83, 171, 261 n. 24, 264 n. 57; homosexuality, 29, 83, 94, 166–67, 261 n. 24, 277 n. 44; paired sex, 84–88, 210–11

Fantasy, sexual, 104–5, 160; during masturbation, 59, 60, 69, 71, 73, 82–83, 86, 95–96, 97–99, 112; private, during paired sex, 64, 76, 80, 105; with pornography, 204, 223–24, 227, 233–34, 235, 238; sadomasochistic, 148, 267 n. 36
Farley, Margaret: Aquinas on contraception, 253 n. 37; sex and love, 252 n. 27
Fellatio: insemination, 124–26, 133, 154–55; by oneself, 61; in pornography, 202, 214, 215, 231–32, 244, 286 n. 89; as silencing, 214, 215; women crave, 231–32, 283 n. 39. See also Condom; Oral sex
Feminism, Augustinian. See Augustinian feminism
Ferguson, Ann: adult-child sex, 32; love and sex, 208–9, 211

Fetishism, 72–73, 81, 261 n. 23, 261 n. 24, 277 n. 44
Fingarette, Herbert: alcoholism as disease, 269 n. 14
Finnis, John: sexual disintegration, 99–102
Firestone, Shulamith: reproduction without sex, 141; romanticism, 278 n. 63
Fisk, Milton: antiessentialism, 265 n. 19
Flirting, 43, 118, 137
Flynt, Larry: as René Magritte, 226
Fracher, Jeffrey, 263 n. 41; sex therapy, 163. See also Kimmel, Michael
Freud, Sigmund, ix, 172, 255 n. 59, 269 n. 13; "Anatomy is destiny," 201, 278 n. 48; beauty and sex, 201, 276 n. 38; homosexuality, 191, 261 n. 24, 277 n. 44; masturbation, 262 n. 36, 278 n. 56
Frye, Marilyn: adult-child sex, 32, 155

Gardella, Peter: sense of sin, 144
Garry, Ann: women servile to men in pornography, 231–32
Gender differences, 177–78; in number of sex partners, 115–17; in role of physical attractiveness, 189, 206–7
Giles, James: theory of sex, 261 n. 23
Gingrich, Newt: oral sex not adultery, 264 n. 6
Glenmullen, Joseph: sex therapy, 164
Goldman, Alan, 138; Kantian respect in sex, 40; sexual act, 68–71; sexual desire, 68–71, 81, 83
Gracyk, Theodore: Le viol as objectifying, 218
Gratitude: produced by good sex, 23, 75. See also Affection
Gray, Robert: sexual activity produces pleasure, 127–30
Greeley, Andrew: adultery, 153–54
Green, Karen: sex and love, 4, 42
Green, Richard: ego-dystonia and sexual health, 158–61
Greer, Germaine, 282 n. 31; re-eroticization, 17, 21, 147
Griffin, Susan: fellatio in pornography, 231–32
Gubar, Susan: Le viol as objectifying, 217–19, 224
Gudorf, Christine: revised Christian sexual ethics, 30, 254 n. 54

Guilt feelings: for masturbating or enjoying pornography, 96, 109, 231, 260 n. 1

Hamer, Dean: biology of homosexuality, 170, 271 n. 55
Hartsock, Nancy: antiessentialism of sex, 123–24
Hawthorne, Nathaniel (Scarlet Letter), 27
Heilbroner, Robert: beauty as natural, 207–8
Hein, Hilde: degradation, 257 n. 96
Herman, Barbara: sex in Immanuel Kant, 260 n. 9
Heterosexuality: as dysfunction, 157, 161; similar to homosexuality, 136, 139, 167, 168, 268 n. 44. See also Compulsory heterosexuality; Explaining, heterosexuality
Hill, Anita, 26
Hill, Judith: women as promiscuous in pornography, 232–33
Hite, Shere: men's masturbation, 260 n. 1; rape motive, 85
Hobbes, 277 n. 42
Hommel, Teresa: fellatio silences women, 214
Homosexuality, 139, 178: as disease or illness, 156–58, 164, 165–68; and masturbation, 60, 61, 63, 94; morality of, 10, 18, 100–102, 154–55, 251 n. 3, 254 n. 54; naturalness of, 10, 29, 66, 166–67, 252 n. 32, 270 n. 42; as sex, 132, 136, 266 n. 27; similar to heterosexuality, 136, 139, 167, 168, 268 n. 44; therapy for, 15, 163–64, 254 n. 51. See also Explaining, homosexuality; Marriage, homosexual
Hornsby, Jennifer: pornography silences women, 280 n. 7
Hume, David: beauty and arousal, 197, 199
Hustler: meat-grinder cover, 226–27

Illich, Ivan: social construction of disease, 143
Incest, 10, 28–29, 90; masturbation as, 60
Infertility, 12, 135, 168. See also Reproductive health
Insatiability, sexual: in women, 29, 169,

230, 236. See also Nymphomania; Promiscuity
Insertion: as mark of the sexual, 62–64, 116, 139
Intergenerational sex. See Adult-child sex

John Paul II, Pope (Karol Wojtyla), 29–30, 252 n. 25; contraception, 13, 14–15, 17, 254 n. 49; sex and love, 3, 41–42

Kant, Immanuel, 58, 90, 177; exchange of rights, 9–10, 55–56; marriage, 9–10, 41–42, 65–66, 101; masturbation, 65–66, 148; Second Formulation, 40, 99; sex objectifies, 65, 100; unnatural sex, 28, 66, 105–6
Kappeler, Susanne: men as brutal, 265 n. 13; women killed in pornography, 285 n. 64
Kimmel, Michael: masturbation, 93–96, 263 n. 41; sex therapy, 163
Kinsley, Michael: fate of the ugly, 204
Kittay, Eva: Hustler cover, 226; rape fantasies, 267 n. 36
Kofman, Sarah: Sigmund Freud, castration, and sexuality, 261 n. 24, 277 n. 44
Kovel, Joel: social construction of health, 168
Kundera, Milan, 1, 30

Langton, Rae: pornography silences women, 280 n. 7; rape proclivity, 284 n. 62
Laumann, Edward (et al.): sex survey, 60, 115–17
LeMoncheck, Linda: sexual thoughts, 99
Lennon, John: masculine role model, 93, 95, 163
Levin, Max: love makes sex healthy, 152–53, 163, 168–69
Levin, Michael: homosexual promiscuity a disorder, 158; point of penis, 167
Le viol. See Magritte, René
Lewontin, Richard: genetics of sexuality, 271 n. 55
Libertarian ethics, 28, 33, 40–41, 43, 49, 56–57; rejection of paternalism, 38–39, 52. See also Consent
Longino, Helen: pornography as harmful and degrading, 220–23, 231–32, 281 n. 13

Love: exculpates, justifies, purifies sex, 2, 3, 4, 17–23, 25–27, 28, 41–43, 153, 208–9, 210–11, 228, 247, 252 n. 27, 266 n. 23. *See also* Affection; Separation of sex and love; Sexual health; Shared intimacy; Woodhull, Victoria

Lucretius *(De rerum natura)*, 199

Lynn, Barry: pornography, 279 n. 1, 279 n. 77, 283 n. 42

MacKinnon, Catharine, 22, 25, 44, 276 n. 37, 284 n. 62; academic texts, 236–38; brutality and violence of heterosex, 137, 240–41, 255 n. 66, 267 n. 36, 268 n. 48, 286 n. 89; consent and coercion, 184–85, 242–43, 245–48; as conservative, 22, 93, 230, 239; erection as mark of the sexual, 111, 125, 227, 269 n. 59; "get her!" 236, 237, 239; all heterosex is rape, 246–47, 255 n. 66, 267 n. 36, 268 n. 42; men love death, 121, 227, 235, 238; men's masturbation, 239, 241, 248, 249; pornography silences women, 219, 280 n. 7; romanticism, 247–49; women barter sex, 190, 235; women killed in pornography, 231, 238–39, 242, 284 n. 61. *See also* Model Antipornography Law (MacKinnon-Dworkin)

Magritte, René: *La connaissance naturelle*, 281 n. 8; *Le viol*, 217–19, 224, 281 n. 8, 282 n. 17; "This is not a pipe," 226

Mapplethorpe, Robert: *Helmut and Brooks*, 225

Marchiano (Lovelace), Linda: coerced into pornography, 245

Marmor, Judd: healthy sex, 153, 160

Marriage, homosexual, 18, 65–66, 106–9, 255 n. 55

Martin, Suzy: Antioch policy, 52

Marx, Karl, 271 n. 55; "hunger is hunger," 123; money transforms ugliness, 207

Masson, Jeffrey Moussaieff: promiscuity as mental illness, 159

Masturbation, 16, 210, 222, 230; adulterous, 60, 64, 112; completeness of, 72–76, 82–83, 95–96; etymology, 260 n. 3; harmful, unhealthy, pathological, 77, 78, 91, 92, 109, 145–46, 148, 151, 155,

170; in Catharine MacKinnon, 239, 241, 248, 249; in men's liberation, 93–99, 163; morally worse than rape (Aquinas), 10–11; obscenity of, 103–4; perverted, unnatural, 11, 66, 72–73, 74, 105–6, 167; and potency, 91, 105, 152, 262 n. 36; to prevent sin, 8, 91; as rape, 59, 60, 109; as sex, 62–64, 68–70, 71, 111, 130, 132–33, 135; utility of, 87, 91–92, 262 n. 37

Meilaender, Gilbert, 2

Men love death, 121, 227, 235, 238

Men's liberation: and masturbation, 93–99, 163

Metaconsent, 57–58. *See also* Consent

Mill, John Stuart: freedom and autonomy, 171, 173

Milligan, Don *(Sex-Life)*, ix

Mirrors: use of during sex, 72, 280 n. 5

Model Antipornography Law (MacKinnon-Dworkin): section 2.1.i (dehumanization), 227–28; 2.1.iv (mutilation), 226–27; 2.1.v (submissive posture), 215, 223–24; 2.1.vi (reduction to body parts), 224; 2.1.vii (whores by nature) 235–36; 2.1.viii (dildos, animals), 229–31; 3.1 (coercion), 242–47; 3.2 (trafficking), 279 n. 1

Mohr, Richard: gay love and marriage, 18–19, 109, 279 n. 72; Robert Mapplethorpe, 225

Money: motive for sex, 34–37, 57, 173–74, 204, 205–6, 245, 248. *See also* Coercion; Prostitution

Montaigne, Michel, 3, 19

Morgan, Robin: marital rape, 34–35, 37, 38; woman's desire and initiation, 39, 215

Moulton, Janice, 20, 53; knowledge and sexual satisfaction, 88–90, 196–97; novelty and sexual satisfaction, 87–89

Moulton's Problem: when is a kiss sexual?, 111, 122

Murphy, Timothy, 265 n. 19, 268 n. 44

Nagel, Thomas: completeness, 71–74, 76, 81–82

Natural family planning, 13–15, 17, 254 n. 47, 254 n. 49. *See also* Abstinence

Necrophilia, 30–31, 284 n. 61

'Net sex, 118
Neu, Jerome: sexual intentions, 131
Nicholson, Susan: Aquinas on contraception, 253 n. 37; Aquinas on rape, 252 n. 31
Noonan, John: Aquinas on contraception, 253 n. 37
Nozick, Robert, 2; fantasies as use, 263 n. 47
Nymphomania, 169–70. See also Insatiability, sexual; Promiscuity; Sexual health

Objectification, 95: in nature of sex, 3, 40, 65, 71, 82, 97–99. See also Degradation, sexual; Dehumanization, sexual; Subject/object
Obscenity, 103–5
O'Neill, Onora: sex and intimacy, 42
Oral sex: as humiliating and degrading, 134, 215–16; not real sex, 63, 139; reifies body parts, 216–17, 224–25. See also Fellatio
Orgasm from breathing, 16, 210. See also Sprinkle, Annie
Orgasmic dysfunction: in women, 162–63, 164. See also Sexual health

Packwood, Robert, 25
Padgug, Robert: antiessentialism of sex, 123
Paglia, Camille: 30, 266 n. 22; sex as threatening, 198–99; sexual objectification, 97–98
Paired sex: as masturbation, 62–63, 65, 89–90; private fantasies during, 64, 76, 80, 105. See also Compulsory pairing; Explaining, paired sex
Parthenogenesis, 141
Passacaglia, 19, 26
Pateman, Carole: fellatio silences women, 214; prostitution, 87, 96; consent, 247, 258 n. 114, 286 n. 81
Paternalism, 32–33, 37–39, 52–53
Paul (Saint): consent into future, 31, 56–57; sex in marriage, 6–9, 15–17, 112, 147; as sexual liberal, 8, 91. See Pauline access
Pauline access, 6, 126, 223; leads to sexual boredom, 86, 88, 90, 144; objectifies, 8,

13, 33; to one self, 67, 86. See also Boring sex; Paul (Saint)
Paul VI, Pope: contraception, 13–14
Pausanias. See Symposium (Plato)
Penis: alien, 134; as balloon, 217; as brain, 283 n. 53; center of universe, 93, 94; as fist, 268 n. 48; as greeting, 167; as nose, 217; point of, 167; as puppet, 141; ugly, 94, 201–2. See also Erect penis; Erectile dysfunction; Fellatio
Perfection in sex: 89, 105, 204
Peterson, Susan Rae: token "no," 46
Petronius, 3
'Phone sex, 74, 118
Pineau, Lois: rape and communicative sexuality, 49, 244, 286 n. 78
Pius XI, Pope: contraception, 13, 260 n. 4
Plato. See Symposium (Plato)
Polysemousness: of acts, 48, 52, 121–24, 128, 131; of body parts, 58; of depictions, 120, 219; of gender, 220; of a kiss, 111, 120, 121–22, 219; of language, 46–47, 50, 219–20; of Le viol, 219; pornography, 220, 225–27, 233–34, 235–36, 237, 242. See also Duck-rabbit
Pornography: beauty in, 203–4, 211–13; causes rape and sexual violence, 193, 282 n. 37, 284 n. 62, 286 n. 89; degrading, 213, 220–23, 227–30, 230–31; effects on relationships, 151–52, 203; heterosex in, is rape, 243, 245–46, 248; polysemousness, 220, 225–27, 233–34, 235–36, 237, 242; prostitution in making, 37, 182, 183–84, 242; sadomasochistic, 193, 239–40; silences women, 219, 280 n. 7; using is sexually unhealthy, 151–52; stupidity of consumers of, 224, 280 n. 7; viewer's input into its fantasy, 204, 227, 233–34, 235, 238; women killed in, x, 228, 230, 231, 238–39, 241, 242, 284 n. 61, 285 n. 64. See also Beaver photograph; Model Antipornography Law (MacKinnon-Dworkin)
Portnoy, Alexander: adultery as masturbation, 64, 114
Posner, Richard: rhythm method, 14; sex in marriage, 34
Potato, hot, 271 n. 55
Primoratz, Igor: libertarian ethics, 33–34, 36, 40, 41
Promiscuity: 29, 169; an illness in men,

158, 159; of women in pornography, 96, 232–33, 235–36, 241. *See also* Insatiability, sexual; Nymphomania

Prostitution, 82, 87, 151, 235; and consent, 33–37, 245, 248; definition, 266 n. 23; in making pornography, 37, 182, 183–84, 242; separates sex and love, 4, 248; as sex, 70, 115, 116, 128, 129; social constructivism of, 125

Prozac: in sex therapy, 148, 269 n. 11

Rapaport, Elizabeth, 204–5

Rape, 20, 24, 25, 45–47, 66–67, 85, 113, 160, 269 n. 11; caused by pornography, 193, 282 n. 37, 284 n. 62, 286 n. 89; conceptually impossible in marriage, 9, 30, 57, 260 n. 8; by fantasy, 59, 60, 109; by fraud, 257 n. 111; heterosex in pornography is, 243, 245–46, 248; all heterosex is, 246–47, 255 n. 66, 267 n. 36, 268 n. 42; as natural, 10–11, 237; and pleasure, 85, 129–31; prostitution as, 36, 245, 248; as sex, 129, 134, 137, 255 n. 65. *See also* Coercion; Consent

Rape, date/acquaintance. *See* Antioch University's "Sexual Offense Policy"; Estrich, Susan; Pineau, Lois

Rape, marital, 34–35, 37, 38, 256 n. 92

Rape proclivity, 284 n. 62

Re-eroticization, 15–17, 84, 91, 147, 175, 188, 197; of homosexuals, to heterosexuality, 15, 163–64, 254 n. 51

Reich, Wilhelm: sexual health, 154

Reidhead, Julia: Antioch policy, 50–51

Reproduction, 137–41; as mark of the sexual, 134–37; the purpose of sex, 2, 5, 13–15, 105–6, 198, 209–10; without sex, 141, 208–10, 268 n. 58

Reproductive health: is not sexual health, 138, 167. *See also* Infertility; Sexual health

Respect: in sex, 1, 34, 220–23, 229

Rhythm method. *See* Natural family planning

Rich, Adrienne: compulsory heterosexuality, 127, 263 n. 54

Right, moral: to sex, 19, 24, 30, 32, 53; to sexual satisfaction, 53–54, 193. *See also* Basic human need; Duty

Rossi, Alice: pleasures of breast feeding, 139–40

Rousseau, Jean-Jacques: masturbation, 59, 60, 109

Rubin, Gayle: on Catharine MacKinnon, 230, 244

Ruddick, Sara: completeness, 74–77

Russell, Bertrand, 24; consent in marital sex and prostitution, 33–35; reasons for sex, 39–40, 70, 206

Russell, Diana E. H.: animals in pornography, 229; rape proclivity, 284 n. 62; racism in pornography, 212

Sade, the Marquis de, 30, 60

Sadomasochism, 60, 221, 271 n. 55; as communicative sexuality, 49–50; fantasies of, 148, 267 n. 36; lesbian, 41, 193, 276 n. 37; light, 114, 265 n. 12; and love, 2–3, 28; in pornography, 193, 239–40

Sambia: fellatio insemination, 124–26, 154–55

Sartre, Jean-Paul, 3

Schauer, Frederick: pornography as sex aid, 234

Schopenhauer, Arthur, 234; adult-child sex, 31; masturbation, 148, 153; sex for reproduction, 198, 209

Schulhofer, Stephen: rape by fraud, 257 n. 111

Scripture: 1 Corinthians 7:1, 6; 1 Corinthians 7:3, 57; 1 Corinthians 7:3–5, 6, 252 n. 24; 1 Corinthians 7:4, 252 n. 29; 1 Corinthians 7:8, 6; 1 Corinthians 7:9, 8; Ephesians 5:22–23, 252 n. 29; Exodus 20:17, 203; Genesis 3:7, 263 n. 48; Genesis 38:9–10, 260 n. 4; Leviticus 20:13, 251 n. 3; Matthew 5:28, 114; Matthew 5:28–29, 99; Matthew 5:30, 59; Romans 7:23–25, 7–8

Scruton, Roger, 4, 90; masturbation, 102–6

Separation of sex and love: in casual sex, 4; by contraception, 13; by masturbation, 93–94; by pornography, 94, 152; in prostitution, 4, 248. *See also* Love

Sex therapy, 113, 147, 148, 163–64. *See also* Re-eroticization; Sexual health

Sexual act: gender differences in definition, 115–17; intentions in, 131–34; as penetrative, 62–64, 116, 128, 139; as producing erection, 111, 125; as pro-

Sexual act *(Continued)*
  ducing pleasure, 68–71, 123–24, 127–
  30, 136–37, 227; relation to sexual
  parts, 115, 117, 118–19, 267 n. 39; as reproductive, 133, 134–37, 139, 140
Sexual addiction, 159–60
Sexual arousal, 123, 138, 227; and beauty,
  182, 194–98, 199, 202, 204; and completeness, 71–74; as mark of the sexual,
  115–17; in rape, 130–31; spiral of, 71–
  72, 82. *See also* Boring sex; Erect penis
Sexual body part, 121; reification of, 216–
  17; relation to sexual act, 115, 117,
  118–19, 267 n. 39; social constructivism
  of, 126
Sexual desire, 39, 68–71, 81, 83, 261 n.
  23, 267 n. 39
Sexual experience, 113, 129, 130
Sexual health, 77–78, 159–60; ego-syntonia in, 158–61; evaluations in judgments of, 93, 110, 144, 145, 146–48,
  150, 152–53, 161, 162–67, 173–174; as
  free sex, 172–74; as functioning sexually, 149–50, 156–58, 162–63; and
  harmfulness, 154–55, 173; as hygiene,
  145, 149–50, 151; in terms of love, 41–
  42, 152–53, 163, 168–69, 270 n. 22; as
  natural sex, 165–67, 170–74; as pleasurable sex, 165, 168; relation to reproduction, 138, 165, 167; social constructivism of, 142, 143, 153, 154–55, 159,
  163–65, 168, 169, 170. *See also* Erectile
  dysfunction; Nymphomania; Orgasmic
  dysfunction; Sex therapy
Sexual perversion: does not exist, 84; psychology of, 71–74, 138; as unhealthy
  sexuality, 170–73. *See also* Adult-child
  sex; Bestiality; Coprophilia; Fetishism;
  Homosexuality; Masturbation; Mirrors;
  Necrophilia; Sadomasochism; Sexual
  health; Voyeurism
Sexual pleasure, 30, 85, 139–40; from
  beauty, 194–98, 204; from knowledge,
  88–90, 132, 196–97, 204; as mark of the
  sexual, 123–24, 127–30, 136–37, 227
Shaffer, Jerome: sexual desire, 267 n. 39
Shakespeare, William: Sonnet 116, 18;
  Sonnet 129, 3
Shared intimacy: and sex, 20, 42, 247–48.
  See also Affection; Love

Sherfey, Mary Jane: women's sexual insatiability, 29, 169, 236
Shrage, Laurie: social constructivism of
  sexuality, 125–26, 154–55
Silence: does not mean "yes," 34, 49, 244
Simmons, Paul: Aquinas on contraception, 253 n. 37
Sinatra, Frank: compulsory heterosexual
  marriage, 107
Singer, Irving: sexual pluralism, 254 n. 52
Socarides, Charles, 172: on homosexuality, 157–58
Social constructivism: of beauty, 197–98,
  207–8; of healthy sexuality, 142, 143,
  153, 154–55, 159, 163–65, 168, 169,
  170; of heterosexuality, 127, 209–10,
  267 n. 34; of homosexuality, 266 n. 27;
  of knowledge, 166; of maleness, 127; of
  prostitution, 125; of the sexual, 70,
  122–27, 154–55; of sexual body part,
  126. *See also* Antiessentialism
Solomon, Robert: sex as communication,
  77–80, 81–82, 84–87
Solomonesque arguments, 85, 87, 210–11.
  See also Solomon, Robert
Sprinkle, Annie: benefits of sex, 133, 160;
  eroticization, 16, 121, 123–24, 147
Statistics, manipulation of: 170, 284 n. 61,
  286 n. 67
Steinbock, Bonnie: adultery, 26
Steiner, George: sex as communication,
  78–79
Sterility. *See* Infertility
Stoltenberg, John, 255 n. 67; antiessentialism, 127; objectification, 97–99;
  pornography, 96, 238; respect in sex, 1,
  30
Strossen, Nadine: *Le viol*, 282 n. 17
Subject/object: person as both in sex, 72,
  74, 82–83, 98. *See also* Completeness,
  sexual; Objectification
Sullivan, Andrew, property rights, 275 n.
  22
Swift, Jonathan ("Strephon and Chloe"),
  199
Symons, Donald: women's sexuality, 236,
  238
Symposium (Plato): Diotima, 16, 213; Eryximachus, 146–49, 152, Pausanias, 26,
  146–47, 159, 202; Socrates, 252 n. 25

Thomas, Clarence, 25, 26
Thomas Aquinas (Saint), 43, 166, 216;
  adultery, 4, 9, 29, 252 n. 32; contraception, 11–12, 253 n. 37; homosexuality,
  10–11, 252 n. 32; incest, 10, 28–29;
  masturbation, 10–11, 74; natural law
  ethics, 10–11, 28–29, 33; natural sexual
  inclination, 6, 14; rape, 10–11, 252 n.
  31
Tiefer, Leonore: healthy erections, 143
Tisdale, Sallie: fellatio, 202
Tissot, S. A. D.: masturbatory insanity,
  148, 153
Token "no," 46–47, 280 n. 7
Tong, Rosemarie: on Catharine MacKinnon, 246, 279 n. 1

Usefulness: of masturbation, 87, 91–92,
  262 n. 37; of (other) sex, 91, 133, 154,
  159–60, 209

Vannoy, Russell: arousal, 196; masturba-
  tion, 261 n. 13
Victimology, 281 n. 13
Voyeurism, 69, 82

Wasserstrom, Richard: adultery, 264 n. 2
West, Robin: harms of consensual sex,
  37–39, 52

"When in doubt, ask," 44–45, 49, 258 n.
  118
White, Vanna: is not Vanna White, 199
Wiewel, Brenda: women's sexuality, 160–
  61
Willard, L. Duane: aesthetic discrimina-
  tion, 181, 186–87, 188, 190–92
Willis, Ellen, 123; sex, love, and abortion,
  20–23
Wolf, Naomi. See Beauty Myth (Naomi
  Wolf)
Wolgast, Elizabeth: pornography, 234–35,
  236, 283 n. 43
Wollstonecraft, Mary: women's beauty,
  275 n. 16
Woodhull, Victoria: sex, love, and mar-
  riage, 27, 34, 40, 70, 256 n. 92, 266 n.
  23, 270 n. 22
Words: as sexual, ix–x, 50–51, 241
Wreen, Michael: adultery, 111–14

Yeats, W. B. ("Crazy Jane Talks to the
  Bishop"), 216